AAV-9838
VC-Griffin

THE WOMEN AND THE WARRIORS

Syracuse Studies on Peace and Conflict Resolution
Harriet Hyman Alonso, Charles Chatfield, and Louis Kriesberg
Series Editors

Syracuse Studies on Peace and Conflict Resolution
Harriet Hyman Alonso, Charles Chatfield, and Louis Kriesberg, *Series Editors*

A series devoted to readable books on the history of peace movements, the lives of peace advocates, and the search for ways to mitigate conflict, both domestic and international. At a time when profound and exciting political and social developments are happening around the world, this series seeks to stimulate a wider awareness and appreciation of the search for peaceful resolution to strife in all its forms and to promote linkages among theorists, practitioners, social scientists, and humanists engaged in this work throughout the world.

Other titles in the series include:

THE

℘OMEN
AND THE WARRIORS

THE U.S. SECTION OF THE WOMEN'S
INTERNATIONAL LEAGUE FOR PEACE
AND FREEDOM, 1915–1946

Carrie A. Foster

SYRACUSE UNIVERSITY PRESS

First Edition 1995
95 96 97 98 99 00   6 5 4 3 2 1

This book is published with the assistance of a grant from Miami University of Ohio.

The paper used in this publication meets the minimum requirements of American National Standard for Information Sciences—Permanence of Paper for Printed Library Materials, ANSI Z39.48-1984. ∞™

Library of Congress Cataloging-in-Publication Data
Foster, Carrie A.
The women and the warriors : the U.S. Section of the Women's
International League for Peace and Freedom, 1915–1946 / Carrie A.
Foster.
p.   cm.—(Syracuse studies on peace and conflict resolution)
Includes bibliographical references and index.
ISBN 0-8156-2625-8. — ISBN 0-8156-2662-2 (pbk.)
1. Women's International League for Peace and Freedom. U.S.
Section—History. 2. Peace movements—United States—History.
3. Pacifists—United States—History. I. Title. II. Series.
JX1965.F66   1995
327.1′72′082—dc20   94-39571

To the two most important people in my life,
both of whom just happen to be women:
my mother, Eleanor Foster,
and my daughter, Rochelle M. Tropf.

Carrie Foster is Associate Professor of History at Miami University, Hamilton, Ohio, and resides in Hamilton. She holds a Ph.D. in history from the University of Denver.

Contents

Preface

THIS BOOK was over fifteen years in the making and there were times when I despaired that it would ever see the light of day. Of the many obstacles to its completion, both personal and professional, probably none was more formidable than my own commitment to superior undergraduate teaching for I began a fulltime teaching career in the very early stages of the book's formation. I now realize that the frantic attempt to achieve perfection in both areas of my professional life was, at best, an exercise in futility. Yet I do not regret the effort because the insights gleaned from the research and writing had a tremendous impact upon my teaching while conversely, the research that informed my pedagogical endeavors provided a crucial interpretive framework for the book.

Like all professional historians, I bring to my work as teacher and scholar a certain ideological perspective. Capable of only vague articulation fifteen years ago, by the time I settled into my first potentially permanent teaching position, the fundamental premise of this ideological perspective, I realized, was very little different from that of the women I was writing about. And that premise can be summed up in one word: democracy.

Based on their belief in the essential equality of men and women everywhere, the women of the interwar WILPF were committed to the idea that this equality should be reflected in all realms of human activity whether social, political, or economic. Ultimate decision-making power in any society, they thought, should be exercised in the interest of the common good in accordance with the wishes of the sovereign people.

The women of the United States Section of the WILPF saw themselves as more fortunate in this respect than many, if not most, of the world's peoples, for however imperfect their own country might have been as a social or economic democracy, they were quite convinced that theirs was at least a political democracy. This fortuitous state of affairs was not insignificant from the WILPF's perspective for it meant that the people possessed the power to reform the American system and move it in a more democratic direction socially and economically.

For the most part, the interwar WILPF was composed of women from the middle class, and I think most middle class Americans today still accept without questioning that, however flawed in practice, the American system was created by the founding fathers to function democratically. It seems to me that this is particularly true of those middle class men and women who are well-educated, for our educational system attempts to instill that notion almost from day one. Yet it is with respect to this very issue that I part company with the women of the WILPF and with most of my friends, neighbors, and colleagues. However much I would like it to be otherwise, the historical evidence has persuaded me that the most egregious error perpetuated by educators with each new generation is this notion that the authors of our Constitution shared our commitment to a democratic society.

I cannot think of anything more important to our understanding of American history than the simple fact that, contrary to common belief, the United States was not created as a democracy to function democratically. Instead, it was established with the superficial trappings of democracy to obfuscate the reality that it was a plutocracy designed to function, as it most effectively has, not in the interests of all of the people but for the benefit of a small, upper class elite.

Analyzing our national history as a plutocratic process rather than as a democratic one sheds a whole new light on events, personalities, and motivation, and goes a long way to explain why so much of our history, past and present, has been characterized by *undemocratic* excess. For me it also clarifies the troubling issue of why reform movements have so consistently failed to achieve their objectives, even in those rare instances when they appear to have succeeded. If the system is not democratic, then reform movements grounded in the belief that it is are doomed to fail, for democratic change can only succeed in a system designed to accommodate the needs and desires of a sovereign people.

As long as Americans unquestioningly accept the notion that their country is and was intended to be a functioning democracy, true peace, freedom, and justice will continue to elude them. And so, too, will any substantial degree of peace, freedom, and justice for other peoples of the world, for contrary to the noble sentiments expressed by generations of American leaders, it is not democracy we wish to further in other countries but plutocracy—plutocracy abroad to serve the interests of plutocracy at home.

There are times, to be sure, when I regret ever having begun my search for "historical truth," for it is often lonely out here on the fringes of the accepted American "democratic dogma." Perhaps if I had known where my intellectual journey was leading me, I might have turned back long ago. As the WILPF's founder, Jane Addams, observed when her adherence to pacifism during World War I went against the prevailing mood of prowar fervor, "The force of the majority was so overwhelming that it seemed not only impossible to hold one's own against it, but at moments absolutely unnatural, and one secretly yearned to participate in the 'folly of all mankind'."[1]

Despite this sense of isolation and alienation, however, Addams's own ideological perspective soon compelled her to conclude that "the ability to hold out against mass suggestion, to honestly differ from the convictions and enthusiasm of one's best friends did in moments of crisis come to depend upon the categorical belief that a man's primary allegiance is to his vision of the truth and that he is under obligation to affirm it."[2] I concur.

One of the things that made it easier for Addams to bear the social opprobrium that accompanied her inability to relinquish her "vision of the truth" was the support of a few close and faithful friends. I, too, have been fortunate in this respect. Without the intellectual, professional, and moral support of my long-time (and long-suffering) friend and advisor, John Livingston, this book never would have been written. Not only did he suggest the topic, but with infinite patience and good humor, he tolerated my occasional outbursts of anti-academic rebellion, was always reassuring in those frequent moments of self-doubt, and never hesitated to chastize me for lapses of intellectual rigor.

To committed democrat and political sophisticate Ace R. Hayes, I owe an intellectual debt that I can never repay. An individual for whom historical truth is an obsession, it was Ace more than anyone else who forced me to acknowledge that that truth is only infrequently illuminated by the conventional wisdom of academia. Moreover, his own experiences as a rebel against the established plutocratic order did more to enlighten me about the way the system really works than anything I learned as a politically naive member of the educational establishment.

Thanks in part to a generous grant from the John Anson Kittredge Educational Fund, I was able to make yet another research trip to the

Swarthmore College Peace Collection in the summer of 1988. As on my two previous trips to Swarthmore, Kate and George Myer welcomed me into their home, making me feel as though I was simply part of the family. Kate's was a double role: first as my host and friend with whom I enjoyed numerous evening strolls through the peaceful streets of Wallingford, and second, when she joined the staff of the Peace Collection, as a professional guide through the vast sources in peace history housed at Swarthmore. She, along with three curators—Bernice Nichols, J. Richard Kyle, Wendy Chmielewski—and other staff—Eleanor Barr, Barbara Addison, Mary Ellen Clark, Wilma Mosholder, Cynthia Sadler, and Marty Shane—made my three lengthy visits to the Peace Collection the stuff of which fond memories are made. Sandy Volpe and Doris Mitterling from the WILPF collection at the University of Colorado made my many weeks of research there much less tedious. I thank them both as well as Jack Brennan, who at that time was the director of the Western Historical Collection.

Without the sympathetic support and encouragement of both faculty and staff on the Hamilton Campus of Miami University, I seriously doubt that I could have successfully balanced the various responsibilities demanded of regional campus faculty in history. In particular, I am grateful to Harriet Taylor, executive director of the Hamilton Campus, and Kathleen Burgoon, coordinator of social sciences. Harriet is the ideal administrator. Her almost perfect combination of professional competence, efficiency, and reliability is tempered by a commitment to high quality education in the broadest possible sense and a compassion for humanity worthy of our emulation. Kathie's advice and understanding were no less important in my struggle against defeatism and just plain exhaustion. Faculty secretaries Jane Ristau and Theresa Troutman deserve my thanks as well; with seemingly endless patience, they typed draft after draft of the manuscript, never once complaining at my insistence upon perfection.

I am also grateful to Mary Ellen Jones of the University of California at Berkeley for her diligence in unearthing among the Anne Martin Papers the information I sought, thereby saving me the time and expense of yet another research trip. To Steve Sunderland goes my appreciation for providing a sympathetic and supportive ear when I found myself unable to keep up with the hectic schedule I set for myself.

A debt of gratitude is owed as well to former student Connie Rickert-Epstein for her thorough and enthusiastic examination of the National Woman's Party Papers. For days on end, she painstakingly went through roll after roll of microfilm, gleaning every possible bit of information relevant to the issues involved, proving beyond the shadow of a doubt what I had already surmised: Here was a young woman of exceptional intellectual curiosity, ability, and determination.

Yet Connie is by no means the only student over the years who has served to remind me of why I wanted to teach history in the first place. I think particularly of Suzanne Wenzel and Debbie Marlow: Both have gone on to excel in the academic world, Suzanne in psychology and Debbie in women's history. These three young women are not only my good friends but are as well trusted colleagues for whom I have the utmost professional respect.

Connie, Suzanne, and Debbie are only three of hundreds of students who have passed through my classroom on their way to the realization that you cannot know where you are going if you do not know where you are, and you cannot know where you are if you do not know where you have been. The faith and confidence of these students in me as a guide on this not-always-pleasant journey has sustained me when I was discouraged, and their eagerness to understand the links between and among yesterday, today, and tomorrow has given me hope that the WILPF's vision of peace, freedom, and justice for all men and women may yet be realized.

Thanks are due as well to an anonymous reader of an early draft of the manuscript whose criticisms and recommendations for revision were invaluable. In this same vein, Harriet Hyman Alonso and Charles Chatfield, two of the editors of the Syracuse Studies on Peace and Conflict Resolution, went much beyond the call of duty not only by closely reading subsequent drafts, but by making indispensable observations and suggestions as well. Eliminating more than three hundred pages from the original text would have been far more difficult had they not offered such incisive and astute editorial assistance. And always there whenever I needed her for any reason was Cynthia Maude-Gembler of Syracuse University Press. Her consistently cheerful optimism when I missed deadlines and plagued her with endless questions has never ceased to amaze me. She is more than an editor; she is my friend.

Last, but as they say, never least, has been my family. The dedication says it all.

Hamilton, Ohio
September 1993

Carrie A. Foster

Abbreviations

AAA	Agricultural Adjustment Act
AAUW	American Association of University Women
ACLU	American Civil Liberties Union
AFL	American Federation of Labor
AFSC	American Friends Service Committee
ALAWF	American League Against War and Fascism
APS	American Peace Society
ASPL	American School Peace League
CEIP	Carnegie Endowment for International Peace
CIA	Central Intelligence Agency
CPS	Civilian Public Service
CIO	Congress of Industrial Organizations
DAR	Daughters of the American Revolution
EPC	Emergency Peace Campaign
ERA	Equal Rights Amendment
FEPC	Fair Employment Practices Commission
FBI	Federal Bureau of Investigation
FOR	Fellowship of Reconciliation
HUAC	House Un-American Activities Committee
IWW	Industrial Workers of the World
ICWPP	International Committee of Women for Permanent Peace
ILGWU	International Ladies Garment Workers Union
KAOWC	Keep America Out of War Congress
LSCO	Legal Service to Conscientious Objectors
NAWSA	National American Women's Suffrage Association

NAACP	National Association for the Advancement of Colored People
NCCO	National Committee on Conscientious Objectors
NCCCW	National Conference on the Cause and Cure of War
NCPW	National Council for the Prevention of War
NCW	National Council of Women
NPC	National Peace Conference
NRA	National Recovery Administration
NSBRO	National Service Board for Religious Objectors
NWP	National Woman's Party
NATO	North Atlantic Treaty Organization
PWWC	Post War World Council
WPC	War Policies Commission
WRA	War Relocation Authority
WRL	War Resisters League
WPP	Woman's Peace Party
WCTU	Women's Christian Temperance Union
WCOC	Women's Committee to Oppose Conscription
WILPF	Women's International League for Peace and Freedom
WJCC	Women's Joint Congressional Committee
WPS	Women's Peace Society
WPU	Women's Peace Union
WWP	World Woman's Party
YWCA	Young Women's Christian Association

THE WOMEN AND THE WARRIORS

1

Introduction

THIS BOOK is about women and peace. Specifically, it is about the
United States Section of the Women's International League for Peace
and Freedom (WILPF) from its beginning in 1915 as the Woman's
Peace Party (WPP) to its near-demise at the end of World War II. It is a
story of pacifism, Progressivism, feminism, and, in a very real sense, of
failure. But it is also a story with its final chapter yet to be written, for
even as this book goes to press, the women of the WILPF continue
their struggle for world peace and social justice, a struggle begun by
their mothers and grandmothers some seventy-five years ago.

Like most of the men and women who were part of the nation's
peace movement in its heyday between the two world wars, WILPF
members recoiled in shock, horror, and disbelief at the carnage and
material destruction of World War I. Determined that history not repeat itself, interwar peace activists, however much they might disagree
over emphasis or strategy, were united by a belief that peace, in the
words of one eminent historian of the subject, was the "necessary reform."[1] For a generation raised at the end of the nineteenth century
—that "grand century of peace and progress," as Bertram Wolfe put
it—a generation that believed that the twentieth century "would surely
be too civilized for war," the impact of the Great War was without
precedent. This optimistic, self-confident generation came to realize
along with Wolfe that "it was not just one single all-embracing war, but
an age of total wars into which we were entering," and thus peace was
indeed the necessary reform if civilized society was to survive, let alone
prosper.[2]

Thus it was that World War I "fired the formation of the most dynamic peace movement in American history."[3] There were, of course,

1

numerous peace societies already in existence; between 1901 and 1914 forty-five new organizations came into being. One such organization was the American School Peace League (ASPL) founded in 1908 by social reformer and teacher Fannie Fern Andrews. Prior to the formation of the WPP after the war's outbreak, the ASPL was the only antiwar organization directed by a woman. The league formed branches in every state, sent out reams of propeace literature to schools and teachers, and was effective in introducing young people to the idea of international cooperation. But "frustrations and failures" characterized the prewar peace movement, for it was unable to command much respect or attention.[4]

Without a doubt, the largest, most influential, and financially stable peace groups prior to World War I in the United States were those founded by and dominated by men. Organizations such as the American Peace Society (APS), active since 1828; the American Peace Union, founded in 1866; the Carnegie Endowment for International Peace (CEIP) and the Church Peace Union, both founded by millionaire steel magnate Andrew Carnegie after the turn of the century; and the World Peace Foundation, incorporated in 1910 by Boston textbook publisher Edwin Ginn, all included women as members and occasionally as officers. But not until the 1920s did women come into their own as active, vocal, and influential members of the peace movement. In the two decades between World War I and World War II, "women provided both animating force and mass audiences," creating the most noteworthy antiwar crusade the United States had yet experienced.[5]

Certainly the ratification of the Nineteenth Amendment in 1920 saw the culmination of a struggle that had demanded truly heroic dedication and effort on the part of suffragists such as Carrie Chapman Catt, which then left her free to create the National Conference on the Cause and Cure of War (NCCCW) in the early 1920s. But the fact that so many women preferred to work for peace in the interwar period through organizations made up exclusively of members of their own sex is more than merely a case of substituting the goal of peace for that of suffrage.

First of all, many women who were active in the older peace groups prior to the war became impatient and frustrated with their lack of power in these organizations. As WPP National Secretary Lucia Ames Mead noted in early 1915, "women held very few offices in the old societies, and had some fresh methods of their own which they wanted to employ."[6]

Second, many women became increasingly unwilling to defer to

the authority of their male counterparts in the prewar peace movement because they were part of the first generation of women to
self-consciously insist that women were quite as capable as men of completing a college education and embarking upon professional careers.
And they had done just that. Jane Addams, Emily Greene Balch, Katherine Devereaux Blake, Madeleine Z. Doty, Anna Garlin Spencer, Amy
Woods were all leaders in the WPP and WILPF; all were college-edu-
cated professionals. Addams and Woods were social workers, Balch was
an economics professor at Wellesley College, Blake was a teacher and
administrator in the New York public school system, Doty was an attorney, and Spencer was an ordained minister. To be sure, they entered
professions that tended to reflect a concern with the welfare of others
before self and could, therefore, be considered particularly appropriate for women. But as career women they enjoyed a certain degree of
respect and influence in their professional lives that did not spill over
into their participation in the peace movement.

Third, the prevailing philosophy of the time among men and
women suggested that women shared certain nonaggressive attributes
as females. Women, because they were biologically the "mother half of
humanity," so the theory went, were by nature nurturing and sacrificing. As life-givers they were seen to be naturally more prone to conciliation, compromise, and cooperation than the male of the species; they
were the "gentler sex." Whereas woman brought life into the world and
thus instinctively sought to preserve it, it was man who, through centuries of warfare, destroyed that life. If ever there was an area of endeavor that cried out for the special and unique attributes of the
woman, it was in the realm of antiwar activity. The concept of peace
was feminine, the concept of war and violence, masculine.

The failure of men to prevent the outbreak of World War I led
women to conclude that formation of a separate women's peace society
was crucial. It was time to give organizational voice to the essential
differences between men and women, differences that were both biological and social. "It may be," thought Balch, "that since war, like
childbirth, is one of the matters in which women have a distinctly different role from men, we should always find room for a special
women's league of peace." In wartime, for example, women, as non-
combatants, had greater freedom of action than men. And, as society's
"earliest educators (in the nursery)," as mothers, and as "the guardians
of life," Balch went on, women brought a unique set of perceptions to
the peace movement.

A fourth reason for maintaining a segregated organization was to provide education and "mutual support" for that half of society who "generally do not think in political terms but in terms of feelings, and are generally concerned less about political questions than about questions of morals, health, social welfare, etc." Last, but by no means least, was the issue of power, that is, of leadership. A separate women's organization, Balch concluded, "gives scope for activity on the part of many women who would be in the background and quite inactive in a joint organization which in practice, to hold men, must be run by men."[7]

For these reasons, then, women came together to form such groups as the Woman's Peace Party, founded in 1915 by Jane Addams on the instigation of Carrie Chapman Catt; the two more radical nonresistance organizations: the Women's Peace Society, formed in 1919 by Fanny Garrison Villard, daughter of the radical abolitionist William Lloyd Garrison, and the Women's Peace Union, created in 1921 by Elinor Byrns and Caroline Lexow Babcock, among others; and the National Conference on the Cause and Cure of War (NCCCW) organized by Catt in 1924. The NCCCW served as an umbrella organization for the peace activities of other women's groups such as the League of Women Voters and the American Association of University Women. These organizations provided an arena of political activity for thousands of recently enfranchised women concerned with the issues of war and violence who might otherwise have remained on the sidelines in the interwar period.[8]

Despite substantial differences in focus and ideology among the women's peace groups, differences that occasionally resulted in harsh words and unfriendly behavior, there was much cooperation. In this respect, the female side of the peace movement operated no differently from the male-dominated organizations. Nor did the women attempt to keep themselves aloof; the conflict and cooperation that characterized relations among the women's peace groups also characterized relations between the female and male wings of the movement as a whole.

United by a belief that peace was the necessary reform, women's peace groups in the interwar period did not differ in any significant way, therefore, from those dominated by men. But the women were united in a second way that *did* set them apart from the male-dominated wing. Almost without exception, women peace activists were unwilling to accept the continued second-class citizenship of women and were, accordingly, feminists who had supported the drive for woman suffrage.

A minority, like Doty and Blake of the WPP/WILPF, were militant feminists who followed Alice Paul into the National Woman's Party after the suffrage victory and thus supported the Equal Rights Amendment. Others, like the outspoken Fanny Garrison Villard and Caroline Lexow Babcock, were not only militant feminists but radical pacifists as well, nonresisters who adamantly refused "to help in, or sanction, any undertaking which involves violence or the destruction of life."[9] Still others, exemplified by Addams, were social feminists, opposed to the Equal Rights Amendment in the belief that its implementation would invalidate protective legislation for women workers, which they saw as vital to the health and well-being of women, children, and the family. Most social feminists reflected a more moderate pacifism as well, opposing all forms of violence but more willing than nonresisters to accept half a loaf in the process. Last, there was the group associated most notably with Catt, women who worked long and hard in the suffrage campaign, but who rejected the militant tactics of Alice Paul's Congressional Union and who did not embrace either pacifism or nonresistance.

As suffragists, women such as Addams and Catt traveled extensively abroad in the international suffrage campaign, coming into close personal contact with women from all across the globe. They quickly overcame the obstacles of language difference and unfamiliar culture in their effort to reach a common goal. Whatever their differences or disagreements, these were subordinated to one overriding concern—obtaining the franchise for the politically dispossessed female.

Just as the suffrage campaign provided these women with invaluable experience in international cooperation and understanding, it also gave them the opportunity to test their organizational skills in coordinating a constituency to support a specific goal in the political realm. This background served them well in subsequently organizing for peace. More than that, the need for cooperation and coordination to achieve the franchise was also reinforced by their professional lives.

As members of the urban middle class, their professions gave them first-hand experience in the turn-of-the-century settlement houses and the communities served by such facilities. Particularly true of WILPF members, this close contact with immigrants, the working poor, juvenile offenders, and others of the dispossessed classes in the cities convinced them that friendship, cooperation, and sharing among such diverse peoples were not only necessary for harmony and progress, but also increasingly possible. As Addams asserted, any institution—like war, for example—that sought to achieve its goals through coercion "not only interrupted, but fatally reversed this process of cooperating good will which, if it had a chance, would eventually include the human family itself."[10]

Such women were, in short, "community internationalists."[11] In a world where militarists and nationalists were becoming ever more bellicose, these social workers and educators, these wives, mothers, sisters, and daughters were thinking in terms of family, community, and the brotherhood of mankind. It was not that they loved their country less, but rather that they loved humanity more. As Balch put it, "lovers of our own lands, we are citizens of the world."[12] Their loyalty transcended the artificial distinction of national boundaries to embrace the entire human race; thus, they were transnationalists rather than merely internationalists.

Although clearly influenced by the precepts of the nineteenth-century evangelical religious tradition, which stressed the golden rule and brotherly love as manifestations of God's saving grace, the women were less concerned with the kingdom of God than they were with the world of man. As secular humanists, their opposition to war and violence was predicated upon a moral philosophy committed to the sanctity of every human being. The goal they envisioned was a world of peace, harmony, and cooperation among all peoples working together for the common good, and the methodology they employed combined reason with social science and selfless benevolence.

As products of the Progressive period of reform, women peace activists in the aftermath of World War I embodied most of those characteristics associated with "the progressive temper": a commitment to democracy, faith in scientific "truth," a concern for morality and social justice, and an unswerving belief in progress and the efficacy of education.[13] They believed that reason, or intelligence, utilized in an ongoing process of education would ultimately dispel the ignorance and fear that prevented people from recognizing their common interests and needs. Although a slow and often frustrating process, such "sweet reasonableness" would, over time, obtain the "inner consent" of all, a necessary prerequisite for international amity and impossible to achieve through the coercive violence of war. As Addams said, "We still believed it possible to modify, to direct and ultimately to change current ideas, not only though discussion and careful presentation of the facts, but also through the propaganda of the deed."[14]

Just as important as reason was a sincere and dynamic attitude of good will and disinterested benevolence toward others. "If you really care about a person, or about a people, if you sincerely and strongly wish them good," maintained Balch, "they will sense it and in time, under halfway normal conditions, they will respond."[15] In like fashion, women peace activists firmly believed that as long as individuals and nations pursued their own selfish ends to the detriment of the common good, hostility, animosity, and eventually war would be the outcome. A world of genuine peace and freedom required an application of the precept to "love thy neighbor as thyself" to political, economic, and social relations among all peoples. This meant that those nations blessed with an abundance of the world's resources must share of their wealth with those countries less fortunately endowed. "To achieve this great socio-economic transformation requires many and costly sacrifices, including a timely and generous renunciation of privilege," Balch pointed out. "It may well prove that the measure of the will to do this is the measure of the capacity of our civilization to endure."[16]

For these women, then, the means of achieving their goal was as important as the goal itself. One could not expect positive results from the utilization of negative means. A war to end war was a contradiction in terms, for war breeds fear, animosity, and the desire for revenge, thus paving the way for future wars. By the same token, there could be no such thing as a war "to make the world safe for democracy," for war involves violence and coercion, and democracy is predicated upon the free choice of the individual and the voluntary consent of the people. And these women were nothing if not democrats; they firmly believed in accountable power and in the right of the sovereign people to control public decision making whatever the issue involved. That was what freedom was all about; that was why peace was necessary.

As Progressive reformers, peace activists of the 1920s believed that private power had corrupted and perverted this essentially democratic society. The solution, as they saw it, was to diminish private power by enlarging the sphere of public power, that is, by democratizing the system. And because public power meant government composed of the elected representatives of the people and sworn to implement the will of the people, the peace movement supported and encouraged government to act in favor of disarmament, outlawry of war, and international treaties and tribunals. They achieved a certain degree of success in that decade, but not to the extent that it altered in any appreciable way the existing distribution of power. And when the propeace effort of the 1920s became the antiwar struggle of the 1930s, many in the peace movement came to view public power—government—with as much distrust and apprehension as they did private power. With growing alarm, peace activists began to perceive in Franklin Roosevelt's domestic and foreign policies a subversion of the American democratic system. The public power of the government seemed to be less and less responsive to the will of the people; public power began to replace the evil of private power.

As much if not more than any other participant in the interwar peace movement, the WILPF exemplified this Progressive ideology and methodology. Thus a study of the organization's evolution from World War I through World War II provides us with yet another perspective on the subject of Progressive reform in the U.S. And because the WILPF combined Progressivism with feminism, its interwar history may also shed light on the feminist movement as it shifted gears from the suffrage campaign to other issues of importance to women. Third, as an organization of peace advocates who were female, the WILPF represents a relatively unexamined aspect of peace history. For despite the prominence of women in studies of the interwar peace movement and reform movements generally, there is only one in-depth study of a *woman's* peace organization.[17]

Of the four major women's peace groups in the 1920s and 1930s, it is generally acknowledged that the two most significant both in terms of size and influence were the NCCCW and the U.S. Section of the WILPF. Unlike Catt's group, the large membership of which was due to the fact that it acted as a clearinghouse for the peace interests of other women's organizations, the WILPF was founded as an entirely separate group. Moreover, the WILPF has been more enduring than the NCCCW. The latter was not created until 1924 and survived only until 1947, having become the Women's Action Committee for Victory and Lasting Peace in 1943. The WILPF, on the other hand, had been functioning for nine years by 1924, survived a serious schism in the early 1940s and a massive restructuring in the immediate postwar period to continue into the 1950s and beyond.

Although drastically reduced in size by the war's end, the WILPF grew slowly during the uncertain years of McCarthyism, became an outspoken critic of U.S. involvement in the Vietnam conflict in the 1960s, and was one of the major sponsors of the massive antinuclear demonstration in New York in June 1982. Whereas the NCCCW was limited in activity and scope to the United States, the U.S. Section of the WILPF has been affiliated internationally since 1919. One final reason for focusing upon the WILPF is its leadership, for until now the only two U.S. women to receive the Nobel Peace Prize have been Jane Addams and Emily Greene Balch.

The story of the women and the warriors is one of courage, commitment, and love. And it is a story of interest group politics and power. If it is also a story of failure, it is worth noting that the failure was not the women's. It is the warriors who bear the responsibility for the failure to achieve peace and freedom after the Great War, for it was these men of power, here and abroad, who continued to rely on force and the threat of force to attain their goals. Yet the story is not over, for the WILPF and others in the peace movement continue their struggle for a nonviolent and just world looking toward that day when the story ends, as ideally it should, with the observation that they all lived happily ever after.

2

Born of War

"WE DO NOT THINK we can settle the war. We do not think that by raising our hands we can make the armies cease slaughter. We do think it is valuable to state a new point of view. We do think it is fitting that women should meet and take counsel to see what may be done."[1]

So commented Jane Addams on 13 April 1915 as she and forty-six other American women set sail for The Hague to attend an International Women's Congress, despite the war that raged in Europe. Although the delegation was composed of well-educated professional women, it was primarily as feminists and pacifists that they were invited to attend the congress as members of the recently formed Woman's Peace Party. The congress had been called to organize women internationally to bring an early end to World War I.

Like the majority of the Progressive generation, the women who formed the WPP three months earlier were stunned by the outbreak of the war, believing as they did that war of such magnitude was a thing of the distant past. Credit for catalyzing the American women into action, however, belonged to two European suffragists, Emmeline Pethick-Lawrence of Great Britain and Rosika Schwimmer, Hungarian journalist, social worker, and pacifist. Both women came to the United States shortly after the war's outbreak to enlist public opinion behind the drive for an early peace as well as for woman suffrage.

Schwimmer, who had met Carrie Chapman Catt in 1904 at an International Women's Congress in Berlin, was one of a number of people who at the time had a plan for neutral mediation of the war. Schwimmer framed hers in the form of a petition that she and Catt presented to President Woodrow Wilson on 18 September 1914. Signed by women from eleven European countries, the petition called for the establishment of a world parliament and international nonmilitary sanctions as well as for neutral mediation. Shortly thereafter Pethick-Lawrence arrived in the United States and in the aftermath of a speech in Chicago in which she endorsed Schwimmer's plan, the Chicago Emergency Federation of Peace Forces was formed. With Addams as chairperson the federation was to provide organizational support for the idea of neutral mediation initiated by the United States.

Neither Schwimmer nor Pethick-Lawrence was satisfied with the formation of a merely local organization, however, so both women urged Addams and Catt to call a national conference of women to address the issues in Schwimmer's petition. Addams generally preferred to work for social change through organizations composed of both men and women, but she found herself agreeing with Catt that the male-dominated peace societies seemed ineffective at best and, too, women appeared to be more eager to bring about an early end to the war.

Catt, although not disinterested in the peace movement, was more single-mindedly devoted to the suffrage cause and thought it best to remain aloof from any women's peace organization so as not to confuse it in the public mind with the suffrage question. Moreover, Catt did not want to be too closely identified with the English suffragist for Pethick-Lawrence was associated with the militant wing of the British suffrage movement which was decidedly anti-German. As president of the International Suffrage Alliance, Catt could not afford to alienate any segment of the suffrage movement. Finally, Catt was concerned that the militant wing among U.S. suffragists might attempt to exert a controlling influence at such a conference because Pethick-Lawrence had ties with members of the Congressional Union, which was meeting at the same time and place proposed for the peace convention.

It may be that Catt's desire to prevent this latter possibility from occurring persuaded her to cosponsor the conference despite her misgivings, for in late 1914 she and Addams sent invitations to all national women's organizations with peace committees to attend a conference in Washington, D.C., on 10 and 11 January 1915. Some 3,000 women turned out for this conference at which the WPP was born. Represented among them was every possible shade of thought within the woman movement. Antisuffragists made the trip as did moderate and militant suffragists, socialists, radical pacifists, and social feminists.[2]

Moderate feminism with a prosuffrage perspective prevailed from the outset, due to the choice of Addams, Catt, and Dr. Anna Howard Shaw as keynote speakers and to the eighty-six-member platform committee that met the day before. All but one of the eleven planks in the platform that resulted from two intense days of debate addressed the issues of war, peace, and international relations. That final plank undoubtedly alienated the antisuffragists present for it was an unequivocal demand for woman suffrage.

The remainder of the platform was, in the words of one historian, "relatively daring."[3] Reflecting the women's first priority of ending the war quickly, it called for the immediate formation of an official conference of neutral nations. Three additional planks called for the democratic control of foreign policies, the removal of the economic causes of war, and nationalization of arms manufacture so as to take the profit out of preparation for war. A fifth plank, like that demanding woman suffrage, reflected a feminist influence as it called for the appointment by the U.S. government of a "commission of men *and women* . . . to promote international peace."[4]

The details of the platform were spelled out in the group's "Program for Constructive Peace," which urged the creation of a world court and an international legislative and administrative body, a permanent League of Neutral Nations, total disarmament, internationalization of world waterways and free trade, and, of course, the extension of democracy by including women in the franchise. That both platform and program were accepted with little dissension is an indication of the women's realistic understanding of the dynamics of international politics as well as their repudiation of a narrow-minded and chauvinistic nationalism.

Although "daring," there was nothing particularly new or earth-shattering in these proposals; they were fairly commonplace to all peace groups at the time, both in the United States and abroad. What was new among peace groups was the justification for the formation of a separate women's peace organization, written into the platform's preamble by Anna Garlin Spencer. This explanation expressed the prevalent belief in the distinct differences inherent in the female sex that made women biologically as well as culturally disposed toward life-sustaining rather than life-destroying endeavors.

"As women," declared the preamble, "we feel a peculiar moral passion of revolt against both the cruelty and the waste of war." This revulsion against war was unique to woman because she was the "custodian of the life of the ages," and had been "charged with the future of childhood and with the care of the helpless and the unfortunate." Over the centuries with patient toil women had laid the foundations of home, family, and "peaceful industry," and now protested the wanton destruction of this social structure by the male half of humanity. As the "mother half" of the human race, therefore, the women demanded the right to be consulted in matters concerning not just the lives of individuals but of nations as well. As the WPP statement of purpose declared, "We . . . give united help toward translating the mother instinct of life-saving into social terms of the common good."[5] Hence, they came together as women to give formal organization to their beliefs and political clout to their demands.

The women who enthusiastically endorsed the platform and program thus reflected the feminist wing of the women's movement, which desired the vote and the moderate wing of the suffrage movement, which called for the vote on the basis of gender difference rather than as a political right guaranteed in a democratic society. This sentiment was essentially that of social feminism and, not surprisingly, social feminists not only dominated the January proceedings but made up the majority of the eighty-five women who became charter members and officers of the WPP. Addams, for example, was elected chairperson and among the other officers were Spencer, Alice Thacher Post, Lucia Ames Mead, and Sophonisba Breckinridge, social feminists all.[6]

As a moderate feminist women's peace society, the newly formed WPP immediately made its presence known. To strengthen the political power of all peace groups through federation, the WPP called for a national emergency conference to be held on 27 February in Chicago, now national headquarters for the women's peace group. The 300 men and women who gathered for the conference formed the National Peace Federation with Addams as chairperson and immediately launched a nationwide campaign for a conference of neutral nations.

In the meantime, the invitation came from Europe requesting the attendance of a delegation of American women at the International Women's Congress to be held at The Hague in late April. Issued by Dr. Aletta Jacobs, the first woman physician in the Netherlands and president of the Dutch National Society for Woman Suffrage, it was the result of the failure of the International Suffrage Alliance to hold its biennial meeting in Berlin in June 1915 as previously arranged. Because of the war, the German branch of the suffrage group withdrew its invitation to host the meeting, a decision with which Catt fully concurred for she thereupon canceled the meeting altogether, fearing that "an attempt to call an International Congress might disturb the harmonious working of the national suffrage groups."[7]

A handful of European women vigorously disagreed with this decision, among them Dr. Jacobs and Scottish lawyer Chrystal Macmillan, secretary of the International Alliance. They were convinced that in this time of animosity among nations, women from all across the globe should meet to demonstrate that they at least could rise above wartime hatreds and come together in friendship and accord. As Holland was neutral and The Hague symbolic of peace, they were determined to bring such a meeting about. Thus a small committee of women from Britain, Belgium, Germany, and the Netherlands met in Amsterdam in February 1915 to plan a preliminary program for an international women's congress. Desirous of a presiding officer of stature and from a neutral country, they chose Addams. She accepted and on 13 April forty-seven women from the United States, the majority of them members of the WPP, sailed for The Hague.

By all accounts, it was an impressive delegation for besides Addams it included Grace Abbott, director of the Immigrants Protective League; Fannie Fern Andrews; Emily Greene Balch, Wellesley College professor; Sophonisba Breckinridge, University of Chicago professor and dean of the Chicago School of Civics and Philanthropy; Madeleine Z. Doty, prominent lawyer and juvenile court investigator; Elizabeth Glendower Evans, women's trade union organizer; Lucy Biddle Lewis, trustee of Swarthmore College; Alice Thacher Post, vice-president of the American Anti-Imperialist League and wife of Louis F. Post, assistant secretary of labor; Julia Grace Wales, English professor from the University of Wisconsin and author of a widely circulated plan for neutral mediation; and Dr. Alice Hamilton, vice president of the American Medical Association and special investigator of dangerous trades for the Department of Labor.

Because congress membership was restricted to those women who agreed that women should have the vote and that international disputes should be settled by pacific means, the 1,135 delegates were not only feminists and suffragists but pacifists. Immediately forming themselves into the International Committee of Women for Permanent Peace (ICWPP), with near-unanimity they quickly adopted nineteen resolutions that reflected both views, including demands for total disarmament, a World Court, woman suffrage, and the participation of women at the postwar peace negotiations. Only resolution number 20, put forward by Schwimmer, created any notable controversy. It stipulated that the congress send envoys to both neutral and belligerent nations to express the women's views as embodied in the resolutions.

Addams and Macmillan, among others, were dubious about the efficacy of such an undertaking but because the majority supported it, both skeptics deferred and agreed to represent the congress as envoys.

Addams, Jacobs, and Rosa Genoni of Italy were selected as the envoys to the belligerent nations, joined by two unofficial delegates, Dr. Alice Hamilton and Frau van Wulfften Palthe of The Hague. Macmillan, Balch, Schwimmer, Cor Ramondt-Hirschmann of Holland, and Baroness Ellen Palmstierna of Sweden visited the neutral countries accompanied by Lola Maverick Lloyd of the United States and Julia Grace Wales who acted as secretary for part of the journey. Each group embarked upon its mission in May, shortly after the congress closed, visiting fourteen countries in five weeks.

It is difficult to assess the real impact that these women had on the twenty-two prime ministers and foreign ministers with whom they visited. The tone in the United States was set by Theodore Roosevelt who referred to the entire congress as being "silly and base,"[8] and there may have been many Americans who silently agreed, but the women thought that their efforts had a definite positive effect. They were received cordially in each country, belligerent and neutral alike, as they presented their foremost proposal that a neutral conference for continuous mediation be held as soon as possible.

An important reason for quickly convening such a conference stemmed from the women's belief, best expressed by Addams, that the prolongation of the war was primarily an issue of ignorance among the peoples of the belligerent nations. The women thought that once challenged by the facts, people's aggressive inclinations would quickly dissipate, and the result would be a European-wide clamor for peace. "The greatest obstacle to the development of public sentiment for peace," Addams believed, "is control of the press by the military authorities. They will not permit any discussion of peace."[9] A conference of neutral nations could provide the public forum necessary to counter the prejudice, misplaced emotion, and distorted propaganda, thus opening lines of communication for an early negotiated end to the conflict.

Although the envoys reported that the official response to their overtures was encouraging, it is quite possible that the statesmen, belligerent and neutral alike, were simply exercising good manners as they patiently listened to the women's recommendations. Whatever the truth of the matter, the women returned home in July 1915 persuaded that an official conference of neutral nations was still in the realm of possibility.

In alliance with the National Peace Federation, the WPP spent the better part of the next few months trying to convince Woodrow Wilson to call such a conference. Peace forces pointed out that "the belligerent countries stand ready to accept collective action and the European neutrals are eager and ready to act." The United States, they went on, was the sole stumbling block for it alone "keeps the world waiting by remaining apathetic." With words designed to appeal to the Progressive sense of moral obligation as well as to its outrage over the influence of private power in the public sphere, peace advocates exhorted Americans to take a stand: "Do you realize what a tremendous burden of responsibility is thus thrown upon us? In an age in which all the world is our neighbor, shall we continue to stand aloof? Shall we justify the charge, already openly expressed by Teuton and Ally alike, that our greed for money and power prompts us deliberately to withhold our co-operation, so that a weakened and bankrupt Europe may assure our commercial and political supremacy?"[10]

Such strong words were backed by action. In early October ICWPP leaders met in New York and issued a public manifesto calling for an official conference of neutrals. A week later the delegates to the Fifth International Peace Congress in San Francisco commissioned David Starr Jordan, president of Stanford University, and Louis P. Lochner, secretary of the National Peace Federation, to visit Wilson with such a plea. The meeting with the president took place on 12 November 1915, four days after a carefully planned national demonstration in behalf of neutral mediation had inundated the White House with 20,000 telegrams. As was the case later in November when Addams, Schwimmer, and Lillian Wald conferred with the president, Wilson temporized on the issue. Disappointed but not yet defeated, the WPP organized a mass meeting in Washington on 26 November to coincide with a visit to Wilson by Schwimmer and Ethel Snowden of England. Despite another 12,000 telegrams to the White House, the women reported that once again the president was unwilling to commit himself.

Members of the WPP were much discouraged by Wilson's obvious disinclination to call a conference of neutrals. Although Jordan reported that the president had been unusually receptive to the idea, the women concluded that Wilson endorsed only his own personal mediation, not a collective effort. The women did not know how right they were, for they did not know that by the end of November 1915 secret negotiations between Edward M. House, Wilson's primary adviser on foreign policy, and Sir Edward Grey, British foreign secretary, had been underway for almost a year. Their negotiations eventually resulted in the House-Grey Memorandum of 22 February 1916. Envisioning an entirely different role for the United States than the one pursued by the peace movement, that document stipulated that when the Allies indicated their readiness, Wilson would call a conference to end the war. Should Germany balk at the idea, the United States would enter the war on the Allied side. If the conference was convened and Germany then refused to accept "reasonable" terms for ending the conflict, again the United States "probably" would enter the war on the side of England and France.[11]

By 1916, this hidden agenda provided an important impetus to the country's preparedness movement, fueled by German submarine warfare in the spring and summer of 1915. In the fall of 1915, Wilson called for an increased military budget, a larger navy, and a 400,000-man army. The WPP protested that such a move at this critical juncture would create distrust and fear of the United States among other nations and this, in turn, would lessen U.S. moral influence once the war was over and would disqualify the president from rendering a truly neutral mediation in the meantime. Moreover, other nations would feel compelled to match U.S. military increases with their own, thereby creating rivalry, suspicion, and burdensome taxation for all concerned.

Given the women's observation that Americans seemed "obsessed by fear of some possible future German invasion," they recognized that any public statement concerning such an emotionally charged issue as war preparedness must also address the issue of national defense. It was clear to them that there was no need for concern on this score: "We believe in real defense for real dangers, but not in a preposterous 'preparedness' against hypothetical dangers."[12] Armaments, the WPP pointed out repeatedly, were not synonymous with defense.

The fight against preparedness was the theme of the WPP's first annual meeting, held in Washington, D.C., in early January 1916. There was easy consensus among the 150 delegates in calling for a congressional investigation of the current state of U.S. military readiness and the likelihood of attack by a foreign country as well as for "action to provide for the elimination of all private profit from the manufacture of armament."[13] But where the women's earlier public stance on preparedness indicated consensus on the issue of national defense, this was no longer the case by January. Radical pacifists wanted the party to adopt their view of absolute nonresistance even in the event of attack, but that was a position that went too far for the majority, pacifist and nonpacifist alike. It was a difference of opinion that caused no serious problems for the time being, but it foreshadowed the rupture that eventually occurred in 1919 when a small contingent of radical pacifists left the WPP to form the Women's Peace Society (WPS).

Following the close of its annual meeting a delegation from the

WPP led by Addams appeared before Congress to testify against any preparedness measures. In a lengthy statement before the House Committee on Foreign Affairs on 13 January, Addams suggested that the demand to increase the size of the military establishment was due to war hysteria emanating from Europe. There was no need to increase arms in this country, she contended, until the United States had an enemy and knew who that enemy was.

When nothing of substance materialized from the hearings, a new antipreparedness group quickly emerged to lead the fight. Formally launched in April 1916, the American Union Against Militarism did not fold when only one month later Congress acceded to almost all of Wilson's preparedness program. Instead, it remained in the forefront of the anti-intervention movement for the next year.

The election that fall changed the situation very little. Although disappointed in the president's stand on preparedness and in his refusal to initiate an official neutral conference, peace advocates found nothing more promising offered by his Republican opponent Charles Evans Hughes. Moreover, Wilson's pledge of U.S. willingness to participate in a postwar association of nations for the promotion of international peace and democracy persuaded peace groups that he still shared their vision of what the world might become once the war was over. The election was close but despite the jingoism of Republicans like Theodore Roosevelt (whom Addams had supported in 1912) and Henry Cabot Lodge, both of whom wanted U.S. intervention on the side of the Allies, the American people returned Wilson to the White House hoping that he would continue to keep them out of war.

Mediation of the conflict became a matter of the utmost urgency by the time of the election for after two years of this war of attrition, the cost to both sides was staggering. Almost prostrate economically, the Allies could win only with direct U.S. military intervention, and that intervention was practically assured if Germany engaged in unrestricted submarine warfare, which was its only hope for victory. Time was fast running out for those who urged a mediated peace.

In mid-December hopes were raised when the German government called for a conference of belligerents. Wilson sought to encourage the idea by suggesting that as a basis for such a gathering both sides specify their war aims, but the results were disappointing. Thus on 31 January 1917 Germany announced her resumption of unrestricted submarine warfare. Its navy would henceforth sink all ships in a war zone around Great Britain and that, of course, at some point would mean U.S. ships. Hoping to forestall any precipitous action by the administration, on 3 February Addams wired Wilson expressing the WPP's hope that he would "find it possible to meet the present international situation in league with other neutral nations in Europe and South America whose interests are similarly involved." Suggesting that "such an allegiance" could provide the framework of a "League of Nations," at the very least it would "offer a method of approach less likely to involve any one nation in war."[14]

Wilson's advisors saw the situation differently. Within a matter of hours the president, albeit with deep regret, severed diplomatic relations with Germany, an ominous sign that catalyzed the country's peace forces into action as never before. The WPP sent a lengthy telegram to Wilson two days later, again suggesting that he call a conference of neutral nations before the United States was drawn into the war, and urging a referendum vote of the American people to ascertain "whether it is their wish to defend American commerce by war."[15]

On 7 February the country's peace groups formed an Emergency Peace Committee to organize the American people behind a massive campaign to pressure Congress into calling for a national referendum and conference of neutrals. WPP members joined hundreds of like-minded Americans in a Lincoln's birthday pacifist demonstration in the nation's capital on 12 February and a little over a week later, unanimously adopted a statement of principles with recommendations for action.

The women urged U.S. citizens to refrain from entering "the danger zone" and beseeched their government in case of an "overt act" against the United States in the stepped-up submarine warfare to limit its response to "the protection of its citizens and commerce through the use of its Navy as a police force without declaration of war." Should such an "overt act" appear to mean imminent war, however, the women called for a referendum of the people before war could be declared. They further reminded their government of the arbitration treaties to which this country was a signatory and expressed their hope that these would be adhered to. After once again imploring Wilson to continue efforts at mediation, they stated unequivocally that should the United States enter the conflict, it should act on its own or with other neutral nations and "under no circumstances ally itself with any of the belligerents, since their aims and ambitions may differ substantially from our own."[16]

Meeting in New York on 22 and 23 February to formulate a national program of action, the nineteen members of the Emergency Peace Committee used the WPP's statement of principles as the basis for their discussion. Despite the unanimous sense of urgency shared by all, disagreement arose over two issues. In drawing up its statement, the WPP's executive board had divided sharply over the issue of a referendum vote. In the desire to present a united front, however, those who opposed the idea agreed to compromise and thus approved the statement. When the same issue was raised in the Emergency Peace Committee the more conservative organizations such as the American Peace Society (APS) opposed it, while the WPP and the American Union Against Militarism supported it. There was also notable dissension over whether or not the committee should vote a resolution of unconditional confidence in the president's leadership. Again the division was between the more conservative groups that favored such a resolution and the liberal-pacifist organizations that opposed it.

Even though the more conservative groups were male-dominated this difference of opinion was not one of gender. Rather, it was a difference of methodological approach stemming from two opposing ideological perspectives concerning the exercise of power. The liberal-pacifist groups envisioned a postwar world where all nations would work collectively to keep the peace by striving to eliminate the causes of war through conciliation and compromise. The more conservative peace societies also supported international cooperation but in a more negative fashion.

The older established APS, for example, took a legalistic view of the postwar world, stressing the importance of enforcing international law through the auspices of a world court. The more recently formed League to Enforce Peace emphasized Great Power maintenance of the peace through a league of nations that would employ military force against any member who threatened the international status quo. Thus where collective power for the liberal-pacifist groups would be exercised positively for peace, collective power for the conservative organizations would be exercised negatively against war.

This difference in approach among peace organizations would surface again in the postwar period because the disagreement over the positive or negative exercise of power remained. The liberal-pacifist wing perceived power in a positive fashion for it envisioned a postwar world of power exercised from the bottom up, one where nations would be organized democratically and, hence, the causes of war would be progressively eliminated as the peoples of all nations worked in concert through their representatives under the auspices of an international association to further justice, economic equity, and political freedom. The conservative wing emphasized the negative exercise of power on the basis of enforcement from the top down. For them peace meant a stable world order that could be maintained only if legal and military institutional arrangements were erected by the Great Powers to ensure that no one among them and no lesser power could attempt to upset the balance.

Although one position was more democratically oriented and the other leaned in the direction of elitism, the difference was not serious enough in February 1917 to prevent compromise within the Emergency Peace Committee's conference. It was a trade-off, with the liberal-pacifist groups winning a limited vote of confidence in Wilson's leadership and the conservatives defeating the resolution for a referendum vote.

Three days later Wilson asked Congress for power to arm U.S. merchant ships, thus apparently vindicating that limited vote of confidence by the peace movement. Two delegations of pacifists, including Addams and Balch of the WPP, called on the president in protest. They left the White House much discouraged, for Wilson made it clear that in his opinion if the United States did not enter the war, it could do little in its aftermath to effect a constructive peace. Addams was keenly disturbed with this view for she perceived him to be saying that a constructive peace was predicated upon his own personal intercession at the peace talks. It seemed to her an overrating of the moral leadership that any one individual can possess as well as a deviation from the principle of democracy that Wilson so strongly espoused. Addams thought, along with others in the peace movement, that Wilson's opportunity to influence the peace talks in a positive fashion would be greater as a neutral than as head of a belligerent nation.

When the Senate failed to act upon his request, the president found an old law that could be used and on 12 March ordered the arming of the U.S. merchant marine. At about the same time Carrie Chapman Catt renounced pacifism, offering the services of her suffrage organization to the government in the event of U.S. entry into the war, and shortly thereafter she resigned from both the WPP and the ICWPP.

In mid-March when it was learned that three U.S. ships had been sunk by submarines, the peace movement had only one straw left to grasp, that perhaps Congress could be persuaded to reject a presidential request for a declaration of war. On 2 April the members of the Emergency Peace Committee converged on Washington with countless other Americans. Prevented by a swollen police force from holding a parade, peace advocates held a meeting followed by a large demonstration at the capitol and heated exchanges with members of Congress.

Tension was high and tempers were short as prowar and antiwar groups waited the arrival of the president at Congress. It was a losing battle for those who still clung to the hope that the United States could remain neutral, because that evening Wilson went before both Houses of Congress and in a moving speech asked for a declaration of war against the Central Powers.

It would be the war to end all wars, he said, it would make the world "safe for democracy." In calling for this moral crusade the president repudiated his earlier position of January that only a peace without victory could lay the foundation of a stable peaceful postwar world. It was an eloquent speech designed to appeal to the Progressive mentality and despite the still-pervasive sentiment among the American people to remain aloof, it succeeded.[17] Congress took four days to debate the issue, during which the WPP and other peace groups lobbied desperately, but on Good Friday, 6 April 1917, the United States entered World War I on the side of the Allied Powers.

3

Struggle to Survive

THE OUTBREAK OF WORLD WAR I had presented women activists of an antiwar persuasion with a number of challenges to their understanding of the way the world ought to be, and they had responded to those challenges quickly and effectively. Intent on organizing an international women's peace group, they met the challenges of the war's violence, the danger and difficulty of wartime travel, and male ridicule with courage and commitment, and successfully formed the ICWPP.

Resolved to do all they could to bring an early negotiated end to the conflict, the ICWPP met the challenge of wartime hatred and suspicion with no less determination. Personally pressuring belligerent and neutral alike, the women were undaunted in their efforts to persuade national leaders to convene a conference of neutrals and accept a negotiated peace without victory.

When statesmen failed to yield to such pressure, the women of the WPP found themselves faced with yet another challenge—how to prevent U.S. entry into the war. They again rose to meet the challenge by utilizing every legal means within a democratic society to stave off this possibility. But the men of power viewed the situation differently, and the result was U.S. military involvement on the side of the Allies.

It is perhaps noteworthy that of the war-related challenges confronted by the women, only the one where the women exercised the power of decision—organizing and sustaining a peace organization—succeeded in achieving its objective. Although this seems to lend credence to the prevailing wisdom of the time regarding women's more conciliatory and cooperative nature, two related challenges posed by U.S. involvement in the war suggest otherwise. First, the "war hysteria" prevalent in the country after April was not restricted to males, and was a phenomenon that the WPP tried valiantly but in vain to counter. Second, by the war's end, the WPP was struggling desperately to meet a challenge to its very existence as an organization because membership had dwindled away to almost nothing.

The war years were difficult for the handful of pacifist members of the WPP who did not succumb to the pro-war hysteria rampant in the United States by the spring of 1917. Shortly after the declaration of war the WPP issued its "Program During War Time," which opposed conscription and compulsory military training and called for a just war settlement and a spirit of good will toward all. Addams testified before Congress against a conscription bill and the Espionage Act, and was one of a committee of pacifists that called upon Secretary of War Newton Baker to urge absolute exemption for conscientious objectors. Such pleas fell upon deaf ears as the Wilson administration "prepared to compel national war loyalty through statutory law."[1] In May the president approved a conscription act and early the following month he signed the Espionage Act into law. Conscientious objectors were given a choice between noncombatant military service and military imprisonment.

Addams attempted to explain the WPP's position in public appearances throughout the country, but her audiences were cool if not actually hostile. One angry letter-writer called her an "awful ass" and condemned her speeches as being "unpatriotic and pro-German."[2] She was under constant surveillance by the government and Secret Service agents broke into WPP headquarters in Chicago searching for evidence of subversive activity.

Two issues of *Four Lights*, the New York chapter's monthly newsletter begun in January, were barred from the mail in the summer. The July issue included a particularly "devastating attack on military preparedness" that suggested rather sardonically that women, too, could play a role in this war. "Women must not feel," the article began, "that because they work in the narrow confines of the home, they cannot help in the great work of destruction. . . . Now is the time for them to prove that they are glad and eager to destroy joyfully all that they and other women have produced. It takes but a minute to destroy a boy into whose making have gone eighteen years of thoughtful care." Within three days an agent from the Department of Justice was in the *Four Lights* office demanding to know the "ancestry of the editors."[3]

The WPP did not fare any better at the hands of private citizens. As Addams later recalled, "It was often far from pleasant to enter the office. If a bit of mail protruded from the door, it was frequently spat

upon, and although we rented our quarters in a first class office building on Michigan Boulevard facing the lake, the door was often be-
fouled in hideous ways."[4]

In October 1917 the executive board of the WPP met for the first
time since U.S. entry into the war. The meeting was held "in a country
house in the suburbs of Philadelphia. The officers, who came from
New York, Boston, St. Louis, Chicago and Philadelphia, appeared in
the role of guests at a house party in order that their hostess might not
suffer from public opinion." Out of this meeting came the first public
response of the organization to the wartime emotionalism. "We gladly
note all the incitements to noble and unselfish action of which these
troubled times bear fruit," proclaimed the women. "Any suspicion or
resentment manifested toward any 'pacifist' group meets with no 're-
prisals' from us. Our business is to help mitigate all the horrors of war
by consistently refusing to make any sacrifice of human fellowship and
good will."

Hoping to reach the essential benevolence and tolerance that they
believed to be beneath the surface of the uglier aspects of the national
temper, they went on: "We throw back no verbal brick-bats; on the
contrary, we set ourselves to sympathetic understanding of those from
whom we differ, and to grateful recognition of their contributions to
that common fund of ethical idealism and of wise mastery of political
problems upon which the reconstruction of the world depends."[5]

By the fall of 1917, however, wartime xenophobia had taken its
toll. Government-sanctioned efforts to silence antiwar opposition combined with the suppression of civil liberties and mob violence against
pacifists, blacks, socialists, ethnic aliens, and radical labor could not be
contained by expressions of "sweet reasonableness," however sincere,
and the WPP suffered accordingly. Vilified and ostracized for their refusal to join in the national orgy of chauvinism and patriotism, women
like Addams and Balch agonized over their position as friends and colleagues, one after another, left the pacifist fold, decimating its ranks.

When Carrie Chapman Catt left the WPP she took with her the
women who were more prosuffrage than antiwar, a defection that from
a purely pragmatic perspective made eminently good sense. It would
serve no useful purpose for suffragists to antagonize the male-dominated power structure after so many years of struggle to win it over to
the cause. Moreover, that cause might actually be furthered if women
could show themselves to be equally as loyal and patriotic in their support of the war as men. Catt was not persuaded that the war would
usher in the millennium, but securing the franchise for women was

more immediately important to her than a principled stand for pacifism. Once the vote was secured women could then use it to abolish war.

Paul Kellogg of the *Survey,* John Dewey, and many social workers also joined the ranks of the prowar enthusiasts. Kellogg declined to publish Addams's speech on "Patriotism and Pacifism in Wartime" because it was too controversial; Dewey envisioned major social reforms as a possible outcome of the war; and Mary Kingsbury Simkhovitch, president of the National Federation of Settlements, broke with Addams over the issue, publicly defending U.S. entry into the conflict. "The force of the majority," Addams wrote later, "was so overwhelming that it seemed not only impossible to hold one's own against it, but at moments absolutely unnatural, and one secretly yearned to participate in the 'folly of all mankind'."[6]

There was also the fear that in "holding one's own," the pacifist would acquiesce in a different but equally as undesirable an evil: "Conscience was uneasy, as well it might be," wrote Balch. "Where is the line dividing inner integrity from fanatical self-will? I do not know whether what held me should be called a religious faith or an irresistible set of the inner self, or fanaticism."[7] Regardless of what "held" her, it was strong enough to cost Balch her job for she was fired by Wellesley College for her pacifist stand and although the school later apologized, Balch never returned to teaching.

Other middle class women, those who endorsed the war, fared much better. Eager to aid in the national cause, they were mobilized by the Committee on Women's Defense Work under the direction of suffrage leader Dr. Anna Howard Shaw who, like Catt, repudiated WPP pacifism. Under the auspices of Shaw's committee, women from the National American Women's Suffrage Association (NAWSA), the General Federation of Women's Clubs, and the National Council of Women (NCW) threw themselves enthusiastically into the war effort by pushing the sale of liberty bonds and obtaining food conservation pledges from housewives. Little of the committee's work was crucial to the national enterprise but it provided thousands of women with a sense of shared purpose and usefulness on the home front in support of their men overseas.

Alice Hamilton was appalled that so many American women seemed to find joy and satisfaction in support of the war but Addams, although saddened by the same phenomenon, understood its origin in that wave of intense nationalism that comes from the belief that one is working for some common good. Despite the pervasive view that anyone who did not openly and enthusiastically endorse the war was thus a coward and a traitor, WPP pacifists, like the Quakers, socialists, and hundreds of conscientious objectors, did not abandon their prewar beliefs. "The ability to hold out against mass suggestion," Adams concluded after considerable inner turmoil, "to honestly differ from the convictions and enthusiasm of one's best friends did in moments of crisis come to depend upon the categorical belief that a man's primary allegiance is to his vision of the truth and that he is under obligation to affirm it."[8]

WPP pacifists paid a high price for that affirmation. They could live with the social opprobrium and even the charges of cowardice and treason, but the resulting isolation and alienation was the more difficult to bear because their repudiation of the majority belief ran counter to their sense of and commitment to, community. "Is there not a great value in mass judgment and in instinctive mass enthusiasms?" Addams wondered. "And even if one were right a thousand times over in conviction, was he not absolutely wrong in abstaining from this communion with his fellows?"[9] These women were neither saints nor martyrs and it was not enough for them as feminists and pacifists to wait out the war until in its aftermath they could begin again to work for women's rights and peace. They were activists, social reformers whose lives had meaning only in doing, and in doing with and for others, with and for community.

Addams finally found a way to restore her sense of usefulness to the community without, in her own mind, compromising her pacifist convictions. In early 1918 she began a speaking tour of the country as part of Herbert Hoover's Department of Food Administration. There was a certain poignant irony in her appeal to the nation's housewives to conserve food and increase its production, for in so doing, she joined the many nonpacifist women of the government's Committee on Defense Work engaged in the same endeavor.

Unlike the women of Shaw's group, however, Addams used this publicly accepted forum to talk about more than food. She stressed the importance of creating an international organization after the war as part of a cooperative global effort to preserve peace by preventing hunger. She suggested that perhaps the Russian Revolution of the previous year was based upon the peasant soldier's "instinct" to till the soil rather than continue the senseless bloodletting of war. And she spoke, thought, and wrote about the long historical connection between the human need for food to survive and the role of women as providers. Reviled when she spoke about women and peace, she was accepted and even again admired when she spoke about women and food. So long as she acted the part she looked, "a woman who has ever mothered humanity," people were willing to listen.[10]

Other WPP members were equally as nonthreatening in their wartime activities. Leaving the more controversial issues of civil rights violations and the plight of conscientious objectors to such organizations as the Fellowship of Reconciliation and the newly created Civil Liberties Bureau, the WPP concentrated on educating the public toward a more rational reconstruction of the world in the war's aftermath. Working closely with the American School Peace League, the Committee on International Relations of the Daughters of the American Revolution, and the World Alliance of Churches, the women pacifists spoke to receptive audiences in schools and women's clubs on topics such as "The New Preparedness," "The Teacher's Task in Wartime," and "After the War, What?"[11] One theme was pervasive: A durable peace could only come through a democratically organized world functioning under the auspices of international organization.

On 8 January 1918 Woodrow Wilson went before Congress and in a major address on Allied war aims, explained his goals for a postwar world of peace and stability. Known as his Fourteen Points speech, it was everything the WPP hoped for: "We are glad to see in the forefront of this statement the fundamental basis of the new world order—democratic diplomacy, freedom of the seas, equality of trade conditions, the greatest possible reduction of armaments, prime regard in colonial matters for the welfare of the population themselves, cooperation with the new Russia, and finally, formation of a general association of nations." The WPP enthusiastically recommended the president's program to the twenty-one sections of the ICWPP, calling it "the most profound and brilliant formulation as yet put forth by any responsible statesman of the program of international reorganization."[12] With renewed hope for the future, WPP members began to prepare for their first postwar reunion with the other national sections of the ICWPP.

One of the resolutions passed at The Hague Congress in 1915 called for the ICWPP to meet again after the war at the same time and place of the official peace conference in the effort to influence the outcome of those negotiations. With the signing of the Armistice on 11 November 1918 ICWPP pacifists all across the globe readied themselves to travel. Rather than meet without the presence of their colleagues from the Central Powers who could not go to France, ICWPP leaders scheduled their Congress for Zurich, Switzerland. In early April 1919 twenty-six WPP delegates sailed for Europe, among them Addams, Balch, Alice Hamilton, Lillian Wald, and Jeannette Rankin, the Montana congresswoman who had voted against U.S. entry into the war.

In late April the women arrived in France where they stayed for the next three weeks. They first went to Paris where they spent a few days consulting with members of the French section of the ICWPP and with Edward House, Herbert Hoover, and other officials at the peace conference. Then a small contingent of the delegation, including Addams, Hamilton, and Rankin, took a five-day tour of the "devastated districts" under the guidance of the American Red Cross.[13] Appalled at the destruction and desolation they saw, it was not difficult for the women to imagine the misery and suffering of the thousands of men who had died there.

With Addams as president, the Zurich Congress opened on 12 May with 147 women from fifteen countries in attendance. Because most had attended The Hague Congress four years before, they looked forward eagerly to this long-anticipated reunion. Yet it was a painful experience as well for the faces of the European women clearly showed that it was not only the combatants who suffered in war. Upon greeting an Austrian woman whom she had not seen since the earlier Congress, Addams could scarcely believe her eyes. "She was so shrunken and changed that I had much difficulty in identifying her with the beautiful woman I had seen three years before," she recalled. "She was not only emaciated as by a wasting illness, looking as if she needed immediate hospital care—she died in fact three months after her return to Vienna—but her face and artist's hands were covered with rough red blotches due to the long use of soap substitutes, giving her a cruelly scalded appearance. My first reaction was one of overwhelming pity and alarm as I suddenly discovered my friend standing at the very gate of death."[14]

Although the war was now over, the suffering continued even as the women gathered: revolutionary struggles in the shattered Austro-Hungarian Empire and in Germany, civil war in Russia intensified by Allied intervention in the summer of 1918, and the Allied food blockade that threatened millions of already malnourished Central and Eastern European people with starvation. The ICWPP cared little about the politics of the situation; that people who had already suffered through four long years of war were now in its aftermath forced to face continued "famine, pestilence, and unemployment" was "a disgrace to civilization." The women sent a telegram to the conference in Paris demanding that the blockade be lifted immediately and that "food, raw materials, finance, and transport" be made available at once to all people in need. Wilson cabled his response: "Your message appeals to my head and my heart."[15] But, he said, there was nothing he could do.

The hopes for a new world order that had been raised by the president's Fourteen Points and by his presence at the peace talks were quickly dashed as the terms of the peace were hammered out. The war to make the world safe for democracy, the war to end all wars had done nothing of the kind. "By guaranteeing the fruits of the secret treaties to the conquerors," protested the women, "the Terms of Peace tacitly sanction secret diplomacy, deny the principles of self-determination, recognize the right of the victors to the spoils of war, and create all over Europe discords and animosities, which can only lead to further wars."

Even the newly created League of Nations was a disappointment, for the covenant omitted a number of "fundamental principles" necessary to make it "a real instrument of peace."[16] Of all the discouraging results of the Paris peace conference, the League Covenant was the most difficult for the women to accept, as they had pinned their hopes for postwar peace and justice on an effective and representative international organization.

As Progressive reformers committed to democracy in substance as well as in form, ICWPP members anticipated a postwar association of nations organized democratically and functioning democratically. As professionals in social work, law, medicine, and education, the ICWPP expected that the enlightened expertise of their various disciplines would be utilized by such a league of nations in the amelioration of world problems that held the potential for rivalry and conflict. As dedicated pacifists, the women envisioned an international organization composed of nations, all of which would repudiate force and the threat of force internally and externally in their effort to maintain the peace. As feminists concerned with women's rights, equality, and social justice, the members of the ICWPP at the very least hoped for if not expected the full and equal participation of women politically, economically, and socially in the postwar world. The League of Nations as it emerged in 1919 was sadly lacking in all respects.

The League failed as a democratically organized body because membership was not made "freely open . . . to any state desiring to join" nor was its "executive power" to be democratically elected. It could be made a more democratically functioning organization, the ICWPP noted, if "Nationalities and Dependencies within any government" were given the right of "direct presentation to the League" of their desires for self-government, and if all nations were guaranteed "free access to raw materials on equal terms." It could help reduce the human misery that so often sows the seeds of unrest and conflict by organizing "international resources to combat disease and improve health" and by adopting "a plan of world economy for the production and distribution of the necessities of life at the smallest cost."

As a peace-keeping organization, it could insist on total disarmament among all member nations as well as the abolition of military conscription. "In order to avoid future wars," it could abrogate "regional understandings like the Monroe Doctrine," and enforce its decisions "by other means than military pressure or food-blockade." In the interest of promoting justice and equality, it could abolish child labor, guarantee "complete freedom of communication and travel," eliminate all government censorship, and establish "full equal suffrage and the full equality of women with men."[17]

It could—and, thought the ICWPP, should—do all of these things. But it provided for none of them. Although they voted their approval of the League in principle, the members of the ICWPP saw the organization as little more than a creation of the Great Powers to serve their own particular national interests. In its espousal of the international status quo as written into the Treaty of Versailles, the League in its present form, concluded the women, would only legitimize the inequities and injustices of a punitive peace.

In contrast to the atmosphere of narrow national self-interest and vindictiveness that prevailed among the Big Four as they drew up the peace terms, the tone at Zurich where the women discussed these terms was set by Addams in her opening address when she spoke of the "co-operating goodwill" of the delegates "free from animosity or sense of estrangement."[18] In indignation and outrage, the German women might have clamored for a strongly worded condemnation of the harsh terms imposed upon their country by the treaty. There was no need; the German delegates sat quietly as Ethel Snowden of England, supported by Jeanette Rankin of the United States, introduced a resolution concerning those terms that expressed the "deep regret" of the congress that the treaty "should so seriously violate the principles upon which alone a just and lasting peace can be secured, and which the democracies of the world had come to accept."

Easily adopted, the resolution criticized the treaty for violating the principle of justice by its "disarmament of one set of belligerents only," and condemned the "financial and economic proposals" to be imposed upon Germany because of the "poverty, disease and despair" that would inevitably result from such demands. With unanimous approval the delegates sent a second telegram to the official conference in Paris "strongly" urging that the allied and associated governments amend the treaty to "bring [it] into harmony with those principles first enumerated by President Wilson."[19] This time there was no response.

Following the close of the congress six delegates, including Addams, went to Paris to present the group's resolutions to officials at the peace conference. The other delegates then headed for home but Addams and Hamilton remained. They had been invited to join a group of English Quakers in a relief mission to Germany. Not until early July were the women granted visas but finally on 7 July, Addams and Hamilton, accompanied by Carolena M. Wood, a U.S. member of the Society of Friends, reached Berlin where they joined four English Quakers and Aletta Jacobs, who had arrived the day before.

While arranging for the distribution of food and clothing among the victims of the blockade, the American women made "every effort to see as many children as possible" so as to ascertain "the effect of long-continued under feeding as registered in their growing bodies." Everywhere they went—Berlin, Leipzig, Breslau—they visited child welfare clinics, playgrounds, homes for convalescent children, hospitals, orphanages, public kitchens, and private homes. Everywhere they went, the faces of the mothers and the bodies of the children told the same tragic story.

Pale, wan, and listless, the children were undersized and emaciated: "The shoulder-blades of the boys stand out like wings, it is really almost a deformity; their ribs and their vertebrae can be counted, and their bony little arms and legs look still thinner because of the swollen joints. . . . The narrow, sunken chests bode ill for the future in a society where tuberculosis infection will certainly be widespread." It was already widespread; so were rickets and other illnesses associated with prolonged malnutrition. Severe loss of weight was accompanied by loss of height: "Already the schoolchildren of Leipzig average 2 to 4 cm. shorter than the pre-war average." Under such conditions education was almost impossible: "It was in Saxony . . . that they spoke with horror of the 'time of turnips' when for three or four months the entire population had almost nothing to eat except white turnips. . . . [I]t was of course impossible for many of the children to digest such food. The village schoolmaster in Barenstein told us that in the course of each morning nine or ten children would leave the room, vomit their breakfasts and stagger back, too miserable and sick to hold up their heads, much less to study their lessons."[20]

Objectively and dispassionately, the twenty-five page report simply documented the facts. There was no need for any righteous indignation or moral condemnation; the statistics were enough. The report placed no blame, called for no revenge, preached no sermon about good and evil. In the neutral scientific language and even tone of the social scientist, it documented horrendous suffering, despair, and daily sacrifices of one human being for the welfare of another. Without editorial comment, it noted the generosity of families in Switzerland and Holland who opened their homes to German children. In understated eloquence the report spoke clearly and unequivocally the women's understanding of the real impact of war and the true meaning of peace; both were measured in human rather than political terms. As Addams and Hamilton continued their journey word came that in Weimer the German government had signed the Treaty of Versailles. The Great War was truly over.

As an orgy of mass murder and material destruction, World War I was unprecedented in human history. Some 10,000,000 young men died and 20,000,000 more were maimed, crippled, burned, and wounded. Thirteen million civilians died and 10,000,000 more had become refugees. The war made widows of some 5,000,000 women and orphans of 9,000,000 children. Its cost was estimated to be somewhere around $331,000,000,000. Economic chaos, political instability, and vast areas of devastation went hand-in-glove with bitterness and fear throughout Europe.

As for the United States, Addams and Hamilton returned home in August 1919 to a country where labor-management conflict and race riots promised a less-than-tranquil return to "normalcy." Earlier hopes of Progressive reformers for the postwar "social possibilities" of wartime government control and planning dimmed with every passing day as the government quickly began to dismantle agencies like the Fuel Administration and the War Industries Board.

The Democratic party had lost control of the Congress and Republicans were intent on "political command of postwar society" with a program that portrayed themselves as the party of "superior patriotism, nationalism, and administrative acumen" while criticizing the Wilson administration for its "insufficient bellicosity, its parochialism, and its bureaucratic incompetence."[21] Politically, it did not look encouraging for the continued Progressive reform of American society; Addams was reported to be "a good deal depressed and has not much constructive to suggest."[22]

If the political situation looked bleak for the reinvigoration of reform measures, it appeared no less so for the achievement of an internationally organized world and a just and lasting peace. In the fall of 1919 Americans condemned the Treaty of Versailles not because it imposed a victor's peace upon the hapless vanquished, but because it was not harsh enough toward the losers. Addams's speeches to raise money to feed starving civilians in Central and Eastern Europe brought a new wave of accusations that she was pro-German and a traitor to her country. The repressive atmosphere of the war years had not waned and it was difficult not to become disillusioned and discouraged. "The war psychology or whatever it is that controls public opinion in the United States," Addams observed, "is still very tense; it seems at moments as if we would never break thru [sic] altho [sic] I comfort myself at times with the scriptural remarks about 'good seed sown in dishonor'."[23]

It was only as feminists that the women pacifists could take heart that autumn. Although not quite yet an accomplished fact, the cause of woman suffrage appeared secure. Wilson had urged Congress to pass a suffrage amendment and by June 1919 both houses had done so. Ratification was by no means guaranteed but the fact that the prohibition amendment, also endorsed by American women, was ratified in 1919 was an encouraging sign. Perhaps women could be persuaded to use that vote in behalf of peace and justice. But if they did, it did not appear that they would do so through the auspices of the Woman's Peace Party.

The success of the Zurich congress testified to the determination of women pacifists the world over to do whatever they could as organized and unified women to implement a just and humane peace. Coming together originally in the attempt to end the war quickly, they had failed in that effort—but now that the war was over, they saw their work as just beginning. Thus they voted to become the Women's International League for Peace and Freedom and to establish their international headquarters wherever the League of Nations, imperfect though it might be, centered its work. In the United States the WPP transformed itself into the U.S. Section of the WILPF, but its leaders harbored serious reservations about its ability to engender any widespread support for peace among American women. The eighty-five charter members of the WPP had grown to 512 in one year's time, organized into thirty-three local branches. With the inclusion of its 132 affiliated groups, the WPP's total membership by the beginning of 1916 was close to 40,000. U.S. entry into the war had done its damage, however, and although by December 1917 the WPP had grown to 200 local branches and affiliated groups, total membership had been cut in half.[24]

This downward trend continued unabated throughout the remainder of the war and by the summer of 1919 Anna Garlin Spencer was lamenting the difficulty of getting "any considerable number of women to see that the WIL [WILPF] needs the actual membership of a large body of women for its own program as a distinct contribution to the union of the women of the world to outlaw war. . . . Many women as well as men, do not see any use in a segregated women's movement."[25] Perhaps because women had supported the war effort with as much enthusiasm as men, perhaps because women had entered the work force in greater numbers than ever before, perhaps because women saw political equality with men just around the corner, perhaps for all of these reasons women no longer saw any compelling need to continue in political organizations composed solely of members of their own sex.

Whatever the reason, WILPF leaders in the United States entered the post-war decade not at all confident that their organization would endure, and not at all confident that if it did, it could ever be more than merely a "representative committee" to support the activities of the international organization in Europe. Equally as discouraging was dissension in the ranks. How could the organization survive if it could not hold current members let alone attract new ones? It was not an auspicious beginning for the U.S. Section of the WILPF, either internally or externally, but as Balch declared confidently, "I know what American women can do when they put their backs into a piece of work."[26]

4

Pacifism and Patriotism

AS THE DECADE OF THE 1920S opened, the U.S. Section of the WILPF
saw its most crucial problem to be that of its own survival. Wartime
defections were staggering. By 1919 there were only fifty-two members
left and dues had not been collected for over a year. The national
mood did not appear conducive to political activism of any kind, particularly if it was linked to the war. The country was determined to return
to "normalcy" as quickly as possible. Disillusioned with the peace talks,
disgusted with the treaty, and appalled at the incredible cost of the
conflict, Americans wished to put the war and everything connected
with it behind them and get on with living the good life.

Those who publicly advocated pacifism and internationalism were
not particularly popular with patriotic Americans who had been persuaded that such ideas were subversive, un-American, and allied with
the evils of Russian bolshevism. Xenophobia was much more difficult
to turn off than it was to turn on, and the government showed little
inclination to help. In January 1919 the Overman Subcommittee of the
Senate Judiciary Committee heard testimony from Archibald Steven-
son, a member of the propaganda section of the New York Bureau of
the Military Intelligence Service, that 100 men and women who "had
not helped to win the war" should be investigated as communist agita-
tors. Among those named were Addams, Balch, and Breckinridge of
the WILPF.

Under such circumstances Addams concluded that the WILPF in
this country was no longer viable as an independent and autonomous
body and could continue to function only as an advisory committee to
the Geneva office. "I do not believe," she wrote, "that there is much
chance for doing propaganda work for peace. . . . I am very much

impressed with the fact that our war psychology is in a much earlier stage than that of the other allied countries and that we will simply have to wait until the present attitude toward movements such as ours is somewhat modified before we can hope for many members."[1]

As alarming as the number of wartime defections was division among those women who remained, resulting in the formation of three additional women's peace groups by 1921. It was clear by mid-decade that none of these new organizations represented a threat to the WILPF's survival, but that fact was not apparent in 1919. Two issues caused this split: One was functional and concerned the way in which power was exercised within the WPP and the other involved an ideological dispute over pacifism as both theory and practice.

The original organizational structure of the WPP included a central coordinating body, the National Executive Board, which had the power to appoint a state chair when a state branch was first organized, to tender advice and assistance to state or local branches, to issue literature, to call the annual and other meetings, to appoint the chairs of the various standing committees and to engage national organizers, and to represent the national organization in all matters of an emergency nature when there would be no time to consult with the branches. With the exception of the first state chair, state and local branches elected their own officers and governed their own membership.

At its annual meeting in December 1917 the WPP decided that in the future each branch should function autonomously with respect to name, policy, propaganda, publications, and activities so long as these were in accord with the organization's constitution and platform. Although the branches were requested to report regularly to the executive board, these structural changes represented a substantial degree of decentralization. The board thought that it would be able to work with the ICWPP more quickly and efficiently if it possessed greater independence from the branches. In addition, U.S. entry into the war was seen to mean new responsibilities for each branch requiring greater freedom of action to meet special local situations.

Despite this decentralization, two of the most important branches, New York and Boston, charged the organization in 1919 with being insufficiently democratic. "The constitution of the league," noted the New York branch, "makes no provision for the participation of the membership in the direction of affairs but rests the entire conduct of business and the disposal of funds in the hands of a New York Executive Board. This Board is elected at an annual convention and is empowered to fill its own vacancies. The constitution can be amended only at the annual convention in the spring. No democratic activity of the membership is possible under these conditions."² Shortly thereafter the Boston branch disbanded and two smaller societies emerged to replace the practically moribund New York branch.

The first of these two groups, the Women's International League of Greater New York, never amounted to much and soon disappeared from the scene. The second group was viable from the beginning, however, due in large part to the forceful and charismatic personality of its leader, Fanny Garrison Villard, daughter of abolitionist William Lloyd Garrison, wife of Henry Villard who was formerly an editor of *The Nation*, and mother of the liberal, outspoken journalist Oswald Garrison Villard.

As a well-educated member of the upper middle class and thanks to her husband's business success, Fanny Garrison Villard was able to pursue a life of philanthropy and public service. In this sense she was typical of the nonprofessional Progressive reformer who became a WILPF peace activist. Instrumental in the founding of Barnard and Radcliffe colleges for women, she was a staunch supporter of woman suffrage as well as an activist in the Consumers League and the NAACP. And true to the heritage of her famous father, Villard was an uncompromising absolutist with respect to the principles she believed in.

Her radical pacifist stance preceded World War I and was based on the simple premise of absolute nonresistance: "a refusal to take human life at any time under any conditions, either on a scaffold, or a battle field, or even in self-defence."³ She was instrumental in the early years of the WPP as head of the New York branch, but became progressively impatient with the organization's unwillingness to adopt a position of radical pacifism as its philosophical base. Others within the New York branch echoed Villard's growing disenchantment with WPP timidity concerning the pacifist issue and by September 1919 this philosophical difference of opinion was compounded by complaints about "lack of unity" among the branch's members, resulting in growing frustration within the executive committee.

The WPP-turned-WILPF welcomed into membership a wide range of antiwar advocates:

> Some of us are non-resistants. Others justify violence in the class struggle. Some put their faith in organization and education, while others believe that revolution alone will ensure peace. Some accept the pro-

posed League of Nations as the first step toward international co-operation; others condemn as reactionary anyone who speaks a good word
for either the Treaty or the League. Some of us wish to build up a
strong, international feminist movement, so that never again will
women be impotent in a world crisis. Others see in feminism only sex
antagonism or a confession of weakness. Some wish us to do relief
work in Central Europe. Some urge a legislative program. Others
scorn political action, and hope to make us part of the direct action,
left wing movement.[4]

That such diversity of opinion represented "a lack of unity" was not
a problem for the majority of WILPF members. It was seen as desirable
because the WILPF, given its depleted numbers, hoped to attract as
many women peace activists as possible whatever their particular concern. For the radical pacifist minority in the New York branch, however, this "heterogeneous membership" was perceived as negative
rather than positive for it prevented the formation of any "permanent
policy." Growing frustration among these members of the branch's executive committee finally compelled their resignation in mid-September 1919, and within a month they organized the Women's Peace
Society (WPS) with Villard as chair and Elinor Byrns, lawyer, socialist,
and feminist, as vice-chair.

The "underlying principle" of the WPS was "a belief in the sacred-
ness and inviolability of human life under all circumstances," and its
immediate goals were "universal and complete disarmament [and] absolute freedom of trade."[5] In these two respects the WPS differed little
from the WILPF; it was over the issue of nonresistance that the two
groups diverged. The WPS member pledged herself "never to aid in or
sanction war, offensive or defensive, international or civil, in any way,
whether by making or handling munitions, subscribing to war loans,
using my labor for the purpose of setting others free for war service,
helping by money or work any relief organization which supports or
condones war."[6]

Such a position of radical pacifism obviously would exclude even
Jane Addams. It was rejected by the WILPF as being too restrictive for
an organization that hoped to have any political impact. WILPF members, by way of contrast, signed no pledge and swore no oath but rather
simply accepted the organization's "Object" as stated in its constitution:
"To promote methods for the attainment of that peace between nations which is based on justice and good will and to cooperate with
women from other countries who are working for the same ends."[7] As

part of the International WILPF, members of the U.S. Section voted
with the Zurich Congress to concentrate on four issues: world peace,
internationalism, political freedom, and social justice.

Although Byrns considered herself something of a socialist revolutionary, functionally the WPS was not organized along those lines. Like
the WILPF, it was a reform organization committed in good Progressive
fashion to democracy as both means and end: "We have faith to believe
that every cause worth winning, every interest worth preserving, can be
won or preserved without resort to murder. We are convinced it is possible to have a government based on agreement, instead of a government based on the use or threat of violence." And the WPS, again like
the WILPF, based its formation on the female's unique role as mother.
"We have decided to have a woman's organization," it noted, "because
women are in a special sense responsible for the preservation and creation of life. They are therefore more likely than men to see that it is
their duty to safeguard life by insisting it be held sacred."[8]

The initial impression among WILPF members was that Villard's
group was to be more of a "study and debating club" than an active
political peace organization that would compete with the WILPF for
members, nationally and internationally.[9] As 1919 passed into 1920,
however, it became increasingly clear that the WPS was indeed intended as a rival organization and, as such, began to create confusion
as to which group in the United States was the duly constituted section
affiliated with the international organization in Geneva.

That European members of the WILPF were more radical in their
pacifism than their American counterparts was common knowledge
within the U.S. Section, and there was concern that Villard's group, in
its efforts to establish an international base, would woo the European
WILPF organization into its ranks. WILPF officer Mabel Hyde Kittredge
was almost in despair over the situation and in expressing her concern
to Addams in the fall of 1920, astutely observed that the U.S. Section,
appearing weak and timid, carried very little weight with public opinion. In contrast, the WPS was making quite a splash "by a stand so
strong as to be noticed, even though it is criticized and laughed at."[10]

In a very real sense Kittredge was right. When the WPP became the
U.S. Section of the WILPF in November 1919 it was little more than a
middle-of-the-road rump organization, having been sheared of both its
conservative and radical wings. The conservatives departed with Catt
just prior to U.S. entry into the war and the government's subsequent
attack on left-wing radicals compelled the moderates to move in a
more conservative direction. As a reform organization dependent on

public support for its policies and programs, the WPP felt it had little choice but to abandon its left wing when wartime public opinion, responding to the government's lead, became increasingly xenophobic. One such casualty was the outspoken feminist, socialist, and intellectual Crystal Eastman. When the State Department refused passports to socialists in 1919, WPP Board members were quietly relieved that Eastman would thus be unable to represent the group at Zurich.

When the WPS broke with the WILPF later that fall, it was a mixed blessing. Moderate WILPF leaders such as Lucia Ames Mead might welcome the departure but the price of such ideological purity was high. Only twenty-five of the original eighty-five charter members were left to reconstitute the WPP as the U.S. Section of the WILPF in November. Anna Garlin Spencer, newly elected president of the group, was discouraged and chagrined. That the U.S. Section was expected to play an important role in the postwar work of the organization had been obvious at Zurich when Addams was elected international chair and Balch, secretary-treasurer. Yet Spencer did not think the U.S. Section could become a "permanent" organization despite her feeling that it was morally obligated to make a "strong and self-sacrificing attempt to get members if we are to keep faith with the European women" and with Balch, busily at work in Geneva organizing the International Office.[11]

When she learned of the discouraging state of affairs in the United States, Balch was quite surprised, and in early September 1919 wrote Addams reassuringly of her faith that "the American branch will . . . become very active and go out after members and come to be actually a political as well as a moral force."[12] With the subsequent dissolution of the New York and Boston branches, however, the International Secretary became more concerned. "I feel I cannot face with any equanimity the idea of New York not furnishing this great international movement with powerful and active backing," she wrote in mid-December. "When you see what our British section and sections in other countries are doing, it seems as if I could hardly bear it not to have America and above all New York do their full share."[13]

As for the concern with Villard's rival peace group, Balch did not believe that the formation of the WPS weakened the WILPF's efforts for peace or made it ineffectual. On the contrary, she often remarked that if certain shades of pacifist thought did not find the WILPF a congenial home, they had a duty to form a separate group. She welcomed eagerly each new peace organization into the movement, convinced that such a proliferation of peace groups would have a greater

public impact. "I should like to see a city like New York," she explained
to Villard, "have half a dozen really active peace groups of different
types following their own lines freely, not worried by one another's
different methods, nor mutually responsible for one another's acts or
policies, but cooperating fully on all their common aims and tactics. I
think ten petitions or deputations to Washington," she went on, "or
newspaper protests coming from ten groups of 100 people, each really
a live organization, means more than a petition, etc., from one group
of 1000 people, even if the 1000 can agree on one form of words or
action, and even if they can act promptly."[14]

So long as all the various organizations cooperated with one another in "propaganda and educational work and trying to exert political influence," this proliferation of peace societies was all to the good.
It was Balch's way of gently chiding her friends at home that their
concern over the WPS and their general malaise toward creating a viable WILPF was inappropriate. "I feel strongly that the American situation is crucial," she argued. "Such enormous questions we face as:
compulsory military training, the expansion of our military establishment and navy, relations with Mexico and Latin America, . . . the Oriental question—Japan, China, Siberia,—our relations to Europe, . . .
our relation to Russia, the League of Nations, the danger of violence
and social and economic changes on both sides."[15] There were so many
urgent issues to be taken up by peace groups, Balch insisted, that ex-
pending energy squabbling among themselves was a tragic waste of
effort.

Perhaps Balch's advice had some impact on the U.S. Section for by
early 1920 Spencer began to strike a more optimistic note. "However
strong a hold the 'mysticism of militarism' still has upon the common
imagination," she remarked, "those who have suffered most during
these last years have learned that we must not have another world war.
They understand that we must end the fragments of little wars that still
further ravage, desolate and bankrupt nations. We are all convinced
that we must learn a better way of living and working together." And
they would find that way, she told WILPF members, through the power
of women-as-mothers: "Women of all races and peoples . . . will for
awhile at least work somewhat by themselves until they become strong
and commanding in their power of motherhood to declare that this
obsolete legalizing of human slaughter must be outgrown. Ours is a
small group," she acknowledged, "but it has the great privilege of feeling the heartbeat and echoing the intellectual leadership of the
women of 21 other countries in the WILPF."[16]

Spencer was right. Despite the effort of Villard's organization to woo the International WILPF away from the U.S. Section to the WPS, European WILPF leaders did not want to further divide the women's peace movement in the United States. They echoed Balch's sentiments, counseling cooperation rather than competition. A number of WILPF members in the United States agreed; like Ellen Winsor, Katherine Blake, and Madeleine Z. Doty, they joined both organizations and like Addams, they spoke at WPS disarmament meetings and attempted conciliation. Winsor voiced the sentiment of many within the WILPF when she wrote to Byrns of her hope that the two organizations could unite. Byrns concurred but thought the nonresistance issue too divisive to bring such a union about.

The nonresistance issue was also divisive within the WPS itself. The pledge required of all WPS members was designed to limit the group's membership to radical pacifists who would be activists in the cause of peace, and up to a point it was successful. But as Winsor pointed out, in times of crisis, "how many women—or men either—will stick to it?" She reminded Byrns of the WPS member who in testifying before Congress on the disarmament issue was asked if she advocated the complete abolition of the U.S. armed forces. "No, I did not say that," she responded quickly. "I said until we can bring about a joint discussion, a joint concert of action, I am willing to leave it to the men of the country, influenced by the women of the country, to keep the army at a minimum. I do not know whether that would be 100,000 or 50,000 at this time, but I hope it will be a great deal less." As Winsor remarked, "If a leader of the non-resistant Women's Peace Society takes that stand, what can you expect from the rank and file?"[17]

Byrns was already aware of the problems that were being created within the WPS because of its moral absolutism, and as a committed pacifist she found the situation most discouraging. It was her understanding that anyone who signed the pledge of nonresistance agreed not to "support, participate in, or in any way justify, any war." But much to her surprise she learned that even Fanny Garrison Villard was unwilling to go that far. Byrns was further "disconcerted" when she discovered that Villard bought Liberty Bonds during World War I: "I felt as if the solid ground had given way under my feet," Byrns wrote to a friend.[18]

The problem of reconciling theory and practice also plagued the WPS. Byrns expected the WPS to be an activist peace organization, not merely a society where women intellectualized about the issues in heated debate; that was an important reason for leaving the WILPF in the first place. But as early as the spring of 1921, Byrns reported, many WPS members were becoming disenchanted with the group, having concluded that it "could get nowhere with Mrs. Villard as chairman because she was merely moralistic and theoretical and was not willing to consider any practical applications of the principle of non-resistance." Byrns did not dispute this observation. Noting that she was "very fond" of Villard and had the "highest respect" for her, Byrns suggested that Villard "has so long thought of non-resistance in the abstract that she has not considered sufficiently the practical side of having to live it, in a militaristic world."[19] Byrns wanted the WPS to be more than merely a protest group and argued that if the WPS did not relate its philosophy to action, it would be "scorned" for being unwilling to face reality or would disappoint those who expected it in a crisis to "stand" on its principles by direct action.[20]

Villard's observation in the fall of 1920 that the U.S. Section of the WILPF had "gone, practically, to pieces"[21] and that the WPS would be the beneficiary of that demise might have been an accurate characterization of the situation a year earlier, but much had changed in that twelve-month period. Partly because the WPS was too radical in its pacifism and internally divided over theory and practice, and partly because neither major political party had a liberal reform wing of any strength, women interested in peace activism, however few in absolute numbers, began to respond to the WILPF's appeal for money and members. By its annual meeting in April 1920 almost 500 new members had joined, paying either the regular dues of one dollar or, if a college student, twenty-five cents. A national office was established with large donations from wealthy women making up the difference between income from dues and office expenses.

By 1921 the WILPF had settled its internal difficulties to emerge as the moderate wing of the women's peace movement. However decimated its ranks by wartime fervor and defections of both right and left, it was willing, even eager now, to educate Americans out of their narrow-minded attitude of nationalistic chauvinism through methods of rational persuasion and "sweet reasonableness." Mabel Hyde Kittredge reported to Addams that the U.S. Section "is doing well now. Every one seems to be at peace," she noted, "and freedom of action inside the organization is all there."[22] While the WILPF was growing in numbers, donations, and confidence, the WPS continued to experience internal problems. Within eighteen months of its formation, it was squabbling internally over the same issues that had prompted its founders to leave the WILPF in the first place.

The cohesive organization of radical pacifists actively involved in the political sphere that Byrns and other leaders had envisioned did not materialize. Disagreement over the role the society was to play in the women's peace movement finally brought a split in the ranks. Joining with a small group of radical pacifists from Canada, Byrns, Caroline Lexow Babcock, and other WPS leaders organized the Women's Peace Union of the Western Hemisphere (WPU) in the summer of 1921. Its objective was to combine absolute nonresistance with political activism and its goal was to promote an amendment to the U.S. Constitution calling for a referendum of the people before that country could go to war.

The threat to its viability as a women's peace organization that the WILPF perceived from the formation of the WPS vanished in less than two years. Although the WPS had 1,500 dues-paying members by October 1921 when the WILPF could boast of only 500 more, by May 1923 the WILPF had attracted 5,000 members; not until 1926 would the WPS reach even half that number. After the death of Fanny Garrison Vallard in 1928, the WPS began a slow decline, disappearing from the scene by 1933. Neither the WPS nor the WPU seriously challenged the WILPF as the preeminent women's peace organization in the interwar years, even though the WPU continued its fight for a referendum vote through a Constitutional amendment into the 1940s. Both of the smaller societies soon came to understand that as the left wing of the women's peace movement, their position of absolute nonresistance was simply too radical for mainstream American womanhood. All three women's peace groups quickly recognized what Balch and the European women had been maintaining all along—the number of peace organizations was not the issue. Cooperation among them was.

Focusing on militarism as the chief cause of war, in the early 1920s the WILPF, WPS, and WPU joined hands behind a drive for disarmament and the abolition of universal military training. They formed an antimilitary coalition that included the Women for World Disarmament, an ad hoc group of the National Women's Party hurriedly formed in response to the National Defense Act of 1920, and the National Council for Prevention of War (NCPW), organized in September 1921 by the Quaker pacifist, Frederick J. Libby. The NCPW acted as a clearinghouse for its member organizations, which included the three women's peace groups among its original seventeen as well as the pacifists of the Fellowship of Reconciliation (FOR) and the Quakers of the American Friends Service Committee (AFSC). Originally calling itself the National Council for Limitation of Armaments, its first task was to make the upcoming Washington Naval Conference a landmark in precisely that cause.

Like the WPS and WPU, the radical pacifist minority within the NCPW used the term "disarmament" to mean just exactly that: the immediate, universal, and complete abolition of arms and military forces. Unwilling to accept half a loaf, neither organization was willing to "endorse legislation or propaganda for reduction or limitation of armament."[23] The majority of moderates, pacifist and nonpacifist alike, agreed with the radicals that disarmament was the ultimate goal but would accept arms limitation, if necessary, as a first step. That the Great Powers that met at the Washington Conference on the Limitation of Armaments in 1921–1922 did not envision disarmament as their objective is clear from the name of the conference as well as from its intent and outcome. The goal was not to eliminate armed force but rather to reduce military spending as part of an effort to stabilize the European economy and promote a climate of peace conducive to the growth of international commerce. The outcome was not what the radicals hoped for. One result, the Washington Naval Treaty, also known as the Five-Power Pact, established a ratio for capital ship tonnage among the United States, Great Britain, Japan, France, and Italy of 5:5:3:1.75:1.75. "It was indeed a very mild form of limitation which emerged from the conference," the WPU observed, "and the war system was left intact."[24]

The moderate wing of the peace movement, encouraged when Congress responded to its pressure in 1920 by appropriating less than $400,000 to the War Department (which had asked for almost $1 million), supported the results of the conference as a step in the right direction. The WILPF, however, may have been "radicalized" by the intransigence of the radical pacifists—a number of women were active in both wings. In less than a year the WILPF was leading an effort to reduce the U.S. armed forces by abolishing the National Defense Act altogether, because it provided for a 280,000-man army buttressed by an army reserve and a National Guard of some 450,000 men. With the November election in mind, WILPF members campaigned against candidates who were promilitary and WILPF leaders testified in Congress against increased appropriations for the military. The Wisconsin WILPF successfully lobbied the state legislature to abolish military training at the state university. Apparently national disillusionment with the outcome of the World War and its tremendous cost was working in the women's favor.

At least War Department personnel seemed to think so. Prior to the election that fall Secretary of War John Weeks "began a public campaign designed to increase the visibility of the army, convince the public of its importance, and counter the headway that peace groups were making in opposition to the War Department's national defense policy."[25] If the formation of other women's peace organizations did not prove a serious threat to the WILPF's survival in the early years of the postwar decade, the military arm of the U.S. government did. Not directed solely at the WILPF but at the peace movement in general and women's organizations in particular, this attack by the War Department actually strengthened the WILPF among more militant women peace advocates and unified the peace movement in its resolve to counter the power of militarism. Yet it was not without its negative effects, for by the end of 1924 American women who had entered the decade "as one of the best-organized interest groups in the country"[26] were seriously divided over the issue of patriotism and national loyalty, with the more conservative peace advocates who might have joined the WILPF turning to an entirely new woman's peace group.

When the secretary of war began his public relations campaign, he targeted "silly pacifists" and their "insidious propaganda" as the major obstacle to stronger national defense policies.[27] Lucia Ames Mead, head of the WILPF's Committee on Education, protested in a letter to Weeks that the United States had no foreign enemy against which the country needed to defend itself: "Our dangers from outside attack are the least that we have to face," she pointed out, asserting that "our chief dangers are from within" and included "gross illiteracy" and a huge national deficit.[28]

Hearkening back to the wave of strikes in 1919 and the Palmer Raids of 1920, Weeks was quick to point out to the WILPF that the purpose of a strong national military was not solely for defense against foreign threats, but that it was essential as well for suppression of threats emanating from within such as strikes and alien political beliefs. The WILPF promptly released the secretary's letter to the press, not an act that would endear the women to the War Department.

By early 1923 the War Department went on the offensive with a vengeance, singling out the WILPF as its primary target. Brigadier General Amos A. Fries, head of the Chemical Warfare Service, condemned the WILPF for what became known as the "slacker's oath." Fries alleged that all WILPF members were required to pledge that they would not in any way support a future war. Said Fries, such an oath was "nothing short of treason." As Mead pointed out to Weeks, no such pledge had ever been required by the WILPF and had, in point of fact, been rejected in April 1922. Although she suggested in no uncertain terms that Weeks take measures to correct these false allegations, not only did he not do so, he emphatically defended those military officers who were being criticized by "forces in America who are preaching revolution and the establishment of a communist government."[29] Shortly thereafter, the so-called "spider web chart" began to circulate, purporting to document with criss-crossing lines everywhere the connection of peace groups and women's organizations with international communism.

The chart emanated from the Chemical Warfare Service, put together by librarian Lucia Maxwell on the basis of information regarding domestic subversion compiled by military intelligence. It listed the names of twenty-one women, including Addams, Balch, and Florence Kelley, and seventeen organizations, fifteen of which were noted as members of the NCPW and the Women's Joint Congressional Committee (WJCC), a coalition of women's groups formed to lobby Congress to pass legislation of interest to women. The chart's heading was a dire warning that "the Socialist-Pacifist Movement in America is an absolutely fundamental and integral part of international socialism."[30] Although it was not published until March 1924 when it appeared in Henry Ford's *Dearborn Independent,* the chart was circulated by the Chemical Warfare Service not long after Maxwell completed it in May 1923.

Fringe elements among patriotic Americans quickly jumped on the bandwagon. A Philadelphia investment broker with no apparent ties to the WILPF denounced the organization as "a purely Communist affair, gotten up originally in the interests of Germany and taken over by the Communists in their own interests and controlled by them. It has found many dupes," declared Francis Ralston Welsh, "because its professed objects appeal to almost everyone, but its chief promoters will be found mixed up with every sort of Communist, criminal and enemy of our civilization." To those who protested the sincerity and integrity of the WILPF, Welsh warned that "one must draw a very strong line between people . . . who believe that its aims are its professed aims, and the people who originated it and carry on its work, who know that its professed aims are not its real aims. Its real aims," he concluded triumphantly, "are in the interests of Communism, and would lead to the worst war and the most frightful carnage this country has ever known."[31]

A pamphlet, "Peace at Any Old Price," a distorted report of the WILPF's 1923 annual meeting, began to circulate at about the same time. Written by a Mr. R. M. Whitney of Washington, D.C., who, like Welsh, apparently spent a great deal of time trying to convince others that the WILPF was a communist organization, it was indirectly given credence by the Department of Justice, a fact the WILPF protested without satisfactory response. The WILPF offered to debate Whitney on five mutually agreed-upon topics in its newsletter, but the man declined, saying that he thought the offer was well-intentioned but that the organization was "undoubtedly under the influence of the Soviet Government."[32]

Shortly after the spider web chart appeared in the press the WJCC responded. In early April 1924 five women from the group called upon Weeks with a letter that accused the Chemical Warfare Service of a "scurrilous, libellous, and criminal" attack on the "twelve million women voters" represented by the WJCC. Pointing out the inaccuracies of the chart and condemning its guilt-by-association innuendoes, the letter implicitly threatened a lawsuit if "immediate redress" was not forthcoming.[33] By mid-month Weeks sent his regrets, informing the women that he had ordered all of the charts destroyed and that General Fries was to notify everyone to whom it had been sent that it contained errors of fact and should be destroyed.

But the damage was done. For months thereafter the public continued its accusations against the WILPF. In voting first to condemn the WILPF as subversive and then to investigate the charge, the patriotic Daughters of 1812 decided that the WILPF was guilty until proven innocent. Rep. M. C. McLeod, Republican Congressman from Detroit, urged the Department of Justice to investigate WILPF members as Soviet agents. The Women's Overseas Service League accused the WILPF of "insidious propaganda" and the adjutant general of the Military Order of the World War, noting that his organization was campaigning against "Pacifists, Reds, Pinks and all subversive individuals or organizations who would undermine our government," included in that group both the WILPF and the NCPW. The American Legion and the Veterans of Foreign Wars passed resolutions denouncing the WILPF, and the Daughters of the American Revolution (DAR) attempted to dissociate itself from any connection with the WILPF by publicly declaring its "absolute" opposition to disarmament.[34]

Although urged by friends to sue for libel, the WILPF chose not to, in part because of the cost involved. A lawsuit would have seriously taxed the WILPF's financial resources in the best of times, and not only was the organization just beginning to get back on sound economic footing when the attacks began, what income the women did raise by

1924 was needed to finance their Fourth International Congress, held in Washington, D.C., the first week in May.

The theme of the congress was "A New International Order" and it was followed by an International Summer School in Chicago from 17 to 31 May. Under the direction of Sophonisba Breckinridge of the University of Chicago, the summer school focused upon the "Biological, Psychological, and Economic Bases of Internationalism."[35] Given the fact that the spider web chart and the War Department had made "internationalism" a dirty word'by the spring of 1924, the WILPF's publicity for its May events only exacerbated the xenophobic hysteria directed against the women pacifists.

Delegates from twenty-five countries, as well as visitors and observers from as far away as Liberia and Turkey, arrived in the United States at the end of April.[36] The majority were able to make the trip only through the generosity of the U.S. members who raised $400 for each delegate's traveling expenses and provided room and board, as did a number of WPU members, after their arrival.

The basis of discussion for "a new international order" was a French memorandum, submitted to each national section a few weeks prior to the Congress. Its underlying principles were two: "(a) that all nations are equal in rights, and (b) that all nations are interdependent." The memorandum anticipated political organization in this "new order" in terms of a League of Peoples to exist either with the League of Nations or to replace it altogether. This new league would have no armed forces and would not be allowed to impose economic sanctions. Economically, the memorandum advocated free trade and the abolition of government protection of private investment in other countries and, last, it included a "World Charter of Labour."[37]

Among the resolutions voted by the congress for immediate political action were demands for the abolition of conscription, the democratic control of foreign policy, the outlawry of war, and the enlargement of the League of Nations. Economically, the delegates called for tariff reductions by all nations and international control of the world's raw materials. The women also stressed the need for radical changes in the social order, including an end to capital punishment, penal reform, and male and female equality of influence in all spheres of life.

On 9 May after the close of the congress, attended by the other women's peace groups as well, delegates boarded a private railroad coach hired by the U.S. Section called the "Pax Special," which began its trek from the nation's capital to Chicago for the summer school. The train stopped at a number of cities along the way, where delegates addressed public meetings and were entertained by local WILPF members. For the majority of the international visitors this trip was their first introduction to the United States, and an exciting one it proved to be, although not necessarily what they had anticipated. For their American hosts it was cause for embarrassment and keen disappointment in the behavior of their countrymen.

The trouble started almost a month earlier as plans were being made for the reception of the Pax Special in cities like Pittsburgh, Cincinnati, and Indianapolis. Paraphrasing only slightly the words of Emily Kneubuhl, WILPF member and director of the Cincinnati League of Women Voters, all hell broke loose in that city when the news was received that the train would be stopping there. The anticommunist fervor stirred up by the War Department and the spider web chart was particularly strident in Cincinnati, "the most difficult place in the country for peace and radical propaganda," according to Roger Baldwin of the American Civil Liberties Bureau.[38] Some patriotic citizens were quite convinced that these pacifist women were nothing less than agents of Moscow, bent on destroying all that was virtuous in American society. The most vociferous opposition to the women's visit came from the American Legion and one of the city's leading newspapers, but the League of Women Voters was a fairly strong and cohesive group of women who were not afraid of meeting this challenge headon. One member held an important position on the city's other influential newspaper and saw to it that the WILPF received some positive press coverage.

As the days passed the attacks upon the WILPF as being unpatriotic and subversive grew more intense and "vitriolic" in Cincinnati and the press refused to publish retractions of palpably false and slanderous statements. Martha Trimble, WILPF coordinator for the Pax Special, was informed by her sources from the press that the War Department itself "has determined to do everything possible to hinder our peace work," and thus had contacted various newspapers across the country, directing them to "give [the WILPF] hell" in their press coverage.[39] When she heard this, Trimble went immediately to Capitol Hill where she spoke with a number of senators concerning the matter. William Borah of Idaho told her bluntly, "if there is any interference with the meetings, I shall make an attack on the floor of the Senate," and a second senator promised to write a note to Secretary of War Weeks asking for an explanation of the War Department's alleged interference.[40]

The accusations against the WILPF generally followed the same pattern: first, that the women pacifists attempted to infiltrate the public schools to obtain an oath from the students that they would never defend their country in time of war; second, that WILPF members themselves were required to take this "slacker's oath"; third, that the women advocated "the abrogation of the marriage vow" (i.e., that they believed in "free love"); and last, that the organization refused to display the American flag on its platform.[41]

There was not a shred of truth to any of these charges, but the viciousness with which they were leveled against the pacifists in Cincinnati finally brought capitulation. The plans for mass demonstrations, public meetings, and poster displays were cancelled. When the Pax Special arrived, wrote Trimble, "we were met by Mrs. Kuhn with a number of automobiles at one of the out of the way stations, and were taken quietly and privately to her home, where we were entertained for breakfast and dinner. Mrs. Kuhn had quietly without any publicity at all gotten over 200 reservations for a luncheon at one of the hotels. Detectives were stationed at the hotel in case violence should be attempted. But nothing happened and the tide of public opinion turned in our favor. Reporters and photographers came to Mrs. Kuhn's home and the investigating committee published its report the day of our arrival. . . . That night a private reception in Mrs. Kuhn's home was attended by hundreds."[42]

At Wheeling, West Virginia, the story was much the same, for there was no reception committee to meet the train, only silence. "In a driving rain, Miss Woods and I made our way to the home of one of our members who took in the 75 of us for the day," Trimble reported. "We scouted about, visited the individuals who composed the opposition and found that they were ready to wilt as soon as we opened discussion with them. The Mayor came to see our guests late in the afternoon and offered to apologize to them and to us for the way his city has acted. Through telephone calls, we were able to work up a splendid dinner for the evening at which many new memberships were received. Wheeling, W. Va. [sic]," she concluded triumphantly, "will not forget the 'PAX SPECIAL.' I think that city will not be so easily fooled again by false propaganda."[43]

And so it went, all the way to Chicago and then back again in June—Dayton, Cleveland, Detroit, St. Louis, and Indianapolis. At each stop west of Pittsburgh, "attacks by such groups as the Daughters of the American Revolution and the American Legion, accusing delegates of subversion and 'spying,' caused panic amongst local committees and the cancellation of meetings."[44]

The summer school, too, had its share of unpleasant incidents but there were also numerous instances of sympathetic support. When asked by the American Legion if he planned to permit the WILPF to hold meetings in university facilities, the president of the University of Chicago replied, "this university has always stood for freedom of thought, and I see no reason for changing its policy. I consider it an honor to have the meetings held here."[45]

By all accounts, the International Congress and the summer school were successes. The publicity, negative as well as positive, brought the WILPF to the attention of people who probably would never have heard of it otherwise. Membership increased and financially the organization was $600 in the black after all expenses were paid.

If the WILPF and peace organizations generally not only survived but even prospered as a result of the government's attempt to discredit them, such was not the case with the women's movement. The WILPF had never been a member of the Women's Joint Congressional Committee and when that group protested the spider web chart to the Secretary of War, Maud Park made that fact quite clear, thereby hoping that the WJCC would not suffer from guilt-by-association. As Catt pointed out to Addams, the WJCC "refuted the charge made against their [sic] own organizations, but . . . left out in the cold all the organizations that were not connected with them."[46] This had the unfortunate effect of alienating the WILPF from such large and influential women's groups as the General Federation of Women's Clubs, the League of Women Voters, and the National Council of Women (NCW).

Individually, the WJCC's dissociation with the WILPF left many women who were active in both groups in something of a quandary, and organizationally it further divided the women's movement when members of the NCW, to which the WILPF did belong, began a drive to get the WILPF to resign. Initiated by a minority within the NCW in April 1924 but rejected by the majority, the effort picked up steam by September, perhaps because of all the publicity associated with the WILPF's International Congress and summer school. In a letter to Amy Woods, WILPF Executive Secretary, Eva Perry Moore, president of the NCW, observed regretfully that even though she knew that the accusations against the WILPF were false, at least four members of the NCW were demanding the peace group's resignation. Apparently these groups were concerned that the WILPF's presence at the NCW's convention in the coming spring would taint the proceeding with an un-American influence. Not wishing to cause embarrassment for the NCW, on 12 September the WILPF's executive board voted to resign from the NCW.

By December, however, much to the consternation of Moore, the

WILPF had withdrawn its resignation, primarily on the advice of Addams. For the NCW the issue was now more than merely guilt-by-association; it was a matter of money. Congress was considering an appropriation request from the organization and was demanding information concerning "disloyal" members of the women's group. In responding to Moore's request that the WILPF resign as "a necessity," Hannah Clothier Hull, WILPF president, noted that "under ordinary circumstances there could be no hesitation or question in instantly complying," but because the present situation was based on the issue of "policies believed to be advocated by the W.I.L.P.F.," the Executive Board did not feel "warranted in complying" as a resignation "would be understood as an admission of current calumnies and an encouragement to further attacks upon pacifists all along the line." Hull expressed the WILPF's "sincere regret" at causing the NCW "further anxiety," but explained that board members "feel that a great principle is involved and that we cannot passively assent to such injustice."[47]

There was not unanimity about the matter among WILPF board members, however, for although they agreed "not to resign under first fire," they discussed the likelihood of doing so "later." That time came within a month when in mid-January 1925, under no pressure from the NCW, the WILPF sent a letter of resignation to Moore indicating that "the League withdraws its membership from the Council of Women in order to concentrate upon its work unhampered." Although formally severing its ties with the NCW, many WILPF members, as Hull had pointed out in her December letter, were also "very actively engaged" in other organizations belonging to the NCW and would "thus be entitled to remain in the Council" despite the WILPF's departure.[48]

Although it did not succeed in destroying the WILPF as the foremost woman's peace organization, the War Department's attack did result in dividing women on the issue. The attempt to discredit the WILPF's national loyalty and patriotism may have attracted the more radical among women peace supporters who were angered at the campaign of lies and innuendos, but it also clearly alienated those more conservative women who, although concerned with peace and justice, did not want to be associated with such a controversial organization. That Catt understood this to be the case is evident from her action in creating the National Conference on the Cause and Cure of War (NCCCW) in 1924.

Although woman suffrage was always Catt's main goal, she had not deserted the cause of peace altogether. Exhausted from the suffrage struggle, she spent the better part of the next two years resting at home, but returned to the peace issue in 1923 with a three-week lecture tour of Europe. She did not join her former colleagues from the WPP when it became the WILPF in 1919 because she considered the organization's program impractical and too idealistic. After the storm of vilification broke against the WILPF in the spring of 1924, Catt was approached by a number of women's organizations with committees interested in doing peace work but leery of associating with the WILPF. Out of this meeting came the formation of the NCCCW, an umbrella organization for groups like the League of Women Voters, the National Women's Trade Union League, and the American Association of University Women, all of which wished to study the issues of war and peace but did not want to engage in direct political action.

Peace societies as such were not invited to the NCCCW's first annual meeting, held in Washington, D.C., from 18 to 24 January 1925, but individual peace activists including prominent WILPF members were included in the program. The fact that 900 delegates attended gave some indication that however virulent the antipacifist propaganda stirred up by the government, not all Americans shared this sentiment.

Catt did not intend to "discredit" the WILPF by creating the NCCCW. As she wrote to Hull at the end of January, her major concern was that Addams' group had "drawn to it a good many of the hysterical variety," thus alienating many women of a more moderate peace orientation. Nor did Catt see the NCCCW as competing with the WILPF in the political sphere. "I think the League is more likely to be the power that will blaze the trail than any other group in the field," she observed, "but when that trail is blazed a road must be found out of it, and the more conservative groups will have to do that."[49]

And they would do it through political education rather than through political action, holding annual conferences throughout the interwar period with such themes as "The Contribution of the United States to World Peace" (January 1928), "War and Waste" (January 1934), and after the outbreak of World War II in Europe, "Choosing Our Direction" (January 1940).[50] By the end of the 1920s, eleven women's organizations representing approximately 5,000,000 women were involved as sponsors with the presidents of these groups, the chairpersons of their committees on peace or international relations, and Catt composing the NCCCW's national committee.

It is doubtful that the NCCCW would have been formed had the Department of War not targeted the WILPF in its attempt to destroy the peace movement. But neither goal was achieved. The WILPF not only survived but grew in numbers and public exposure while ironically becoming more radicalized in the process. The peace movement emerged more unified by the experience and, thanks to the formation of the NCCCW, larger than ever before.

It is not surprising that in its effort to consolidate and enhance its wartime victory that the military would attempt to discredit the peace movement and women's peace groups in particular. As one officer in Military Intelligence commented, "All the work of industrial and physical preparation for defense will have been wasted if the younger generation are [sic] going to turn out to be pacifists and internationalists."[51] Because women as mothers and teachers had a greater influence on the younger generation than men, and because women were believed to be more pacifistic than men, women's peace groups were the logical target. And because the WILPF was the foremost women's peace organization, it made perfectly good sense for the military to "divide and conquer" the peace movement by attacking the WILPF.

Such a strategy of "divide and conquer" could not be implemented by attacking the public policies and programs of the peace movement for it was clear that disarmament and the abolition of universal military training enjoyed widespread public support in the early 1920s. The War Department could, however, capitalize on wartime xenophobia by a propaganda campaign that equated pacifism and internationalism with disloyalty and, by innuendo, with communism. With respect to the peace movement generally, this strategy resulted in only limited success by widening an already existent philosophical gap between antiwar advocates and patriotic nationalistic organizations like the veterans' groups and the Daughters of 1812.

The War Department achieved its most notable success by dividing, if not conquering, the women's movement. If there was such a thing as a "women's vote," and it was by no means certain in the early years after the suffrage victory that there wasn't, and if women were by nature antimilitaristic, then women as a class represented an even greater potential threat to the military establishment than did the peace movement. Thus it was no accident that women not only became the focal point of the War Department's attack on the peace movement, but that women's organizations generally were targeted. Yet although the strategy of "divide and conquer" succeeded in splitting the women's movement by setting (alleged) radical against moderate and conservative, this kind of external pressure could not have so easily created such a schism had there existed among women a strong sense of "collective self-consciousness" as they emerged from the suffrage campaign.[52] It may be that the War Department's attack only sped up a process of "fractionalization" already well under way.

As for the WILPF, after 1925 it became the only political action arm of any significance among women peace activists. Joan Jensen is probably right in her assertion that as women in patriotic societies began to denounce the peace movement during the loyalty controversy, women peace advocates became "much less willing to claim motherhood as a cause of pacifism." As a result the WILPF, as well as the WPS and WPU, became less visible as *women's* peace organizations and more important as women's *peace* organizations as they became "increasingly involved in mixed groups with men who agreed with their political principles rather than with women who joined them in a special crusade against war."[53] Having inadvertently become more radicalized as a result of their confrontation with the War Department, WILPF members began to move away from "feminine" concerns such as relief work and antiwar education to focus instead on such "masculine" issues as economic imperialism and power politics as causes of war.

5

Challenging Economic Imperialism

FIRMLY ENTRENCHED BY 1925 as the only sizeable women's peace group with both a broadly based program of action for peace and justice and intent on direct political action to achieve these goals, the WILPF became an influential part of a much larger peace movement determined to realize a world without war. In this struggle, this coalition of pacifists and antiwar groups focused on three main objectives in the latter half of the 1920s: to eliminate government protection of private business investment abroad, to obtain global support for the idea of making war an international crime as the first step toward universal disarmament, and last, to ensure disarmament in the United States and overseas.

Although many historians have characterized the nation's peace movement in the interwar period as part of a prevalent mood of isolationism, the facts of the matter do not warrant such a conclusion, particularly in the case of the WILPF. In pursuing its goals from the mid-1920s through the early 1930s, the WILPF was one of only two U.S. peace groups to be truly internationally organized, the other being the Fellowship of Reconciliation (FOR).

Despite efforts by the War Department to divide American women over the issue of national loyalty by the mid-1920s, the peace movement emerged stronger and more active than ever. Most numerous were the moderate and radical pacifist organizations, which included the women's groups—the WILPF, WPS, and WPU—as well as the War Resisters League, which was founded in 1924 by Tracy Mygatt, Frances Witherspoon, and Jessie Wallace Hughan and included men and women. Also important among pacifists were the American Friends Service Committee (AFSC), the American branch of the FOR, founded in

1915 by a group of Quakers, YMCA officials, and Social Gospel clergy-men; and the Committee on Militarism in Education, created in 1924 by FOR leaders to combat military training in the schools. Liberal but generally nonpacifist reformers in the NCCCW and the NCPW formed the second group, and the more conservative internationalists of the League of Nations Non-Partisan Association (1923), the Carnegie Endowment for International Peace (1910), and the Foreign Policy Association (formerly the League of Free Nations Association of 1918 but renamed in 1921) composed the third.

Ideologically, all three wings were opposed to war as a method of settling international disputes, but where the conservative internationalists emphasized collective security and thus the threat, if not the use, of coercion in the quest for peace, pacifists focused on the nonviolent creation of economic, political, and social justice to remove the causes of war. Liberal reformers tended to oscillate between the other two positions, depending on the issue and strategy involved. There was also a good deal of overlap between one wing and another, both organizationally and individually. The WILPF, FOR, and AFSC, for example, were all members of the NCPW and individual members of the WILPF were also members of one or more of the women's organizations that composed the NCCCW.

The glue that held them all together in one very vocal and active peace movement in the 1920s was their belief, as DeBenedetti has put it, that "peace was the necessary reform."[1] This confidence that peace was right, desirable, and necessary forged a positive, energetic drive to persuade the electorate and their governmental representatives to embark upon a systematic program of creating a climate internationally to give peace a chance. Such a program involved the interrelated issues of disarmament, outlawry of war, and mechanisms of a global nature to establish international communication and cooperation, such as the League of Nations and a World Court. And because economic instability within nations created political instability that could lead to war, a program for peace also meant confronting the problem of economic inequity between and among nations as well as the related issue of economic imperialism.

It was a formidable task that peace seekers set for themselves, and the immediate postwar period was not auspicious for ultimate success. Party politics played upon American anger, resentment, and frustration over the peace settlement to reject the Treaty of Versailles and U.S. membership in the League of Nations. The military's attack upon the peace movement and women's organizations had been part of the same phenomenon. Yet there were hopeful signs as well. Coalition politics among peace advocates pushed the Harding administration into calling the Washington Naval Conference. That resulted in some degree of naval arms reduction as well as a moratorium on additional buildup. Not long thereafter the president came out publicly in support of U.S. membership in the World Court (the League of Nations' Permanent Court of International Justice). Should the United States agree to participate in the Court, reasoned peace reformers, perhaps U.S. membership in the League would not be far behind.

Regardless of the issue involved, cooperation among the three wings of the peace movement was more prevalent in the propeace effort of the 1920s than during the antiwar struggle of the 1930s. The most significant example of such coalition politics in the postwar decade was the formation of a group of over thirty organizations in 1927 to work for a peaceful resolution of the growing crisis between the United States and Central America. This crisis was the result of over two decades of smoldering resentment against "Yankee imperialism" in Mexico and Nicaragua, resentment that had been exacerbated by U.S. policymakers.

U.S. economic imperialism was at the heart of the problem, not only in regard to Latin America but in terms of U.S. foreign policy as a whole in the interwar period. U.S. leaders envisioned an international order wherein each and every nation would keep an "open door" through which the capitalist businessman could come and go at will, whether in search of cheaper raw materials, new markets, or areas of investment. This "Open Door World" would be controlled by the industrial-creditor nations, Great Britain, France, the United States, Germany, Italy, and Japan—all of which, asserts diplomatic historian William Appleman Williams, shared a "community of ideals, interests, and purposes"—under the domination of the strongest among them, the United States.[2]

Peace and stability throughout the world were absolutely essential to the success of this "Open Door" vision, and therefore it would be necessary for these "great powers" to police the underdeveloped areas of the world to ensure that nationalistic revolutions did not occur; such upheavals interrupted the free flow of trade and, if allowed to succeed, reform-minded governments in those Third World countries might embark upon policies detrimental to the economic and financial interests of the industrial-creditor nations. Ideally, as Williams points out, this "commercial conquest of the world" would not come as the result of military force, but rather by "political intervention of the subtle and behind-the-scenes variety that would not arouse the antagonism of the natives or the American public."[3]

The WILPF viewed economic imperialism of whatever variety as one of the most serious threats to world peace because the government of a creditor nation invariably used the indebtedness of weaker countries "to acquire control over those countries" and because private business interests of the creditor nation relied upon government support "to secure their ventures." For both of these reasons the WILPF perceived that economic imperialism was "big with menace";[4] in the former case it was a matter of the weak being exploited by the strong and this was morally unacceptable. In the latter instance imperialistic policies could too easily result in military coercion, that is, war.

There was a philosophical issue at stake here as well, one that had to do with the quality of life rather than with quantity of things. As Madeleine Z. Doty observed, "The competitive struggle to acquire possession of things has always been a cause of violence." Although she had enthusiastically supported it, she pointed to the Russian Revolution as an example of this struggle. "The thing that is so disastrous to life," she lamented, "is this willingness of workers and capitalists alike to bring all life down to an economic basis. All morality, all Christianity, all spiritual values are reduced in the last analysis to the economic standard. This spells death to beauty, death to truth, death to life. It seems to me," she concluded, "we women have to set up another standard, a standard that does not make 'economics' the end and all of existence." The implication was clear: The female value system stressed quality of life—the male value system destroyed that quality by a focus on material acquisitiveness.

If U.S. bankers or industrialists decided to invest in foreign countries, then, declared Doty, the WILPF could respond by pointing out to these businessmen that "friendship, understanding, and love are more important than any material possessions." It may be, she acknowledged, that a financier benefits the foreign country by helping to build a railroad. But he does not aid that country "if he brings in the army and navy to protect 'his interests' and kills hundreds of foreigners and Americans alike in the securing for himself the benefit of his investment. Killing men," she asserted emphatically, "is a moral issue. It has got to come right out of the realm of economics."[5]

With these concerns in mind the WILPF persuaded Senator E. F. Ladd of North Dakota and Rep. Roy O. Woodruff of Michigan to introduce in Congress a resolution on the subject of economic imperialism on 1 December 1924. Originally drafted by E. C. McGuire of the Institute of Economics, who was reputed to be highly knowledgeable about Latin American affairs, and subsequently modified by Senator Edward Costigan of Colorado at the request of the WILPF upon the suggestion of Senator Ladd, this concurrent resolution provided that, first, "the United States government shall be relieved of all necessity of using the United States army to protect the business man who invests in foreign countries," and second, that "the United States government shall not recognize any arrangement which will commit the country to military intervention in connection with claims against foreign debtors."[6]

The sentiment expressed here was a direct outgrowth of the 1915 Hague Congress where the women, voicing their opinion that "the investments of capitalists of one country in the resources of another and the claims arising therefrom are a fertile source of international complications," urged that all nations adhere to the principle that such investment be made at the risk of the investor alone, without claim to the protection of his government.[7] An even stronger statement of this policy was made at the WILPF's Board meeting in November 1923 when the women passed the following resolution:

> Whereas, powerful business interests of the United States have loaned many millions of dollars in various parts of the world, and,
> Whereas, these interests have often called upon our government to protect their investments, and
> Whereas, such protection has often resulted in the limitation of the sovereignty of the borrowing nations,
> Be it resolved, that we urge upon the Congress of the United States the passage of a bill forbidding the use of the army or navy in collecting private debts or in protecting the investments of private individuals in foreign countries.[8]

By 1924 the WILPF's concern over the issue of governmental support for private business ventures abroad was heightened, for by the end of that year over two decades of U.S. imperialism in Latin America was compounded in the women's minds by the question of "what commitments, on the part of the United States, the Dawes Plan may involve in case the bonds should be defaulted on."[9] Formally announced in early April 1924, the Dawes Plan involved U.S. loans to Germany for reconstruction as well as for her reparations payments to England and France.

In the 1920s the plan was just one in a series of attempts by U.S. policymakers to promote a peaceful stable world conducive to the economic well-being of U.S. business enterprise. It was important from the

U.S. point of view if for no other reason than it would get Germany back on her feet so that she might join the other industrial-creditor nations in a stable world order geared to the growth and prosperity of capitalism. In addition, the financial experts who designed the plan ensured that German economic stabilization would bring a tidy sum into the coffers of U.S. banking institutions such as J. P. Morgan and Company, which agreed to underwrite $110 million of the initial $200 million loan.

Not without validity did the WILPF, among others, see this plan as a blatant example of the most undesirable kind of economic imperialism.[10] The major concern of the women pacifists was whether the bankers would insist on U.S. military intervention to collect their millions in the event that German prosperity did not materialize to the degree anticipated. Given that such a pattern had developed over the years in Latin America, where U.S. armed forces had intervened twenty-one times between 1898 and 1924, the WILPF had cause for alarm.[11] Certain members of Congress shared this concern, so the WILPF-sponsored bill, now Senate Resolution No. 22 forbidding the use of the U.S. military to secure the foreign investments of U.S. business, was introduced immediately upon the convening of the 68th Congress in December 1924.

As part of their campaign to get the resolution translated into legislation, WILPF leaders urged their members to write their senators and representatives, solicited the support of seventy-eight other organizations interested in the cause of peace, furnished a copy of the resolution to sixty leading journals, and sent a press release to a selected group of large daily newspapers. The next step was to push for a congressional hearing, no easy task even with the cooperation of William Borah, chairman of the Senate Foreign Relations Committee. The WILPF had just about given up hope when suddenly Senator Henrik Shipstead of Minnesota, now in charge of the bill, announced on 18 February 1925 that hearings would begin on 25 February.

With only a week to gather a delegation in support of the resolution, the WILPF worked feverishly, contacting as many influential people as possible. On the twenty-fifth the committee room was filled to overflowing. Jeannette Rankin spoke for the WILPF and statements supporting the resolution from Professor John Dewey and James Weldon Johnson, U.S. consul in Nicaragua from 1909 to 1913, were read into the record. Other speakers for the bill during the two-day hearings were writer Dr. Ernest Gruening and Lewis S. Gannett, assistant editor of *The Nation*.

Citing the examples of El Salvador, Costa Rica, and Panama, Gannett commented that the United States "has found at its doors unorganized governments, peon labor, great undeveloped resources. These offer the opportunity to the more highly developed country to secure from government officials, eager to mortgage the future for present personal profit, the rights to monopolize trade, to keep labor subservient, and to control [the] economic policies of these backward people." Gruening's observations about the U.S. military occupation of Haiti paralleled those of Gannett.

Gannett and Dewey stressed the undemocratic nature of U.S. economic imperialism. "We have unawares been committed to a policy of empire," Gannett commented. "The people of this country have never been consulted about it. Their elected Representatives in Congress have never been consulted about it." Dewey concurred; passage of Resolution No. 22, he asserted, would "protect the country from the evils of secret diplomacy, and from the making of arrangements which, while apparently made openly, nevertheless commit the people of the country to later actions which they never intended and about which they have never been consulted."[12]

Nothing concrete materialized from the hearings before Congress recessed so in the summer of 1925 the WILPF concentrated its efforts toward preparations for a new hearing in the fall. Rankin's suggestions for a plan of attack were fairly typical of the way in which the national office would continue to enlist its members' support for legislative programs. She advised all WILPF members to write their senators and representatives, requesting a copy of the resolution and suggesting that these officials familiarize themselves with it. Each WILPF member should then study it and publicize it as much as possible among local organizations. Last, she should again write her senators and congressman asking their opinion on specific items in the bill. As 1925 passed into 1926, however, hopes for a new hearing dimmed. From the WILPF's standpoint it was more important than ever that Congress address the issue, for by 1926 an already tense situation between this country and Mexico was deteriorating rapidly.

The key to understanding U.S.-Mexican relations in the early years of this century was oil. The development of this vast natural resource fell largely to foreign investors, especially Americans, and in December 1925 the Mexican government passed two new laws detrimental to the interests of American oil companies. U.S. oil magnates naturally protested, resulting in negotiations between U.S. Secretary of State Frank B. Kellogg and the Mexican Minister of Foreign Affairs, which continued throughout 1926 with no settlement in sight. For their part, U.S. oil investors refused to comply with the new laws and commenced injunction proceedings to prevent their implementation.

These alarming developments between the United States and Mexico prompted the WILPF to even greater efforts to spur Congressional action on its resolution. By the end of February 1926 Dorothy Detzer, WILPF Executive Secretary, suggested that perhaps interest in the bill could be renewed with a new bill to supplement Resolution No. 22. It would require the War Department to submit a public report whenever it was called upon to serve any other department within the government, any organization, or any U.S. citizen either to preserve peace, collect debts, supervise elections, or in any other way to employ the military when not authorized by Congress. No action on this idea was taken by the women, however, and congressional interest was now focused on the World Court. Borah asked the WILPF not to urge him to reintroduce the bill, now Concurrent Resolution No. 15, because of the amount of work involved in this latest and, to his mind, more pressing issue.

Congress adjourned in the spring with the matter still unresolved, a situation that alarmed the WILPF, particularly in light of the opinion in some quarters that lack of Mexican cooperation might compel the United States to "carry prosperity and education" to her southern neighbor by force of arms. "A war," declared an April editorial in *Liberty* magazine, "may be necessary to remove this obstruction to [American] economic advancement."[13] The situation remained unchanged by fall. By then another problem arose: The persistent resentment of the Nicaraguans over U.S. imperialistic policies down through the years was coming to a head.

Relations between the United States and Nicaragua in the early years of the twentieth century were no less exploitative than those with Mexico. Uprisings directed against the U.S.-controlled Nicaraguan government in 1912, 1921, and 1922 were quickly suppressed with the aid of the U.S. military. By 1925 the situation was considered to be under control and the U.S. Marines, stationed in Nicaragua for over a decade, departed for home in early August.

Fresh revolutionary activity against the U.S.-backed government erupted again in October of the following year, and as 1927 approached, Kellogg, under growing pressure to settle the Mexican problem, decided upon an indirect tactic that would tie his problems with both Central American countries together and, it was hoped, result in a demand for military intervention to settle the mess once and for all.

As diplomatic historian L. Ethan Ellis put it, Kellogg "countenanced, if he did not engineer, an inflammatory news report" in mid-November 1926, charging that Mexican communists were deliberately fomenting unrest throughout Central America.[14] Kellogg warned the Mexicans that the United States would not tolerate such subversion, prompting Detzer to observe that it was the old tried-and-true "red-baiting" technique always useful in obfuscating the real issue.[15]

The WILPF's response was swift. "The habitual interference of the United States in Central American affairs," noted Detzer in a letter to the Secretary of State, "would seem to have set a most unfortunate precedent for the alleged action now taken by Mexico with regard to Nicaragua. The President and other government officials are continually assuring the citizens of the United States that our military and naval forces exist solely for the defense of this country and not for aggressive warfare nor for the pursuit of empire." If this was true, she continued, then it seemed that there were a few questions that Kellogg should answer:

(1) On what legal ground can the Department of State threaten to risk the lives of American soldiers because of reported or actual interference by one Latin-American country in the affairs of another? (2) How can the "warning" to Mexico by the State Department as reported in the press be interpreted in terms of "national defense"? (3) If the United States Government holds a warship in Nicaraguan waters [,] what is the explanation for the State Department's refusal to countenance the alleged or actual military presence or activities of another nation there? (4) To what extent does the reported loan by American bankers to the present government of Nicaragua influence the "warnings" of the Department of State?[16]

The State Department declined to respond to the WILPF's "interrogatories" as it was contrary to department practice "to indulge in general or hypothetical discussions with private individuals or associations regarding its position with respect to current questions of foreign policy."[17]

The fact that the War Department had requested all state governors to ready their militias for mobilization increased the seriousness of the situation as far as the WILPF and the NCPW were concerned. Both groups redoubled their efforts to obtain a congressional hearing on the WILPF's resolution dealing with economic imperialism, more crucial than ever in light of the current administration's attitude to-

ward utilization of the military. By a tortured definition of the word
"war," Calvin Coolidge was able to argue that at least as far as Latin
American countries were concerned, U.S. "interventions undertaken
'to discourage revolutions' were not war 'any more than a policeman
on the street is making war on passers-by'."[18]

Growing revolutionary activity in Nicaragua finally forced President
Adolfo Díaz, now almost bankrupt, to request direct U.S. intervention
on his behalf in December 1926. Unfortunately, the Nicaraguan problem was made all the more serious by the developing crisis in Mexico.
All foreign investors on Mexican soil were required by the 1925 laws to
obtain, prior to 1 January 1927, "confirmatory concessions of limited
scope and duration" from the Mexican government.[19] With less than a
month until that deadline, not one U.S. oil company had complied nor
did any intend to.

As far as the WILPF was concerned, the situation in Mexico involved "something deeper and thicker than oil." It concerned two dif-
fering concepts of private property. Writing to Doty, then international
secretary of the organization in Geneva, just prior to Christmas 1926,
Detzer noted that Mexico "is no more Bolshevik in the academic Marx-
ian interpretation of the word than the United States, but if one inter-
prets Bolshevism as meaning a change in a country's attitude toward
property, the Central American countries are developing a very different conception from that of the United States. It is this new development which is apparently at the bottom of the difficulty now."[20]

In the "Latin tradition," as Addams pointed out, property vested in
land and in the natural resources beneath that land were perceived as
belonging to the whole people, to be developed in the interest of all, a
concept at variance with the operative premise of U.S. capitalism,
which dictated that property vested in land and natural resources belonged to the private owner to be developed as he saw fit.[21] As for the
communist issue, the WILPF noted that the "sinister reports" of Bolshevik influence and plots in "certain administration newspapers have
been definitely traced to certain officials in the Department of State."
The WILPF was very much aware, however, that Kellogg's revival of "the
red menace" had precisely the effect on the American public he desired. The American Federation of Labor, for example, and "groups of
that kind which might be friendly [to the Mexicans] are of course,"
reported Detzer, "panic-stricken at the very suggestion of 'red'."[22]

On Christmas Eve 1926 Coolidge ordered the military to Managua
and began to make noises about rescinding the 1926 arms embargo to
the region, a move that peace groups feared would only increase the

likelihood of war. The U.S. Marines arrived in Nicaragua's capital on 6 January 1927 and shortly thereafter, "Kellogg presented his semi-hysterical memorandum on 'Bolshevik Aims and Policies in Latin America' to the Senate Committee on Foreign Relations, and a small public furor ensued."[23] Behind this "furor" was the united strength of the country's peace organizations, appalled at the belligerency of their government and its use of scare tactics, and more determined than ever that war between the United States and Mexico, which now appeared imminent, would not erupt.

In late 1926 and early 1927 a "Peace With Mexico" committee was organized, and pressure on the secretary of state to submit the dispute to The Hague Court of Arbitration was stepped up when it was learned that Mexican President Plutarco Elías Calles was willing to do so. With only three days notice, on the evening of 16 January approximately sixty representatives from thirty-three organizations, including those of the "Peace With Mexico" committee, held an emergency meeting in Washington to discuss the most effective strategy for the immediate future. Three WILPF members attended; among the other organizations present were the American Federation of Teachers, the National Women's Trade Union League, and the Socialist League for Industrial Democracy as well as various other peace groups such as the War Resisters League, the FOR, and the NCPW.

"Gravely concerned" over deteriorating relations between this country and Central America, the assembled peace advocates, now calling themselves the "Peace With Latin America Committee," drew up a statement of position on the issue for each delegate to take back to his or her membership for consideration. With respect to the growing tension between the United States and Mexico, they affirmed their belief that "the present differences with Mexico should be settled through peaceful channels, and [we] emphatically protest against any attitude toward the Mexican government savoring of coercion. . . . In coercion we include the movement of troops toward the Mexican border, the sending of warships into Mexican waters, the lifting of the existing embargo on arms, or the severing of diplomatic relations." As for Nicaragua, the conference called for the removal of the Marines as the first step toward an equitable solution to the "present difficulties" there. Planned pressure on the Coolidge administration included a massive press campaign, dissemination of the "factual information" regarding both disputes, and a telegram-and-letter campaign to both the president and Congress.[24]

Conference members reminded their national policymakers of "the oft-declared purpose of this and preceding administrations to adjust all international differences through the peaceful channels of arbitration." Nor did they stop there: The president's own words from a 1925 speech were thrown back at him. "Our country definitely has relinquished," Coolidge had said in Omaha, "the old standard of dealing with other countries by terror and force and is definitely committed to the new standard of dealing with them through friendship and understanding. . . . I shall resist," the president concluded, "any attempt to resort to the old methods and the old standards." Very good, exclaimed the peace seekers: "No excuse," concluded the delegates flatly, "will exist for coercive measures" in the present situation until "all peaceful methods have been fully tried and entirely exhausted."[25]

Detzer sent a letter to every WILPF member, asking cooperation in a campaign to inundate the White House with 10,000 telegrams within two weeks. She contacted other organizations to that same end, and wired Will Hays, former postmaster general, Presbyterian elder, and now "moral arbiter of the motion-picture industry,"[26] protesting the belligerent and jingoistic headings in the newsreels, which proclaimed that "if the call comes for Nicaragua or Mexico our boys are ready,"[27] and urged all WILPF branches to follow up with telegrams of their own.

By the end of January 1927 the peace organizations were also actively supporting two bills in Congress, the first of which stipulated that no troops would be deployed without congressional action. The second called for the complete withdrawal of U.S. troops from Nicaragua. Mass meetings of peace activists were being held in any number of large urban areas—New York, Baltimore, Milwaukee, Chicago. A "small public furor" indeed.

So long as Congress remained in session, peace groups felt relatively confident "that there will be no suggestion of war." It was after Congress adjourned with the subsequent "nine months of executive control" that worried the pacifists.[28]

The peace seekers' faith in the power of Congress to influence the decisions of the executive branch was not wholly warranted. The situation in Nicaragua quickly deteriorated as the revolutionary forces of Juan Sacasa fought their way inland from the east. The State Department was besieged with pleas from the Díaz government for immediate, full-scale U.S. military intervention. Despite a 25 January vote of seventy-nine to zero in the Senate to submit the matter to arbitration—credit for which the WILPF not incorrectly attributed to the concerted action of a unified peace movement—"within a month 2,000 troops were on Nicaraguan soil."[29]

Naturally enough, Resolution No. 15 on the "evils of American imperialism" acquired a greater sense of urgency in the first few weeks of 1927 and at long last, Senator Shipstead agreed to take up the matter again. Detzer quickly went to work to round up speakers for a new hearing before a subcommittee of the Foreign Relations Committee, which was finally held on 16 February 1927. Despite intensive preparation the hearing was a rather "dismal" affair.[30] Two of the scheduled speakers failed to show up and Shipstead refused to accept testimony from a Nicaraguan citizen whom Detzer had persuaded to appear. After two years of futile effort on the part of the WILPF to have it written into law, for all intents and purposes Resolution No. 15 was dead. Although frustrated and disappointed, the WILPF and the Peace with Latin America Committee still had urgent work to do; of great concern to peace forces even as Resolution No. 15 died was the April expiration of a treaty with Nicaragua that contained the all-important arms embargo clause.

By mid-March rumor was rampant in Washington that the U.S. ambassador to Mexico, just recently back at his post from a conference with State Department officials, carried with him the message that Kellogg planned to use "coercive measures" on 1 April after the expiration of the arms embargo.[31] Thus the Peace with Latin America Committee, including journalists from the *New Republic*, the *Nation*, the *World Tomorrow*, and the *Christian Century*, decided to call upon the secretary of state, to question him about the rumor and to renew the demand for arbitration.

According to Detzer, Kellogg told the committee's deputation on 16 March that as far as lifting the arms embargo after 1 April was concerned, "embargoes were such difficult things and so troublesome he didn't know whether they could bother with it any more." Calling the embargo a "nuisance" and refusing to commit himself on the issue, Kellogg's blasé attitude "frightened" the peace workers and only served to reinforce them in their determination to keep the embargo from being lifted. Moreover, his mental and physical condition—"so terrible that they could hardly look at him"—gave the pacifists added cause for concern, and reports that he had sent "secret instructions" to Nicaragua convinced some of the committee members that "the time had come for a nationwide demand" calling for the secretary's resignation. Although he denied the allegation that he had sent secret instructions to anyone about anything, "the opinion is here," wrote Detzer to Balch, "that his word cannot be trusted as he has already denied things and then affirmed them within a few days."[32]

Described by DeBenedetti as "the single most successful anti-war undertaking of the decade,"[33] the efforts of the peace movement to prevent open hostilities between the United States and Mexico and to guide Kellogg in the direction of arbitration or at the very least, negotiations, finally bore fruit. Disconcerted by the public uproar, at the end of March 1927 Kellogg sent for Henry L. Stimson, Secretary of War in the Taft administration, and requested the former New York district attorney to depart as soon as possible for Nicaragua to "straighten the matter out."[34] On 9 April Stimson, accompanied by his wife, departed for the troubled Central American country.

Although the State Department hoped that U.S. supervision of the 1928 Nicaraguan election would not be required, Stimson believed that it would be "absolutely necessary" if any degree of peace was to be maintained.[35] Such indirect intervention, thought the diplomat, would be more likely than military coercion to persuade the Sacasa revolutionaries and the anti-Díaz liberals to settle the unrest on U.S. terms.

Gaining the agreement of the Díaz regime to accept U.S. supervision of the upcoming election was accomplished almost immediately. Getting the forces of Sacasa, particularly the army under the authority of General José Maria Moncada, a Liberal, to accept the continuation of President Díaz in office was another matter. Stimson's warning to the general—a not-too-veiled threat—that the United States was adamant on this issue, plus his written statement "that forces of the United States were authorized to take custody of all arms and to disarm forcibly those who would not voluntarily give up their weapons," apparently convinced Moncada to acquiesce. On 2 May 1927 both the Sacasa-Moncada forces and the Díaz conservatives signed the Tipitapa Agreement. Among the provisions of this settlement were "an immediate grant of peace and amnesty, the opportunity for Liberals to participate in the existing government, the creation of a nonpartisan constabulary, trained by Americans, and the supervising of elections in 1928 and succeeding years by Americans."[36]

Stimson returned home satisfied that a potentially threatening situation had been resolved, yet Nicaragua's internal difficulties were far from over. Only eleven of Moncada's generals agreed to the Tipitapa terms; the twelfth, General Augusto C. Sandino, refused. A true patriot committed to a Nicaragua for Nicaraguans, Sandino and his followers saw the agreement as a continuation of U.S. imperialism and they were determined to fight until the Yankees went home for good. For the next six years the Sandino forces fought a popular guerrilla war against the liberals and conservatives.

The U.S. Marines remained in Nicaragua until 2 January 1933. In the intervening years, sporadic incidents between U.S. troops and Nicaraguan nationals persisted, costing the lives of some 42 Marines and over 3,000 Nicaraguans. Detzer sent a protest to the White House each time a death resulted from one of these clashes. With what must have been annoying regularity from the perspective of both Coolidge and his successor, Herbert Hoover, telegrams and letters arrived from the WILPF. That of 21 July 1927 was typical:

> Today's press dispatches indicated Nicaraguan catastrophe more serious than first reports. Since the landing of troops December 24th the Women's International League has repeatedly urged you to use your great power to prevent the resort to violence which are [sic] so often the inevitable results of military occupation in a foreign country. . . . We pray that you will recognize this present crisis as an opportunity to manifest American forbearance and to demonstrate a spirit of non-violence dictated in accordance with the judgment of the righteous by immediately withdrawing American troops from Nicaragua.[37]

In the meantime, while Stimson was working out the Tipitapa Agreement, Kellogg still faced an equally threatening situation in Mexico. In mid-summer 1927, Dwight W. Morrow, former Amherst classmate of the president and an attorney with the House of Morgan, was appointed ambassador to Mexico, a move, according to historian L. Ethan Ellis, that marked "the overt transition from hostility to conciliation in Mexican-American relations."[38] Morrow's appointment combined with Stimson's efforts in Nicaragua brought a sigh of relief from the Peace with Latin America Committee, although it was aware that months could elapse before negotiations produced anything concrete.

Praised by historians of U.S. foreign policy as an astute diplomat in a touchy situation, Morrow succeeded in winning over the good will of the Calles government and in obtaining thereby a compromise in the controversy over the 1925 Petroleum and Alien Land laws satisfactory to all but U.S. oil producers. They continued to protest well into 1928 but to no avail. Morrow's settlement, in which the Calles government recognized the "binding validity of property rights" from the former regime, and in which the United States recognized Mexican sovereignty over her own natural resources, was accepted by both governments.[39]

With the success of the Stimson and Morrow missions the crisis in Central America was over, at least for the moment, and peace workers could congratulate themselves for having played a critical role in averting war. But the issue of economic imperialism was still a live one, as the WILPF understood now more clearly than ever. And so the women reaffirmed their unequivocal opposition to the economic exploitation of one nation by another:

> The increasingly open and cynical advocacy of imperialism and the constant extension of American control, financial and political, over weaker countries call for our utmost exertions to try to strengthen the true American doctrine and practice of respect and neighborliness toward all, strong and weak alike. We are convinced that it is possible to help backward countries forward to the point where they can maintain orderly conditions, and in general to assist their progress in civilization, without occupation or overlordship. The W.I.L.P.F. stands for co-operation, without any imposition of our national will upon other peoples, and as occasions arise we propose to do all in our power in favor of this policy in every case.[40]

As for government protection of private investment abroad—"the complicated and difficult problem of the rights and duties of a home government in the matter of the protection of its citizens abroad and especially of the foreign investments of its citizens"—Balch, acting in her new capacity as WILPF Director of Policies, proposed that the issue "needs to be made the subject of international study and . . . agreements . . . reached constituting a code of the most enlightened practice to replace the present legal confusion."[41] To this end, she suggested that the League of Nations might undertake such a task.

The Peace with Latin America Committee, as an ad hoc group, dissolved once the crisis ended. Coalition politics to create peace did not terminate, however, for antiwar organizations were already gearing up to support a diplomatic effort to outlaw war forever throughout the civilized world. In this endeavor, the WILPF again played a major role.

6

Cruisers For "Crime"

COALITION POLITICS IN THE 1920s enabled the peace movement to mobilize strong public pressure against the threat of military intervention in support of economic imperialism. The larger goal remained, however: to create positive conditions of justice for all people that would prevent such threats. Peace seekers saw the issue of imperialism as part of a larger, peaceful adjudication of disputes among nations. In particular, they promoted the outlawry of war in relation to their opposition to arms increases, especially for the navy, because they believed that international law and disarmament had to be complementary if either was to constrain war. One goal was to obtain universal adherence to a pact declaring war illegal. Once this was accomplished, the logical next step would be disarmament among the signatories. For if war was a crime and men were rational and law-abiding, weapons of war would not only be unnecessary, they would be immediately anachronistic. Then, with coercion as a method of settling international disputes no longer possible, differences arising between and among nations would have to be resolved through a system of international justice that would include both a World Court and treaties of arbitration.

Not only was this a logical and reasonable approach to the peace issue, it had the added advantage of focusing upon goals that could bring together both pacifists and nonpacifists. Whereas the legalistic aspect of outlawry combined with disarmament and a global judicial system would appeal to nonpacifist antiwar advocates such as the Carnegie Endowment or the Foreign Policy Association, the nonviolent emphasis would assure the support of pacifists. Moreover, with universal acceptance of the idea that to wage war was to break the law, to commit the most heinous of crimes, and with concomitant elimination of national war-making machines, capitalists with investments in foreign countries would find protection for their "property rights" only through the legal system of a World Court. No longer would the "might makes right" of gunboat diplomacy be operative.

The 1921–1922 Washington Conference on the Limitation of Armaments, although disappointing to the more radical pacifists in its results, seemed to be a good beginning. And when William Borah introduced an Outlawry of War resolution in Congress in 1923, followed by Senator Claude Swanson's resolution in the spring of 1924 supporting U.S. participation in the World Court, antiwar advocates were even more encouraged. Although Congress adjourned that spring without taking action on either resolution, the prospects at least for outlawry appeared brighter with the Coolidge and Dawes election victory in the fall because the new president referred to outlawry by name as one of the issues his administration would address. The elevation of Borah to the chairmanship of the Senate Foreign Relations Committee, the most powerful position in Congress with respect to foreign policy, raised the hopes of the peace movement even further.

Because outlawry and the World Court as strategies for U.S. participation in international affairs outside the League of Nations were legalistic in approach, it was not long before their advocates produced an amalgam of the two. Thus in early 1925 the "Harmony Plan" was put forward by an interesting group comprised of pacifists (Kirby Page and socialist Norman Thomas), outlawrists (Salmon O. Levinson, the Chicago attorney who originated the idea, and Charles C. Morison, editor of *The Christian Century*), and World court supporters (James T. Shotwell of Columbia University and James G. McDonald, chairman of the Foreign Policy Association).[1]

Intrigued by the plan, the women of the WILPF, after hearing its proponents discuss the issue at their annual meeting in April, decided to work for its implementation. By September, however, there was apparently enough division within the rank and file over the specifics of the plan that WILPF leaders now urged members "to work for entry into the Court in whatever way seems to them to promise to be most successful."[2]

The World Court issue was finally brought before the Senate in December, and by the end of January 1926, senators voted in favor of U.S. membership, seventy-six to seventeen. Because such participation was predicated upon the acceptance by all court members of a number of "reservations" demanded by U.S. leaders, peace seekers had grave doubts as to the eventual outcome. In March the League of Nations

Council called for a September conference of all concerned, including
the United States, to discuss the situation. In the meantime, uncer-
tainty prevailed as to the status of the United States in the Permanent
Court of International Justice.

Dorothy Detzer undoubtedly voiced the sentiment of the majority
of WILPF members when at the organization's annual meeting in the
spring of 1926, she noted that regardless of "what the future of
the United States' participation in the World Court is going to be," the
affirmative vote in the Senate represented "a gesture in the direction of
international cooperation." That in itself was important, she maintained, but equally so was its indication that perhaps nationalistic
Americans were beginning to think internationally. Moreover, Detzer
thought, the vote pointed to "the value of united services and united
efforts on the part of peace groups on a single issue. The World Court
fight," she concluded with some satisfaction, "brought conservative and
radical groups into definite co-operative activity."[3]

Detzer was referring to the formation of the National Legislative
Committee during the previous winter, comprised of representatives
from the American Federation of Labor, the YWCA, the WCTU, and
the NCPW, which in itself represented forty-three member organizations of the peace movement. Although the World Court issue was not
the primary focus of the committee, created to "follow legislation on
peace and war" in Congress, the WILPF was encouraged by the fact
that such diverse organizations could unite on any specific piece of
legislation at all; it seemed to auger well for the future influence of
peace forces on Capitol Hill.[4] And the WILPF was right, for many
of the committee's groups would join forces in the Peace with Latin
America Committee when the crisis with Mexico and Nicaragua
emerged some few months down the road.

With the World Court issue hanging fire, with no renewed effort
on Borah's part to push outlawry in Congress, with the demise of the
Harmony Plan because of division within the peace movement, and
with the growing crisis in Central America occupying an increasing
share of the antiwar activists' time and energy throughout the remainder of 1926, the role the United States would play in international
peace-keeping, if any, was left up in the air. By the end of the year,
however, pressure from outlawrists upon Borah finally pushed the senator once again into presenting his resolution on the subject. But there
was no stirring speech to accompany its introduction and it was immediately referred to the Foreign Relations Committee where Borah quietly let it die. He was more intent on utilizing his oratorical talents to

castigate administration policy in Central America than to push for an issue for which, at present, there would be no political pay-off. Thus when Congress adjourned in the spring of 1927, there had been no further effort on Borah's part in behalf of outlawry.

Disarmament was faring no better. Steadily deteriorating relations among the Great Powers in the years following the Washington Naval Conference portended a new arms race in naval forces. When the League of Nations in 1925 and 1926 convened a Preparatory Commission for a General Disarmament Conference, it seemed to offer a way out of an undesirable situation, all the more so when the Coolidge administration, much to the delight of the WILPF and other peace groups, agreed to participate. But by early 1927 the conference had made little progress and so on 10 February 1927 Coolidge invited the major naval powers to a conference to discuss further arms limitation.

The intervening years had taken their toll, however, and within less than a week of Coolidge's proposal France declined to attend and shortly thereafter Italy followed suit. Although Japan and Britain, along with a number of lesser powers, accepted the invitation, British leaders let it be known that they did not favor any far-reaching reduction plans. Thus less than one month after the initial proposal, the prospects for the conference that would open in Geneva on 20 June 1927 looked slim indeed.

Yet by then the outlawry cause had been reinvigorated, thanks to French Foreign Minister Aristide Briand. In a major address on 6 April 1927, the tenth anniversary of U.S. entry into World War I, he declared his government's willingness to sign an Outlawry of War pact with the United States. Unfortunately, his timing was rather poor as both Secretary of State Kellogg and the American public were deeply involved in the developing crisis in Central America. Hence, the proposal made little impact on either Washington or public opinion.

Briand's message was well timed for the WILPF, however, because it preceded the organization's annual meeting by a mere three weeks. It was eagerly seized by the women as a proposal of great potential promise. As Balch put it after quoting at length from the foreign minister's speech, "We trust that these words addressed to the American people will not fall on sterile ground and we propose to do all we can to give them effect."[5] A letter from the women expressing these sentiments was immediately dispatched to Briand.

As for Borah, Briand's message was received with lukewarm enthusiasm at best but at the urging of outlawrists, within a week of the WILPF's annual meeting and in the same city, he, too, publicly re-

sponded. In a speech on 9 May the senator, noting that he was opposed to a pact solely between France and the United States, made it
clear that if the French and the Americans were agreed as to the meaning of "outlawry of war," then he could envision a bilateral agreement
to that end as a stepping-stone to one that would include all nations. If
we can take Detzer's word for it, it appears highly probable that WILPF
pressure upon Borah was partially responsible for his suggestion of a
multilateral arrangement, for the WILPF had already gone on record
accordingly. At its annual meeting prior to Borah's speech, the women
announced their decision to draw up a petition calling for outlawry
treaties among the United States, Germany, and England as well as with
France.

Other than a letter to the *New York Times* from Nicholas Murray
Butler, president of Columbia University, praising the Briand proposal
for its possibilities for future action, there was little more in the way of
response. Kellogg was still grappling with the crises in Nicaragua and
Mexico as summer came, and renewed attempts by Briand in June to
obtain a more positive response from Washington backfired because
this time Kellogg was overtly negative. There the matter remained
throughout the summer of 1927. Even more discouraging for the
peace movement was the failure of the Coolidge Disarmament Conference; on 4 August it ended by mutual agreement when attempts to
resolve the differences between the United States and Britain fell on
deaf ears.

If there was little the WILPF could now do with respect to disarmament, the women did their utmost to keep the outlawry issue alive.
They corresponded with Levinson, offering encouragement and support. They sent out over 20,000 petitions, which "called on the president to initiate Treaties to outlaw war beginning with France and
England." They sent telegrams on the issue to the president. They even
suggested to Jane Addams that she invite Briand to speak to the WILPF
on the subject when they heard that he was planning a trip to the
United States.[6] Little more could be done until Congress acted that
winter.

In the fall the situation changed. By late October Borah was taking
a stronger position on outlawry, and yet he almost lost his leadership
role on the issue. On 8 December 1927 Republican Senator Arthur
Capper of Kansas introduced a resolution that authorized the president to sign a multilateral treaty renouncing war as an instrument of
national policy with all signatories pledged to settle disputes between
and among themselves by peaceful means only. The resolution also
allowed the government to rescind protection of any citizen found

guilty of aiding and comforting an aggressor nation, and stipulated
that government action must never be used to impede the implementation of collective sanctions against an aggressor nation.

Because the Capper resolution raised the problem of defining an
aggressor nation and also committed the United States, albeit indirectly, to the principle of collective security, Borah thought it went too
far. He quickly introduced a counterresolution that embodied a multilateral agreement to outlaw war. Almost overnight the idea of outlawry
was thrust into national prominence and it was Borah who began to
push the administration in that direction. He was fearful that the Capper resolution, gaining as it was more adherents with each passing day,
might become law over his more innocuous measure and thus jeopardize traditional American neutrality, which rejected collective security
in favor of unilateralism.

The peace movement, although united on the general principle,
was divided on outlawry as it now emerged in Congress. The problem
revolved around that section in the Capper resolution that provided
for "the use of economic pressure . . . upon aggressor nations."
Hannah Clothier Hull, Quaker president of the U.S. Section of the
WILPF, explained the objection of the Friends to this provision by noting that it brought up "the question of economic sanctions and the
possibility of a hunger blockade."[7] The devastating results of such a
blockade by the Allies in Eastern Europe at the end of World War I
made it impossible for the pacifist Quakers to endorse any resolution
that could have the same effect.

NCPW leader Laura Puffer Morgan expressed regret that the outlawry idea had not been kept separate from the issue of treatment of
aggressor nations in the Capper resolution but, nevertheless, supported
it in preference to Borah's more bland proposal. The WILPF initially
favored the Capper resolution, but when Borah countered with his
more general proposal dealing solely with the idea of outlawry, it became the focus of the women's allegiance because it avoided the divisive issue of economic sanctions.

Kellogg initially supported the Capper resolution, but persistent
pressure from Borah combined, perhaps, with a Jane Addams-led
WILPF presentation to the president of over 30,000 signatures on its
petition favoring the outlawry concept only, brought a change in the
administration's position. By the first week of the new year Briand accepted the secretary's proposal of negotiations to extend the idea of
outlawry to all nations although he rejected the suggestion that such a
pact cover all wars, not just those deemed wars of aggression.

Kellogg found himself without a formula to ease Briand's concern on this score but Borah quickly provided him with a way out of his dilemma. In early February 1928 the senator remarked that "a multi-lateral pact such as he had in mind interfered with no other agree-ments. Without machinery or provisions for determining aggressor," he concluded sagely, "a resort to war by any of the signatories automat-ically would release the others from the pact; they would be free to take whatever action they wished."[8]

Kellogg was pleased with Borah's "solution"; Briand was satisfied; and those within the peace movement concerned with the implication of economic sanctions in the Capper resolution could take heart as the administration transferred its support to the Borah formula of Out-lawry. By April 1928 matters had progressed to the point where Detzer, noting "the concrete proposal by the Secretary of State," could urge WILPF members everywhere "to write to the President and to the Sec-retary of State thanking them and commending them on their action. We have so often criticized government policy," she pointed out, "that we should be eager to acknowledge all the splendid efforts for Peace as we are quick to oppose all the forms of militarism."[9]

The proposal to which she referred would commit signatories to the renunciation of war "as an instrument of national policy." It avoided completely any distinction between "defensive" and "aggres-sive" war and it was totally without teeth. Bland, innocuous, and thor-oughly inoffensive, the proposed treaty could have been signed with a clear conscience by the most belligerent of militarists. By this time, however, a fresh dilemma had emerged for the peace forces. Why, they queried, support outlawry of war with such enthusiasm while at the same time backing a bill providing for the largest naval appropriation in the nations's history? Outlawry was supposed to be coincident with the elimination of arms, not an *increase* in a nation's warmaking power.

The WILPF was interested in outlawry as part of the whole disarma-ment issue. The importance of sea power to national economic expan-sion had been stressed ever since the turn of the century, and was an important part of U.S. and British intransigence leading to the demise of the Coolidge Disarmament Conference. In fact, the resulting deteri-oration of amicability between the two imperialistic powers was one of the more significant factors behind the 1928 naval appropriation bill.

It was this very fact of economic motivation that concerned the women of the WILPF. They agreed with maverick Army General Billy Mitchell who in the spring of 1925 pointed out to the group that if U.S. leaders were really sincere in their insistence that they were only interested in ensuring the defense of the country against external attack, then "airships were all that would be needed." The WILPF agreed that the only need for a navy "lay in the fact that we must protect our capital abroad."[10]

Throughout the mid-1920s, therefore, the WILPF closely monitored all efforts in Congress to increase the size of the navy, lobbying along with the NCPW against such legislation whenever it was proposed. It was an uphill struggle and when the outlawry idea began to take hold, "Big Navy" advocates were beginning to push a "two-part program for naval increase." First, the WILPF reported, "there will be an investigation of the Navy with a great deal of publicity by the Naval Committee,"[11] and second, a bill appropriating money for a five-year naval construction program was anticipated to come up in the House sometime early in the year. Despite the demands on their time and energy due to both the Central American crisis and the outlawry issue, the women resolved to counter this "Big Navy" push.

Introduced in Congress in February, the Cruiser bill called for the construction of seventy-one ships at a cost of $740,000,000: twenty-five cruisers, thirty-two submarines, nine destroyers, and five airplane carriers. This money, to be spent over the next five years was, as the WILPF noted, only the "appalling beginning of a twenty-year program which involves the staggering amount of two and a half billion dollars."[12] Peace workers were now confronted with the formidable job of limiting the influence of one of the most powerful sectors of U.S. business enterprise, the armaments industry. Although they wished that Congress would reject the Cruiser bill entirely, peace groups were realistic enough to realize that the best they could probably do would be to obtain a reduction in the total number of proposed vessels.

This effort produced some heated exchanges between antiwar forces and self-styled patriots as hearings began in mid-February before the House Naval Affairs Committee, chaired by Fred A. Britten of Illinois. According to one newspaper account, "angered by circulars which Mr. [Frederick] Libby has sent throughout the country, members of the committee prompted witnesses to make derogatory statements about him and then denied an opportunity to one of Mr. Libby's associates [Laura Puffer Morgan] to put in a defense."[13]

Referring to the anti-Cruiser bill material of the NCPW as "radical trash," Britten denounced the absent Libby and then, with the eager assistance of representatives from the DAR and the Dames of the Royal Legion, castigated pacifist Dr. William I. Hull, husband of WILPF President Hannah Hull, who was also absent from the proceedings. Britten and the women patriots concluded that such a menacing individual should be removed from his professorship at Swarthmore College. Even Detzer was not exempt from the scathing attacks upon pacifists. When she attempted to state the WILPF's objections to the bill, Mrs. Noble Newport Potts, president of the National Patriotic Council, leaned over to warn Britten, "That's a dangerous woman you've been talking to."[14]

The storm of public protest over the Cruiser bill instigated by the peace groups, particularly the NCPW, WILPF, AFSC, and the Federal Council of Churches, equaled if not exceeded the outcry over the Mexican crisis of the previous year. "Tons of mail" flooded the House Naval Affairs Committee, according to the WILPF, and an emasculated bill providing for only sixteen new vessels was finally accepted.[15] In mid-March it went to the Senate for consideration. Detzer reported with delight the rumor that Britten had grumbled that credit for the drastically revised version had to go "the efforts of two women—Mrs. [Laura Puffer] Morgan, who is the mind behind the National Council [for Prevention of War], and Dorothy Detzer." The statement was "inaccurate," Detzer noted, as were "most of Britten's statements," but, she concluded gleefully, "it is pleasant to have him consider us so dangerous."[16]

At the WILPF's 1928 annual meeting in early May, the three major issues commanding the women's attention during the previous year brought united response in the form of three related resolutions. With regard to the Central American crisis, the women went on record in deploring "the recent action of the Senate in sanctioning the marine occupation of Nicaragua," and urged the State Department to replace the military supervision of elections there with a "civilian commission," preferably composed of Latin American members. Again noting the "great inconsistency of offering peace treaties to the world and at the same time reaching out for naval supremacy," the women voted to send to the Secretary of State an expression of their "very deep satisfaction . . . for the lead he has taken in promoting the multilateral treaties" to outlaw war. Then, concerning the naval issue, they resolved:

> WHEREAS, An increase in the naval establishment can only create a
> new race in armaments with friendly nations, and
> WHEREAS, President Coolidge has assured the American public
> within the past year that our Navy is second to none, therefore be
> it
> RESOLVED, That we urge the Senate to abandon any program look-
> ing to an increase in the Navy.[17]

With the approach of the national political conventions in the summer, looking toward the presidential election in November, the WILPF began to plan strategy for influencing the party platforms. Out to the branches from the National Office on 31 May 1928 went a letter requesting that each branch appoint two individuals or committees, one for each party, to pressure their respective party's delegates. Detzer suggested that they push for only one or two specific planks and recommended either "the multilateral treaties denouncing war as an instrument of national policy," or one concerned with economic imperialism which would oppose intervention abroad "for the protection of our Nationals."[18] There was no need to concern themselves with naval legislation any longer, she wrote, for at adjournment in spring 1928 the Cruiser Bill was dead.

In the meantime, negotiations between Washington and Paris on the outlawry treaty made slow but steady progress. Once the political conventions were history and the election campaign began in earnest, the many months of endeavor for outlawry finally culminated in success. The signing of the Kellogg-Briand Pact (27 August 1928, Paris) committed the fifteen initial signatories, including the United States, to "condemn recourse to war for the solution of international controversies and renounce it as an instrument of national policy in their relations with one another."[19]

As Borah pointed out months earlier the total absence of sanctions gave the treaty absolutely no credible means of enforcement, a weakness, as Charles DeBenedetti has noted, which most scholars attribute "to the naivete of American peace leaders and the gullibility of American public opinion." In point of fact, he asserted, "there is little evidence to believe that American popular opinion was more successful in initiating substantive negotiations toward the peace pact than it was in realizing other peace ideals during the postwar years."[20] Not only were peace leaders not responsible for the pact's adoption, they were not altogether "naive" or "gullible" either.

First, as diplomatic historians have pointed out, only an antiwar treaty so completely devoid of teeth would have been entertained at all by either the Coolidge administration or William Borah. It was precisely because it fit so perfectly into the Republican scheme of presenting the United States as a "peace-seeker" in the postwar world, while at the same time pursuing goals of economic expansion abroad, that the Kellogg-Briand Pact ever got off the ground. Second, as a measure that reinforced the status quo of the postwar world as provided for in the Treaty of Versailles, it was made to order for those power brokers intent on preventing or suppressing nationalistic revolutions. Last, as a "public relations" maneuver to impress national and international peace advocates as well as others skeptical of U.S. intentions in the postwar world, it was without equal—and it *was* without equal precisely because it was so totally vacuous.

To charge the peace forces in this country with "naivete" as so many scholars have done with respect to this issue, and others as well, is a distortion of the facts. There undoubtedly were women within the U.S. Section of the WILPF as well as others within the peace movement as a whole who truly believed that even without any provision for enforcement, the Kellogg-Briand Pact meant the dawn of a new age, an age pledged to the peaceful resolution of disputes between and among nations. Yet with respect to the WILPF (and it was fairly typical of the majority of peace organizations), the evidence does not indicate that either leaders or followers were quite that naive.

In fact, it appears that certain European sections of the WILPF were somewhat frustrated and perplexed over the "ho-hum" response of the U.S. Section to the idea of outlawry as it began to emerge in concrete form in the summer of 1928. Detzer indicated as much in a letter to Balch in late June when she reported that "the European countries" could not understand why the American women were so "lukewarm" with regard to the "Kellogg proposals." The basic reason was very simple: "It is almost impossible," she noted, "for the Peace Movement to go in with great and wide enthusiasm when Kellogg continues his policy in Nicaragua and says that it should not at all interfere with a big Navy." It was extremely difficult, she concluded, "to get people to accept his sincerity" on the outlawry issue.[21]

Now this position, it is true, suggests that the women's lack of enthusiasm for the outlawry negotiations was predicated less on the concept itself and more on the personal role of the secretary of state who, if past behavior was any measure of future conduct, was not to be trusted. His negative behavior belied his positive words. Yet this was only part of the question, for although the women of the U.S. Section harbored some legitimate skepticism with regard to Kellogg's sincerity, they also recognized that even if the idea of outlawry was realized in a multilateral treaty, it would be an exercise in futility unless such a treaty was made the "basis for real disarmament." A letter from the women to the Secretary of State of 22 July put the matter unambiguously: "It is a self-evident fact that no treaty for the outlawry of war, however widely accepted, can have more than a purely theoretical and academic value unless all the signatory powers give practical form to their avowed abandonment of force by taking immediate steps toward disarmament. No country can sincerely talk arbitration while at the same time maintaining a large military establishment. Under such circumstances a treaty might easily become 'a scrap of paper'."[22]

In other words, the Kellogg-Briand Pact as it subsequently emerged was perceived by these pacifists not as an end in itself, but as a *means* to an end—disarmament among all nations. Thus the WILPF, in the United States and abroad, called upon the various nations not only to "renounce war through the signing of this multilateral treaty," but at the same time "to institute measures for immediate disarmament."[23] It was clearly understood that the Kellogg-Briand Pact in and of itself was meaningless without this further step toward world peace. Even the European women in their enthusiasm for the Pact saw it as nothing more than the possible "beginning of a series of steps towards the substitution of law for war."[24]

As the U.S. Section of the WILPF looked to the 1928 presidential election, its overriding concern was with the twin issues of the pact's ratification—without reservations—and disarmament, particularly as it feared the re-introduction of the Cruiser bill. The problem of reservations emerged in September, and in the opinion of Professor Edwin Borchard, a respected authority on international law, the pact when hedged about with these reservations ceased to be an agreement that outlawed war. Instead, he asserted, it became "in fact and in law a solemn sanction for all wars mentioned in the exceptions and qualifications." He concluded, therefore, that "it would be difficult to conceive of any wars that nations have fought within the past century, or are likely to fight in the future, that cannot be accommodated under these exceptions."[25]

The election of the "right" men in November might spell the difference between success and defeat for their cause, so the women went to work to determine just who these men were. As a nonpartisan organization, the WILPF sent questionnaires to Congressional candidates of both major parties and the socialists to ascertain their position on these two issues as well as on related matters. Nor were the presidential candidates overlooked. Addams and Lucy Biddle Lewis presented the questionnaire to Herbert Hoover, Lillian Wald led a WILPF deputation to the New York Democrat Al Smith, and a third group headed up by Detzer visited the Socialist candidate, Norman Thomas.

At the same time Detzer and Morgan of the NCPW requested that Borah bring the Kellogg-Briand treaty to the floor of the Senate for consideration just as soon as he received it from the president. He agreed to do so but then confirmed the women's fears that the Cruiser bill would be re-introduced. He might not receive the treaty, he pointed out, until after the Senate took action on the naval bill, which, he admitted unhappily, would undoubtedly pass this time. Acknowledging that Borah was probably right, the WILPF's National Board directed Balch to draft a letter to Coolidge "asking for precedence for the Kellogg treaty over the Navy Bill" which would not be sent until the most propitious time for pressure in this regard.[26]

It is interesting to note in this unfolding drama as to whether the Kellogg treaty or the Cruiser bill would win first consideration once the Senate reconvened, that the WILPF women were among that handful of individuals who, for all their alleged "naivete" and "lack of realism," were astute *and* frank enough to characterize this anomalous situation for precisely what it was—an "absurdity."[27] To be sure, there were those who agreed with that senator, who disdainfully referred to the Kellogg treaty as "an international kiss" or a second, who commented that the treaty was not worth much more than "a postage stamp." And although historians like Selig Adler have written that "with a straight face, Vice-President Charles G. Dawes told the senators that the outlawry of war and the measure to build fifteen new cruisers concordantly formed the current American foreign policy,"[28] neither those senators nor Adler were as perceptive as the women of the WILPF.

Trying to control their impatience, these pacifists pointed out that it was ridiculous to ratify the Kellogg-Briand Pact making war a crime and then immediately do an about-face and pass a bill appropriating $270 million for the construction of fifteen new cruisers and an aircraft carrier, quite clearly implements of war regardless of what other name might be used to describe them. As Detzer observed, "For some unaccountable reason quite remote from logic there is an effort to pretend that the treaty to outlaw war and a bill to increase the Navy have no possible relation or consequence."[29]

As election drew closer the White House and State Department were inundated with letters and telegrams from WILPF members all across the country, urging that the Kellogg treaty be given top priority when Congress re-convened. Each letter writer received the same response from the State Department: "The General Pact for the Renunciation of War will be submitted promptly after the convening of Congress." Detzer, by now an old hand at discerning deliberate ambiguity, was not satisfied; she headed straight for the State Department. There she confronted Prentiss Gilbert, acting chief of the Division of Western European Affairs, and asked him pointedly "if he could interpret the word 'promptly'." He had to admit that he was simply acting upon orders from the Secretary of State and thus did not know whether the word meant days or weeks. Although rumors were rampant throughout Washington and in the press that Borah and Senator Hale, who was sponsoring the Cruiser bill, had entered into a backroom agreement whereby the latter bill would come up first, Borah denied knowledge of any such arrangement, reiterating his intention to introduce the Kellogg treaty as soon as he was able.[30]

As expected, Coolidge's Secretary of Commerce, Herbert Hoover, was elected to the presidency in November, bringing a Republican-dominated Congress with him. The time was now fast approaching for the new Congress to convene and so the WILPF doubled its efforts in behalf of the Kellogg-Briand Pact, already supported by fifty-eight other nations, all but one of which were waiting to see what the United States would do before finally ratifying the agreement. Detzer, for one, was determined to have U.S. ratification by Christmas.

By early December the treaty was in the hands of the Senate Foreign Relations Committee, each member of which now received a copy of the letter drafted earlier by Balch that gently prodded him into action: "It is hard for anyone who has not happened to have opportunities of mixing as an unofficial person with similar people of many countries," she wrote, choosing her words carefully, "to realize how deeply respect for the United States is undermined when public and official undertakings of executive representatives of our people are contradicted and overthrown by its legislative representatives."[31] Similar sentiment was expressed by the 350 "representative citizens" who signed "a Memorial to the U.S. Senate" on 17 December, and again at a Conference on the Cruiser bill, organized by that same citizens committee in Washington on 8 January 1929.[32]

Nor did Detzer let up on the pressure. Enlisting the support of her good friend Ludwell Denny, chief editorial writer for the twenty-five Scripps-Howard newspapers, she fell only three weeks short of her goal for ratification. Adopting "a committee report spelling out the right of self-defense and eliminating sanctions from measures available for enforcement," the Senate ratified the Kellogg-Briand Pact by a vote of eighty-five to one on 15 January 1929.[33] When Coolidge signed the treaty two days later the United States became the second nation formally to adhere to a renunciation of war as an instrument of national policy; only the Soviet Union had ratified earlier.

Then those same senators immediately began consideration of the Cruiser bill. Having just committed themselves to the position that the waging of war was a crime, they passed the bill that provided for the construction of sixteen ships that would increase the likelihood of U.S. success in fighting a war, now a crime. As Roger Baldwin of ACLU commented a few weeks later, "I do not think that the diplomats who signed [the Kellogg-Briand Pact] . . . mean more than an empty gesture in the direction of peace."[34]

Despite the fact that it really did not make much sense to outlaw war and at the same time increase one's power to wage war, the U.S. Section of the WILPF recognized that whatever the Cruiser bill may or may not have represented in the way of U.S. militarism, the United States was just one nation among many (albeit the most powerful), and the Kellogg-Briand Pact was an international treaty. If peace forces across the world could prevent the other signatories of the pact from embarking upon similar arms build-up, the United States would find itself isolated with sixteen spanking new but anachronistic naval vessels. Thus the theme of the WILPF's 1929 International Congress was quickly decided upon: "How to Make the Kellogg Pact a Reality."[35] Not surprisingly, the focus was disarmament.

7

Disarmament Hopes Dashed

ALTHOUGH THE COOLIDGE DISARMANENT CONFERENCE ENDED an abysmal failure in August 1927, the League of Nations' Preparatory Commission for a General Disarmament Conference, convened in 1925–1926, was still sitting in Geneva as the Kellogg-Briand Pact was ratified. While the commission continued its work, looking toward the conference scheduled for 1931, plans went forward for a 1930 naval disarmament conference in London as a preliminary step, its goal being to extend the 1922 naval treaties among the Big Five. The Anglo-American discord left over from the Coolidge Conference dissipated quickly in the early spring of 1929 as President Hoover embarked upon negotiations with the British. The WILPF could not have been more pleased and as summer came continuing negotiations between the two great naval powers indicated a growing willingness, if not eagerness, to accomplish something of substance with respect to naval arms cuts.

Proposals and counterproposals continued into the fall, however, and no satisfactory compromise was reached. Adding a new dimension to the conference, now barely two months away, was the revelation that certain "steel and shipbuilding corporations" had hired one William B. Shearer in 1927 to do whatever he could to thwart the Coolidge Conference in Geneva.[1] This covert pressure on the delegates from the armaments industry might never have become public knowledge were it not for the fact that Shearer, who apparently lived up to his end of the bargain, was now filing suit against his former employers for failure to provide promised recompense.

The Shearer lawsuit brought a Senate investigation of the matter, and Dorothy Detzer attended as many of those sessions as she could that fall. Her conclusion that the shipbuilders—"the great captains of industry"—made a "pathetic anemic appearance" with regard to any display of "courage or responsibility" was supported by other observers at the hearings. Journalist George Seldes remarked caustically that "to escape the charge that they hired a lobbyist to defeat the American government's hopes, the great American business men, the builders of the American navy and the . . . merchant marine, deliberately made themselves foolish on the witness stand. They didn't know what it was all about. They had been victims of an over-zealous over-patriotic agent. They had been jazzed off their feet and out of their minds. They were innocent." Helmuth Engelbrecht, associate editor of *The World Tomorrow*, agreed with both assessments. As Detzer exclaimed in disbelief, "passing the buck was the one thing in which [the shipbuilders] excelled. . . . One wondered how any self-respecting men could make themselves out either such fools or such irresponsible citizens."[2]

The Senate investigation produced nothing in the way of tangible results. Barely suffering a slap on the wrist, the builders of U.S. warships endured no recriminations, morally, legally, or financially. "They had admitted," wrote Seldes, "that they did not fire Shearer until March, 1929, the 15–cruiser bill having been passed in February and eight ships awarded the private manufacturers. The smash-up at Geneva had resulted in business orders for millions of dollars for them and the creation of the revolving fund of $250,000,000 for loans in the construction of new vessels. Truly Shearer said, 'As a result of my activities . . . eight 10,000 ton cruisers are now under construction' by the firms which employed him."[3] The public uproar over this disclosure apparently encouraged Hoover to take a stronger public stance on disarmament. In an Armistice Day speech he announced that the United States would reduce its naval strength as far as any other nation was willing to go.

On 20 January 1930 British Prime Minister Ramsay MacDonald provided the United States with the opportunity to act on the president's words, for on that day, just twenty-four hours before the formal conference convened, he called for the abolition of all battleships. Then after negotiations were underway France countered with a demand for the abolition of submarines. Peace forces were jubilant but not so those groups with a vested interest in maintaining or even expanding the world's naval forces. "The lobbyists for the great shipbuilding firms, the steel industry, and certain of the labor unions," recalled Detzer some years later, "descended on senators in a powerful phalanx, urging them to denounce this Socialist sacrilege."[4]

While these "Big Navy" proponents pressured Congress, peace groups were hard at work at home and in London, attempting to mobilize public opinion on behalf of naval reduction. The methods employed were an interesting blend of prewar Progressivism with postwar public relations. The Progressive stress on education, on replacing ignorance with knowledge, was still critically important and went hand-in-glove with the Biblical adage, know the truth and the truth shall set you free. But it was no longer enough to spread the way, the truth, and the light via the printed word and the lectern; mass communication was now in vogue.

Each year an increasing number of American families joined their neighbors in becoming proud owners of at least one radio, and the peace movement was quick to take advantage of this technological advance in disseminating its message. The publicity that could be gained from the "hoopla" of mass demonstrations, colorful parades with bright, snappy banners waving in the wind accompanied by the peppy music of the high school band was not overlooked either.

While publicity and public relations committees attempted to mobilize public opinion through eye and ear appeal, political pressure on lawmakers and other government officials became less personal and more professionalized. The days of genteel persuasion over brandy or tea were fading fast. It was no longer sufficient to be a Jane Addams, simply one respected and admired individual of some status and prestige sitting down with a head of state to discuss the ethics or morality of an issue. Now more than ever before, it became a matter of power. How many potential votes did a Jane Addams represent? How much economic or political clout could a group muster from its constituency, and how quickly could it be mobilized? It was a much faster-paced world, where talent and ability in playing the political game of give-and-take was not only a plus but a real necessity.

The WILPF adjusted quickly to this new postwar reality and by the late 1920s had perfected the new techniques in public relations, thanks particularly to leaders such as Mabel Vernon and Anne Martin who had gained invaluable experience in just this kind of mass publicity from the suffrage campaign. Every possible tactic that might mobilize the American people to support their government at the London Disarmament Conference was utilized by the WILPF, from personal pressure to mass demonstrations. Through the efforts of Rosalie Jones Dill, wife of a Washington senator, NBC agreed to provide the half-hour from six-thirty to seven every Saturday evening for a Radio Peace Program as long as the London conference was in session. Had Ford

Motor Company sponsored an entertainment program in this time slot, wrote Detzer confidentially, it would have had to pay the network $10,000. The WILPF was given this thirty minutes of "prime time," estimated to reach from thirty to forty million listeners, for nothing.[5]

Out of a desire to have immediate and first-hand knowledge of the conference's proceedings as well as to keep pressure on the delegates, the U.S. Section of the WILPF sent Madeleine Doty to London as its representative. The NCCCW also sent a delegation with a resolution to present to the negotiators, and the Women's Peace Crusade, an association of eighteen British organizations, including the WILPF, presented a memorial to the conferees in early February urging them to make the Kellogg-Briand Pact a reality by agreeing to a "large decrease . . . in the naval armaments of the world."[6] In addition, two Japanese women, one a WILPF member, presented a peace resolution to the conference with the signatures of 180,000 Japanese women.

By mid-February Doty was reporting the discouraging news that the conference was deadlocked. "There is a great depression at the moment," she wrote to the international secretary of the WILPF in Geneva. "Things are not moving. There is a vicious circle which no-one seems to dare to break. Gt. [sic] Britain and America have come out for total abolition of the submarine. France refuses any reduction and demands increase. Italy says small nations will abolish submarines if big nations will abolish battleships. Japan is watching the other Powers."[7]

As the talks continued, the principle of "parity" began to emerge as official U.S. policy—naval parity between England and the United States, naval parity between France and Italy. Because parity meant that the United States would actually be permitted to build *more* battleships and cruisers rather than reduce her naval force, the WILPF was not only keenly disappointed when the conference took this tack, it was beginning to grow a bit impatient.

Then when the U.S. delegates refused to support either the idea of an "Atlantic security pact whereby these naval powers would agree not to go to the aid of an aggressor nation," or even a consultative pact under which the nations would confer in times of a threat to peace, the national office of the WILPF in Washington began a protest campaign of telegrams sent every night to the president, who was then vacationing in Florida. Rerouted to the State Department, these telegrams and the thousands of letters from WILPF members throughout the country prompted Prentiss Gilbert to call Detzer on the phone "to inquire how long this W.I.L. barrage was going to continue."[8] Detzer's reply was unequivocal. She would continue to urge the women to protest U.S.

policy at the naval conference until that policy was brought into line with the pledges so earnestly put forth by the government prior to the conference, pledges calling for naval reduction, not increase.

After Hoover returned to Washington, Detzer and WILPF President Hannah Clothier Hull composed a lengthy letter to him, which Detzer then hand-carried to the executive department. The letter reaffirmed the WILPF's support for Hoover's expressed policy of desiring naval reduction and indicated concern over what was clearly a repudiation of this policy by U.S. delegates to the conference. Acknowledging that as "private citizens" they might not be privy to any extenuating circumstances that accounted for this situation, they nevertheless concluded that should the conference fail, that failure "would rest squarely on the United States."[9]

The letter brought an immediate response. At four o'clock the following afternoon at Hoover's request, Detzer sat across the desk from the president while he attempted to explain the dynamics of the conference. "He recognized . . . the sincerity of the W.I.L. in pressing for more affirmative action," she reported, "but he felt sure . . . that we would not be so vocal and persistent if conversant with all the facts." So the chief executive of the United States insisted that the executive secretary of the WILPF read for herself each of the official dispatches sent to him from the U.S. delegation in London. For the better part of an hour there was silence in that office as Detzer went through the thick pile of correspondence, item by item.

Rather than being persuaded that the WILPF had been operating under a "misapprehension," however, when she looked up from the last of those dispatches Detzer told Hoover that what she had just read only confirmed her earlier opinion that the responsibility for a conference failure would rest with the United States. Despite what she had learned concerning "other factors which must be considered in this situation," she was no less convinced that ultimate responsibility for the conference's failure to conclude a naval reduction agreement rested with the man sitting across from her. When he then turned to her and asked what she would do at this juncture were she in his shoes, she responded:

> "We both know what war means to all the little people. If I were President of the United States I would never forget for one moment all those little people. Remembering them, I would discard all ideas of 'parity' and 'reduction' and I would offer at London a program so audacious and inspiring that the world would rise up and call me

blessed. You can do that; you have the power. You would be opposed and vilified, of course, by the vested interests in war, but those are the ones who are never shot at or starved. . . . Why can't you do that?"

"I can't," said the President, swinging his chair around toward the window again. "I can't. Besides, you forget that this is not a disarmament conference. This is a conference on limitation."

"I haven't forgotten that, Mr. President," I said. "But certainly you can limit things down to nothing. . . . If you would offer a program of real naval disarmament, supplemented perhaps with a positive economic program, think what that would mean for peace? Why can't you do something like that before it is too late?"

"I can't," he said. "I can't."

"Well, if you can't do all of that," I pursued, "why can't you accept the proposals for the abolition of battleships and submarines? If the other nations are making those proposals just as a bluff, why don't you call their bluff? But if they are honest, what a good start that would be. If the United States doesn't respond now, it may be forever too late."

The President was silent for a long moment; then he raised his hands in a gesture of futility, and dropped them on the desk. "I can't," he fairly whispered. "I can't."[10]

Detzer left the White House that lovely evening in April 1930, still believing that Herbert Hoover was no less committed to peace and disarmament than she was herself, but that he could not act on that commitment with respect to the London conference because he was "trapped." Occupying the most powerful position in the world's most powerful country, the president of the United States, Detzer thought to herself in amazement, "for some reason . . . is not a free agent." Not knowing whether Hoover felt himself powerless to act because of the "horse-trading" of party politics or because of "secret factors not revealed in the dispatches" she had read, Detzer walked slowly back to her office to type up a memorandum of her conversation with the president. The one thing she *did* know was that not only would the results of the naval conference fall far short of the expectations of the peace forces, but that this disappointment could be traced to the White House where Hoover now sat in the gathering dusk, "defeated by circumstances he conceived to be now beyond his control."[11]

The results of the 1930 London Disarmament Conference were indeed a disappointment for peace advocates. On 22 April a treaty signed by the five major powers—England, France, the United States, Japan, Italy—called a halt to the construction of capital ships until 1936 and limited the size and armament of submarines and aircraft carriers. A treaty signed by Japan, England, and the United States achieved parity only for the latter two nations. Japan was permitted to build only seven destroyers for every ten allowed the western powers. In addition, the treaty included a provision allowing for increased construction should any one of the three nations feel that its national security was threatened. The conference adjourned with France and Italy still at loggerheads over the latter's demand for parity with the former, and France adamantly refusing to sign any limitation agreement without a military defense pact with England. A conference that was expected to limit the naval forces of the major powers as a preliminary step to the upcoming Geneva Disarmament Conference had, with respect to the United States, accomplished precisely the opposite. By achieving parity with England, the United States could now embark upon a program of naval increase.

Despite the opinion of some highly placed political figures close to the international peace movement that the London conference "was a great step forward," some of the more radical among peace advocates, including the WILPF, WPU, and NCPW, could not agree that the Five Power treaty, in particular, "had given a great boost to the general cause of disarmament."[12] Detzer and pacifist writer Devere Allen organized a Pacifist Action Committee to "frame suggestions with regard to pacifist action . . . which would include a recommendation not to support the Naval Treaty."[13] More likely to give "a great boost" to the disarmament cause was the joint resolution passed by Congress only two months later establishing the War Policies Commission (WPC).

Created on 27 June 1930, the WPC was composed of four members each from the House and Senate, plus the attorney general and the secretaries of War, Navy, Commerce, and Agriculture. It was headed by the Secretary of War, Patrick J. Hurley. Its stated purpose was "to promote peace and to equalize the burdens and to minimize the profits of war, . . . to study and consider amending the Constitution . . . to provide that private property may be taken by Congress for public use during war, . . . together with a study of policies to be pursued in the event of war."[14] Although the resolution exempted from consideration the "conscription of labor," what it amounted to was clearly a consideration of the conscription of capital, a proposal much to be feared as far as peace groups were concerned. Norman Thomas and Detzer, among others, warned that the kind of constitutional amendment necessary for the effective conscription of capital would encourage "a fascist-like regimentation of every detail of American life."[15]

Public hearings began on 5 March 1931 and shortly thereafter, government testimony revealed the existence of an Industrial Mobilization Plan within the War Department, the first public indication that such a plan had even been under consideration. As Seymour Waldman, who attended all of the hearings, noted in his 1932 study of the WPC, under this plan U.S. business firms would be offered "tentative contracts on a non-competitive standby basis with a guarantee of full production and satisfactory prices and profit margins in the event of war."[16] Not without reason, therefore, did the peace movement view the WPC's primary concern as being the problem of military preparedness despite the noble and high-sounding phrases given as reasons for its creations. As Arthur Ekirch, Jr., noted in his introduction to Waldman's study, with the Industrial Mobilization Plan governmental emphasis shifted "from legislation for peace to legislation that would make war, or the preparation for war, cheaper and more efficient."[17]

That commission members were unenthusiastic at best over the prospect of peace advocates testifying at the hearings was made clear by the treatment accorded those scheduled to appear. Originally the representatives of the peace organizations were informed that they would be called to speak during the week of 25 May 1931. Norman Thomas, Director of the League for Industrial Democracy, and Nevin Sayre, executive secretary of the FOR, were both on speaking tours that spring and so planned their schedules accordingly, as did Detzer and Tucker Smith, executive secretary of the Committee on Militarism in Education. Suddenly on 16 May Detzer was notified that the time for their appearance had been moved forward to 20 May. "It was with a great deal of inconvenience," she wrote to Balch in Geneva, that she, Thomas, and Smith managed to rearrange their plans at the last minute. "Norman Thomas even canceled his engagements in North Dakota to come back," she reported wryly.[18]

These three spokespersons for the peace groups arrived for the hearings on the morning of the twentieth only to find that someone else was scheduled to speak first. Finally Tucker Smith was called, but unfortunately, according to Waldman, he was not the most impressive of witnesses. Not only were his comments "a bit vague" but he seemed "perilously in danger of sinking into a bog of abstractions."[19] At this point Detzer picks up the story:

> After he [Smith] finished, an Assistant Secretary of the Treasury took up all the rest of the time in the morning. It was about 12:30 when he finished, whereupon Secretary Hurley . . . announced that the commission would adjourn for the day. This was quite unusual, for up to

this time, they had not adjourned at the noon hour but had sat right through the afternoon. Norman, Nevin, and I protested, as each one of us was leaving Washington that day. Norman spoke first, and when he had finished, the Secretary of War asked him who he was. Norman said, "I am Norman Thomas." The Secretary of War said, "Who?" as though he had never heard of him even though he had run for the presidency of the United States. There was a hurried conference and finally Hurley came in and stated that he had canceled the engagements he had made and said we could speak. Thereupon Norman Thomas, Nevin Sayre, and I presented our testimony, but were not cross-questioned at all, the decision being apparently that we could read our stuff into the record but that we would not be dignified by a process of cross-questioning.[20]

Although Detzer made a number of salient points with reference to the purpose of the WPC when her turn came to speak, her main thrust centered on the commission's goal of promoting peace by studying methods to remove the profits of war. "It would seem obvious," she pointed out, "that if you would take the profits out of war you must first take the profits out of preparations for war; in other words, remove any private gain from preparation." She was quick to add that she was not suggesting that wars resulted solely from the machinations of greedy munitions makers. Arms manufacturers and other industries that profit from the war system "must have a return on their investment," she acknowledged, but if taking the profits out of war would help to promote peace—and clearly it would—then the focus should be on some kind of control over the munitions and other war-related industries that "gain now through the preparations for war." She concluded that it would be almost impossible to do anything in the current situation "except to check in a small way the profits of war"; hence, the solution was "a complete nationalization not only of the raw materials, but of all manufactures" connected with war.[21]

On 5 March 1932 "after hearing nearly fifty witnesses and taking over eight hundred pages of testimony," the WPC sent its final report with recommendations to Hoover who then turned it over to Congress within two days. The WILPF's suggestion to nationalize the munitions industry was not included. Twelve of the thirteen commission members agreed that an amendment to the Constitution should be adopted to give Congress undisputed power "to prevent profiteering and to stabilize prices in time of war." While this cumbersome process was being effected, a "revenue law should provide for the recapture of excess profits by taxing 95 per cent of all individual and corporation income above the average profit made by the individual or corporation during the three years immediately preceding a war."[22] Finally, the majority report firmly warned against any congressional consideration of a Constitutional amendment that would allow governmental confiscation of private property for public use during war without compensation.

Representative Ross Collins of Mississippi was the lone dissenter. He protested the majority proposal that the army be entrusted with control of U.S. industry during wartime. Collins firmly opposed the idea of the military having the power to regulate prices or any other form of civilian activity during war. And although his minority report did not point this out, in effect the WPC recommendations meant that the government would only *fix* profits at a certain level but not prevent profits, and this only in times of war, not during peacetime. The WILPF's emphasis on the importance of removing the profit from the preparation for war had fallen on deaf ears. This fact underscored the warning of Army Chief of Staff General Douglas MacArthur in his testimony before the WPC that "the acceptance of the War Department proposal to guarantee a profit . . . to industry would place a premium on the institution of war, especially in periods of economic depression, and would merely provide certain vested interests with another incentive for war."[23]

For whatever reason, the WPC report died in committee that spring, perhaps because members of Congress realized that to consider proposals dealing with wartime profits for munitions makers while the United States was in the midst of a high-level international disarmament conference was a bit ludicrous if not hypocritical. For in January 1932 the General Disarmament Conference for which the Preparatory Commission had been planning intermittently since 1926 opened in Geneva.

Convinced in the aftermath of the London Conference that peace propaganda could not wait until the diplomats were actually in session, the peace movement's efforts to influence the outcome at Geneva began immediately. Most conspicuous among these efforts was the WILPF's national campaign for signatures on a petition calling for total and universal disarmament.

The idea of such a petition was quickly seized upon by the international WILPF and as the winter of 1930 became the spring of 1931, the number of signatures on the petition in the United States and abroad continued to grow. At the end of January the U.S. Section had collected approximately 11,000; by mid-March the women were boasting of over 15,000; and by the end of April, 25,361 had signed. Yet the national goal was one million signatures by the time of the petition's presentation to the conference in early 1932. At the rate they were going the women of the U.S. Section would fall far short of their goal. The final push for signatures came with the organization's annual meeting in mid-June in Los Angeles. Planned around the theme of disarmament, the five-day meeting culminated on Sunday 21 June with a "Disarmament Caravan Ceremony." A 3:00 P.M. ceremony in Hollywood's Griffith Park sent off amid music, speeches, and much fanfare a WILPF caravan of automobiles to travel from coast to coast, stopping at various towns and cities along the way to publicize their cause and collect signatures on the petition.

Only one car, known as the "Petition Car," was scheduled to make the entire journey. Driven by the young and energetic Dorothy Cook, a 1931 honors graduate of Goucher College, it was escorted across the country by relays of automobiles from state to state. By the time it reached the East Coast it had traveled through twenty-five states, stopping in the capital city of each to present the petition to the governor. It also visited approximately 125 other communities where meetings were held with local officials, the press, and the public. Organized and directed for the most part by Mabel Vernon, veteran activist of the Congressional Union in its struggle for woman suffrage during the Wilson administration, the caravan created tremendous publicity for the WILPF and the cause of disarmament, and although the number of signatures collected was running well behind the number already obtained in the major European nations, the women were pleased with the enthusiastic response that greeted the caravan as it made its way across the country.

Despite the solemnity of its cause, the journey had its humorous side as well. In recounting her adventures as Petition Car driver, Dorothy Cook remarked that had she kept a diary, it would have read something like this:

July 1—Tail wind; car boiled all day.
July 2—Higher altitude; car boiled all day.
July 3—Neither tail wind nor mountains but—car boiled all day.
Repeat until July 15.[24]

Then there was the town through which the peace caravan was led by the local Boy Scouts, marching to an earnest bugler's rendition of "We're in the Army Now." Or the occasion when an inexperienced and very nervous young peace worker addressed a gathering of the male

Carpenters Union by referring to the assembled members as the "mothers of the coming generation."[25]

The final leg of the caravan down Pennsylvania Avenue to the White House in October was accompanied by the same massive publicity and fanfare as its send-off from California had been. Six hundred eighty-five women participated in the procession through the capital. "In automobiles bearing the names of the states they represented, members of the delegation met the caravan as it entered the District of Columbia from Maryland and escorted it to the Capitol where a procession was formed, headed by a band and Boy Scout trumpeters. The procession, a mile long as it moved down Pennsylvania Avenue from the Capitol to the White House, was the first Peace Parade witnessed by the national capital since the war."[26]

Addams presided at ceremonies inside the White House where Hoover was presented with the disarmament petitions. With only 150,000 signatures, however, the U.S. Section was embarrassingly short of its goal of one million. As he accepted the petitions, Hoover spoke in glowing terms of the importance of public opinion in a democratic society, expressed his gratitude to the WILPF for its effort to mobilize the American people behind the disarmament cause, and declared as he had prior to the London conference that where this issue was concerned, he personally needed "no urging."[27] After her experience with the president during that earlier conference, one cannot help but wonder what went through the mind of Dorothy Detzer as she listened to those words.

Signatures on the disarmament petition had been the primary purpose of the WILPF caravan, but a secondary objective was to drum up support for the appointment of a woman to the official U.S. delegation to Geneva. The WILPF's first choice was Addams, but she declined, suggesting instead that the various women's organizations unite in support of some other prominent woman such as Catt or Judge Florence Allen of the Ohio Supreme Court. When Catt, too, removed herself as a candidate, the women drew up a list of potential candidates, which was then approved by the WILPF and the numerous groups making up the NCCCW.

The State Department was a little taken aback when both the WILPF and the NCCCW began to pressure for a woman delegate. Pointing out that a woman on an official U.S. diplomatic delegation was without precedent, State Department personnel quite clearly indicated their unhappiness with the fact that the issue had even come up. But when the women refused to withdraw their demand, the State Department finally agreed that if all the major women's organizations could unite in support of one particular candidate, it would keep an "open mind" as to her possible appointment. Detzer, for one, was just a bit miffed with this particular stipulation. "To the officials [of the State Department]," she noted dryly, "it seemed wholly irrelevant and illogical for us to ask if the men all had to get together, too."[28]

But the women came through. Stressing that they did not want a woman appointed simply because she was female, but rather that they wished to have a woman appointed who had "taken a real peace stand," the nation's female peace activists united behind Judge Florence Allen and so informed the State Department and President Hoover.[29] Judge Allen was more than willing to serve in such a capacity and felt confident that the Ohio Supreme Court would grant her a leave of absence. But, as she confided to both Catt and Hannah Hull, she was concerned about the issue of money. She did not think it would be proper for her to accept her salary as judge if appointed to the Geneva conference, but with no other source of income and her elderly, ill father totally dependent upon her, she simply could not accept the appointment unless she received some sort of financial remuneration. Neither Catt nor Hull thought it wise to try and raise the necessary money through their respective organizations for fear that a group like the Navy League "would spread the charge that [Allen] had been subsidized by pacifists."[30] Neither peace leader knew how the government ordinarily handled the financial arrangements with its representatives in such cases, so Detzer was instructed to find out. The information gleaned from her State Department contacts was not encouraging.

In cases such as the London Naval Conference in which all of the delegates were also government officials, there was no problem; they simply continued to receive their regular salary. In instances where delegates were not already on the government payroll they received "rather generous expense money" from the government but no salary. Hence, should Judge Allen be appointed as delegate, she would not be paid for her services. As Detzer noted in her letter to Catt conveying this information, it was time "to make it quite clear to the government that persons should not be prevented from becoming delegates to so important a conference merely because they were unable personally to support themselves. It would be most terrible," she concluded, "if delegates to international conferences must be limited to the rich who can afford to pay their own way."[31]

It may be that it was the issue of money that prompted the judge to withdraw her candidacy, for within a week or so, Florence Allen informed Catt that she was no longer to be considered in the running. By this time it ceased to matter, for Hoover informed the women that he would not even consider the judge as a delegate because she was a Democrat. "We thought Democrats were persons, too," Detzer recalled later, "and we didn't see the Disarmament Conference in terms of a Republican caucus; nevertheless, we accepted this decision meekly, and we all got together again." After more meetings and more discussion, the women's organizations came up with the name of a good Republican woman, Dr. Mary Woolley, president of Mount Holyoke College. Amazed that the women had come through a second time, the State Department reluctantly agreed that "Dr. Woolley would be appointed when the proper time came."[32]

A few days later the phone rang in Detzer's office. The president, said Washington newspaper correspondent Drew Pearson, would be announcing the names of the delegates to the Geneva Conference that very afternoon and Mary Woolley's name was not among them. Pearson apparently had finagled a copy of the confidential list of appointees from an office worker in the State Department and, knowing how important the issue was to Detzer, a close friend, he thought that she should be apprised of the situation as soon as possible. Detzer immediately put in a call to the State Department and made an appointment to see Assistant Secretary of State James Grafton Rogers.

She stormed into his office full of righteous indignation over the administration's "breach of faith." Rogers, of course, was curious as to where Detzer had obtained her information. She simply said she did not "feel at liberty" to reveal her source and continued to protest the administration's decision. Rogers made a valiant effort to explain, but Detzer thought his reasons were more in the way of excuses and, although the discussion was frank and even friendly, Rogers could do no more than express his regret over Detzer's obvious disappointment. "Its just too bad," he concluded sympathetically.

"It's not only too bad, Mr. Rogers," she replied, "it's also stupid."

"Stupid?" he said.

"Yes, really stupid," she repeated. "Has the Administration forgotten that elections come with fair regularity in this country?" She opened the door. "And, Mr. Rogers—*women and elephants never forget.*"

Rogers threw back his head and laughed uproariously. Quickly sobering, he pondered a moment and then picked up the phone and asked to be connected with the White House. Minutes later, he had an appointment with the president. Within a couple of hours he was back on the phone with Detzer who was still fuming but now somewhat hopeful as she awaited the outcome of the meeting between the two men.

"I have some news that I think will please you," came Mr. Rogers' nice voice.

"Good, what is it?" she asked excitedly.

"The President will announce the delegation at four o'clock this afternoon as planned," he said, "and *your* Dr. Woolley will be on it."

"Hurrah," she said, "that's wonderful, wonderful. How did you accomplish it? What did you do?"

"Oh, I just borrowed the words of a lady I know," he replied. "I said, 'Mr. President—this is serious; women and elephants never forget'."[33]

With the opening of the conference just a little more than a month away, the WILPF could also take heart at the world-wide response to its disarmament petition. With 1,400,000 signatures Great Britain collected the most names, but Japan was not far behind with its one million. The United States came in a poor third with only 400,000 but as the International Office of the WILPF in Geneva reported, all told the response to the petition was impressive. Over twenty-seven nations had circulated the call for disarmament from places as obscure and distant as Ceylon and Tasmania, and each day that went by brought another batch in the mail. The ultimate question, of course, was whether or not this world-wide expression of the people for "universal and total disarmament" would have any influence on the sixty-odd nations soon to be assembled at Geneva.

With the official U.S. delegation scheduled to depart for the conference on 20 January 1932, a massive peace demonstration orchestrated by the WILPF was held at the Belasco Theater in Washington, D.C., on the tenth, "a final demonstration to impress the delegates to the Disarmament Conference of the interest of the American people in its success."[34] A resolution adopted by the assembled groups, which included Dr. Woolley as guest of honor; Silas Strawn, president of the U.S. Chamber of Commerce; Oswald Garrison Villard, editor of *The Nation;* and John A. Simpson, president of the National Farmers Union, stressed the interrelatedness of armaments and worldwide economic depression. Noting that in the "worst economic crisis in history" the conference had the opportunity to free people everywhere from "a large part of their crushing armaments burden," the resolution called upon the president to "leave no stone unturned to prove to the Conference the readiness of the United States" to initiate "genuine disarmament."[35] Also present and in agreement with this sentiment were a number of women's groups; Protestant, Catholic, and Jewish organizations; educators (John Dewey was a member of the sponsoring committee); World War I veterans; numerous journalists; and spokesmen for the American Legion.

On 20 January another mass demonstration was organized by the WILPF in Madison Square Park in New York as a send-off to the departing U.S. delegates and the three unofficial observers whom the WILPF was sending from its own membership: Hannah Clothier Hull, national chairman of the U.S. Section; Meta Berger of Wisconsin, wife of Socialist Victor Berger; and Katherine Devereaux Blake, member of the WPU and WPS as well as a WILPF National Board member. Laura Puffer Morgan of the NCPW and Bess Howard of the League of Nations Association were also sailing for Geneva where they would set up an information center dealing with conference activities. After speeches by various dignitaries, the crowd proceeded from the park to the pier where the final farewell took place amid flowers, photographs, and fanfare.

The Geneva disarmanent conference continued its sessions throughout that spring of 1932, accomplishing little or nothing. Perhaps it was a case of "great expectations, great disappointments," but by July "all that had been accomplished was the drafting of a general resolution as a proposed basis for further negotiations."[36] The pleas of the struggling German Republic under Chancellor Heinrich Bruning that its survival in the contest for power with the growing popularity of Adolf Hitler and his National Socialist German Workers Party depended on the modification of the disarmament clause in the Versailles Treaty went unheeded. "The German government," Bruning urged anxiously, "ask their [sic] own disarmament be followed by general disarmament."[37] Neither Bruning's cry for help nor the sudden and unexpected proposal on 9 February by Soviet Foreign Minister Maxim Litvinov for total and universal disarmament elicited any degree of cooperation from the other nations present. As Detzer later recalled, "the Soviet plan outlined in the most careful and minute detail the process by which disarmament might be accomplished." A proposal that would have saved these nations billions of dollars in military expenditures during the most crippling economic depression experienced by the modern world was overwhelmingly defeated on 25 February. "Support for it came only from three nations—the German Republic, Turkey, and Persia." Two months later elections in Germany resulted in "an enormous increase of Nazi seats in the Prussian and Bavarian diets."[38] And in less than a year Adolf Hitler was in power.

On 23 July 1932 when the conference delegates voted on the "bastard" resolution proposing further negotiations, the only section of substance being that outlawing chemical warfare, Detzer was seated in the visitor's gallery. That vote to temporarily adjourn "this tragic farce," she observed sadly, passed with forty-one votes in favor, two against, and eight abstentions. "The room was very tense and hushed," she noted, "when Bruning for Germany voted a resounding 'No.' But the high point came when Litvinov simply shouted, 'The Soviet Union votes *Yes*—for Disarmament; *No*—for this resolution.' The gallery, packed with bourgeois women, was swept into such spontaneous, riotous applause for the Soviet delegate that the guards couldn't get order, and cleared most of us out. I was perfectly willing to go. Why stay to see the murderers of peace toss earth on the coffin of disarmament?"[39]

The Geneva Disarmament Conference would not reconvene until February 1933, just prior to the inauguration of the new Democratic administration of Franklin D. Roosevelt and just after the appointment of Hitler as the new German Chancellor. The WILPF, although still keenly interested in the issue of disarmament, was by this time much less enthusiastic and optimistic over the possibility of anything in the way of positive results from the continuation of the conference. Detzer's opinion of the U.S. delegation's performance during the first six months of meetings was not particularly laudatory and she found it difficult to whip up any real enthusiasm for certain individual members of that delegation. "I have always felt," she wrote in retrospect, "that had the U.S. delegation one outstanding personality—a personality fired with conviction and infused with deep moral responsibility—the results might have been different. But we had no such person. One could hardly expect the suavity of Hugh Gibson, the big-navy mentality of Claude Swanson, the solemnness of Norman Davis, and the timidity of Mary Woolley to stir and sway the conference. Some of us, in our limited way, tried to stir and sway *them*. But how does one sway the soul of a cabbage?"[40]

Detzer's disgust with Woolley's "timidity" stemmed not only from that delegate's uninspired performance at Geneva, but also from her public statements after she returned home "that her business on the commission was not to antagonize and thus to establish woman's place on official commissions."[41] As Detzer wrote to Balch and Hull, for herself she preferred to make another try for Florence Allen when the conference reconvened; after all, she pointed out, the Democrats would soon be in power. Apparently her sentiment was not shared by the other women, for Mary Woolley remained.

At its annual meeting in April 1932, while the delegates to the Disarmament Conference were still haggling among themselves, the U.S. Section of the WILPF passed a resolution calling for a government investigation of the munitions industry. Because it was apparent to the women that the statesmen of the great powers could not or would not agree to any meaningful degree of disarmament, perhaps thought the women, the issue of arms control could be more effectively addressed with a different approach.

Various suggestions were made by WILPF members in the United States and abroad as to activities that would call attention to the munitions problem and thereby both complement and supplement an official investigation in the United States. One woman advocated "universal picketing of munitions factories" while another suggested "putting international pressure [for disarmament] directly on certain governments of the progressive smaller countries where we already have friends and allies."[42] Without a doubt the most creative suggestion came from Amy Woods who waxed enthusiastic over the idea of arranging a meeting between representatives of the peace groups and "the leading DuPont brothers" so that the former could persuade the latter, "as leading citizens, for the great welfare of this country and humanity to throw their influence against private manufacture of arms by stopping it in their own production."

Woods broached this idea with Zara DuPont, sister of the munitions manufacturers and a WILPF member, who responded, "It is worth trying." She pointed out to Woods, however, that her brothers would probably counter with, "Why don't you ask the Remington Arms people to stop?" to which Woods blithely responded, "But we need point out their supremacy in the commercial field today and say 'somebody must be patriotic enough to lead off, and we ask you'."[43] The WILPF, however, chose not to act on Woods' idea, deciding instead on the more promising method of a Congressional investigation of the arms industry.

In good Progressive muckraking fashion, the sordid facts of exorbitant profits made from death and destruction by the industrialists while the "common man," now suffering from the most severe depression in the nation's history, was expected to lay down his life for his country, would be revealed to an unsuspecting public. Justifiably outraged over such revelations, millions of Americans would rise up as one and demand of their weak-willed and vacillating officials an immediate halt to this business of "iron, blood, and profits." If one could not rid the world of war through outlawry pacts, if government representatives could not agree among themselves to dismantle their military apparatus, then, perhaps, one could remove at least one major incentive behind the continuation of military build-up—profit. As Addams declared to the national Democratic convention that summer, "We regard with horror the results of unrestricted trade in armaments and of the profits derived from their manufacture and sale. We believe that an important advance in disarmament could be secured by international agreement among the governments as to the nationalization of arms and munitions, which would not only eliminate private profits accrueing [sic] to the great armament factories but also reduce the war scares, often deliberately fomented by them."[44]

Ever since its inception the WILPF had considered the sticky subject of the international trade in munitions, legal and illegal, to be of critical importance to the issue of world peace, and thus was keenly disappointed when neither a 1923 nor a 1925 international conference concerning arms trade, both convened by the League of Nations, accomplished anything of substance. Although not a League member, the United States had participated in both conferences. In 1923, however, the United States "had refused to interfere with the private manufacture of arms," and in 1925, the conference delegates quickly restricted the scope of their discussions to the illicit arms trade.[45]

In the years following the latter conference the flagrant attempts of munitions manufacturers to thwart any meaningful disarmament implementation internationally only steeled the WILPF in its resolve to establish some kind of control over arms manufacture, both in the United States and in Europe. These pacifists were convinced that so long as exorbitant profits could be made in this bloody business, wars would continue. In other words, arms manufacturers clearly had a vested interest in war or, at the very least, in preparation for war and thus, concluded the WILPF, might even go so far as to foment wars to ensure a continuation of their profits.

Directed by the WILPF National Board in April 1932 to begin the arduous process of obtaining a congressional investigation of the armaments industry, Detzer put together a list of the ninety-six senators then in office, selecting twenty whom she thought might be willing to sponsor such legislation. Only George Norris of Nebraska and Wisconsin's Robert LaFollette evinced any interest or concern. But Norris was "too old and too sick" to undertake such a controversial and taxing endeavor, and LaFollette was "carrying all the legislative fights" he could handle.[46] With the national election in the not-too-distant future promising a group of fresh new liberal faces in Congress, Detzer waited until autumn to pursue the issue.

Although energetically supported by the NCPW, FOR, and the

NCW, the WILPF did not succeed in finding a senator willing to sponsor such a measure until the fall of 1933, and by then the matter of traffic in arms and arms limitation took on added significance. Hitler was in power in Germany and Japan had begun her drive for hegemony in the Far East, thus transforming the pro-peace efforts of the 1920s into the antiwar struggle of the 1930s.

It is somewhat ironic that in the late 1920s and early 1930s when the peace movement and peace-minded women were united as never before that the results of their determined efforts would be so meager. Although such cooperation appeared to have been a significant factor in preventing war in Central America, U.S. imperialism, which had given rise to that crisis in the first place, simply continued under a different, less militaristic, guise.

Similarly, while the nations of the world eagerly committed themselves to the Kellogg-Briand Pact, the agreement's lack of enforcement provisions and its multitudinous loopholes made it a rather empty gesture. The United States's quick endorsement of new naval vessel construction after ratifying the pact was almost an insult to the intelligence of the American people. Last, if peace-loving people here and abroad were encouraged by the convening of three disarmament conferences, the failure of all three to achieve any real progress toward arms limitation, let alone disarmament, was further evidence that what the people wanted and what their government wanted were apparently two different things.

William Shearer's covert lobbying at the 1927 Coolidge Disarmament Conference, the administration's "red-baiting" techniques during the Central American crisis, Hoover's failure to acknowledge the truth about the disarmament treaty during his lengthy meeting with Detzer at the White House, the need for political "blackmail" to obtain Mary Woolley's appointment as delegate, the influence of men of wealth from big business in government and diplomatic circles—all were valid reasons for the WILPF to have questioned the accepted notion of the United States as a functioning democracy.

But the women pacifists entered the depression decade with that faith still unshaken, no less convinced than before that in the United States the people were the sovereign power and that government existed, as it should, to serve the interests and needs of those people. Within a few short years, however, events would compel the WILPF to re-evaluate its understanding of the system and, in the process, many of its members made a sharp turn to the left, economically as well as politically.

If the WILPF's Progressivism, and its pacifism as well, were thus radicalized, such was not the case with the women's feminism. By the mid-to-late 1930s women activists, although still cooperating for peace and in basic agreement that women should be equal with men in all spheres of activity, were hopelessly divided as to how to define and how to achieve that equality.

8

Tensions of Transition

ALTHOUGH THE VARIOUS ORGANIZATIONS of the peace movement were disappointed over the failure of the disarmament conferences, they could not fault themselves for that failure. And there had been successes as well. Whether women's groups or those of both genders, whether pacifist or simply antiwar, peace activists created a strong coalition that cooperated in pressuring the Coolidge administration for a peaceful resolution of the Central American crisis and triumphed in pushing the idea of outlawry through to international agreement.

The WILPF did yeoman service in forging this post-World War I peace coalition, actively soliciting the support and cooperation of numerous organizations and institutions, including colleges and universities, churches and other religious groups, and trade unions as well as women's organizations such as the WCTU, League of Women Voters, Council of Jewish Women, and the Council of Catholic Women. Throughout the 1920s the WILPF persistently sought to exchange speakers, publications, and ideas with other like-minded groups and, in turn, requested their backing for WILPF-sponsored legislation, programs, and special events. As Dorothy Detzer put it, "If there is one thing . . . which is better than giving the organization a definite piece of work to do[,] it is to cooperate with some other organization on that work."[1]

Despite the divisiveness among the women's organizations fostered by the War Department in the early 1920s over the issues of loyalty and patriotism, by the end of the decade, the majority of the women involved reestablished a cooperative working relationship. A renewed effort of the War Department and "superpatriots" in the late 1920s to brand the peace movement and women's organizations as communist and subversive did not have the desired effect of destroying either the coalition of peace groups or the new cohesiveness among women's peace societies. In fact, it gave added impetus to the unity of all women activists, save those of self-styled "patriotic" societies such as the Daughters of the American Revolution (DAR), the one organization, ironically, to be torn apart as a result. A new assertiveness among women peace workers and other women activists was also strengthened as the decade of the 1930s opened. The extraordinary demand of the State Department that all of the women's organizations unite in support of one female delegate to the Geneva Conference was a case in point. That the women came through, not just once but twice in meeting this demand, was telling evidence of the great distance they had come in cooperating and unifying in just a few short years after an acrimonious beginning.

And yet there was conflict within the WILPF, as in any association of diverse individuals regardless of ideological consensus. Based primarily on class and generational differences, few of these disagreements, however exasperating and unpleasant as they undoubtedly were to participants at the time, were serious enough to prevent the effective functioning of the organization. In the early- to mid-1930s, however, a conflict of personality and power in the ranks of national leadership not only dragged in the rank-and-file, but threatened to paralyze the organization at a time when its cohesiveness was crucial to the peace movement as a whole, given the increasing signs of danger to world peace from abroad.

Only one of the WILPF's internal disputes involved a policy issue, and given the nature of the issue, was not confined to the peace group. A minority of WILPF members also belonged to Alice Paul's militant feminist organization, the National Woman's Party (NWP). In the 1930s, when the NWP attempted to obtain the peace group's endorsement of the Equal Rights Amendment, there was conflict within the WILPF and between it and the NWP.

Whether internal or external, personal or organizational, ideological or methodological, such conflicts reflected the tensions of transition: political transition as peace societies and women's organizations shifted from coalition politics to create peace in the 1920s to coalition politics to prevent war in the 1930s and generational transition as younger and more "liberated" women came to dominate the ranks as leaders and followers. The WILPF thus confronted a whole new series of challenges not directly related to its reason for being, and although its response ensured its effectiveness as part of the peace movement, it also had the unfortunate effect of contributing to a schism within the feminist movement.

Although three separate women's peace organizations—the WPU, WILPF, and NCCCW—entered the decade of the 1930s they did so with their differences reconciled. From 1924 on, the much smaller and more militant WPU concentrated on obtaining a constitutional amendment to outlaw war and in this effort it easily won the cooperation of the WILPF. Coming to an equally satisfactory modus vivendi with the NCCCW was not quite so easily done, but was accomplished by the end of the 1920s nevertheless. Carrie Chapman Catt did not endear herself to WILPF members in January 1925 at the first Conference on the Cause and Cure of War, referring to "Miss Addams and her peace organization as the lunatic fringe,"[2] but this did not prevent the WILPF from becoming involved in the activities of the NCCCW from the outset.

Although women's peace groups as such were not permitted to be NCCCW sponsors, individual WILPF members participated in its programs, for ideologically they had much in common. Both organizations stressed economic rivalry and imperialism as well as secret and unjust treaties as causes of war, and both emphasized the outlawry of war, international organizations, and arms reduction as political measures to "cure" war. These similarities augured well for the possibility of future cooperation as did their basic difference. The NCCCW's focus on education nicely complemented the direct action approach of the WILPF. Despite similarity of program and policy, however, what really brought the two groups together was a fresh outburst of vilification against both by self-styled "patriotic" women, most notably from the DAR.

After the Pax Special incident of late spring 1924, the attacks against the WILPF as being bolshevik and subversive died down rather quickly. A few unpleasant incidents occurred in the next year or so, prompting Oswald Garrison Villard to raise again the suggestion that perhaps the WILPF ought to sue, but on the whole, things remained fairly quiet. Then in late spring 1926, the military started in on the WILPF and other peace groups again and, as before, individuals and other organizations wasted no time jumping aboard the bandwagon.

It all began on 26 April when Army Major General Eli A. Helmick addressed the Daughters of 1812 on the subject of "Menaces Facing Our Country Today." According to Helmick, "the insidious arm of the soviet government of Russia" was reaching into U.S. schools through the efforts of some thirty-one pacifist organizations "to abolish military training in high schools and colleges." His inclusion of the WILPF among such Russian-manipulated groups brought a quick response from Hannah Clothier Hull who wrote Secretary of War Dwight F. Davis, demanding "a complete retraction."

Davis' response essentially provided a green light for a renewed attack on peace groups as subversive. "It is the view of the [War] Department," he wrote, "that the address of General Helmick was made before an unofficial gathering upon a subject in no way related to his official duties. . . . Obviously the Department is not responsible for views thus given public expression by an officer of the Army appearing in his private capacity as a citizen."[3] Having thus ignored the issue of the truth or falsity of Helmick's remarks, Davis concluded by noting that he had referred Hull's letter to the Major General.

The NCPW was also singled out as an "arm" of the Soviet Union in Helmick's speech, and Frederick Libby, who received a letter from the secretary of war not unlike that sent to Hull, protested indignantly. Pointing out that Helmick had most certainly not addressed the women's group as a private citizen but rather, specifically as an army officer, Libby suggested that because Helmick's "tirade" of "false and misleading character" was only one of several such public utterances by military men, the War Department, "far from discouraging such conduct, . . . is itself inciting its employees to this action."[4]

Libby was probably more right then he knew when he suggested that the War Department was behind such inflammatory tactics. In late April and early May 1926 Congress was holding hearings on the Welsh bill against compulsory military training, and peace organizations in the NCPW, the WILPF in particular, were urging members to write their representatives in Congress to support the bill. The military was again on the defensive and it would be only reasonable for it to counter the pacifist offensive by arousing public opinion against it.

Always striving to increase membership, the WILPF that spring focused on establishing new branches in the Midwest. With the military intent on defeating the Welsh bill, the WILPF's organizing efforts were unfortunately timed. The successful creation of a new branch in Sioux City, Iowa, precipitated a storm of protest from the local post of the American Legion in which the WILPF was denounced in terms almost identical to those of Helmick. Admitting that "some pacifists are sincere," these veterans also proclaimed that "many of them are bitter enemies of our government." Accordingly, they passed a lengthy resolution giving "hearty approval" to the "present policy of the government in offering facilities for military training in schools and colleges," condemning as "unpatriotic and un-American" all efforts to abolish such training.

Not wishing to arouse the wrath of local womanhood, the legionnaires praised those "outstanding women of Sioux City whose patriotism is unquestioned." But in joining the recently organized branch of the "notorious" WILPF, "these good women have been deceived by the 'wolf in sheep's clothing'." In reality, proclaimed the Legion, the WILPF was "one of the most vicious and unpatriotic organizations in the United States. It is directly affiliated with the Communist Government of Russia."[5]

Hannah Hull immediately demanded a retraction. Commander S. G. Eaton of the Sioux City Legion acceded, provided that the WILPF send proof that the Legion's allegations were unwarranted. Detzer pointed out that the proof "should come from *their* side," but nevertheless, put together a statement outlining the inaccuracies and misrepresentations of the Legion's accusations.[6] The Legion, however, did not print this statement as Eaton had promised, so as part of a speaking tour that summer, Detzer went to Sioux City to discuss the issue with Eaton and legionnaire Jesse Marshall, author of the original article attacking the WILPF.

Detzer sat down with the two men and went over the Legion's statement of allegations point by point and, in a few instances, word by word. As for calling the WILPF "notorious," "vicious," and "unpatriotic," Detzer was finally able to get the men to admit that "they would consider such words insulting if used with regard to the Legion." They apologized, acknowledging that the terms were "too strong."

When Detzer inquired as to the source of the Legion's information for the charge that the WILPF was "affiliated" with the Soviet government, Marshall responded with the following logic: Madeleine Z. Doty was the WILPF's international secretary. Doty was the wife of Roger Baldwin. Baldwin was director of the American Civil Liberties Union. The ACLU's board of directors included William Z. Foster. Foster was a Communist. Thus, the WILPF was "directly affiliated with the Communist government of Russia." In attempting to demonstrate the ludicrousness of such convoluted reasoning, Detzer asked innocently if she would be considered "directly affiliated" with the Legion because her brother was a Legionnaire. Finally, the men agreed that the allegation was a "misstatement" and should not have been included.

It went like this until the entire document had been scrutinized and each innuendo, exaggeration, and falsehood acknowledged by the men for what it was. Eaton continually apologized, saying "over and over again, 'Of course, that never should have been written','" thereby discrediting Marshall who grew angrier with each apology, all the more so since he had written the article using information sent by the general staff of the army, surely a trustworthy source.[7] Once again Eaton promised to print a retraction.

Back in her Washington office after visiting a number of U.S. cities as well as making an extended trip to Europe, Detzer observed soberly that "attacks on Miss Addams and the Peace Movement generally have been instigated in all parts of the country. It is the most serious situation that we have had to face since I have come into the W. I. L."[8] Still not enamored of the idea of suing, yet convinced that "pacifists must be more aggressive in the future—not so timid"[9]—the WILPF attempted a reasoned rebuttal that summer to the persistent and irrational accusations.

Dismissing the charge that the WILPF had some "mysterious connection with Soviet Russia" as "moonshine," a lengthy statement by Emily Greene Balch pointed out that the organization "never receives instructions or suggestions from any government." The WILPF, she declared, was "diametrically opposed to any form of dictatorship, to red armies as to armies of every color, to violence in revolution as elsewhere, and to the class war." Acknowledging that the WILPF advocated the diplomatic recognition of the Soviet Union, as did "many statesmanlike men, in and out of office," as well as the release of all political prisoners, Balch noted that such policies were not based on the approval of any philosophy held by individuals or nations, but, rather, on the principle of "fair play" and the need to return to "normal conditions" if peace and "world order" were to be realized. As for allegations that the WILPF was guilty of disrespect for the flag and "made attacks upon the Government of the United States," they could only be described accurately, exclaimed Balch in an uncharacteristic moment of impatience, "by that 'shorter and uglier word'."[10]

Whatever positive effect Balch's statement may have had in friendlier quarters, it apparently had no impact on the American Legion. Shortly after the WILPF moved into its new headquarters in October 1926, the Legion began to pressure the WILPF's new landlord, the Allies Inn, to evict the women. "Certain members of the Army" began to boycott the inn's cafeteria and vowed to continue so long as the inn housed the WILPF.[11] Although the threatened eviction never materialized, nothing the WILPF said or did could stem the onrushing tide of antipacifist propaganda. Even a pamphlet aimed at "penetrating the fog of misunderstanding and recrimination that characterizes the present quarrel between the advocates of disarmament and of preparedness" written in early 1927 by the Director of the National Americanism Commission of the Legion failed to have any effect. A "veritable wave of hysteria is sweeping the country," wrote Carrie Chapman Catt.[12]

By the early months of 1927 the women's "patriotic" societies, most notably the DAR, were in the forefront of the attack.[13] As damning to pacifists as anything the DAR said or did was the dissemination of two colorfully written pamphlets, one entitled "The Common Enemy," and the other, a reprint of thirty-six pages read into the Congressional Record in July 1926, which was put out by the Woman Patriot Publishing Company with a masthead that read "Against Feminism and Socialism."

The basic thesis of the first pamphlet, author unknown, was that "Communism, Bolshevism, Socialism, 'Liberalism' and UltraPacifism tend to the *same end*": the abolition of government, patriotism, inheritance, religion, the right to private property, and "family relations." Thirteen organizations, the WILPF among them, were cited as espousing these goals and were allegedly part of a "world revolutionary movement" aimed at the destruction of "civilization and Christianity."

The second pamphlet was "a wholesale attack upon the patriotism and honor of individual women and women's organizations," including Addams and the WILPF and Florence Kelley and the Consumers League. Both women and both organizations were accused of being Bolshevik and attempting to establish communist doctrines, practices, and policies in the United States. Additional literature circulated by the DAR made similar charges against other women's organizations such as the League of Women Voters, the General Federation of Women's Clubs, the Women's Christian Temperance Union (WCTU), and the Young Women's Christian Association (YWCA).

At the DAR's spring convention, George L. Darte, adjutant-general of the Military Order of the World War, spoke out as he had in 1924 against the "nationwide conspiracy" of communists he had uncovered, which were composed primarily of persons "whom others consider worthy Americans." Singling out Rose Schneiderman, president of the National Women's Trade Union League, Darte characterized her as a Bolshevik, an anarchist, and a revolutionary.

Such obviously scurrilous and slanderous commentary, whether written or verbal, was more than Catt could take. That summer she wrote "An Open Letter to the D.A.R." in *The Woman Citizen*, a lengthy and scathing indictment of the organization's "mendacious and brutal attacks upon thousands of Americans who never saw a Bolshevik in their lives." Her ringing defense of both Kelley—"a very great woman

[who] is not and never was a Communist or a Bolshevist"—and Schneiderman—"a trade unionist and a working woman" who was not an anarchist, Bolshevik, Communist, or "Red"—was equaled in eloquence only by her tribute to Addams and the WILPF.

With respect to the WILPF, Catt wrote bluntly, "I am not a member of this organization. I have attended none of its meetings, am not in sympathy with all of its policies, and I carry no brief for it. I do not, however," she stated emphatically, "approve of the use of libel as a campaign method." She went on to refute in specific detail the charges made against the organization, citing chapter and verse from WILPF policies, meetings, and programs. "It is truly shocking," she concluded, "to note how untrue, how misleading, how contemptible are the charges made against this body. Call it radical if you wish, but cease charging it with conduct almost treason."

Then she turned to the accusation-by-innuendo of communism made against Addams. Quoting from former Secretary of War Newton Baker, Democrat, and President Coolidge, Republican, both of whom had nothing but the highest praise for this alleged Bolshevik, Catt outdid them both in her concluding remarks about the Hull House director: "Miss Addams," wrote Catt with authority, "is one of the greatest women this republic of ours has produced. She has given her life to serve others. She knows no selfish thought. You slap her on the right cheek; she only turns the left. Sticks, stones, slanders, you cast upon this highest product of American womanhood and not a protest passes her lips. . . . The literature distributed by you persuades the uninformed to believe what is not true about an honorable citizen."

Given the subsequent "DAR revolt" between leaders and the rankand-file, it appears likely that Catt's magnificent defense of women activists had some effect on the women "patriots." At the very least, it symbolized and may very well have contributed to the growing cohesion among women's organizations, pacifist or otherwise, which was clearly manifested by the decade's end. It is also representative of the more assertive character of the women's peace movement as the 1930s opened, and indicates as well that the shift from defining women-as-mothers to perceiving women as politicized activists in a democratic society had taken place in less than ten years' time. The DAR's attack on women's organizations as communist was no different in this gender-related sense than the military's accusations against all peace activists, male or female. Men and women pacifists alike were assailed—and defended—on their politics alone. The issue was political ideology, not gender.

Although accusations of communist subversion against the WILPF did not cease after publication of Catt's "Open Letter," they decreased sharply, and throughout the remainder of 1927 into the first half of 1928, the DAR was in the throes of a massive upheaval. From chapters in the east and midwest came challenge after challenge to the organization's leadership and policies. A blacklist of eighty-seven women speakers was circulated by the national board, which included almost every notable female activist in the country. Detzer and Balch were blacklisted for their WILPF membership, but Hannah Clothier Hull made the list for being an "international pacifist." Florence Allen's "crime" was partly that she was a judge; Elizabeth Gilman's that she was a member of the ACLU; Mary Woolley and Ida Tarbell had sinned as "radicals"; and Julia Lathrop and Elizabeth Glendower Evans shared the dubious distinction of being condemned in four categories: as pacifists, feminists, internationalists, and socialists.[14] Even DAR member Lucy Biddle Lewis made the list! The only name included with no reason at all given was that of Jane Addams; apparently her qualifications for inclusion were considered obvious.

By March 1928 the upheaval became open revolt. A New Jersey woman, accused by DAR leaders of being "subversive" because she "dared to investigate" the reliability of a speaker at an organizational function, wanted a new policy implemented with respect to future speakers.[15] A Kansas delegation demanded a referendum of the entire membership with respect to organizational policy and others drew up petitions challenging leadership tactics.

At the DAR's April convention leaders were clearly on the defensive but they gave not an inch. Honorary President General Mrs. George Thatcher Guernsey hotly denied the existence of any speakers "blacklist," calling it instead simply "a list of undesirable speakers for patriotic societies." Incensed at the "impertinence of any little Kansas chapter" for trying to "dictate policies to the National Board," Guernsey reminded delegates that "our policies are formed above and handed down by the Board of Management to the Chapters. The Chapters were created just for the convenience of the National Society."[16]

Yet the damage was done; the antifeminist, antipacifist, and antidemocratic stance of DAR leaders had discredited the organization in the eyes of its more liberal members. In the aftermath of this "DAR revolt," antiwar advocates, pacifist and nonpacifist alike, enjoyed a new sense of community based on a shared sense of mission that left the "patriotic" women out in the cold.

WILPF pacifists continued to support the WPU's fight for a Constitutional amendment outlawing war, and the WPU frequently worked in tandem with the WILPF on other legislative matters. WILPF members, although consistently in attendance at NCCCW meetings as representatives of other organizations, were for the first time in 1929 allowed to have their own peace literature table. When making plans in February of that year for its Sixth International Congress in Prague, Addams suggested Catt as a featured speaker, and when Kathleen Courtney of the British Section of the WILPF began planning a speaking tour of the United States in mid-1929, she found herself equally as interested in speaking for the NCCCW as for the WILPF. This time no female peace feathers were ruffled in the United States by what appeared to be a conflict of interest. Instead, Detzer of the WILPF and Henrietta Roelofs of the NCCCW painstakingly worked out together the details of Courtney's tour.

Even the National Council of Women, so eager to be rid of the WILPF in 1924, did an about-face. In January 1929 Dr. Valeria Parker, the new president, sent the WILPF an invitation to rejoin. The WILPF's national board made no immediate decision but appointed a committee to look into the matter. Brought up at its annual meeting in early May, the NCW's invitation was unanimously accepted by WILPF delegates. As Balch wrote to Parker of the decision, "Please believe that we deeply appreciate the spirit in which you have written to us and trust that we have before us years of happy and mutually helpful co-operation between these two bodies of women devoted to the common cause of better human relations and conditions."[17]

Such harmony did not mean that peace workers no longer were subject to suspicion or animosity, nor should it suggest that all women active in the political sphere, with only the exception of the super-patriots, enjoyed a blissful existence free from discord and dispute. On both counts, quite the contrary was true. Although there may have been no concerted attack on peace advocates accusing them of communism, free love, and other related crimes of equally heinous nature, they periodically encountered the kind of hostility exemplified in a February 1929 response to the WPU's solicitation for support of its Constitutional amendment. An Arizona attorney wrote back saying that "it is such addle-pated ideas as this one . . . that make it difficult for red-blooded American citizens to restrain themselves." Calling the amendment idea "wholly unAmerican, insidious, communistic, and entirely disastrous," he heartily wished the women "the most complete failure" and signed off with "patriotically yours."[18]

There was harassment of the international WILPF as well. A mysterious group calling itself the "Entente International Against the Third International" linked the WILPF to the highest levels of the Soviet government.[19] No names appeared on the documents issued by the group, and no office of the entente was located in the building given as its address in Geneva, Switzerland. Equally as bizarre as the entente was evidence indicating that a person or persons unknown periodically entered the WILPF's U.S. office after working hours, used the typewriter, and tampered with the files and mimeograph machine. This went on for over a year during which time address name plates of members continually turned up missing. Not until the WILPF vacated its office in the Allies Inn in mid-summer 1929 did the harassment cease.[20]

Then there was the infamous "passport case." In the summer of 1929, as part of her preparation to attend the WILPF's August International Congress in Prague, Detzer went to the State Department for renewal of her passport. The process was just about complete when the clerk learned that not only was she a pacifist, she had gone to Russia after World War I as part of an international relief effort. Thereupon, the clerk insisted that Detzer take the oath of allegiance. "Read that," he ordered, pointing to a block of fine print at the bottom of the application blank. "When you have read it, sign your name, then stand up, and I shall administer the oath."

She sat down and began to read the fine print. "I swear," it ran, "that I shall support and defend the Constitution of the United States from all enemies, foreign and domestic. . . . I take this oath without any mental reservation or purpose of evasion, so help me God."

"But I am afraid I harbor a 'mental reservation'," she said. "Though, perhaps, you can interpret some of these phrases for me; just what is the exact meaning of the word 'defend'?"

"It means," he said emphatically, "defense by *force of arms*."

"I don't think I can sign it then," she said.

"Then you don't get a passport," he announced triumphantly.[21]

Leaving the office, Detzer crossed the hall and spoke with another official who reminded her of the much-publicized Supreme Court decision of just two months earlier when in late May, it denied citizenship to Hungarian pacifist Rosika Schwimmer because of her refusal to bear arms in defense of the United States. After protesting that the Schwimmer analogy did not apply since she was already an American citizen, Detzer returned to her office and drafted a letter to Secretary of State Henry Stimson. Reiterating her "mental reservation," she requested that she be allowed to take the oath in the form ruled acceptable by the State Department for pacifist Roger Baldwin some three years earlier. In that modified form, the words "swear" and "defend" were omitted so that the oath read, "I affirm that I will support the Constitution . . . so help me God."[22]

Within a week, the State Department acceded to Detzer's request. Accepting her distinction between a citizen and a noncitizen, Stimson ruled that "citizens may be granted passports although they specifically refuse to take the oath to defend the country." Detzer took the modified oath and obtained her passport.

Pacifists also experienced the day-to-day disputes that inevitably color any organization simply because imperfect human beings inhabit an imperfect world. Certainly the WILPF had its share of conflicts, few of them serious enough, however, to result in any long-standing divisiveness or to threaten the effective functioning of the organization. When examined in their totality, these internecine problems, occasionally centered on ideological or methodological issues, appear most often to reflect the difficulty of adjustment to both class and generational changes at the national level of leadership.

Not until the group's annual meeting in April 1922 was it clear that the U.S. Section would survive the period of postwar reaction and prosper as an autonomous organization only if directed by a paid full-time administrator in the position of executive secretary. In mid-October Amy Woods, a moderate pacifist who would not alienate the group's more conservative members, was hired to fill this all-important position. Self-confident, with international knowledge and experience, Woods was a capable administrator.

She was also a strong-willed woman who was not always as tactful or considerate of other's feelings as Board members thought she might be, and by spring 1924 she had elicited "friction and opposition" in the national office by her attempts "to decide for the members what they should think and do." Although the incident was resolved, it confirmed board members in their opinion that their executive secretary had a somewhat "difficult" personality and was "hard to work with."[23]

Woods' failure that fall to obtain the unanimous vote of confidence by the board that she desired may have led to her request for a leave of absence after 1 December to tour South America. Whatever the case, the board refused to grant a leave, thus forcing Woods' resignation as of that date. The negotiations must have been fairly amicable, however, for the board asked her "to act as a Special Representative of the W.I.L. during her stay in South America."[24] As it was, Woods vacated the office of executive secretary on 15 November 1924, before Lucy Biddle Lewis and Madeleine Z. Doty, a committee of two appointed by the board to secure a replacement, had recommended a successor.

Perhaps this need to find someone quickly was one reason why, when Detzer was hired in December, it was only for a period of two months and temporarily thereafter on a month-to-month basis. But it is also possible that the board's initial hesitancy to consider Detzer's employment as permanent was due as well to class and generational differences. Unlike Woods (who was Boston Brahmin born-and-bred) and the majority of WILPF leaders in the immediate postwar period, Detzer's background was more like that of Addams, Midwestern and middle class. But Detzer had not achieved the stature or international reputation of Addams.

When she graduated from high school just prior to the outbreak of World War I, Detzer (1893–1981) reflected an image of wide-eyed serious innocence that concealed the impatience she felt for the "tincan type of education" that she saw on college campuses around her. Choosing instead to spend her education fund on an extended trip to the Far East, she traveled for a year and a half to China, Japan, and Hawaii, settling down for another year in the Philippines.

Upon her return home, she became a resident of Hull House where she worked with the Juvenile Protective Association. She spent long and frequently anxious hours investigating child labor law violations, yet still found time and energy to attend the University of Chicago's School of Civics and Philanthropy. In early 1920, when the AFSC approached Addams about procuring able-bodied and experienced young people for overseas relief work, Addams recommended Detzer. Shortly thereafter, Detzer found herself in Vienna as part of a relief effort providing food to hungry children and expectant mothers.

After two years with the Quaker mission, Detzer returned home to middle class America where she found herself a stranger among family and friends. Unable to adjust to a life that revolved around the summertime pleasures of boat racing and golf, she wired the Quakers, pleading to be sent to "the worst place in the world." In mid-September 1922 she sailed for the Soviet Union where she joined a Quaker mission in the Volga Valley famine region. It was this experience that provided the impetus for her conversion to a "vehement and militant" advocacy of the cause of international peace.[25]

Once back in the United States, while speaking of her experiences overseas before student, church, and civic organizations, Detzer contacted a number of peace groups, hoping to find one interested in offering her a position. Acting upon the suggestion of Frederick Libby,

Detzer approached the WILPF and in December 1924 became its acting executive secretary. As it turned out, it was not an auspicious beginning to a working relationship that would eventually endure for over twenty years.

The dynamic, self-confident, and assertive Dorothy Detzer who emerged by 1930 was not the woman of whom Doty spoke only a few short weeks after Amy Woods departed for South America. Already there was talk of letting Detzer go as Doty seemed quite convinced that she was "not yet capable of swinging such an important position."[26] The problem apparently stemmed from rumors that Detzer was living quite openly with a man without the usual formality of matrimony, followed shortly thereafter by accusations that she was the "other woman" in a love triangle. Such unorthodox behavior did not meet the rather rigid standards of morality implicitly demanded by the WILPF Board of Directors for its most conspicuous national officer.

Doty, however, failed to substantiate the truth of the rumors before recommending dismissal of the young executive secretary. No less strong-willed than Amy Woods and accustomed as an attorney to wielding a certain amount of influence among those around her, Doty may have harbored some resentment over the fact that Detzer had won the position with the support and recommendation of Addams over her own choice of Jeannette Rankin. At any rate, an investigation of the rumors concerning the conduct of Detzer's personal life indicated that there was no basis in fact to either allegation. By mid-May she was completely exonerated of any wrong-doing in this whole "sordid and ugly" affair, and was therefore retained in her post even if only on a temporary basis.[27]

There were other factors that probably made the board cautious about hiring her as a permanent officer. Detzer knew inwardly that she had the talent and energy to make her new position a resounding success, but outwardly she seemed insecure, unsure of herself, and at best, indecisive. Undoubtedly a good part of this exterior demeanor stemmed from an almost child-like eagerness to please the board, a group of predominantly older women, imperious in both manner and bearing. Hesitating to strike out on her own out of deference to these women who seemed to expect such deference from their employees, Detzer found herself at the same time chastised by the board for her apparent lack of initiative.

Detzer may also have felt constrained by her lack of a college education and her middle class roots in the Midwest. Raised to give due obeisance and respect to those of patrician upper class family background, Detzer now faced the potential scorn and contempt of that very class if she did not live up to a standard of excellence that was little short of perfection. The majority of board members, coming as they did from "old" established Eastern families of a fair degree of status and affluence, suffered no financial difficulties in acquiring a college education, generally at one of the more prestigious women's colleges along the Eastern seaboard. They had that special air of self-confidence unique to the privileged few and many were professionals in those fields open to women. Yet here was Detzer with just a high school diploma from Ft. Wayne, Indiana, attempting to win the approval of a most imposing elite of America's finest womanhood. It was a formidable group that confronted Detzer, and the harder she strove to please them, the less she seemed to succeed.

Although as international president Addams wielded the most influence in major policy matters for the U.S. Section, the other eleven national officers and board members in 1924 and 1925 were not mere figureheads expected to follow the dictates of their more famous leader. As chair and vice-chair of the U.S. Section, Hannah Clothier Hull and Emily Greene Balch exercised a not inconsiderable degree of authority. Both had long-standing credentials in the peace movement (Balch having been a charter member of the WPP), and were much respected by board members and the rank-and-file. Board members Katherine Blake and Alice Thacher Post as well as Lucy Biddle Lewis and Madeleine Z. Doty were also charter members of the WPP, and all were accustomed to exercising a substantial amount of power within the organization and having their opinions and decisions deferred to. With the exception of Addams, all of them came from the Eastern elite of wealth and prestige.

Alice Thacher Post (1849–1947), already seventy-one years of age in early 1925, probably possessed the most impressive family credentials, coming as she did from an old and established Boston family of the mid-1700s. Her maternal grandfather, Thomas Worcester, was a Boston clergyman and it was difficult to be more "established" than that. She was educated in private schools in Massachusetts and New York and in 1893 married Louis Freeland Post, assistant secretary of labor in the Wilson administration. A Swedenborgian, Post was also a political and social reformer in the best Progressive tradition with membership in both the Anti-Imperialist League and the American Proportional Representation League. She was a charter member of the WPP and remained a committed peace activist until her death.

Madeleine Z. Doty and Katherine Devereaux Blake had family credentials almost as impeccable as Post. Doty, born in 1879, was reared in the rather exclusive community of Bayonne, New Jersey, and graduated from Smith College in 1900 before going on to receive a law degree from New York University in 1902. Blake (1858–1950), who never married, came from a North Carolina family with aristocratic roots going back to earliest colonial times. Twenty-one years older than Doty, Blake was of Post's generation. Doty was a mere forty-six in 1925 while Blake was already sixty-six.

Although born in New York City, Blake's earliest memories were of her family's North Carolina plantation and its many servants, a number of whom shortly before had been slaves. Her mother had inherited considerable wealth as a young woman and spent it freely during the early years of her marriage. By 1859, the inheritance was exhausted and when the father committed suicide, mother and daughter moved to Washington, D.C., where Lillie Devereaux was forced by economic circumstance to employ her writing talent as a correspondent for the *New York Sun*, becoming the country's first woman journalist.

Blake attended a private girls' school but also received a great deal of her education at home, particularly after Lillie's second marriage. Like the Detzer family in subsequent years in Ft. Wayne, the Blakes were avid readers and held lively discussions on a variety of topics over the dinner table. Katherine became a suffragist early in life and like so many of the charter members of the WPP, pursued a career in one of the few professions then open to women. She began teaching in the New York public school system after her graduation from Hunter College in 1876. Teaching soon evolved into administration when she became principal of an elementary school named after her mother, a position she held for thirty-four years.

A charter member of the WPP, Blake was active in the peace movement and in the field of education throughout the 1920s and 1930s. She chaired the Education Committee of the New York City Federation of Womens Clubs for twelve years and in 1928, traveled to the Soviet Union with John Dewey and nineteen other educators to study its school system. In 1943, she wrote a biography of her mother and gave her last public speech in 1944 when she addressed a gathering in Washington on behalf of the National Woman's Party.

There can be little doubt that the matriarchal figures of such an imposing triumvirate as Lewis, Post, and Blake would cause the thirty-one-year-old executive secretary some trepidation. They were elderly enough in 1925 to look upon the youthful Detzer as a daughter or even a granddaughter from whom they expected deference. Also commanding respect was their status as American patricians and, at least for Blake and Doty, as members of a professional elite.

The same can also be said for WILPF officers Hannah Clothier Hull and Emily Greene Balch for they, too, came from old established Eastern families. Hull was the daughter "of one of Philadelphia's oldest and most respected families"[28] and Balch, like Blake, was a professional educator, having been fired from her professorship at Wellesley College for her pacifism during World War I. Perhaps due to their Quaker affiliation, Hull and Balch were less imperious in both bearing and manner than the "terrifying triumvirate" noted previously, yet their quiet dignity combined with the Quaker way of "gentle persuasion" made them appear almost saintly. Consequently, it would have been easy for Detzer to chastise herself as being mean and petty for an occasional conflicting point of view.

In terms of age, Balch and Hull fell in the middle. Born in 1867 in Jamaica Plain, Massachusetts, where she continued to live throughout most of her long life, Balch at fifty-seven was five years older than Hull. Both women came from large, closely knit families with roots in colonial America. The members of the Hull family of Swarthmore, Pennsylvania, had been pacifists for generations and Balch's father, Francis Vergnies Balch, was a lawyer and Charles Summer's secretary. Balch and Hull graduated from college, Balch as a member of Bryn Mawr's first graduating class in 1889 and Hull from Swarthmore College two years later. Balch went on to study economics as a graduate student abroad, returning to accept a position teaching sociology and economics at Wellesley in 1896. Hull did graduate work at Bryn Mawr in 1896 and 1897 and then married long-time peace activist and Swarthmore history professor, William I. Hull. Balch, like Addams and Blake, never married.

There was really little reason for Detzer to feel either insecure or inadequate before this group of women, for even though she did not share their elite background, her midwestern, middle-class roots and traditions were certainly nothing to feel ashamed of. Born in Ft. Wayne, Dorothy Detzer and her twin brother, Don, were the middle two of four children born to August Jacob and Laura Goshorn Detzer. Karl was two years older and August, Jr., nicknamed Gus, came along about five years later. Dorothy's father was a respected businessman, owner of a drugstore, one of the community's first business establishments to install electric lights and a telephone. Her mother was a librarian and later became a silent partner in the Lehman Book Store, "the largest bookstore in the state north of Indianapolis,"[29] thus leaving the daughter a life-time legacy of love for reading. That the family's nearest neighbors and closest friends were the Hamiltons—one of the wealthiest and most respected families among Ft. Wayne's elite—suggests that Dorothy was no stranger to America's upper class aristocracy when she first encountered the members of the WILPF's board of directors in 1924.

Whether or not Detzer's sense of personal and professional inadequacy in 1924 was justified, it is nevertheless the case that bringing her on board represented a transition for the WILPF in terms of both leaders and followers. Gone by 1924, or at least vanishing quickly, was the woman activist characteristic of the prewar Progressive Era whose geographical locus was the Eastern seaboard, whose socioeconomic class background belonged to the leisured elite of an upper or middle class aristocracy, whose education more often than not included a college degree from a woman's institution in the East, whose feminist ideology stressed the maternal instinct, and whose political activism was grounded in the suffrage movement.

Detzer belonged to the new breed of American woman, to the generation that came of age in the innocent and naive optimism of the prewar world, but grew to intellectual maturity in the postwar world of disillusionment, crass materialism, and deferred idealism. This was the world of the emerging Jazz Age where the image of the flapper would take hold. The women who came to the WILPF from the early 1920s on were much like Detzer: middle class, generally well-educated with college degrees if not careers, knowledgeable, concerned about and up-to-date on current events, and from stable family backgrounds. Few were black or Southern or from the working class, and most shared an urban upbringing. They were as "liberated" as women could be in the interwar period. Although suffrage was now simply assumed, they took it seriously, were politically active and socially aware, and although many of them married and had children, they rarely entertained the thought of being "merely" housewives. They drove (and owned) cars, went on organizing trips and WILPF caravans, and attended conventions and meetings far from home unchaperoned by either maiden aunt or male family members. They openly enjoyed the new focus on fashion, cosmetics, and hair style. They spoke their minds, albeit with consistent good manners, and like Detzer, took pleasure in a small glass of wine and smoked cigarettes with a vengeance. This was not the prewar female world of gentility, conservatism, and "good breeding."

However liberated these younger and more independent WILPF members, they were not particularly militant in either ideology or method. They may have rejected their Progressive mothers' life-style, demeanor, and dress, but they accepted the Progressive reform ideology, a liberal ideology firmly committed to the U.S. system as a democracy which, although by no means perfect, worked pretty well for most of the people most of the time. Like the older peace activists, the younger women believed that the system required only the healing power of "new men and new laws" to eliminate those defects that did exist.

If not convinced pacifists, at the very least these younger women were passionately antiwar, and if they came too late to the suffrage campaign, they were still feminists to one degree or another who benefitted from that campaign. Yet only a distinct minority joined the militant feminists of Alice Paul's National Woman's Party, suggesting that either the majority was opposed to an Equal Rights Amendment or simply felt no need for one. It is quite possible that after the suffrage victory, many women, even those who became politically active (or, perhaps, particularly those who became politically active) simply assumed that voting equality with men translated, or soon would translate, into equality in all other spheres of activity. Certainly the greater freedom and independence experienced by women socially and economically in the interwar years gave at least superficial credence to such a view.

Many of the older women who were veterans of the suffrage struggle knew from first-hand experience as professionals in social work, education, and medicine that although the franchise was a crucial element in women's emancipation, it did not guarantee either justice or equality. Yet these women, like Addams and Lillian Wald, having labored long and hard for the passage of protective legislation for working women in the Progressive Era, were adamantly opposed to the Equal Rights Amendment (ERA), not because they opposed equal rights for women but rather because the NWP's amendment would invalidate such legislation. In their view, the ERA would return the working woman to the days of long, grueling hours, starvation wages, night shifts, and physically dangerous jobs. Such exploitative conditions threatened a woman's life and health as well as adversely affecting home and family. Although in essence acknowledging that the NWP was right in arguing that protective legislation was discriminatory, it was so, said these opponents of the ERA, in a necessary and positive way.

In addition, there was the issue of method. Although WILPF members staunchly advocated equal rights for men and women "in industry, in society, and before the law in every way,"[30] many of them opposed achieving the goal through a constitutional amendment. Like the moderate wing of the suffrage movement under Catt's leadership, they believed that such equality should come through action by the states.

ERA proponents, however, maintained that until men and women were equal in all respects under national law, protective legislation set women apart as a special category of humanity, which implied that separate was not only biologically different, but inferior, and thus required special laws. Moreover, they argued, protective legislation restricted women's freedom of choice in the economic sphere, which was discriminatory in a negative fashion. Laws stipulating the maximum number of hours a woman could work limited her earning potential, and laws prohibiting women from holding certain jobs or working at night unfairly advantaged male workers. The employer's propensity to exploit all workers, male as well as female, asserted the NWP, was a persuasive argument for protective legislation for *all* workers across the board regardless of gender.

However radical or militant the WILPF may have become on the issue of peace, it was not so when it came to feminism. And although there was a substantial degree of dual membership and cooperation between and among the three major women's peace societies in the interwar period, as well as among other women's organizations, such was not the case between the peace groups, other women's organizations, and the NWP. Still, a number of NWP members shared the WILPF's understanding of the interrelatedness of human equality, democracy, and a warless world. As militant feminists politically experienced in lobbying for suffrage and the ERA, they were attracted to the WILPF, given its legislative strategy (unlike the NCCCW) and its broad program of peace-related issues (unlike the WPU). Moreover, the feminist proclivity of WILPF members provided an excellent opportunity for NWP members to proselytize for the ERA.

Convincing the newly appointed executive secretary of the WILPF to join the NWP could go a long way by example to gain other ERA adherents within the rank-and-file. If we can take Detzer's word for it, however, she was not in her new position for more than twenty-four hours when an unpleasant encounter with an NWP delegation so angered her that despite her commitment to equal rights for women, she swore that she would never join the NWP. She never did. But every year thereafter for the next twenty years or so, at the WILPF's annual meeting an NWP member who was also a WILPF member introduced a motion to dismiss Detzer as executive secretary. Each time it was defeated.

It is unfortunate that the U.S. Section of the WILPF, not unlike Congress with respect to the *Congressional Record,* made a regular practice of editing controversy and disagreement out of the minutes of its various meetings. Thus there is no way to independently verify the accuracy of Detzer's recollection with respect to either her initial encounter with the NWP or any subsequent attempts to "wreck her career." Whether or not the initial contact between Detzer and the NWP was as confrontational as Detzer remembered is less important, however, than the fact that she did not join the organization and did not support the ERA. And this fact may have contributed to the subsequent difficulties between Detzer and both Doty and Blake who were members of the NWP.

Detzer and Doty clashed early on over the U.S. distribution of the WILPF's monthly newsletter, *Pax International,* which was put together in the Geneva office by the international secretary. In late 1925 Doty held that position, and she was upset because too often U.S. members did not receive *Pax* until late in the month after publication, by which time, of course, the news was outdated. Because the Washington office was responsible for distributing the newsletter after receiving it from Geneva, Doty concluded that for whatever reason, members of the Washington office were holding it up. And Detzer was in charge of the Washington office.

Doty was at least partially right. Detzer personally had taken on the responsibility of seeing to it that *Pax* was distributed. If the copies arrived while she was on a speaking tour or otherwise caught up in other work, the newsletters waited until she herself could get to them. It was also the case, however, that Doty underestimated the time it took to get *Pax* to the Washington office or from there to members. Had she been willing to acknowledge that her projected timetable was too optimistic, and had Detzer been agreeable to delegating responsibility, the problem probably could easily have been resolved.

But that is not what happened. The conflict between the two women kept leaders in an uproar throughout most of 1926, suggesting that more than the distribution of *Pax* was at issue. What can be conjectured is that class, generational, and ideological differences were sufficiently keen between Doty and Detzer that a minor issue became a major bone of contention.

It may also be possible that the clash represented an early example of a power struggle between leaders as the still acting executive secretary attempted to establish an office routine and prove to the board that she was an efficient, capable leader and administrator. That this may have been the case is buttressed by Detzer's subsequent conflicts with Katherine Blake. Here again, class and generational differences were operative, and because Blake, like Doty, was a member of the NWP, it is possible that conflicting feminist ideologies also played a part.

At the June 1928 national board meeting, Blake and another long-time WILPF member, Margaret Loring Thomas, obtained greater board control over the national office, which was subsequently required to make detailed reports of its routine work. Moreover, the board demanded that "all communications sent to important people should bear the signature of the National Chairman, or Acting Chairman as well as that of the Executive Secretary; so should also suggestions or requests for work sent to State Chairmen and Board members and the general membership."[31]

In reports that summer and fall, Detzer's secretary, Mary Louise Marriott, outlined in far more detail than was necessary what she had done with her working days. In her own polite way, she let it be known that it all seemed a bit silly: "You will understand, of course, that this report can only contain a resumé of the purely mechanical work which my desk carried. . . . It is indeed difficult to compile a report of this sort that will do justice to the endless amount of time spent in doing small, but nevertheless important secretarial duties."[32]

By the end of November a second office secretary, Eleanor Patterson, was on the verge of open revolt over the issue. "It has been necessary each day," she reported, "to concentrate upon the most emergent of several important tasks and neglect the others, with the result that although I have taken no lunch hour for weeks and have put in considerable extra time, there are still many loose ends which it has been impossible to tie."[33]

Detzer was so perturbed over the situation that following the board meeting of mid-October she issued a two-page summary of "Work to be Done by the National Office, Rising Out of One Meeting of the National Board." The forty-three items added up to an exhausting amount of work to be accomplished by the three-person staff, a situation that Detzer indirectly but succinctly noted under item No. 22: "Circularize our entire membership of 7,300 for FOREIGN AFFAIRS. *Extra assistance is forbidden.*"[34] The board did not back down, however, and the staff continued to submit the required "busywork" reports, although on an irregular basis, throughout 1929.

Blake further asserted her authority in early 1930. On a particularly busy January day when the entire staff was quite rushed with preparations for an important event upcoming the following day, she walked in unannounced and informed those present that she was a member of the "office committee," and as such, was responsible for ensuring that all tasks were carried out efficiently and effectively. Compounding the turmoil, she "asked each one of the girls to write out in detail what their duties were."[35] Detzer could find no reference in the board minutes to an "office committee," let alone one with Blake's name, and she promptly informed Balch and Hull of the incident. By the end of 1930, office reports were reduced to a one-page "Annual Statistical Report," and in 1931 to few statistical summaries. By 1932 such reports simply disappeared.

The conflict between Blake and Detzer, however, did not. As chair of the WILPF's Committee on Personal Disarmament, it was Blake's responsibility to push for legislation regulating the purchase, transportation, and use of concealed firearms. In early spring 1930 the board asked Blake to testify on firearms at the Interstate Commerce Commission hearings in April and Blake wrote to Detzer, asking for assistance. Detzer was not inclined to put aside her other responsibilities to assist the older woman in this matter. On the morning of the hearing Blake appeared at the National Office and asked Detzer to accompany her. Detzer declined because she was preparing for her own testimony at a war referendum hearing the following day. Blake concluded her report on personal disarmament at the next month's annual meeting by resigning as committee chair. "I do this," she said, "in order that someone may be appointed with whom Miss Detzer will be willing to cooperate."[36] The board accepted her resignation without recorded comment. Blake continued to criticize Detzer nonetheless and in early 1933, Detzer wailed to Hull, "Isn't it possible, after eight years of work in the WIL, for members of the board to trust my intelligence in matters like this?"[37]

Yet Detzer was quite capable of being aggravating. She had a tendency to take criticism too personally, and sometimes took offense when others made suggestions regarding either office procedure or legislative work. A brilliant public speaker with a quick and frequently biting wit, Detzer's astute political sense was a distinct asset when it came to the wheeling and dealing necessary for success on Capitol Hill. But she was not the efficient administrator that Amy Woods was, having little patience with the details of day-to-day office activity, and this tendency was often a source of frustration to those who worked with her. Most of the internecine conflict within the WILPF during the interwar years, therefore, involved Detzer to one degree or another. It was seldom serious enough to actually threaten the effective functioning of the organization, and it rarely involved more than a handful of women in the upper echelons of WILPF leadership.

In the early-to-mid-1930s, however, a series of disputes between Detzer and other leaders affected the membership-at-large, and threatened to tear the group apart. Although differences of class, generation, and ideology all played important roles, this ongoing conflict also involved power struggles evolving out of personality clashes. Although the WILPF weathered the storm and the peace movement experienced no perceptible negative impact as a result, the cause of women's rights suffered.

According to Detzer, writing many years after the fact, the U.S. Section in terms of both leaders and constituency was composed of "three main groups." There was, first, the majority of women who followed the lead of Addams and Balch:

> They actively supported the policies formulated at the Annual Meetings . . . and the programs to implement those policies thru [sic] political undertakings. Then there was a minority group—but a very vocal minority—who advocated passage of the Equal Rights Amendment and who interpreted (and limited) the concept of Freedom in the W.I.L.'s name . . . as signifying freedom for women. They wanted the organization to make the Equal Rights Amendment its primary concern and the issues of peace as secondary. Then there was a third group, a small minority, who were absolutists; non-resisters who were bitterly opposed to those of us who were prepared to accept a political half-loaf if it constituted what we conceived to be a forward step for Peace. This little band of absolutists were [sic] an irritating thorn-in-the-flesh to the majority of members. They were zealots and . . . inflexible and humorless. They considered it a betrayal of pacifist principles if the W.I.L. employed a flank maneuver in dealing with the military-minded rather than bludgeoning them with a frontal attack.[38]

Only Mabel Vernon had a foot in all three camps at one time or another in the 1930s, and she was with the WILPF for only five years, from 1930 through 1935. With a history of activism in both the militant wing of the suffrage campaign and subsequently in the NWP, her brief tenure with the WILPF had an enormous, albeit short-lived, impact upon the organization.

Born into a Delaware Quaker family in 1883, Vernon was of Hull's generation. She earned a degree in German from Swarthmore College in 1906 and went on to teach high school German and Latin in Wayne, Pennsylvania, until 1913. Invited by Alice Paul, her friend and former classmate at Swarthmore, to join the suffrage movement that year, Vernon quickly became one of the more radical and outspoken members of the militant wing of the suffrage campaign, the Congressional Union (subsequently the NWP). She became both an officer and leader and "led the celebrated suffrage caravan across the country; she spoke be-

fore audiences in every part of the United States; and she was among
the first six of the famous pickets at the gates of the White House to be
taken to jail."[39]

After a brief trip to Europe following the successful suffrage campaign, Vernon enrolled at Columbia University for graduate work in
history and political science, receiving her master of arts degree in
1923. She then went to work for the NWP to obtain for women an
Equal Rights Amendment to the Constitution, and served as Executive
Secretary of the organization from 1926 to 1930.[40]

By 1930 the WILPF had grown to the point where the responsibilities of the executive secretary were simply too much for one person to handle. Thus the board put Detzer in charge of legislative
matters and created two new positions, a finance secretary whose primary responsibility would be to raise money, and a full-time field secretary to coordinate the National Office with state and local branches
and do organizing work to bring in new members. Upon the suggestion of Blake, who thought that "that Washington Office should be
strengthened," Vernon was appointed finance secretary.[41] She was also
named campaign director because of her successful experience as an
administrator and coordinator of public relations events, the need to
mobilize public opinion behind the upcoming disarmament conference, and the expectation that Detzer would become international secretary in Geneva some time early in 1931.

Detzer was not in favor of the arrangement. She wrote to Mildred
Scott Olmsted that "it would be fatal" to the WILPF: the peace group
would lose the cooperation of the other women's organizations by being so closely identified with the politics of the NWP through its new
finance secretary. Commenting on Blake's recommendation of Vernon,
she added that "from now on we have to go after young people. This is
an old woman's organization. Tired people who belong to a feminist
age which is past—in which conflict with men, and looking as unattrac-
tive as possible just is past. Either we put some younger women in, and
wait till we get the right one . . . or we are going to lose ground."[42]

As events were to prove, Detzer was right, but for the wrong reason. Bringing Vernon into the WILPF as a national officer did prove
almost "fatal" for the group, not because of her age nor because other
women's organizations were thereby alienated, but because of conflicts
of power and personality. The result was not only discord between and
among the women of the WILPF, but a major setback for the ERA.

Vernon began her responsibilities with the WILPF immediately,
and on the surface the new system seemed to work well. She joined

Detzer in the Washington office where she began organizing the group's finances and the disarmament campaign. By April 1931 it was clear that Detzer would not be the new international secretary, however, and friction began to surface in the Washington office.

Detzer very much wanted the international position and had been fairly confident that she would be so appointed, and when Camille Drevet of France finally decided to accept it, Detzer must have been keenly disappointed. Because leaders in the U.S. Section had made it clear that they did not think her "capable" of the position, Detzer may have felt that Drevet's appointment reflected a similar lack of confidence on the part of the International leadership. Given the enthusiastic endorsement of Vernon only months earlier by the WILPF Board, it is also possible that by the spring of 1931 Detzer began to fear for her job at home as well. Not only is such a conclusion reasonable under the circumstances, it is supported by Olmsted's later observation that Detzer was "insanely jealous" of Vernon and "fearful that Mabel and her friends are going to displace her." In recalling her own difficulties with Detzer a few years earlier, Olmsted remarked that "Dorothy's relations and mine improved as soon as Dorothy became convinced that I did not want her job."[43]

Prior to Vernon's coming on board, Detzer ran the national office pretty much as she saw fit, taking on certain responsibilities as her own and delegating other tasks among a few clerical staff members. Nothing in the way of letters, literature, or other material left the office without Detzer's prior approval. With the arrival of Vernon and her staff, this routine changed abruptly as Detzer had no control over work related to disarmament and finances. Very quickly the office divided into two opposing camps: Detzer with her loyal staff members on one side and Vernon and her staff on the other. Tension was aggravated by "sneers and gossip" and factional "intrigue."

The problem, according to Detzer, was Vernon. "I don't try to run her kind of work," wrote Detzer to Olmsted. "The trouble is that she tries to run mine. . . . If she would remain in her own field there would be no trouble."[44] The evidence she cited would, at first glance, tend to support her allegation; yet upon closer examination it becomes apparent that the basic issue was that of overlapping responsibilities involved in the disarmament campaign. What Detzer perceived as Vernon's encroachment was seen by Vernon as part of her responsibility.

Olmsted was persuaded that much of the problem was Detzer's fear for her job, but she also acknowledged that Vernon's "headstrong and individualistic way of working" gave Detzer some legitimate cause for complaint. As she wrote to Balch, Vernon "certainly doesn't have the charm and personality that Dorothy does, but she is a far more mature and responsible to deal with. They are both so different and so valuable to us," she concluded, "that I feel some way must be found for holding them both."[45]

Vernon assured Olmsted that she had no interest in Detzer's job. Although she admitted that she thought the Washington office was "very badly run," she claimed to have "had enough of that executive work in the Woman's Party," and had tried in vain to convince Detzer of that fact.[46] Whatever the truth of the matter, it was clear by 1932 that of the two disputants, Detzer was the more distraught. Efforts were made to persuade Vernon to work out of the Philadelphia office so as to separate the two women, but Vernon refused, arguing that the records she needed were located in Washington.

Attempts by board members to enlist the cooperation of the staff in the national office to defuse the tension had some positive effect on Detzer, and by the end of March it was Vernon who was showing signs of stress. "I think you ought to know that Mabel Vernon is ill," wrote Olmsted to Balch. "She looks very badly and is pretty discouraged. I think she is much disturbed mentally and is, therefore, wearing herself out with the strain." But, she added, "things seem to be going pretty well between her and Dorothy at the moment," so she felt that it was best to leave the situation alone for the time being.[47]

Other than some minor board-related matters, this modus vivendi between Detzer and Vernon continued for almost the next two years. While Detzer was deeply enmeshed in the arms embargo issue, efforts to obtain a Congressional investigation of the munitions industry, and problems relative to Liberia and Ethiopia, Vernon's energies were devoted to the critical work of raising money and managing the disarmament campaigns of 1932 and 1933. With these separate spheres of activity and Detzer's three months' stay in Europe in the summer of 1932, apparently the crisis was over.

Although the feud between the two women and their respective staffs would erupt again in 1935 with even greater intensity, by 1934 Detzer was under attack from the third group to which Detzer referred in 1979, that small minority of "absolutists" who were "inflexible humorless zealots." It was best represented by Lola Maverick Lloyd and Anne Martin, although because Lloyd was also a militant feminist, ERA proponent, and NWP member, she was part of the radical feminist minority within the WILPF.

Lloyd played an important role in the 1934 challenge to Detzer's leadership, but the attack was precipitated by Martin, militant feminist, veteran of the suffrage campaign, and an early member of the NWP (although she resigned from the organization to pursue a political career not long after it was formed). Like Jeannette Rankin of Montana, Anne Martin was also a product of the West, having lived first in Nevada and later in California and Colorado.

As the WILPF expanded in the early 1920s it looked westward. In early fall 1926 the national board enthusiastically appointed Martin, "a person of . . . fine personality and ability," as regional director for the Pacific Slope states.[48] The WILPF provided expense money but not salary.

Martin became a member of the national board in April 1927 and continued as regional director throughout 1927 and into 1928. Her organizing efforts took her from Colorado to Utah to California, and by May 1928 she reported that the two California branches of the WILPF that existed in 1926 (Palo Alto and San Diego) had grown to include sections in San Francisco, Berkeley, Carmel, and Los Angeles, with a membership increase from approximately 100 to 600. Smaller WILPF groups were also started in Denver, Colorado Springs, and Boulder, in Tucson and Phoenix, in Santa Fe and Albuquerque, and in Salt Lake City.

However successful she was at recruitment, she managed to thoroughly alienate Catherine Cumberson, a long-time WILPF member and local leader in San Francisco. Having formed an intense dislike for the militant feminist because of her "attacks upon Miss Addams for her pacifism" during World War I, Cumberson was angered anew in 1929 by Martin's propensity to "ride roughshod" over anyone who got in her way. She also mistrusted Martin's close association with Dr. Margaret Long of Denver, an "out and out feminist of the extreme type" whose activity in the NWP "had completely cut off and alienated some of the more important people in the groups that might have been ready to join [the WILPF]."[49]

Detzer attempted to soothe Cumberson's feelings after the story came out, explaining that although "we always have this Woman's Party conflict," some of the most devoted WILPF pacifists were also NWP members and the WILPF was grateful for their contribution. In any case, she added, the problem was a matter for the board's consideration, the more so since "Miss Martin [is] very critical of me, and my work."[50]

The board continued its unwavering support of Martin; within a month of Detzer's discussion with Cumberson, Martin was named to its nominating committee, and she attended the WILPF's International Congress that summer in Prague as a delegate from the U.S. Section. By April 1930 she was quite ill, however, and was unable to attend the annual meeting in late May. Nevertheless, she was re-elected to the board at that time, but in early June her deteriorating health finally compelled her resignation as national board member, regional director of the Pacific Coast, and consultative member of the International Board. Not until early 1934 did Martin re-emerge in the written record as an active WILPF member, and then only indirectly by way of letters of complaint regarding Detzer as executive secretary.

Martin was not at the 13 January Board meeting when two board members read her letters of criticism, precipitating a lengthy and "frank" discussion of the executive secretary's performance. Although neither the identity of the two board members nor the nature of the complaint is made clear, it seems likely that Lloyd was one of the two members involved, and Detzer's handling of the Griffin naturalization bill, one of the key complaints. According to Hull, the meeting ended with a "consensus of opinion" that the discussion was "well worth while,"[51] but apparently Lloyd was not part of that consensus.

Lloyd must have expressed her impatience with the "lady-like" and "unbusinesslike" methods of the meeting,[52] for shortly afterward Hull sent a letter to all in attendance urging them to "give our comments and criticisms, and Miss Detzer, fair play. It is one thing to give criticism and ask to have it taken in a sportsmanlike fashion. It is quite another to nag about it afterwards. . . . All of us have enough devotion to our cause," she concluded, "to put aside personal preferences and prejudices for the larger issues."[53] Lloyd was unmoved. Convinced that Detzer was undermining the Griffin bill, "which I know better than our secretary or anyone else on the Board," Lloyd wrote Hull to "notify" her that she considered Detzer "unreliable" when it came to matters of WILPF policy, and she would henceforth bypass the executive secretary and deal only with Hull.[54]

The basic problem between Detzer and Lloyd was not the Griffin bill or a new naturalization measure, the Cutting bill. Both women agreed that aliens applying for citizenship should not be "debarred because of their religious or philosophical views."[55] There were four divisive aspects of their relationship. First, Lloyd was methodologically more militant in support of an issue than was Detzer and less inclined to compromise. In her work for the WILPF, she exasperated Detzer with her use of polemical language and tactics, which Detzer believed would only antagonize the individuals or groups the WILPF wished to influence. For her part, Lloyd had no patience with methods that to her were soft-pedaling or half-way measures, and cared little whether she antagonized or not.

The second part of the problem between the two women concerned power and authority. Lloyd considered herself the organization's expert on the naturalization issue and resented any interference in the matter. To her credit, she probably worked harder than anyone else in the group to obtain passage of a broader naturalization bill, if for no other reason than that she was a close friend of Rosika Schwimmer who had been denied citizenship because of her pacifism. Detzer did not try to subvert Lloyd's efforts; rather, she and others in the peace movement were concerned that the wording of the Griffin bill "would not accomplish what it was originally intended to do."[56] When the more carefully worded Cutting bill was introduced upon the recommendation of ACLU lawyers, therefore, the majority of peace advocates transferred their support from the Griffin bill, much to Lloyd's anger and frustration.

Third, it may also be the case that Lloyd, a veteran of the suffrage campaign like Martin and Vernon, harbored a none-too-veiled contempt for Detzer because she lacked the political experience of the older woman and thus, should have deferred to Lloyd's expertise on policy matters. And last, Detzer's adamant refusal to join the NWP or support the ERA certainly could not have advanced her position in peace matters with the militant Lloyd.

The Martin-Lloyd dissatisfaction with Detzer as executive secretary seemed to have blown over by fall 1934 when Detzer enthusiastically wrote to Balch after an October board meeting, "The Executive of the Board is such a congenial group, and we work hard, but as Mrs. Hull said afterward, no one was tired, because we were all so nice to each other!"[57] However amicable were relations between the board and its executive secretary, within three months the Detzer-Vernon feud resurfaced with a vengeance in the National Office.

As campaign director, Vernon spent 1934 organizing public relations events in support of disarmament, pressuring for continuance of the Congressional munitions investigation, and protesting budget increases for the military. Her work overlapped with Detzer's responsibilities as the officer in charge of legislative matters. In lobbying Congress, distributing literature, and issuing letters to branches, Detzer and Vernon accused each other of "crossing each other's lines" and countermanding the other's directives without prior consultation.[58] And when it came to requesting specific action on the part of the rank-and-file for certain measures, Mildred Scott Olmsted, named organization secretary in the spring of 1934, was dragged into the ongoing dispute.

In late January 1935 Hull and Lacy Biddle Lewis attempted a solution, but as they acknowledged, "a great deal of difficulty arises from personal relations." Because there was plenty of space in the Washington office for the work of both Detzer and Vernon, they concurred with Olmsted that "general incompatibility and conflicting temperaments" were the culprits.[59] Not surprisingly, therefore, their suggestions for office reorganization had no effect.

From Geneva where she was temporarily the acting international secretary, Balch wrote of her hope that Olmsted could soon come to Geneva and take over the secretary's position for a few months. This was out of the question, Olmsted replied, primarily because "part of my work here is to try to clear up the cause of friction between Dorothy and Mabel and to work out some sort of functioning organization."[60] Although the goal seemed to be achieved by summer, behind the scenes, chaos reigned.

Vernon had been responsible for making the early May annual meeting a gala celebration of the WILPF's twentieth anniversary. She had "completed a brilliant affair," reported Hull. "The dinner was the largest ever held in the Willard Hotel; the broadcast was perfect. . . . Everyone is still marvelling. The people left McPherson Square as if from a religious service, so perfectly was it carried out to the very half second."[61] But appearances were deceiving. Although known only to a select group of five women at the time, Detzer tendered her resignation to Hull, effective as of 1 October 1935, and "refused to consider a reappointment except under certain conditions."[62] Her resignation was not accepted, however, apparently on the understanding that the board, which gave her a vote of confidence at the annual meeting, would try to meet her "conditions."

Shortly after the annual meeting, a frustrated Hull reported to Balch that "we have had the most trying time we have ever had with D. D. and M. V. We have come to such an impasse that I do not know *what* we are going to do. . . . We have had three awful days of discussion in which nothing has been accomplished. Both Mabel and Dorothy are nervous wrecks." Olmsted corroborated Hull's sense of desperation. She informed Balch in mid-May that "things between Mabel and Dorothy have been going from bad to worse. . . . [I]t is a life and death struggle between them, at least so far as the WIL[PF] is concerned.

Dorothy flatly refuses to allow Mabel to continue in Washington . . . and Mabel refuses to leave Washington and open special headquarters in New York or elsewhere."[63]

Up to this point the dispute remained essentially confined to a small group of national leaders; even the international joint chairs in Geneva with whom these leaders kept in close contact were unaware of the ongoing problems. A decision made at the annual meeting changed all this. The delegates "went on record in favor of a campaign this summer to carry a Peace Mandate to the various governments."[64] The idea was to circulate a petition among all peoples calling upon their respective governments to live up to the pledges made in the League of Nations Covenant and Kellogg-Briand Pact, to call an immediate halt to arms production, to secure a world treaty for immediate arms reduction, and to create an international agreement "to end the economic anarchy which breeds war."[65] This would require a closely coordinated effort on an international scale, and all WILPF sections as well as the joint chairs in Geneva would have to approve and cooperate.

Most important, this "Peoples Mandate to Governments" raised the question of leadership. The idea originated with the U.S. Section. Did that mean that such a massive project would be directed from the Washington office? If so, how would responsibility be delegated between the two officers, Detzer and Vernon, who were the logical choices to direct such an enormous undertaking? An executive board meeting was scheduled for 22 May to discuss these and related matters.

In the middle of all this confusion and turmoil, Jane Addams died. The overwhelming sense of loss and grief suffered by Addams' long-time associates and friends in the U.S. Section of the WILPF were undoubtedly much greater for Detzer than for Vernon who had never worked closely with the Hull House director. The board was prevented from dealing with much of substance by the shock of Addams' death on 21 May and the upcoming funeral in Chicago, but it did make key decisions concerning the proposed people's mandate.

Although Vernon was vacationing at the time and thus did not attend the meeting, she was named director of the Mandate Campaign, a decision with which Detzer concurred because she had made it clear that she was not interested in the position. Along with that decision, however, went "an ultimatum . . . about her [Vernon's] management of the future campaign work."[66] Vernon apparently concurred with the ultimatum and agreed to take charge of the Mandate Campaign, and at the 12 June board meeting presented an outline of her ideas for the project, hoping to launch the campaign on 6 September, Addams' birthday.

Shortly thereafter the board began to implement a series a measures designed to end the internecine strife in the national office. Hull sent a letter on behalf of the board and executive committee to all staff members. "Constructive criticism of your own department," she wrote, "will always be helpful to the head of that department or to me, but personal criticism of other departments than your own and of those working in them is demoralizing, out of harmony with our cause, and not to be tolerated."[67] A copy of this letter went to every staff member, including Detzer, Vernon, and Olmsted.

Then in mid-October the board passed a resolution that all future appointments to the staff would be made only with the approval of the president "in consultation with the Executive Secretary." Second, the board voted to make the executive secretary responsible "for the entire work of the National Organization," and last but certainly not least, agreed "that there should but one National Headquarters, and that all departments of the work should be located as the President and Executive Secretary direct."[68] In addition, the Mandate Campaign under Vernon's direction was to operate from the Willard Hotel in Washington, thereby separating completely the two disputants and their staffs. Needless to say, with this show of support from the board, Detzer withdrew her resignation and, as Hull observed, the executive secretary seemed "much refreshed in mind and spirit."[69]

Three board members then met with Vernon and went over the minutes of the October meeting in detail with her, explaining the decisions and the reasons for them. "We could not have been more explicit," Hull asserted, but that was not quite true, for Vernon was not informed of Detzer's prior resignation. Although Vernon "felt something was being held back" from her, she "left us," reported Hull, "in a very good frame of mind."[70] Convinced that the long-standing dispute was finally resolved, Hull was chagrined shortly thereafter to learn otherwise, and her patience with her Quaker colleague was beginning to wear thin. "I am much concerned over the whole situation. I do not feel that we succeeded in putting across to thee the Board's actions— or else thee is not facing it. For sometime past we have struggled to smooth matters over and the situation would not be smoothed—Now we are attempting it another way and it is necessary for thee to accept things as they are—If thee does I am sure that all will go well. If thee does not, the situation go awry again."[71]

When a day or so later Detzer wrote Hull that she felt Vernon should be told the whole story, Hull sent a second letter to the campaign director, explaining everything. She reiterated the board's appreciation of Vernon's work for the WILPF—"thee must not doubt it"— and although determined to keep Detzer, the board, she said, was no less intent on retaining Vernon. "Please do, Mabel dear, accept the situation," Hull wrote in closing, "and cooperate as we have asked thee to do."[72]

Apparently Vernon was willing to do so, at least for the time being. Not only did she launch a successful campaign with much publicity and fanfare both at home and abroad, she continued to work diligently on behalf of other WILPF concerns throughout the remainder of that autumn. But at some point thereafter she began to separate the Mandate Campaign from the auspices of the WILPF and to create an entirely distinct Peoples Mandate Committee. It may be that she did not feel that she had the wholehearted support of the WILPF behind the project or, perhaps, by the winter of 1935 she no longer wanted or felt the need for WILPF sponsorship. Vernon always preferred being her own boss and by December, it was clear that the Mandate idea was garnering enough support from other organizations and countries that she could strike out on her own with little risk of failure.

Whatever the reason, on 19 December the campaign was separated from the WILPF with the enthusiastic approval of the U.S. Section and the international officers. Dr. Mary Woolley, president of Mount Holyoke College, was elected chair of the newly organized Committee for the Peoples Mandate to End War, Carrie Chapman Catt continued as honorary chair for the Western Hemisphere, Hannah Hull became chair of the executive committee, and Mabel Vernon remained as campaign director. When Vernon departed from the WILPF as mandate director, she also relinquished her roles of finance secretary and campaign director. The internal division between her and Detzer that had plagued the organization for five years was at long last over.

The WILPF's internal difficulties were, however, far from over. Beginning in mid-1935, as Olmsted put it, "Anne Martin seems suddenly to have become active." That spelled trouble, which continued until Martin's acrimonious resignation at the end of the following summer. Although no longer a WILPF board member nor the regional director of the Pacific Coast in 1935, Martin had not completely severed her connection with the organization. She was the acting state chair of the Colorado branch, although if we can take Olmsted's word for it, not a particularly satisfactory one. In her role as organization secretary, it was Olmsted's responsibility "to develop Branch work and new organization as approved by the National Board or National President," and "to maintain close contact with the Branches and assist them with their particular problems."[73] In this capacity, Olmsted had become concerned about the Colorado branch's lack of activity, but her letters to Martin went unanswered. When Olmsted then contacted the chair of one of the local branches, urging her "to develop a real state organization," Martin quickly responded by complaining that Olmsted had communicated with anyone but herself. As Olmsted indicated, "it puts me in rather a quandary, as I have a feeling that some of the Colorado members are not satisfied with her leadership, which has certainly not been vigorous, and yet, if I can not communicate with them, I can not find out, either the cause of the difficulty or what help they want."[74]

At about the same time, Martin wrote Hull, suggesting that instead of being acting state chair, she be re-appointed regional director of the Pacific Coast division. She was interested in doing organizing work for the WILPF in neighboring states, but only if she was "given a title— one, I suspect," Olmsted mused, "that will make her a more or less permanent member of the Board as well as lend dignity to her."[75] Board members either declined Martin's request or simply procrastinated on the matter, for by the following spring, she was still acting state chair for Colorado and still openly dissatisfied with Detzer as executive secretary. In the meantime, she had become the Western Regional Chair of the Peoples Mandate Committee, no doubt because of her close friendship with Mabel Vernon.

Later that spring Olmsted began making plans with her new field secretary, Eleanor Eaton, for summer organization work in the Midwest. That trip plus the WILPF's work in conjunction with the Emergency Peace Campaign and a severe heat wave was precisely the right formula for a bitter confrontation, not just between Anne Martin and other WILPF leaders, but between the WILPF and the mandate campaign as well. Had the dispute remained confined to leadership circles, it would have been serious enough, but when it also involved the rank-and-file, it nearly became disastrous for the U.S. Section.

By the time of the debilitating mid-summer heat of 1936, Eaton was in South Dakota, where day after day of high temperatures and oppressive humidity made her work increasingly difficulty. So Olmsted wired her to head west to the cool high country of Colorado, where she could continue her work until the drought ended in the Midwest. But Colorado was Martin's territory and even though by July she had resigned as acting state chair, Olmsted warned Eaton that she could expect to encounter problems. Martin "is most antagonistic toward both Dorothy Detzer and me," Olmsted explained, "and has resented it if we corresponded with anyone else in Colorado, while, at the same time, largely ignoring instruction sent to her." It was a serious dilemma for the WILPF, Olmsted told Eaton, for there had been "various revolts" of members against Martin's "leadership."[76]

Not only Eaton but Detzer and Olmsted would be invading Martin's territory that summer. In the spring Detzer was appointed to direct the legislative work of the Emergency Peace Campaign, which involved a field trip to the Pacific Coast then back through Colorado to the Midwest. One reason for stopping in Colorado was to try to salvage the state's 159 WILPF members and arrange the election of a new state chair. The news that Detzer's trip would include a visit to "her" state precipitated Martin's resignation. She protested Detzer's "inefficiency" and alleged that the Colorado branches would not welcome the executive secretary at their meetings. The WILPF must remove Colorado from its membership list, Martin insisted, as "all the good workers have gone to the Colorado Committee of the Peoples Mandate."[77]

Although Olmsted had no desire to "emphasize the differences between Miss Martin and Miss Detzer, or to have the Peoples Mandate Committee and the W.I.L. antagonistic instead of cooperating," she told Eaton that she did not want to lose the Colorado members or just the state "drift."[78] Eaton's arrival in Colorado coincided with Detzer's and, not surprisingly, it was the latter who had the most serious difficulties with Martin and the mandate campaign. Part of the problem, although neither Detzer nor Eaton was aware of it at the time, was the circumstances surrounding Martin's resignation not only as acting state chair of Colorado, but from the WILPF.

Martin accused Hull of confiscating her 30 June letter of resignation, thereby preventing it from reaching eighteen other board members, past as well as present, to whom Martin had directed it be forwarded. Hull's version of the incident was substantially different, but Martin was not persuaded that anything less than malevolent intent on Hull's part was involved. The major portion of her letter of resignation was a scathing indictment of Detzer and a later letter to board members of 30 July was equally condemnatory of Hull. She was resigning, she said, because she found it "a waste of time and strength longer to be associated with an organization whose national board is . . . so ignorant of what constitutes good work and so unappreciative of it." In continuing her none too thinly veiled allusion to Vernon, she accused the board of sacrificing "its most disinterested, industrious and able workers, the authors of its most brilliant achievements, for those who are selfseeking [sic] and inefficient."

Having covertly brought up the subject of the executive secretary, Martin became explicit: "By its continued employment of Miss Detzer as executive secretary . . . [the WILPF Board] has undoubtedly taken a long step toward wrecking the League. On the record, her work is centered on herself and her personal reputation as a speaker. . . . Why then not employ her merely as a speaker, as I have in the past urged. . . . Her branch letters and reports alone reveal her unfitness for the position. . . . They reveal little grasp and no interest in the problems of state, national and Congressional work." As for Hull, Martin referred to her as a "petty politician [who] suppressed" a series of letters from her in 1933 and 1934 in which she had urged "the appointment of a competent executive secretary with the desire and ability to concentrate on building up the state branches."[79]

There is no question that after her early, tentative years Detzer had developed into a self-confident, assertive administrator (even if impatient with detail), a skilled politician, and an effective if not actually charismatic public speaker. She could also be difficult to get along with and did not take kindly to those who challenged her authority or policies. She did not possess the self-effacing personality of Balch nor did she dedicate herself to the cause of serving others in the self-sacrificing manner of Addams. Detzer was a tough-minded determined woman who knew what she wanted and worked incessantly to achieve it. She became a skilled lobbyist (however much she rankled at being called a "lobbyist") and welcomed controversy rather than as before, shrinking from it; she admittedly enjoyed the public spotlight that followed her. She thrived on a lifestyle that not only brought her into constant contact with men and women of power, wealth, and social position, but also involved numerous trips abroad where she was further admired, respected, and squired by such notables as England's MP Fenner Brockway.

This does not mean, however, that Detzer's work with the WILPF was primarily self-centered, nor should it suggest that she had "little grasp and no interest" in the work. The record provides overwhelming evidence of Detzer's keen political understanding and her intense interest in matters of importance to the peace movement. She also had the "ability" to "concentrate on building up the state branches" and proved that ability every time she made a speaking tour. As for the "desire" to do so, "building up the state branches" was not the executive secretary's responsibility; this was the primary reason for Olmsted's appointment as Organization Secretary in 1934 and 1935. Detzer might legitimately be faulted for being something of a prima donna, but she was an invaluable asset to both the WILPF and the interwar peace movement, as contemporaries and historians have acknowledged.[80]

The conflict that erupted between Martin and Detzer in mid-summer 1936 stemmed from three interrelated matters. First, there was Detzer's candidacy as the peace movement's female delegate to the upcoming Inter-American Conference for the Maintenance of Peace, scheduled for November in Buenos Aires. Second was the Mandate Campaign's efforts to raise money among WILPF members and, third, was Detzer's scheduled interview with Republican presidential nominee Alf Landon at his home in Topeka, Kansas.

When Detzer arrived in California in mid-July, she was "shocked" to learn that Vernon had written to all of the state's WILPF branches requesting their support for Caroline O'Day, Democratic political figure and peace advocate from New York, as delegate to the Inter-American Conference. Assuming that Vernon was merely "on loan" to the Mandate Campaign from the WILPF, the branches dutifully complied with her request. When they learned that Vernon was no longer with the WILPF, many felt that they had been used unethically for they wrote their letters of support for O'Day on the understanding that she was the official WILPF candidate.

Outraged, Detzer declared that Hull should immediately resign from the Mandate's executive committee. Given Vernon's alleged duplicity as well as Martin's attempt to woo the Colorado WILPF into the Mandate campaign, Detzer pleaded with the WILPF president not to "go Quaker" on her, but to resign "without delay." Recognizing Detzer's propensity to occasionally overdramatize, Hull did not resign but wrote Vernon concerning the "relation of the Peoples Mandate and the W.I.L.," which "troubled" her. Carefully omitting any reference to source, she noted that she was "getting now very trying reactions against a letter to our Branches about Mrs. O'Day's candidacy for the Inter-American Conference without mention of Dorothy. This would be all right from the Mandate Committee, of course, were it not that it went to all of our Branches as if directed by W.I.L.—Now comes to them further word about D.D. and it is not understood."[81] She chided Vernon for circularizing the WILPF's membership without prior consultation, and there the matter stood.

In the meantime Detzer traveled north to San Francisco where she encountered Mary Moss Wellborn, Vernon's assistant. As Detzer reported to Hull, Wellborn "talked to me about where I was going and like an innocent lamb I told her—Everywhere on the coast she preceded me and asked for money" for the Mandate Committee. And when Detzer arrived in Denver where she met Eaton, "as usual Mary Moss had been there first."

Eaton had been in Denver about a week and had met with Wellborn and Martin; neither encounter was particularly pleasant. Martin held a meeting of Denver WILPF members in Wellborn's honor, and when Eaton attempted to announce Detzer's imminent visit, Martin "forbade it." After the "loyal W.I.L." sent announcements of Detzer's upcoming arrival, Martin apparently telephoned "person after person telling them not to come" to the meeting arranged by Eaton. Martin "even persuaded one of the newspapers" that Detzer was an "imposter" and not to interview her. Almost one hundred women showed up regardless, and Detzer was never in better form. She won them over with an impassioned speech in which she presented her view of the continuing troubles with Martin and Vernon, and when she departed Denver for Topeka to see Landon, she "left a determined, comforted group who [sic] will be ready for Mildred when she comes [at] the end of the month."[82] But she never saw Landon nor even stopped in Topeka.

Before leaving Washington on her trip west, Detzer had made an appointment to interview Landon on 30 July. When she reached the coast she learned that a Mandate Committee delegation was going to Topeka that same day. Because Detzer had informed Wellborn of her plans, she assumed that in "meanness," Wellborn and Vernon had quickly scheduled a meeting with Landon on the same day to foul up her own plans. She was perfectly livid. But as Hull attempted to explain later, "the engagement by the Mandate people for July 30 was made and sent out long ago. . . . Doubtless Landon made all such engagements on the 30th."[83] Other evidence corroborates Hull's explanation, but Detzer was still not convinced.

Back in her Washington office by early August Detzer "felt fresh as a daisy," despite the strenuous trip with all of its tension. As she wrote Hull, "It certainly was lovely coming back to this delightful office . . . where I know there will be nothing but cooperation and friendliness, and no sense of conflict."[84] Vernon and Martin were both gone, and although a handful of WILPF members continued their affiliation with the Mandate Committee, the confusion over the relationship of the two groups and a vote of the International WILPF "to discontinue active work with the Mandate abroad" finally compelled Hannah Hull to resign from its executive committee in May 1937.[85]

Lola Maverick Lloyd continued to be active in both organizations as well as to "censure" Detzer for her work as the WILPF's executive secretary. Yet Lloyd's capacity for hard work, her militant feminism, and her desire to wield authority were all wisely channeled in a more constructive direction. She became chair of the WILPF's Committee on Minorities where she could, and did, focus on the problems faced by "a group that must be classed legally as a minority, the woman half of the world."[86] Lloyd was also a central figure in the NWP's ongoing effort to obtain the WILPF's endorsement of the ERA.

The WILPF had always supported full equality for women, but its conception of equal rights did not include the abolition of protective, or "welfare," legislation for women in the workplace. The majority of WILPF members did not support the ERA, therefore, because its wording meant precisely that, and so they did not join the NWP.[87] Because of their divergence on this basic issue, there was little organizational interaction in the United States between the WILPF and the NWP in the interwar period. Such was not the case internationally.

In 1925 when Alice Paul organized the International Advisory Committee of the NWP with representatives from one African and eleven European nations, three of its most prominent members were WILPF leaders. Members of both organizations joined forces in behalf of women's rights on the Inter-American Commission of Women, founded in 1928 as an advisory and policy-planning group within the Pan-American Union (later, the Organization of American States) designed "to investigate the legal, social, economic, and political problems of women in the Western Hemisphere."[88] In 1929 the NWP was on the organizing committee to create the Open Door International, which focused on equality for working women; by the mid-1930s WILPF leaders Gertrude Baer and Chrystal Macmillan were two prominent Open Door leaders. The NWP and WILPF worked together in Geneva as part of the Women's Consultative Committee of the League of Nations and, after its formation in 1930, through the auspices of the Equal Rights International as well. Such cooperative efforts on behalf of women internationally increased in the 1930s due in large part to the fact that Alice Paul lived in Geneva for most of the depression decade, leaving the U.S. organization to the direction of others.

When the NWP proposed the adoption of an Equal Nationality Treaty in 1930 as a way to eliminate discrimination against women on an international basis, a number of other women's organizations supported it including the International Council of Women, the International Alliance of Women for Suffrage and Equal Citizenship, Equal

Rights International, and the WILPF. In mid-1932, prior to the League of Nations Assembly meeting that year, Alice Paul and Lola Maverick Lloyd, as part of the Women's Consultative Committee and affiliates of Equal Rights International, submitted a report on the issue of equal nationality rights for women. Despite a determined effort by the women and much to their disappointment, the League rejected the Equal Nationality Treaty that fall.

A new administration in Washington by 1933 signaled a renewed NWP effort for the ERA in the United States. Successful in getting the amendment introduced in Roosevelt's first emergency session of Congress, the NWP, for the first time since the amendment was originally introduced ten years earlier, enjoyed the support of other women's organizations in testifying for the measure. Among these were the General Federation of Women's Clubs and the National Federation of Business and Professional Women. Although the WILPF was not included, it was one of ten women's groups, including the NWP, that persistently worked for the repeal of Section 213 of the 1932 Economy Act, which required that whenever personnel reductions were necessary in national government jobs, married persons whose spouses were also employed by the government would be dismissed first. Worded as "married women" in one early version of the bill, the intent of the section was to dismiss all married women workers whose husbands were also government employees.

In 1934, thanks notably to NWP lobbying, Congress made the United States the sixth nation to establish equal nationality laws; internationally, the NWP, WILPF, and other women's organizations continued to pressure the League of Nations to endorse both the Equal Nationality Treaty and the Equal Rights Treaty. This growing cooperation between Alice Paul and the WILPF abroad tended to foster greater communication, if not interaction, between the groups in the United States. Madeleine Doty, for example, like Paul a member of both organizations who made her home in Geneva, worked as hard for women's rights under the auspices of the NWP as she did for peace with the WILPF. A high point of cooperative endeavor for the two organizations was reached in autumn 1934 when ERA proponents Vernon, Lloyd, Blake, and Paul were all U.S. delegates to the WILPF's International Minorities Committee and Paul was appointed "Rapporteur on the Nationality of Women." The Zurich conference also approved the Equal Rights Treaty, although according to Hull, some delegates did so without a full understanding that the Treaty "involves suppression of all protective legislation."[89]

Hull and Addams declined the NWP's November 1934 request to serve on its National Advisory Committee, but they did so in a spirit of harmony; Hull sent "best wishes for the work of the Party always."[90] When later that month the NWP held its national convention, Vernon was one of the keynote speakers, and when she began organizing the Peoples Mandate Campaign for the WILPF in 1935, Vernon solicited the support of Paul and the NWP.

Throughout the interwar period the NWP sought endorsement of the ERA from the other women's organizations with only a limited degree of success. By the mid-1930s the WILPF was one of the most active and vocal of these groups and with its membership broadening beyond the ranks of social feminists who supported protective legislation, it seemed to NWP leaders an auspicious time to obtain WILPF backing for the amendment. As Paul pointed out to Lloyd in 1935, "We cannot hope . . . for the passage of the amendment by Congress until we have secured its endorsement by at least a few of the national organizations in our country. If the W.I.L. would lead the way it would be the first big group to take its place by our side."[91]

By early 1935 seven women's organizations had endorsed the Equal Rights Treaty in Europe as had the Inter-American Commission of Women in the Western Hemisphere, so there was a momentum underway that Paul felt should be capitalized upon. She also pointed out that "since the W.I.L. endorsed the Equal Rights Treaty at the Zurich Congress, . . . it would seem that there would be an excellent chance— almost a certainty—that the United States section would act in harmony with its International if the question were brought before it."[92] Thus Paul sought a favorable vote on ERA at the WILPF's May annual meeting.

When Anita Pollitzer of the NWP (and a WILPF member) went to see Detzer about the issue prior to the meeting, Detzer told her that she "had never been sure that she was for the Amendment, that it was, of course, very different from the Treaty," and that she questioned the "wisdom" of the ERA because of the protective legislation issue. Pollitzer put the two documents side by side and showed Detzer that the Equal Rights Treaty, approved by the International WILPF at Zurich, was identical to the Equal Rights Amendment "in everything except jurisdiction." Pollitzer reminded Detzer of the statement in the Zurich resolution that called for all national sections of the WILPF to support equal rights legislation for women in their own countries. Detzer promised to request the Resolutions Committee to report out the ERA measure for action at the annual meeting, but noted that this was "all" that she could do. When Pollitzer subsequently reported Detzer's response to Vernon and Lloyd, both "thought this quite a gain."[93]

The pro-ERA faction led by Blake managed to get Lloyd appointed to the resolutions committee to ensure discussion on the issue, and Blake, Lloyd, Pollitzer, and Vernon worked feverishly among delegates obtaining signatures on a pro-ERA petition. When discussion time came, those in support of the resolution decided to have Blake take the lead—"she was perfectly wonderful," Pollitzer reported to Paul. One speaker after another in favor of the measure followed in rapid succession until Hull, presiding as national president, announced that she was "going to ask that one speak for it and then one speak against it. This meant," commented Pollitzer, "that even tho [sic] there had been no apparent clamor to speak against the resolution, she would wait and ask those who were on their feet if they wished to speak against the Amendment—if not, to wait their turn."

Because Hull made it clear that she opposed the ERA, pro-amendment forces were probably correct in concluding that her debating maneuver was designed to take the wind out of their sails. Finally Hull left the chair to speak against the resolution, "citing the names of Jane Addams . . . and of Dr. Alice Hamilton as opponents." Since this meeting was in celebration of Addams' founding of the organization, the amendment's proponents now felt certain of defeat, but were somewhat heartened when Vernon followed Hull with an "impassioned and beautiful speech" for the ERA. Then suddenly Olmsted moved to table the resolution and before anyone knew what had happened, the motion carried and it was all over. Pollitzer was "disheartened," Alice Hamilton was apparently rather hostile to Vernon afterwards, Lloyd concluded that approaching Detzer beforehand only gave the opposition the upper hand, and NWP member Jane Norman Smith later called the outcome "a pity," but suggested that just having the subject discussed was a hopeful sign for the future.[94]

A year later the NWP tried again. With Vernon's departure from the WILPF by January, Lloyd became the NWP's foremost ERA proponent within WILPF leadership ranks. Paul was again optimistic about the ERA's chances with the peace advocates, but despite a concerted effort led by Lloyd, the delegates to the 1936 annual meeting defeated the amendment by the slim margin of seventeen to fifteen. As Lloyd subsequently reported in complete exasperation, "with the popular D.D. [Detzer] rushing here and there organizing the opposition and speaking violently against us herself . . . and everyone on the platform rising to vote no and also counting our vote, we were lost."[95]

Further dividing the NWP from the WILPF in late 1936 and early 1937 was the "Women's Charter," a statement of women's rights drafted by a group of women under the leadership of Mary Anderson, director of the Women's Bureau of the Department of Labor. Although the WILPF carefully avoided taking any overt stand on the charter, to the disgust of many pro-ERA members, Detzer encouraged WILPF members to discuss it in their meetings and sent a copy to each board member. The bone of contention was again that of protective legislation. ERA proponents considered the charter "extremely dangerous because it starts off by demanding complete freedom for women and ends up by asking for 'labour legislation which the world's experience shows to be necessary' and is therefore contradictory and highly objectionable."[96] Planning to try once more at the WILPF's 1937 annual meeting to gain endorsement for the ERA, NWP members within the peace group worked as hard against the Women's Charter that spring as they did in coordinating strategy for the ERA proposal.

NWP leaders assembled packets of pro-ERA literature and asked their colleague on the WILPF Board, Dr. Mary Wilhelmine Williams, if she would be willing to sign a cover letter sent out on WILPF stationery (but drafted by the NWP) to accompany the packets to each board member. Williams agreed, but advised omitting Detzer, Olmsted, and Elisabeth Christman of the Women's Trade Union League and newly appointed chair of the WILPF's Labor Committee, from the NWP mailing list. All three, Williams pointed out, were "connected with the National W.I.L. Office and . . . it is just as well to keep them in the dark as long as possible regarding what we are doing."[97] Asking that Board members read the Charter and the enclosed NWP material carefully, Williams' letter urged them to reject the Charter if it came up for a vote.

In early April Lloyd obtained Detzer's agreement to send anti-charter literature to the same women who earlier received a copy of the "What and Why" pro-charter leaflet from the WILPF. Hull consented to provide time at the meeting for a discussion of the document. Each side was allotted ten minutes to present its point of view and then the floor would be open for general discussion. The immediate tasks for the NWP were to decide what anti-charter literature to distribute among the 450 WILPF women involved, and whom to select as the most effective pro-ERA speaker to fill that ten-minute time slot.

Party leaders decided in mid-April to write a new ERA leaflet despite the fact that time was of the essence if WILPF delegates were to receive it prior to the meeting on the 30th. As for choosing a speaker,

it was the NWP's understanding that not long before, Detzer had remarked that a speech made by Party member Helen Bitterman "was
the best or one of the best she had ever heard."[98] Thus Party leaders
were delighted when Bitterman consented to do the ten-minute talk.

As promised by Hull, in mid-afternoon at the Saturday session the
ERA was brought up. In her speech opening the discussion, Bitterman
pointed out that "there can be no peace or freedom or justice for
women under present conditions since constitutionally women have no
citizenship rights except the vote." Without equal opportunity for
women under national law, she continued, "war will come not between
communism and fascism, but between the sexes." Addressing the protective legislation issue, Bitterman stressed the NWP's point that such
laws under the ERA would "be secured according to the nature of the
job, rather than the sex of the employee," and thus would cease to be
discriminatory in limiting economic opportunities for women.[99]

As Bitterman took her seat, Kathleen Hendrie of Detroit immediately moved that delegates endorse the ERA; Blake seconded the motion. Hull then quickly "ruled in accordance with the recommendation
of the executive committee" that a forty-five-minute discussion take
place with a speaker against following every speaker in favor, each one
being allowed three minutes.[100] Four of the five pro-ERA speakers were
active NWP members: Williams, Pollitzer, Blake, and Doty. Of the five
opposed, Detzer, Hamilton, and Rose Schneiderman must have made a
strong impression upon the delegates for when the vote was taken, the
ERA again went down to defeat, seventy to forty-four.

Nor did the WILPF endorse the Women's Charter. In fact, it never
came up for a vote nor is there any indication that it was even discussed. Continued opposition to it from women's labor groups as well
as from the National Federation of Business and Professional Women's
Clubs effectively killed the Charter's chances for implementation by
the end of 1937.

In the spring of 1938 a small group of NWP members was ready to
try again with the ERA at the WILPF's annual meeting in Minneapolis.
Alice Paul thought they ought to keep at it every year until they succeeded and asked Lloyd to again lead the fight. Numerous state and
local organizations had endorsed the ERA by this time as had eleven
national groups, but the only one of any size or influence was the National Federation of Business and Professional Women's Clubs, so the
WILPF's support was still deemed vital. Mary Wilhelmine Williams, no
longer a WILPF Board Member, thought the NWP ought to make the
effort both because the issue was now before Congress, and because a

"special committee of the AAUW had brought in an adverse report of the Amendment. It would seem well," she said, "to try once again to get favorable action from the WIL before the AAUW membership has time to study the matter and, as a membership . . . solidify against" it.[101]

Lloyd and Martha Souder, a WILPF member crucial to the NWP's efforts in 1937, both agreed with Williams but overall, there seemed to be a marked lack of enthusiasm or real interest in making much of a fight in 1938. Not surprisingly, when Lloyd brought the matter up, WILPF delegates again voted it down. Although Paul, Lloyd, and Doty continued their cooperative efforts on behalf of equal rights for women internationally thereafter, the ERA was a dead issue for the U.S. Section of the WILPF as World War II loomed on the horizon.

Whether or not the WILPF's failure to endorse the ERA influenced Alice Paul to organize a new international women's peace society with a feminist emphasis can only be conjecture, but in November of the following year, the World Woman's Party (WWP) was founded. With headquarters in Geneva, the WWP was an outgrowth of the rise of totalitarianism in Europe where in Spain, Italy, and Germany not only was the peace movement under attack, so, too, was the women's rights movement. A number of prominent European WILPF members participated in the formal establishment of the WWP with lavish ceremony at Geneva in August 1939, and the NWP voted to become its U.S. affiliate. Within two weeks of its formation came Germany's invasion of Poland, thus beginning World War II, which, of course, severely curtailed the activities of the WWP in Europe as it did with the WILPF and other peace groups.

When trying to make sense out of this almost decade-long series of disputes between and among various WILPF members and factions, it is obviously impossible to separate the personality conflicts from the political, ideological, generational, and class differences involved. That policy issues were almost insignificant is clear, given that the only one of any substance was that of the Equal Rights Amendment—and even here there was fundamental agreement that men and women should be equal in all spheres of activity. Nor were methodological differences of any great import. Whether militant feminist or liberal pacifist, no one advocated direct action, or confrontational, protest and demonstration as a means of reaching a goal.

The most severe crises that created discord and divisiveness among the women of the WILPF in the 1930s were the products of power, authority, and personality clashes, all inextricably intertwined. And although these factors seem to have had little overt impact on the organization's ability to function as an effective component of the peace movement, it is impossible to ascertain whether or not there were negative effects of a more subtle nature. Could this lack of harmony, for example, have alienated some women sufficiently to have prevented them from taking a more active role in the organization? Did it prevent other women from even joining the WILPF—or the peace movement? It is possible that the WILPF might have been an even more effective part of the peace movement in these critical years had it expended less time and energy on its own internal difficulties? Would the peace movement have been more influential had these conflicts not intervened?

As for the ERA, there is no reason to think that even with the WILPF's endorsement it would have passed Congress in those years. Yet the message that was sent by this continued failure of women's organizations to unite behind the amendment could only have led that male-dominated body to conclude, rightly or wrongly, that women did not know what they wanted. It was not a message that did the cause of feminism any good, and it can be fairly conjectured that it was not one the WILPF would have wished sent.

9

Repression at Home and Abroad

IF THE WOMEN OF THE WILPF disagreed among themselves over the means of achieving equal rights for women, they did not dispute the goal. Believing in the fundamental equality of all human beings, the WILPF had little patience with policies that discriminated against any people whether for reasons of race, religion, ethnicity, or gender, and strove diligently throughout the interwar period against such practices, nationally and internationally. As abhorrent to the WILPF as any other undemocratic feature of the American scene was the blatant discrimination of white America against black America; not only was it undemocratic, it was morally and legally wrong.

Writing in 1907, Jane Addams stated her understanding of democracy as not merely "a sentiment which desires the well-being of all men, nor . . . a creed which believes in the essential dignity and equality of all men, but as that which affords a rule of living as well as a test of faith." Addams and the women who followed her into the WILPF lived their democratic creed. Not perfectly, to be sure, but as one of the founders of the National Association for the Advancement of Colored People (NAACP) who "identified with the common lot," which she herself called the "essential idea of Democracy," Addams could never have accepted leadership of an organization that functioned in any other way.[1] Although it is true that the WILPF began as an organization composed overwhelmingly of white Western middle and upper middle class women, its immediate and successful efforts to attract as members women who were not Caucasian, not imbued with Western values, and not part of a socioeconomic elite clearly indicated that all women who shared a belief in the goals of peace and freedom were welcome with enthusiasm into the new group.

With respect to the U.S. Section, the bleak economic circumstances in which most black Americans lived made sheer survival an imperative that prevented the vast majority of black women from working for any social or political issue, regardless of how strongly any individual may have felt about it. Moreover, de facto as well as de jure discrimination all across the country made it the better part of wisdom for all black Americans to maintain a low public profile. Despite such second-class citizenship, however, there was that handful of middle class black women with the educational background and economic stability to have the requisite leisure for pursuit of such goals as peace and social justice. In the immediate post-World War I period one such woman was educator, suffragist, and social activist Mary Church Terrell.

As president of the National Association of Colored Women from the late 1890s through the early years of this century and as an activist in the National American Woman Suffrage Association, Terrell and Addams came into frequent contact with one another prior to the formation of the WPP in 1915. Although not a charter member of the WPP or an avowed pacifist, Terrell joined the organization shortly thereafter and was elected to the national board, despite her wartime work for the War Camp Community Service, which complied with the government's request "to interest the public in this country's efforts to aid the Allies."[2]

When the time came for the women of the ICWPP to meet at the 1919 Congress in Zurich, the Executive Board of the WPP elected Terrell as one of thirty delegates from the United States. The director of the War Camp Community Service granted her a leave of absence, but when the State Department allowed passports for only fifteen women, "it would have been easy," she observed, "to leave the colored delegate out." But Terrell remained among those fifteen, in all probability because she *was* the only non-white woman and her presence would provide evidence that the peace group welcomed minority women into its ranks.

Recalling the congress some twenty-five years later, Terrell remarked that she was "about to say that women from all over the world were present. But on sober second thought," she mused, "it is more truthful to say that women from all over the white world were present. . . . [I]t was my privilege to represent not only the colored women of the United States, but the whole continent of Africa as well. . . . In fact," she concluded, "since I was the only delegate who gave any color to the occasion at all, it finally dawned on me that I was representing the women of all the nonwhite countries in the world." Although such an exclusive situation was not characteristic of the WILPF for long, it nevertheless remained a predominantly white Western-oriented organization internationally, and in the United States, black women as well as working-class women of any race were always a distinct minority.

Terrell had the honor of delivering a keynote address representing the WPP at the Zurich Congress. Introduced by Addams, who made "a slight reference to the Race Problem in the United States," Terrell endeared herself to the packed hall by giving her talk in flawless German. "When I had finished," she recalled, "there went up such an outburst of approbation as I had not heard since I addressed the International Congress of Women which had met in Berlin fifteen years previously." Her own harshest critic of herself as a public speaker, for "once" in her life, Terrell "was satisfied" with her effort and gratified by her audience's response.

Ten years after the Zurich Congress, Balch's recollection of Terrell's performance was somewhat at odds with that of the black delegate. Commenting rather pointedly on the fact that the WPP had paid for Terrell's passage to and from the meeting, Balch remembered how her speech "rather shocked us all for its decidedly unpacifist tone" because Terrell "glorified the Civil War as the means of liberating her people." Balch went on to observe that once the Congress was over and WPP delegates had returned home, she could not remember Terrell attending even one board meeting of the newly organized WILPF nor doing "the least thing" with respect to peace activity.[3]

Whatever the case, Terrell was not re-elected to the WILPF's National Board after 1920, and whether or not that caused her to lose interest in peace work, since she subsequently became inactive, can only be conjecture. But it may very well be that an unfortunate incident in early 1921 involving a conflict between Terrell and the board concerning an issue of race was at least partially responsible for her failure to get re-elected only a couple of months later.

According to Terrell, in March 1921 she, along with other board members, was asked to sign a petition "requesting the removal of the black troops from occupied Germany." Because the other women were willing to sign it, Terrell's signature was important for unanimity and, of course, because she was the only black member of the board. Told that "the most horrible crimes" against German women had been perpetrated by these black soldiers, Terrell expressed her sympathy for the women if indeed such stories were true. After all, she pointed out in a letter to Addams, "I belong to a race whose women have been the victims of assaults committed upon them by men of all races."

But, she went on, "I am certain that the black troops are commit-
ting no more assaults upon the German women than the German men
committed upon the French women or that any race of soldiers would
probably commit upon women in occupied territory." Having it on
"good authority" that the charges of such behavior by the black soldiers
"are not founded in fact," and convinced that such propaganda "is
simply another violent and plausible appeal to race prejudice," she
could not in good conscience sign the petition. Not wishing to be a
stumbling block to the board's desire for unanimity, however, she decided that the best course of action was to resign, and wrote Addams of
her decision in mid-March.

Addams, who had chaired a committee of the WILPF's Chicago
branch concerned with the issue of "colored troops on the Rhine,"
agreed with Terrell "that we should protest against the occupation of
enemy territory—not against any special troops."[4] She thus refused to
accept the black woman's resignation from the board. But Terrell did
not sign the petition and at the WILPF's annual meeting in May, she
was not re-elected. The national board, therefore, was left with no
prominent black member, a matter of some concern to WILPF leaders.

This state of affairs apparently remained unaltered for the next few
years, although at the 1924 summer school in Chicago, James Weldon
Johnson, secretary of the NAACP, presented a program on "The Race
Problem and Peace," and among the organization's "accomplishments"
noted for 1925 was the invitation extended to "foreign and colored
residents of Pennsylvania, such as Armenian, Hindu, Dutch, Colored
American, Japanese, Italian, German, Mexican and Chinese, to a series
of 10 social evenings in private homes to exchange ideas."[5] And at its
meeting in May 1926, the national board requested that one of its
members approach a number of black organizations in the effort to get
WILPF speakers placed on their summer programs. Clearly the interest
in attracting black support for peace, and black members as well, had
not waned.

Within two years, the U.S. Section had a budding Inter-Racial Committee under the direction of one of its few black members, Addie
Hunton. As for its structure and function among the branches, Hunton
proposed that each interracial committee be kept small, ideally composed of four women, two white and two black, with the national committee advising them as to program and leadership. She indicated to
Mildred Scott Olmsted that she already knew of at least eight black
women in four states who were interested and hoped Olmsted "would
forage for white members to match these."[6] In that same year Olmsted

also managed to arrange for Detzer to be one of the featured speakers at the Biennial Convention of the National Association of Colored Women. Confusion over dates and time prevented Detzer's appearance, much to Olmsted's keen disappointment.

Much of the progress made by the WILPF to forge a closer working relationship between white and black women by the late 1920s was due to Olmsted's efforts. She was convinced that black organizations were an untapped mine of potential peace workers. By late fall 1928 Olmsted was spearheading such a drive among WILPF members, which resulted in numerous contacts with black churches and schools, the distribution of peace literature among black young people, and helping to plan "peace pageants" in black community centers and among scout troops—even enlisting her husband to speak before a black American Legion post. Such activities continued into the following year when Hunton made a number of speeches at various black schools and universities as well as to a variety of interracial groups, always stressing "why Inter-Racial co-operation is necessary for Peace."[7] She was one of two black U.S. delegates to the WILPF's Sixth International Congress in Prague that August and had attended the summer school that preceded it, giving well-received talks at both places.

As the WILPF's director of policies, Balch presented a statement of organizational sentiment with respect to discrimination against racial and ethnic minorities at the group's annual meeting in April 1929. Noting that "in Europe we hear much of minority populations, as the Germans in the Tyrol, or the Jews and Hungarians in Roumania," she pointed out that the United States had its counterparts in "our Negro fellow citizens and the Indian wards of the Nation, and all groups who feel themselves in any way discriminated against." Calling for increased appropriations by Congress for the Department of Interior so as to adequately provide for native Americans, and voicing the women's strong opposition to racial discrimination in terms of immigration and the granting of citizenship, Balch condemned "the Negro problem" because it stemmed from "the stupidities and the cruelty of race prejudice." Anticipating that future time when "there will be no more inconvenience or self consciousness connected with race than with the possession of blue eyes or brown eyes," the women urged Congressional passage of an anti-lynching bill.[8]

The first major test of this racial policy for the WILPF came the following spring as plans were being made for the 1930 annual meeting in the nation's capital. Of the various accommodations available in Washington, the Grace Dodge Hotel offered the best combination of meeting facilities, central location, and reasonable rates for meals and rooms. The problem with the Grace Dodge, as Detzer pointed out, was that while all WILPF members could attend the meetings in the hotel's Garden House with its separate entrance, the black members "could not come into the hotel corridors." According to the hotel manager, this policy was fairly recent, implemented "to protect colored visitors themselves" because at an earlier Episcopal convention, black ministers "were very much insulted by white southern women who were guests at the hotel." Detzer, in asking for the Board's feelings on the matter, indicated that the racial issue in Washington had become "much sharper" because of a recent communist demonstration in which "colored and white paraded together."[9]

When the board met two weeks later it wasted no time in coming to a decision. It voted to hold its sessions at the Friends Meeting House, also centrally located, and its banquet at the nearby YWCA, and followed this action with a letter of protest to each of the city's hotels that practiced racial discrimination. At the annual meeting, when it was learned that the Grace Dodge Hotel was not "a purely commercial enterprise, but . . . is controlled by the National Board of the Young Women's Christian Association," a specific letter of protest was sent to its manager for its policy of discrimination "on account of race and color."[10] When later that fall, the NCPW scheduled its annual meeting at the Grace Dodge, the WILPF, soliciting the support of the Pacifist Action Committee and the FOR, requested Frederick Libby to choose instead a place where blacks were welcome. The NCPW complied.

By mid-1931 the WILPF was reporting with no little pride to numerous achievements with respect to "race recognition."[11] Organizationally, such accomplishments included black speakers at WILPF programs and white speakers at meetings of black organizations; black women on the national, state, and local boards of directors and committees; black office workers at both the state and national levels; participation in a racially mixed Committee of Inquiry and Goodwill sent to Haiti in 1926 with subsequent publication by Balch of a book entitled *Occupied Haiti,* two chapters of which were written by the two black members of the Haitian Committee; and a growing number of speeches and programs organized by Addie Hunton among the branches.

Politically, the WILPF distributed a wealth of literature portraying American blacks in a positive light, including a pamphlet entitled "Achievements of Negro Women." The organization protested in a number of cases where racial discrimination was practiced by places of public accommodation and it expanded its activities concerning racial equality and international peace in the public schools and colleges. Its most important organizational focus, however, was directed toward the long-established practice of lynching. Although the number of lynchings steadily decreased in the first thirty years of this century, beginning with the depression decade they were on the rise again.

"Unalterably opposed to discrimination between people on account of race, creed or nationality," the women declared in 1930 "that the recent lynching and burning of the bodies of negroes is a blot on our civilization."[12] Thus they resolved to step up their efforts to obtain Congressional passage of an antilynching law. When, in the fall of 1933, there was a particularly brutal lynching at Princess Anne, Maryland, the state branch of the WILPF wrote the governor demanding not only speedy prosecution of the culprits, but enactment of a state antilynching law as well. A similar letter was sent to President Roosevelt from the WILPF's National office, asking for his support for such a law at the national level.

When the Costigan-Wagner bill against lynching was introduced in Congress in early 1934, WILPF President Hannah Clothier Hull testified for the measure at the March hearings. During the hearings, when four black women went to the dining room of the Senate office building for lunch, they were refused a table. One of the women, "a Negro Ph.D.," protested and was physically escorted out by two policemen and taken to the "detention room of the Capitol." This incident so outraged certain segments among the radical peace organizations that they "decided to organize a demonstration."

Every day of that week, mixed parties of white and black men and women from the WILPF, FOR, the Quakers, and the Socialist Party went to the Capitol's various restaurants. In the House, restaurant service was refused the group and the Congressman in charge would not talk with the demonstrators about the incident. In the Senate building, the group was served at "a special table set apart for Negroes," and in a restaurant on the Senate side of the Capitol, "service was given if members of the committee sat by themselves at a separate table." As a result of this action, all of the restaurants involved simply implemented a policy restricting service to members or employees of Congress. Making these heretofore public restaurants now private establishments was seen as a "real step in advance" by the WILPF because, by law, "such discrimination is not allowed in a public government restaurant."[13]

Yet an antilynching law failed to pass Congress that spring, prompting another letter to the president from the WILPF in the fall. This time the women took a different tack to impress upon Roosevelt the international implications of the issue. "Apart . . . from the question of human suffering," wrote Balch, "every example of lawlessness and violence in one country reacts in every other and intensifies existing tendencies to resort to intolerance, cruelty and tyranny. The 'Nazi' justifies his persecution of Jews by reference to the American attitude to Negroes," she concluded pointedly, "and the abuses in Concentration camps and prisons, which shame mankind are interrelated with excesses in other countries."[14]

Balch's letter was particularly well-timed, for it reached Roosevelt not long before a national conference on crime, called by the attorney general, met in Washington. Given the Justice Department's view that "the gangster business" was of greater importance, the crime of lynching was not considered.[15] The NAACP thus decided to picket the conference, asking the WILPF to participate. Twenty women were ready to go but when the NAACP could not obtain a permit, it called the demonstration off, not wanting the WILPF participants to be arrested for illegal picketing. Detzer was keenly disappointed, convinced that it would have been "excellent to have had about 20 of our members locked up. It would have been a big story," she lamented, "and probably forced the situation out."[16]

By early 1935 the Costigan-Wagner bill was the most important issue on the WILPF's agenda. With a second hearing soon to be scheduled, the national office urged the branches to write the president and their representatives in Congress and to hold special meetings on the bill. With the depression hanging on, the WILPF noted the interrelatedness of race prejudice and economic insecurity: "The economic tension between whites and blacks, when jobs are at a premium," wrote Detzer, "has invariably been the real cause behind the violence of lynching. A lynching can so terrify Negroes in a given community that they can easily be driven out or so intimidated that they will not attempt to hold jobs which can be filled by whites." Suggesting various lecture topics and books on the issue, the WILPF urged those branches without an Inter-Racial Committee to become involved as part of their responsibility to ensure "no sense of separateness."[17]

By mid-March when the antilynching bill was reported favorably by the Senate committee, the national office had nothing but praise for the WILPF branches in response to its January appeal. And on 15 April, when Detzer reported that the bill was due to come up for action in the Senate that afternoon, she again lauded the branches for their support of the measure, urging one final telegram campaign to counter a threatened filibuster. It was for naught; once again, the antilynch-ing bill failed to pass.

Hunton and other prominent WILPF members felt that interracial work within the organization was neither extensive enough nor suffi-ciently systematic. Reporting to the group's annual meeting that May, Hunton noted that despite the national appeal for creation of more interracial committees among the branches, none was formed. Long-time WILPF member Zonia Baber was of the opinion that "Race Re-lations should be a real feature of the program of the League or altogether abandoned," a position heartily endorsed by Hunton who felt that "treatment of so serious a matter at this time in a haphazard manner" would hurt the cause rather than help it.[18]

Other women in the peace movement apparently agreed, for at the January convention of the NCCCW, women from both organizations met to discuss the issue, and the ideas expressed were subsequently implemented by five WILPF branches—Baltimore, Philadelphia, Bos-ton, the District of Columbia, and Detroit. Hunton praised the various activities of these branches, from greater cooperation with local black organizations to more active recruitment of nonwhite members to in-creased efforts to end racial discrimination in the public schools, and urged other branches to follow these examples.

Hunton's report for the Inter-Racial Committee was not the only one to deal with the race issue at the Annual Meeting that spring. Detzer gave a moving account of the organization's recent experience with the Southern Tenant Farmers' Union, which was led by Howard Kester, former secretary of the FOR. Earlier in the month he had brought to Washington a group of sharecroppers, white and black, to protest against conditions in Arkansas that Detzer referred to as "peonage." A few had been injured in the reign of terror and violence, but none of the city's white hospitals would accept them, and the hos-pital for blacks had no room, even in the hallways. So the WILPF's national office was used as their headquarters, where secretaries Lois Jameson and Huldah Randall made them as comfortable as possible, creating "a little hospital" on the office floor.[19]

As part of its "Principles and Policies" for 1935–1936, voted at that same annual meeting, the WILPF included three principles, peace, freedom, and justice. "We believe that there can be neither peace nor freedom without justice, and that the existing economic system is a challenge to our whole position. It is shot through with force, injustice, and actual violence often employed in the name of public order. Our duty, therefore, and also our opportunity as pacifists, is to work for a better economic and social order by every non-violent means." Under "Domestic Policies," the group reaffirmed its support for the "struggle to overcome the discrimination and race prejudice under which Negroes and other minority groups suffer throughout the United States," and voted "to recognize that covert forms of violence, inherent in the inequalities of our present economic system, are as unethical and cruel as overt types of violence."[20]

The brutality of Arkansas white landowners against all sharecroppers and the Southern Tenant Farmers' Union continued into early 1936. In late January Howard Kester "just escaped being lynched by a band of armed planters and deputies who disrupted a meeting of the white and colored workers at which Mr. Kester was speaking."[21] Reports came back of mass evictions of tenant farmers of both races, thanks to the provisions of the Agricultural Adjustment Act (AAA), which paid farm owners to take land out of production. Across the South where sharecropping and tenant farming became commonplace after the Civil War, particularly for newly freed slaves, the land taken out of production during the Depression was farmed by the children and grandchildren of the original tenants. Although the AAA may have been designed to aid farmers by raising prices for agricultural commodities, it created untold hardship and misery for thousands of poor, landless tenant families in the South. The WILPF's National Board sent a telegram to Roosevelt urging him "to use all his power to prevent violence among these tragic American citizens of the South," and pressed the branches to send similar messages.[22]

In May the National Office sent Lois Jameson on a fact-finding trip through the "terror belt of Arkansas." What she saw gave credence to Detzer's warning of February that the sharecroppers' situation smacked ominously of "incipient fascism":

> The drama of the experience was its sense of contrast. We were driving comfortably . . . on a hot, drowsy afternoon through an unutterably dull, dreary countryside that looked as though nothing ever happened in it. And yet here was a church from whose steps a young teacher had been hauled off to jail for "anarchy" because he was speaking for the Union, and here was a brown cotton-field where a young boy had been shot dead at dusk because he was frightened and had started to run when an angry deputy called to him. We saw places where Union meetings were broken up by violence; and we saw a cabin that had been fired into by a planter's machine gun. It was a tale of terrorism and it was all true.

We made a tour of about 150 miles through Marked Tree, Tru-
mann, Parkin and Earle, and everywhere were scenes of the most
dreadful poverty. The sharecroppers' shacks were, without exception,
ugly and dilapidated. They were one or two room sheds, almost, with
holes in roofs and mostly no glass in windows. They looked as though
they had never been painted; they sagged. Many of them had no sani-
tary facilities whatever. . . . They were all set in the middle of cotton
fields, but you cannot eat cotton. A diversified farming has never been
practiced or allowed so they had no milk or vegetables. . . . The people we saw were intelligent-looking enough, some were even fine-look-
ing, but many of them seemed ill and tired. They have rickets and
pellagra; they were working in the fields long after sunset.[23]

The WILPF's concern that the situation for southern sharecroppers carried with it the potential for an American-style fascism was
echoed by the organization's Labor Secretary Eleanor Fowler. Attending the American Federation of Labor (AFL) convention later that year
as a WILPF representative, Fowler, recognizing that the AFL "is a very
conservative organization," was heartened "by the splendid work of the
delegate from agricultural workers unions who put up a fine fight for
an international charter in order that they might progress more rapidly
in organizing the three million agricultural laborers in this country."
She reported that one of the delegates stressed the need for agricultural organization and unity "as a step in the fight against fascism,
since unorganized rural workers, living on the verge of starvation, are
most easily swayed by demagogues." Indicative of the convention's
sense of solidarity with its rural brethren, it unanimously adopted a
resolution, introduced at Fowler's behest on behalf of the Southern
Tenant Farmers' Union, "condemning the vicious attacks on civil liberties in Arkansas."[24]

Although encouraged by the AFL's action concerning the plight of
farmers and rural workers, Fowler was equally distressed by the gathering's condemnation of pacifism in the same breath as its condemnation of militarism and its call for a strong national defense, and the
"fascist implication" of anti-Semitic references as well as the "attack on
the Negroes implicit in the speeches against the Scottsboro resolution."[25] The racism manifested in the latter instance was particularly
disturbing for the evidence in the Scottsboro case clearly pointed to
the innocence of the nine young black men accused of criminal assault
in the alleged rape of two white women in Alabama some five years
earlier.

Still in litigation on appeal by early May 1937, the Scottsboro case was the subject of a WILPF resolution voted at its annual meeting that year:

> WHEREAS the Scottsboro case has been the occasion of a terrible display of racial and social prejudice;
> WHEREAS it has been a long-continued source of ill feeling and a cause of distrust of our courts; and
> WHEREAS five years of imprisonment have already been undergone by the defendants;
> BE IT RESOLVED that we urge the Governor of Alabama in the name of justice to issue a full pardon to the defendants.[26]

Three months later, the Ninth World Congress of the WILPF, meeting in Luhacovice, Czechoslovakia, added an international appeal to the pressure on Alabama's governor. Pleased that the guilty verdict had been reversed and the death sentences withdrawn for four of the defendants, the women inquired as to what recompense Alabama planned to provide for the long years of misery and injustice suffered by these young men, and demanded the release of those still imprisoned.

While the WILPF worked to bring justice to the "Scottsboro boys," it continued to labor in behalf of a national antilynching law. When the House Judiciary Committee held hearings in early April 1937 on the issue as two such bills were before the House and one in the Senate, Eleanor Fowler testified for the WILPF, stressing the international implications of the problem, "and the lack of faith of other countries in our good faith when we protest about outrages abroad and allow lynchings to go on at home." Detzer observed that a "principal objection" of the committee to such legislation was "fear that federal intervention would interfere with the rapid progress which has been made in cutting down the number of lynchings in recent years."[27]

Here is where the issues of lynching and cases like that of the "Scottsboro boys" come together. As historian Dan Carter has pointed out, Southerners had learned that "lynchings were untidy and created a bad press," and that realization plus the "possibility of a federal antilynching law" combined as the 1930s wore on to act "as a mild restraint" on lynching. But that did not mean the end of mob violence against blacks. It meant, rather, that "lynchings were increasingly replaced by situations in which the Southern legal system prostituted itself to the mob's demand. Responsible officials begged would-be lynchers to 'let the law take its course', thus tacitly promising there would be a quick trial and the death penalty."[28] The "Scottsboro boys" was a case in point, yet despite an increasing use of the legal system to deal with their race "problem," white Southerners continued to resort to lynching, almost as a kind of sport, thus making a national law imperative as far as groups like the WILPF were concerned.

The House voted favorably on such a bill in mid-April 1937, but despite that fact and the stepped-up activity of the WILPF to obtain a positive vote in the Senate, the bill had not yet been acted on by fall. As Thanksgiving approached, Congress was in the midst of a filibuster on the bill, and by March 1938, national leaders of the WILPF were still exhorting members to apply pressure on their Congressional representatives. By the end of January 1939, the WILPF was praising the U.S. Attorney General for his plans to create a civil liberties bureau within the Department of Justice. The women saw its creation as an opportunity to "expose the urgent and imperative need of federal protection through law of an American minority from the crime of lynching."[29] Yet World War II came and went, and still Congress did not pass an antilynching law.

Although striving at home for greater racial and economic justice, the WILPF did not ignore similar instances of racial injustice and economic vulnerability abroad. Beginning in the 1920s, economic imperialism in the African nations of Liberia and Ethiopia (then more commonly referred to as Abyssinia) involving two U.S. business enterprises, the Firestone Corporation, and the J. G. White Company, also demanded a good deal of the women's time and energy.

The situation in Abyssinia surfaced in June 1930 when John Harris of the British-based Anti-Slavery and Aborigines Protection Society approached Mary Sheepshanks, also British, who was then the WILPF's International Secretary in Geneva. It seems that a U.S. engineering firm, the J. G. White Company, had contracted with the Abyssinian government for a mining concession and the construction of a dam. The problem, according to Harris, was not only that the emperor—the newly crowned Ras Tafari Makonnen (later known as Hailie Selassie I)—had allegedly offered slave labor as an incentive to the company, but that the company had apparently accepted the offer.

After Sheepshanks informed the U.S. Section of Harris's allegations, Detzer visited the State Department where she was assured that "no American corporation would contemplate the use of slave labor."[30] Determined to find out for herself, in mid-August Detzer met with Gano Dunn, president of the J. G. White Company. Contradicting the information received from Harris, Dunn told Detzer that the emperor was "bitterly opposed" to slavery and had abolished the institution by decree three years earlier. He also informed her that there was no written contract of any kind between his company and the Abyssinian government, merely a "verbal arrangement" about which he did not elaborate further. Detzer quickly pointed out that if indeed Dunn's company had accepted an offer of slave labor, she did not expect that it would be written down "in black and white." "I also realized," she reported to Sheepshanks later, "that a decree made three years ago . . . did not abolish slavery any more than prohibition had stopped drinking in this country."

Detzer then inquired of Dunn how his company intended to hire its workers, what scale of wages would be paid, and if those wages "would be such as would be approved by the International Labor Office." He assured her that the labor would definitely be free and although no wage scale had yet been set, when it was, "there would be no secret about it and would be at a level which the civilized world" considered proper for such work. While pointing out that the J. G. White Company, like all international corporations, was not "doing business in other parts of the world as a matter of charity," Dunn noted that his company worked in "the closest cooperation" with local missionaries in the interest of all concerned. As the discussion drew to a close, he expressed his concern over the entire affair, hastening to point out that "the most precious thing in the world" to his business was its reputation. Detzer left, quite convinced that if the J. G. White Company had ever contemplated using slave labor in Abyssinia, it would not do so now and would be "much more careful in its relations to the men it hires than it would have been before."[31]

Apparently this was the case, for by April 1931 Detzer was informed by a reliable source that the J. G. White Company "had given up the building of the Abyssinian dam"; preliminary surveys indicated that the dam "could not be built without too great expense." When queried by Detzer, the State Department responded that the rumor might very well be true, but it had not yet received such information from the company. If the story was accurate, Detzer conjectured, "it is possible that without some kind of forced or slave labor, they could not put through their project and make sufficient money." Detzer's sources were correct. A year later, the WILPF reported unequivocally that "plans for the project were dropped."[32]

The issue resurfaced, however, when in early 1933 the Democratic administration of Franklin Roosevelt was about to take office. It may be that J. G. White Company officials thought that the Democrats would be less favorably inclined toward its economic interests in Africa, and thus made a last-ditch effort to finalize its Abyssinian plans while the Republicans were still in power. Whatever the reason, once again the papers were reporting that a meeting was being held in Abyssinia "to consider definite plans made by the J. G. White Company . . . for the building of a dam." Apparently no contract had yet been signed, so the WILPF hastily wrote the State Department, reminding it that the United States had signed the Anti-Slavery Convention in 1929, and asked if the terms of any such contract would be made public before it was signed.

The State Department's reply was less than satisfactory. It referred the women to the public statement made by Gano Dunn back in August 1930 in response to his interview with Detzer indicating in carefully chosen words that "the employment of slave labor by us or by any other foreigners contemplating work in Ethiopia would be obnoxious to the Emperor." All workers would be treated "as free men," the statement concluded, and living and working conditions "will meet the approval of enlightened humanitarians in the United States and elsewhere."[33]

And there the matter remained for at least two reasons. First, as Detzer herself acknowledged, the incoming administration had its collective mind on the economic problems of the Depression and thus it was difficult to get it to consider matters of foreign affairs, especially when there was no crisis involved. Second, by 1933 the WILPF was caught up in a more serious and complicated matter involving the nation of Liberia and the Firestone Tire and Rubber Company.

Liberia had been mentioned when the storm broke over possible slavery in Abyssinia because an international commission to investigate allegations of forced labor and slavery was sent by the League of Nations to Liberia in 1930. But the story really began in the early 1920s at a time when Britain, the colonies of which produced 75 percent of the world's rubber, held a monopoly on the rubber supply, while the United States, beginning its love affair with the automobile, was consuming 70 percent of all the rubber produced. Casting about for other sources of rubber, Harvey Firestone sent researchers into Liberia in 1923. They reported that both rubber and labor were plentiful. In the subsequent negotiations of June 1924 between Firestone and the Liberian government, only a land concession for rubber plantations was discussed. That was finally agreed to on 18 November 1926 when Firestone was given a ninety-nine year lease on a million acres of land for which he would pay six cents an acre. Then, as the WILPF put it later, "true to imperialistic tradition, loans followed the concessions."[34]

The U.S. State Department supported the idea of a loan that would be "guaranteed by governmental revenues and administered by foreigners, [and was] necessary in light of Liberian 'instability',"[35] but the Liberian government, already burdened with substantial debt, did not. Yet less than a month after the land concession contract with Firestone was signed, Liberia also ratified a loan agreement. She did so on the understanding, and with the assurance of the State Department, that the money was not to come from Firestone. A forty-year loan of $5 million at 7 percent interest was thus floated through the Finance Corporation of America. Not until early 1932 did it come to light that the Finance Corporation of America was a Firestone subsidiary, established by the rubber magnate to circumvent Liberian opposition to a Firestone loan.

What brought the whole matter to public, and particularly the WILPF's attention was the issue of labor. The Liberian government had assured Firestone of an adequate labor supply, but it soon became apparent that the rubber plantation demands for workers interfered with a pre-existing arrangement whereby the government aided in the export of Liberian natives to the neighboring Spanish-controlled island of Fernando Po. According to later investigators, this labor system was "hardly distinguishable from organized slave trade, and . . . in the enforcement of this system the services . . . and influences of certain high Government officials, are constantly and systematically used."[36] If Firestone was to see a satisfactory return on investment, these government officials and the native chieftains who supplied the laborers would have to be persuaded to abandon this system in favor of Firestone's needs. Apparently this was done, for in his 1928 publication of *The Native Problem in Africa*, Harvard political science professor Raymond Buell reported that an almost identical system was arranged between Firestone and the Liberian Labor Bureau; labor that before went to Fernando Po now was being rerouted to rubber plantations.[37]

This system, wherein the Liberian government and native chieftains were paid by Firestone to "procure as much labor as possible," was an open invitation to abuse, and workers soon began to complain that they were not receiving wages due them. The U.S. State Department was aware of the situation, as indicated in a June 1928 memorandum sent by William Castle to the U.S. minister in the capital city of Monrovia in which he acknowledged that "it appears that the methods of the Liberian Labor Bureau in recruiting labor for Firestone have a tendency to result in conditions analogous to those of forced labor and are likely at some time to draw the well-merited censure of civilized opinion." Agreeing with Firestone and U.S. officials in Liberia that "it would be unfortunate from many points of view if the question were to be aired at this time," the State Department and the Liberian president attempted to discredit Buell's continued allegations of U.S. collusion, public and private, with the Liberian government in a system of forced labor to benefit Harvey Firestone.[38]

Despite these efforts, Firestone's activities in Liberia gained wider attention—and criticism—until finally in June 1929 the State Department was moved to publicly censure the black government for unseemly labor practices. Apparently the primary reason for this move was the State Department's wish to keep both itself and Firestone from being related in the public mind to any questionable business activities in the African nation. More publicity from various sources followed, and in 1930 came the investigation by the League of Nations. Its report, released in 1931, revealed that "indigenous Liberian workers . . . were being crudely exploited" by the ruling elite, and the scandal that ensued resulted in the resignations of president C. D. B. King and his vice president.[39]

The League's report, however, went beyond the issue of labor practices. It also disclosed the serious financial difficulties of Liberia, difficulties directly traceable to the 1926 loan agreement with Firestone's financial corporation. A special committee of the League Council, chaired by Viscount Robert Cecil of Great Britain, was formed, and after a six-week fact-finding mission to the beleaguered nation in late summer 1931, it made its recommendations. It urged a modification of the loan agreement in Liberia's favor and called for foreign economic administrators directed by a chief advisor who would be answerable to the League. Despite the considerable power and influence this advisor would have, Firestone and the U.S. government not only demanded greater authority for this administrator, they insisted that an American be named to the post, something to which Cecil was adamantly opposed. To make matters worse, Firestone stubbornly refused to renegotiate the terms of the loan.

Although not yet actively involved with the Liberian situation, the WILPF began to take greater notice of the ongoing problems experienced by the African nation. Balch was "uneasy" over the "loan situation" and thought the terms of the Firestone concession "perfectly inconceivable in their disregard for the most elementary protection of the negro population." In discussing her concerns with Raymond

Buell, NAACP Secretary; Walter White, *Crisis* editor W. E. B. DuBois, and Roger Baldwin of the ACLU, she noted that "they all feel as I do."[40]

The Liberians were also concerned, believing the League's plan to be a violation of their sovereignty and in May 1932, they submitted to the League Council an unequivocal statement that Liberia would not accept "any assistance, plan or suggestion relating to matters other than social, health, or finance reform."[41] Neither would they agree to foreign advisors from any country that held colonies bordering on Liberia nor an American as chief advisor on the grounds that an American could too easily become a Firestone sycophant.

The WILPF first became actively involved in the Liberian issue a few months later when in mid-summer 1932 Anna Graves, a Baltimore member at that time living in Switzerland, brought two representatives from the Liberian government to the WILPF's International Office in Geneva. Graves, who had worked with crippled children in London during World War I and subsequently taught English and history in China, Peru, and Mexico, introduced the Liberians to Detzer, temporarily working in the Geneva office, in the hopes that when she returned home, she would enlist the aid of the U.S. Section on behalf of the Africans.

Detzer did more than that. Before departing Geneva, she went to see Cecil of the League's Liberia Committee. He was most displeased with Firestone's refusal to negotiate and with U.S. demands for a chief advisor from the United States. "If the Council of the League is to take responsibility for the plan," he pointed out, "the chief administrator must be subject to it; an American could not be, since America is not in the League." Acknowledging the reasonableness of this position, Detzer also noted that Liberia's refusal to accept a chief advisor from a colonial power was reasonable as well, and thus suggested that Cecil appoint a Scandinavian or Swiss administrator as a compromise move. Cecil was not persuaded and brought the interview to an abrupt close, calling Detzer's views "extreme" and "radical" and the WILPF's position "unrealistic."[42]

By the end of 1932, frustrated over continuing inaction, the Liberian government suspended payment on the Firestone loan until such time as governmental revenues reached $700,000 annually. When Stimson condemned Liberia for its repudiationism, which he said amounted "in effect to the confiscation of moneys due to an American corporation," Cecil condemned Firestone's refusal to negotiate, informing Stimson "that several members of the Committee have arrived at the conclusion that the object of the Firestone Company was, by insisting on the rigid execution of what was, after all, a very onerous agreement, to drive the Liberian Government into such straits that they [sic] would be at the mercy of the corporation."[43] Somewhat chagrined, Stimson told a Firestone representative that continued State Department aid would be forthcoming only if and when the company commenced negotiations. Firestone agreed only if the State Department succeeded in persuading Liberia to rescind its payment moratorium. In the meantime, he wanted an armed invasion to coerce the Liberians accordingly.

It may be that the WILPF got wind of Firestone's demands for military intervention, for in January 1933 Detzer and Graves visited J. P. Moffat, chief of the Western European Division in the State Department. The visit did not go particularly well, and the situation continued to deteriorate until finally, just before leaving office, the Hoover administration appointed a special commissioner to Liberia. General Blanton Winship, "steeped in the traditional attitudes both of the army and the old South toward the Negro,"[44] as Detzer put it, sailed in February accompanied by Ellis Briggs, Chief of Liberian Affairs in the State Department and personal friend of Harvey Firestone, Jr. Perhaps this final effort on Hoover's part plus the knowledge that the Republican president would not have the desired four more years prompted Firestone to act. He soon presented his proposals for a settlement, termed "monstrous" by the British Foreign Office and characterized by Sundiata as having the effect of creating a "financial dictatorship."[45]

Negotiations could at last take place, however, and in June 1933, Winship and the League accepted a modified version of the Firestone proposals. The Firestone Company reduced the interest rate on Liberia's loan from 7 to 5 percent, and agreed that servicing the loan would not be the government's first financial priority. The Finance Corporation of America also agreed not to collect interest when Liberia's annual income was less than $500,000 a year. Yet at the same time, the Liberians were denied the right to use any funds for education as this function was to go entirely to foreign missionaries, and Liberia was forbidden to grant any concessions to another foreign power without the consent of the chief administrator whose authority would be strengthened; this virtual dictator had to be an American. As Detzer observed, "this plan of assistance, as it was quaintly called, would in reality have permitted an American corporation to hold Liberia in bondage for a century: in economic bondage through the concession; in financial bondage through the loan; through prohibition of Liberia's own educational institutions, in cultural bondage; and through the appointment of [an] American government administrator, in political bondage."[46] Liberia agreed; it refused to accept the plan.

Working closely with both the NAACP and other organizations within the peace movement that summer, the WILPF continued to pressure the State Department on behalf of the Liberians. When asked why the United States continued to insist on an American advisor, department officials blandly responded that the "traditional interest" of the United States in Liberia "made it natural for the United States to wish to see Liberia protected from any possible encroachments of European imperialism."[47] When Detzer asked if the department believed that Liberians cared whether the imperialism they suffered from was European or American, a smile was the only reply.

Although Detzer subsequently reported that according to her sources, State Department officials were "worried about further publicity and agitation" on the issue, in a memorandum to Roosevelt, J. P. Moffat noted that he did not take "the criticisms of either the radical negro groups, the pacifist groups or the professional anti-imperialists, such as Raymond Leslie Buell, too seriously."[48]

Intent on breaking the summer's stalemate, in the fall Britain and the United States delivered a joint note to Liberia demanding her immediate acceptance of the plan of assistance. Outraged, Detzer quickly wired L. A. Grimes, Liberia's Secretary of State: "Don't yield,"[49] and then stormed to the State Department where Ellis Briggs, surprised that the WILPF knew about the note, initially denied its existence. Detzer insisted otherwise, demanded to see a copy, and sat down, determined to wait indefinitely until Briggs produced it. Some few hours later, he did, but refused to provide her with a copy. Thoroughly frustrated, the WILPF was only partially mollified when not long thereafter the State Department told Firestone that the United States would no longer support the necessity of an American as chief advisor.

It may be that this decision was then relayed to the League's Liberia Committee, for in October it finally agreed that the chief advisor would be neither an American nor from a colonial power with territory adjacent to the country. The committee also responded to the education issue by allotting a certain portion of Liberia's income for public schools. The State Department approved and urged Liberia to do so. The Liberian government, however, had some serious reservations, mainly concerned with the powers accorded the chief advisor, which seemed to conflict with the country's constitution. Liberia's January 1934 acceptance of the plan was thus predicated upon its being modified accordingly, but the League simply responded by setting a May deadline for the country to accept or reject the plan as proposed in October. Libera refused, Firestone demanded military intervention, and black organizations and the WILPF continued to pressure the State Department. Continuing stalemate ensued, with frustration on all sides.

On 18 May 1934, with Liberians still opposed to the plan without modification, the Liberia Committee withdrew it altogether. The situation remained in limbo until July when the State Department sent a special investigator to the African republic. Upon his arrival, Harry McBride (a financial advisor to Liberia during World War I) learned that the new president, Edwin Barclay, was just completing his own three-year plan of development and assistance. Although McBride thought Barclay's plan inadequate with respect to the power of foreign advisors, he found the financial aspects sound, especially in light of the country's improving revenue picture. By the end of the year the Liberian legislature had approved the plan and two foreign advisors were already on the job.

McBride implicitly recommended the Barclay plan to the State Department, which also found it acceptable, but Firestone vacillated. Informed by State Department officials that military coercion was out of the question, Firestone weakened and, finally, on 1 January 1935, the Liberian government, the Finance Corporation of America, and the National City Bank of New York signed an agreement incorporating the financial provisions of Barclay's plan. Two months later, the two sides signed a second agreement pursuant to the land concession and in May, the United States extended diplomatic recognition. Liberian sovereignty remained intact.

But what of the labor issue that had given rise to international attention in the first place? Somewhere along the way this aspect of the situation seemed to have been lost in the controversy over the Firestone loan and land concession. As soon as Barclay took the reins of government in 1931 his administration enacted a whole series of reforms. With respect to labor, the legislature passed laws prohibiting labor export and forced labor. Governmental machinery in the interior of the country was revamped and a public health service established. Despite some internal opposition to these and other reforms, by the end of 1936 stability was restored, and the Barclay regime endured until 1944.

Just how significant were the efforts of the WILPF in influencing U.S. policy toward Liberia? After all, as a letter from the organization soliciting funds for the cause noted in September 1933, "one of the members of our staff [Detzer] is devoting practically her entire time to Liberia—speaking, interviewing officials, sending delegations to the State Department, securing publicity."[50] Certainly the Liberians thought such effort valuable; a committee "representing the women of Liberia" wrote Detzer of its "thanks and appreciation for the very laudable, timely, and singular efforts you are putting forth,"[51] and L. A. Grimes offered Detzer a token of his gratitude "in the form of a diploma and insignia of the Order of African Redemption. I sincerely feel," he wrote in the autumn of 1933, "that the modified view of the American government . . . is due more to your efforts than to those of any other single individual."[52]

Yet as historian I. K. Sundiata notes, those who have studied the influence, or lack thereof, of black organizations "and their friends" on U.S. policy toward Africa generally and Liberia in particular, conclude that such influence was negligible at best. The State Department, as he points out, knew "the establishment of a virtual American colony in Africa might render the continued espousal of the Monroe Doctrine difficult to justify, and would unquestionably arouse the suspicion of Europe and South America." Moreover, as Stimson saw it in early 1931 when under pressure from Firestone to intercede militarily, "no compensating gain, in profit or prestige, would accrue to the United States if it took over Liberia."[53]

If U.S. policy toward Liberia reflected only the realpolitik of national self-interest, what impact did the humanitarian concerns of the WILPF or NAACP have on either the Hoover or Roosevelt administrations? Was it all just wasted effort? Sundiata thinks not, suggesting that "while American blacks and their friends did not set policy on Liberia, they delimited it."[54] And they did so by virtue of the black vote, restricted as it was. There is ample evidence among memoranda circulated internally between and among State Department officials and the White House in both administrations indicating that a 1933 WILPF observation that "thirteen million [black] votes are not to be ignored" was not taken lightly.[55] Thus it would seem that although the policy of the U.S. government toward Liberia was not motivated by the same altruistic concerns of the liberal black and white groups, that policy was at least influenced in a less imperialistic direction.

But by the time the Liberian crisis was settled, the WILPF confronted a far more menacing world than when it began, not only overseas but at home as well. In both respects, racial and ethnic discrimination joined hands with economic insecurity as the peace movement faced the ultimate challenge to its hopes for a democratically organized world—fascism.

Pacifist organizations such as the WILPF deplored fascism not only because it threatened militarism and war, but because it meant totalitarianism. And totalitarianism signaled the death of participatory democracy as well as the surrender of the individual to the power of the state, particularly as the state came to be symbolized in the figure of one apparently all-powerful and charismatic individual. Clearly Adolf Hitler was such a figure and the WILPF, particularly in its European sections, was quick to see the threat to democratic institutions and processes that the Nazi leader posed.

Of all interwar WILPF activists, none was more intellectually astute or politically perceptive than the brilliant Gertrude Baer. Born in Czechoslovakia in 1890 and the first woman to become under secretary of state in the Ministry of Social Welfare in the Bavarian Republic prior to World War I, Baer was a staunch feminist and pacifist who was "completely emancipated" from the nationalistic fervor so prevalent among others of her generation. As early as the mid-1920s Baer warned her colleagues about Hitler, "a man on horseback" who was "stirring up the discontent and humiliation of the defeated German people and molding it into a dangerous force."[56] Baer took seriously the plans and doctrines outlined by the Nazi leader in his 1924 book, *Mein Kampf,* and as a major figure in the WILPF's German Section, she watched with foreboding the growth of Hitler's National Socialist German Workers Party, aware that it was neither socialist nor representative of the working class.

It was not that the U.S. Section was blind to the issues of territorial aggrandizement, persecuted minorities, or anti-Semitism before Hitler's rise to power. At the 1924 WILPF International Congress delegates adopted resolutions condemning all such undemocratic manifestations of power. The women urged the League of Nations to organize a "special permanent Committee on National Minorities" and agreed "to strive against Anti-Semitism" and economic imperialism. At the summer school following the Congress, a pamphlet on "Anti-Semitism, an Aftermath of the War" by Auguste Kirchoff was among the literature distributed for discussion among participants.[57]

In condemning the Treaty of Versailles as a punitive peace settlement that sowed the seeds of future conflict, the WILPF, supported by a number of equally concerned organizations, called upon President Coolidge "to convene a conference of the debtor and creditor nations to make definite settlement . . . of reparations, interallied debts, and disarmament, in order to achieve a new peace."[58] These issues, along with a persistent call for abolition of customs and tariff barriers, U.S. diplomatic recognition of the Soviet Union, and an end to economic imperialism continued to be an important part of the WILPF's program throughout the 1920s.

So, too, with the WILPF sections in Europe where peace sentiment was especially strong, particularly among the German women, thanks to the effective and capable leadership of Lida Gustava Heymann, Anita Augspurg, and, of course, Gertrude Baer. In the 1920s the forty-two branches of the German Section were active against imperialism, drug trafficking, anti-Semitism, military spending, *Anschluss*, and the death penalty. They worked diligently in behalf of progressive and pacifistic education, penal reform, an eight-hour work day, release of political prisoners, appointment of women to political office, free trade, total disarmament, and a "broad and generous treatment of minorities." Although Bavaria "had to face the 'Hitler' militaristic agitation, . . . the Munich group of the W.I.L. had a pacifist exhibition which attracted great attention and which has been loaned to other towns."[59]

As the decade of the 1930s opened, not much progress had been made with respect to either the economic or related problems stemming from the Great War. As the WILPF pointed out in the early autumn of 1930, "in spite of the Locarno Pact, the Kellogg Treaty, the Naval Conference, nations continue to arm, to build high tariffs, to suppress minorities. The Peace Treaties, the War Debts, the burden of German Reparations, are ugly and staggering problems."[60] In the United States, the WILPF opposed the Hawley-Smoot tariff, despite a protest resignation of some members who believed that the issue was not "germane" to a peace program. WILPF leaders thought otherwise. A prohibitively high tariff, they asserted, "will provoke foreign retaliation against our exports; . . . increase unemployment . . . and the general cost of living, and will inflate the profits of a few at the expense of the majority."[61] As the Depression deepened from 1931 into 1932, the WILPF called for settlement of these economic issues with even greater urgency, and in light of the upcoming disarmament conference, stepped up its pressure for both repudiation of the "Sole German War Guilt" clause in the peace treaties, and U.S. recognition of the Soviet Union. In this effort, the women were aided by the FOR, NCCCW, EPC, the Pacifist Action Committee, and Senator William Borah.

It may be that the WILPF's persistent call for U.S. recognition of the Soviet Union triggered the new wave of attacks against the organization for being "Red" which picked up again in 1931. At least that's what Detzer thought many years later. Although the WILPF advocated recognition of Russia throughout the 1920s, with the deteriorating economic scene in the early 1930s and a major disarmament conference in the offing, recognition of the largest nation on the face of the globe by the richest and most powerful nation seemed more important than ever. As Borah put it to Detzer in the early spring of 1931, "We ought to be on speaking terms with Russia, as Russia and the United States are the most important and powerful nations in the world, and . . . as a great nation, we ought not to go to the Disarmament Conference and not have proper official relations."[62] Thus the WILPF became more visible politically as it increased its pressure for recognition accordingly.

By early May of 1931, Francis Ralston Welsh was on the attack again, this time with an even greater intensity than in the mid-1920s. In an article written for the American Legion, Welsh linked the WILPF, the ACLU, the left-wing Industrial Workers of the World (IWW), the League for Industrial Democracy, and Bryn Mawr College with communism. He even accused Leopold Stokowski of the Philadelphia Symphony of putting "communist propaganda in some of his orchestra performances." Reserving to Jane Addams the dubious distinction of being "in more pink and red affairs than any other person in the United States," Welsh's racism also emerged in his observations about WILPF leader Lucy Biddle Lewis.

According to Welsh, Lewis, when asked whether she advocated interracial marriage, replied, "eventually." That was proof enough for Welsh. Members of the WILPF, he said, "swallow Communist doctrines even up to that point." Naturally, therefore, any organization that would support racial equality *and* "recognition of the bestial Soviet government of Russia" was "shamelessly unpatriotic."[63] Convinced that Welsh's diatribe was libelous, the WILPF nevertheless did not sue.

Welsh's totally unfounded charges were among the more ludicrous of the various attacks against the WILPF in the early 1930s. In the opinion of E. H. Shaffer of the *New Mexico State Tribune* in Albuquerque, the War Department was again the major culprit: "Through its military intelligence service, [it] is still maintaining a rather thorough espionage system that has for its purpose the discouragement of all peace movements on the part of the citizen." Referring to recent incidents in which WILPF member Louise Weir was accused of radical and "sinister designs" by a local minister (and former military chaplain) and "a Captain John Schmidt, on detached service here from the regular army," Shaffer concluded that "its the same old story. . . . The whole thing smacks of the covert espionage system."[64]

In August 1931, a prospective WILPF member was informed that the group was a "menace," a "subversive" organization of communists and Bolsheviks. When asked for evidence of such allegations, the accuser simply responded that the War Department could confirm the charges. The War Department subsequently answered a letter of inquiry by stating that in peace time it did not give out information against organizations or individuals, but that the desired information concerning the WILPF could be obtained from the DAR. When Hannah Hull and Detzer pointed out that the Department "had overstepped" its own policy "by referring persons to an organization which, according to past experience, obviously would give derogatory information" regarding the WILPF, neither the Assistant Secretary of War nor the Assistant Chief of Staff was "able to see the connection." When then asked "if inquiries regarding the Daughters of the American Revolution would be referred to the Women's International League for information," the two men still "claimed to see no parallel."[65]

Allegations of the WILPF's communism and subversive activities continued throughout the remainder of 1931 into 1932, but there were some encouraging notes as well. In February a former American Legion Post Commander in Pennsylvania who was also a disabled veteran from World War I wrote a "dramatic answer" to those attacking the WILPF, and in May, a Legion chaplain from Delaware wrote a lengthy rebuttal to the WILPF's detractors, asserting that it was "not a communistic organization nor does it have communistic affiliations." Refuting point by point the various items of anti-WILPF propaganda circulating among Legion members, he noted that the WILPF's programs and policies were "based on high ideals and motives of justice, freedom, and service" and observed that "servicemen who fought in the 'war to end war' certainly can have no valid objection to an organization pledged to carry out the ideals for which thousands of our comrades died."[66]

In early 1933 Hamilton Fish, Jr., of the House of Representatives went on record in support of the WILPF against the charges that it was "anti-religious and friendly to communism." Defining briefly a communist as someone "who preaches class hatred, atheism, the destruction of private property and advocates the overthrow of our republican form of government by force and violence," Fish did not think such a description could be applied to the WILPF. Commenting that he did not always see eye-to-eye with the women pacifists, "I see no reason why anyone who differs with me should be charged with being a Communist," he added.[67]

The flurry of attacks against the WILPF did not deter it in its calls for diplomatic recognition of the Soviet Union, or for adjustment of war debts, reparations, tariffs, and other related issues stemming from World War I. The women praised President Hoover for his 1931 "moratorium relief" and by 1932 noted "the fast growing conviction among many people in this country that readjustment of debts must be linked with disarmament."[68] The advent of a new administration in Washington with the November victory of the Democrats did not hold particular promise as Roosevelt had made no statement with respect to the debt issue, and his party had "come out specifically against" their cancellation.[69] While the Eighth Conference on the Cause and Cure of War, organized around the theme of "War and Waste," devoted an entire session to the debt issue, the WILPF hoped "that every effort possible will be made to utilize the debt situation in favor of disarmament," and even before Roosevelt took office in March 1933, urged the president-elect accordingly.[70]

As for recognition of the Soviet Union, the WILPF was encouraged; as Borah pointed out, the major stumbling-block in the Hoover administration had been the president himself. Now the senator indicated that because the Democrats wished recognition for such a move, he would push the issue in the Foreign Relations Committee just as soon as the new administration came into office. But by the time Roosevelt began to act on the many pressing problems confronting the country, the political situation in Germany had taken a decided turn for the worse, thus drawing the WILPF's attention to events overseas.

Although the peace movement in Germany was strong, with the WILPF an integral part of it, Gertrude Baer did not cease to warn her colleagues of the growing revolutionary power of Hitler's political party. Yet when Balch visited Germany in November 1931 after an absence of some thirty-five years, her reaction was very different. "I went to two Hitlerite meetings," she reported, "and did not find them impressive. I got no sense of a gathering storm, none of a reservoir of power, will, energy, enthusiasm, or a thought-out purpose, and certainly of no great enthusiasm for the person of Adolf Hitler." Commenting on the "weedy undernourished ineffectual-looking types of boys and men" who made up the Hitler supporters, she contrasted them with the students she met at an "academic lecture" who were "of a quite different type from the 'Nazis'. . . . My impression when I started to Germany in the beginning of October," she concluded, "was that it was on the eve of Revolution. This impression was changed by what I saw and heard. I give it for what it is worth, but it is not mine only but also that of very competent observers—and it was that a Revolution was not impending."[71]

Within eight months Baer was reporting a much different story. "The Reichstag elections of July 31, 1932 stood, even more than previous Parliamentary elections, under the sign of force. Fists and weapons," she wrote, "wordy courage and unexhausted financial reservoirs were decisive factors. Real conviction, qualities of the mind and spirit and reflection were more and more crowded out." Documenting the extensive effort of the peace forces to counter the "brute force" of the opposition, including many letters to the government "taking a stand against private military organizations, civil war, terrorism and force," she nevertheless concluded that "neo-militarism is triumphing."[72]

Baer's observations were corroborated by Detzer when she visited Europe that summer. In "talking, talking, talking" with members of the peace movement and various political figures, she reported that a major concern was "how to swing the coming revolution in all countries with as little violence as possible." Left-wing groups were "all hopeless of any kind of peace and are preparing for the Fascist rise the next few years," even in Holland. "Queer," she remarked with trepidation, "but after these months over here my whole view of the international situation is shifted[;] that is, things seem more dangerous than I knew." And part of that danger, Detzer believed, threatened Baer. "I am so anxious that some way be found to get her out of Germany. I am so afraid they will kill her. . . . She ought not risk her life in Berlin. . . . Some of the younger members [of the German WILPF] . . . are so worried about her being there."[73] And with good reason: Gertrude Baer was not only a pacifist, feminist, and socialist; she was a Jew.

With Nazism triumphant in early 1933 by virtue of Hitler's appointment as chancellor, the violence attendant to the new Reichstag elections, and the Enabling Law, the political threat that Hitler posed to communists, socialists, and Jews became real. With civil liberties quickly suspended, the terror and persecution began in earnest and not only was Baer's life in jeopardy, so, too, were the lives of all German WILPF women. The officers of the International WILPF met in Cologne at an emergency session in early March to try "to work out some way by which we can help our friends in Germany. It seems that protests from groups abroad might be helpful," wrote staff member Anne Zueblin Forsythe to the U.S. Section, "and anything you can do in that way would be valuable. Protests should be sent to the German government, especially as far as we are concerned, at the arrest of pacifists." But, she warned, "Our own friends in Germany should *not* be written to."[74]

Balch was horrified at the accounts of terror coming out of Germany, writing to Camille Drevet in the Geneva Office that she had read that "60 pacifists (among others) have been arrested." She immediately wrote the Secretary of State of her "deep concern about present extremism in Germany" and her hope that the State Department "in endeavoring to safeguard American citizens will also find ways consistent with diplomatic usage and national friendship for Germany to make it clear that American opinion is most unfavorably affected by the news reaching us."[75] A few days later the National Board of the U.S. Section adopted a resolution to be sent to Hitler through the German Embassy in Washington. "We are shocked and dismayed at the reports coming out of Germany as to instances of illegality, violence and torture," wrote the women. "If true they constitute a terrible strain on the name of a great country which has contributed so much to culture and science. We look to those now in power in Germany to reassure the opinion of the world, and to afford justice and civic protection to all, without regard to class, religion, race or political opinions."[76]

By the end of March, Balch joined James T. Shotwell, John Dewey, Reinhold Niebuhr, and Roger Baldwin, among others, in forming a Provisional Committee For Protest Against German Fascist Atrocities. Despite the emphatic denial of fascist sympathizer George Sylvester Viereck to this committee that "a wave of terror is sweeping Germany" and insisting that the stories of Nazi atrocities "are 99-1/2% invention,"[77] the committee was not so persuaded. WILPF leaders urged the branches to send letters of protest to the German Embassy in Washington, to a nearby German Consul, or to the Geneva Office without delay; the response was overwhelming. From cities all over the country came letters not unlike the following one from San Diego:

> The Women's International League of San Diego is keenly aware of the injustice of the Treaty of Versailles and of the fact that the allied governments, including our own, have not kept faith with the German people in regard to the reduction of armaments. Our League has always protested against the treaty, and we have constantly urged our own government to accept the same armament status as that required of Germany.
>
> Today we are saddened by the policy of repression and persecution adopted by the present German government toward Germans of the Jewish race and of dissenting political and economic opinions. We base our judgment not on newspaper stories but on the authorized statements of Nazi leaders encouraging psychological and economic pressure.
>
> In joining our voice to other protests, we are not forgetful of the

fact that some of our own countrymen are guilty of shocking racial discrimination. We do not fail to oppose this discrimination at home with all our strength.

We are convinced that no healthful development for Germany can come out of a policy of repression, that such a policy serves to delay the settlement of Germany's just international grievances, and that it is foreign to the genius of the German people for whom we feel the deepest sympathy and admiration.[78]

At the end of May Detzer and Balch called on German Ambassador Hans Luther in Washington who told them of the "many protests" his office had received from WILPF branches. Luther was not upset over the flood of letters, but "regretted" that the women "did not understand that Hitler was saving Europe from communism." He, like Viereck, denied that any atrocities were occurring, blaming "newspaper propaganda" for the distortions of truth.[79] Yet Danish WILPF leader Thora Daugaard was arrested while crossing Germany in the attempt to get home; noted WILPF pacifist and German political activist Emma Machenhauser was arrested and briefly imprisoned; Anita Augspurg and Lida Gustava Heymann, traveling abroad when Hitler came to power, could not safely return home; nor could Gertrude Baer, who was in Zurich for health reasons when the terror began. Many other German WILPF members fled the country in fear for their lives. As Forsythe wrote from Geneva, "the situation everywhere seems very grave and critical and our German friends are in a most precarious position."[80]

Nor was the fear and intimidation confined to Germany. On 6 June the Swiss government, bowing to outside pressure, ordered Camille Drevet of France, the WILPF's International Secretary in Geneva, to leave the country by the twentieth. At first denied an extension, intervention on her behalf by the French ambassador and other prominent European political figures may have had a positive effect, for although she was denied permission to remain in Switzerland indefinitely because of her "anti-militarist and revolutionary propaganda," she was soon given an extension until 14 July. A second extension to April 1934 was subsequently granted, but as Forsythe exclaimed in disbelief, "This is democratic and free Switzerland! Alas, all countries are about equally democratic today!"[81]

According to other WILPF reports, Chancellor Engelbert Dollfuss had dissolved Austria's Parliament by emergency decree; freedom of speech and assembly were abolished. While trying to counter the challenges from both communists and socialists, the government's most serious threat came from the Nazis, "young men fond of uniforms and parades." Fascism was growing in Belgium where "the press was being muzzled" and an expanded police force was being equipped with military weapons and powers. Fascism was beginning to gain in Czechoslovakia, but the government "strongly punished" paramilitary organizations so the situation remained fairly calm for the moment. Although the French were "conscious of the danger of fascism" and were "reacting against it," signs of its growth were seen "in arrests of Communists and preventive arrests." Although peace sentiment was increasing in England, the middle class in Denmark was "turning towards support of Hitler." The fascist groups in Holland were "small" and were "ridiculed," but in fascist Italy women workers who organized and participated in strikes were "arrested and tortured." "Feverish military preparations" were taking place while every day "propaganda for war in Italy" intensified. Fascism in Germany alarmed the Polish "because of danger regarding Danzig," but nevertheless, "the economic crisis" overshadowed everything else there.[82]

For the WILPF the "economic crisis" everywhere was the key to fascist growth with its terror, intimidation, and persecution. As Heymann asserted with respect to Germany, the Hitler movement was "largely the result of the terrible unemployment." Baer concurred, but stressed the links between capitalism and fascism. The latter was always "the common front of capitalism and the privileged classes." Even in the United States, reported Amy Woods, economic crisis had brought "a dictatorship with capital in the saddle," although of a different type from either communism or fascism. Although for the first time in U.S. history a woman, Frances Perkins, was appointed to the president's cabinet, "government relief for the unemployed has tended towards military control" and there "has been increase in the military budget." Madeleine Doty was not much more optimistic, for although she acknowledged that "at the moment there was greater freedom in the U.S. than there had been and a more progressive attitude," she also believed that "in all probability fascism would come ultimately in the U.S. as it had elsewhere."[83]

Given the WILPF's understanding that the depression was the primary reason for the emergence of fascism, it called upon President Roosevelt in mid-April 1933 to address himself to a number of critically important issues at the upcoming Economic Conference. First, noted the women, "the extreme urgency of situation requires that the Conference should begin its work . . . without delay," and second, that when it did, "each delegation should be prepared to make sacrifices in behalf of the whole." These included the reduction of tariffs and the elimination of "world debts . . . by a policy of generous concessions. The principle of economic nationalism . . . should be repudiated" with the "prosperity of the people" kept uppermost in mind, "not the advantage of those who direct industry."[84]

Responding to the recent violence and terror abroad, the WILPF's International Executive then passed two resolutions accordingly. It urged all governments to prohibit the sale of arms or munitions to any country that resorted to violence, and to forbid loans and credits to any nation deemed by the League of Nations to have "violated its international engagements." More strongly worded was the resolution regarding the treatment of Jews: "The measures of repression and the special laws treating Jewish citizens as an inferior class because they belong to a different race are degrading not to Jews but to humanity. The Women's International League for Peace and Freedom protests . . . against the dissemination of hatred of Jews . . . and the refusal to them of the protection of the regular police; against depriving Jews of all means of livelihood within Germany and at the same time compelling them to remain inside the country; . . . against the fact that Jews . . . are deprived of the rights of citizens in general without being given the rights of a minority."[85]

With respect to stronger economic measures aimed at nations which violated international law or human rights, the U.S. Section was not of one mind. In March 1932 when the issue of an economic boycott arose at the National Board meeting, the women voted "that the United States should not become involved in the policy of boycott or the application of economic pressure except in conjunction with the Great Powers." As for a personal, or "private" boycott, the board chose to leave that decision up to each individual, but noted its "unqualified disapproval of any propaganda for boycott based on ill will or likely to call forth ill will."[86]

A little over a year after the Hitler terror began, the subject of an economic boycott came up again, this time with respect to the WILPF "good-will tour" of Europe planned for the summer. Earlier arrangements had the women sailing on the North German Lloyd steamship line, now a focus of protest not only because of Hitler's repression, but also because it was widely believed that the steamship company was subsidized by the German government. Even after being informed by the German Consul that such was not the case, many of the women still wished to cancel the WILPF's plans with the North German Lloyd line. Others, however, pointed out that this action "would establish a precedent of boycott." As Detzer noted, "for several years members of the National Board . . . have discussed at great length the whole policy of sanctions, and there is a divided opinion about it, but up to date the Board has not agreed to a policy of boycott. To do so now in connection with this German situation," she agreed, "would definitely commit the organization to this policy."[87] Given the lack of consensus, the WILPF decided to arrange for alternate passage as well, leaving the decision up to each individual.

Later that year the boycott issue emerged again at the October Board meeting. A formal vote was taken, showing five members in favor of such a step but ten who were opposed. That negative response was the WILPF's answer to a request by the American League for the Defense of Jewish Rights later that month to join a "National Boycott movement to combat the diabolic forces at work in Germany." As Hannah Hull explained, the WILPF had been "constantly working to do all that we can to oppose the actions of the Hitler regime. We have written . . . Hitler several times, have interviewed the German Ambassador concerning certain individuals in vain and have extended hospitality to German refugees in Geneva."

But as far as a boycott was concerned, she said, "most of us feel that it is wrong in principle, and especially inadvisable in Germany's case." First, she noted, "the Allies are largely responsible for Hitlerism through the Treaty of Versailles and the refusal to disarm." Second, a boycott would "open the way for propaganda for Hitlerism in Germany and lead them to say, 'Now you see what we told you is true: the whole world is against us' with the result of even greater unity within Germany and a stronger determination to prepare to fight the world." Third, a boycott could thus be used as "justification for a great increase in armaments," and last, because Hitlerism involved persecution of pacifists and socialists as well as Jews, a boycott might increase "persecutions of liberals" in Germany while contributing to a growth of anti-Semitism in the United States. Hull concluded, therefore, "I am more and more persuaded that the only way to deal with Germany's situation is by the so-called peaceful methods of protest and persuasion."[88]

As the situation in Europe deteriorated, the WILPF continued its protests and attempts at persuasion. When the Austrian government cracked down on socialists in early 1934, Emmy Freundlich, WILPF member, President of the International Cooperative Women's Guilds, and former deputy in the Austrian Parliament, was arrested and imprisoned without charge. In its letter of protest to the Austrian government, the women noted that the "outrages in Vienna" against socialists had "caused astonishment and dismay in the United States. . . . We are also informed," the women continued, "that Austria is going to follow the unspeakable example of Germany in organizing concentration camps. . . . May we, as friends of Austria, protest against such action and urge the early release of all political prisoners?"[89] After a visit to the Austrian Embassy, WILPF leaders asked all branches to write letters of protest and inquiry regarding Freundlich's situation.

The severe conditions for female political prisoners in Germany, reported by a British WILPF member whose close friend from Berlin was imprisoned for several weeks, prompted the New York branch to send the following resolution to Ambassador Luther that fall: "Resolved, that we ask the German Ambassador to transmit to the German Government our request that concentration camps for political prisoners be abolished, and that all women now in prison or in concentration camps for political reasons be immediately released."[90] In December the National Office sent another letter of protest to Luther occasioned by the "accounts of the barbarous mistreatment of certain German women." Naming specifically seven women involved, the WILPF protested their arrest "in the strongest possible terms" because it involved, "contrary to all legal principles, retroactive application of the law."[91] Balch sent a telegram to the same effect to Hitler.

By early 1935 Baer reported that Europe was "going Fascist everywhere," and that the world was plunging toward war with ever-accelerating speed. Detzer agreed and felt that "a peculiar type of American Fascism" was emerging in the United States as well. At a public meeting where she had recently given a speech, an avowed fascist leader, unnamed, openly welcomed its coming and acknowledged, after being pressured by Detzer, that when it did, "women would be thrown back into the kitchen, as they had been in Germany. . . . [H]e said *he* liked to cook, and that he thought that women were better off in the kitchen than in offices." She was concerned about the political trends in the United States because she was learning how difficult it was to persuade Americans of the dangers; "they refuse to see them," she remarked unhappily.[92]

The threat to peace posed by fascism abroad and the danger to democracy at home from like-minded sentiment compelled pacifists to work more closely with all factions opposed to war and, particularly after Hitler's rise to power, with communists and socialists. Because both left-wing groups were among those targeted by the Nazi leader for annihilation, it was only logical that they responded quickly in a more

active and militant fashion than other antiwar advocates. Thus when
the communists organized the American League Against War and Fascism (ALAWF) in September 1933, the WILPF lent the new group its
cooperation, despite the fact that such affiliation would only feed the
animosity of anti-pacifist "red-baiters."

As Detzer explained the WILPF's position to pacifist Kirby Page,
editor of *The World Tomorrow*, who was more skeptical of affiliation with
the communists than the women, the WILPF "had no illusions about
Communists" and their often "confused ethics, sophomoric tactics, and
insufferable arrogance." But, she added, the WILPF was more concerned that in this time of "terrible crisis," a "united front" of all antiwar groups was the only possible way of preventing in the United States
what had so recently transpired in Germany. There, she reminded
Page, "division among the radical groups . . . destroyed pacifists, liberals, socialists, and communists alike. . . . By a similar division in the
United States or elsewhere in the world, the radical organizations are
bound to go down if a real war crisis comes in these days of Fascist
dictatorships, while in a united front," she asserted, "there is at least
the possibility of preventing such a crisis from developing into war
itself."[93]

And prevention of war was the ultimate issue for the WILPF. If
allying itself with the ALAWF might aid in that effort, then the risk of
alienating the more timorous among antiwar advocates or even breath-
ing new life into overly zealous "patriotic" organizations was well worth
it. For by the time of the ALAWF's creation, it was clear that coalition
politics to create peace was no longer an appropriate response to a
drastically changed reality. Not only was fascist repression on the march
in Europe but militaristic aggression had reared its ugly head in the
Pacific as Japan began to challenge the status quo in that region of the
world. The politics of coalition to create peace of the 1920s quickly
gave way to coalition politics to prevent war in the 1930s.

10

Munitions and Manchuria

THROUGHOUT THE 1920S and into the early 1930s there had been hope and optimism among pacifists that their "propeace" struggle would be rewarded. As Progressives, they were inclined to see the issue of peace more as a matter of "when" rather than "if," and there was good reason for such faith. There had been real progress in the postwar decade, or so it appeared. Washington held the Conference on the Limitation of Armaments; war was averted in Central America, the Kellogg-Briand Pact was approved; three disarmament conferences took place; and, after a shaky beginning, Europe settled down. France and England seemed to be as strong as ever, Germany had made a remarkable recovery from the impact of the Versailles Treaty, the Locarno Pact was signed, and people everywhere appeared to be enjoying a higher standard of living.

With the onset of economic depression this all fell apart. The signs of progress toward peace, freedom, and justice showed themselves to be more apparent than real. The gathering storm of World War II began to rumble accordingly and when Japan made an aggressive move in the fall of 1931 by invading Manchuria, the optimistic propeace effort of the 1920s slowly became the desperate antiwar struggle of the 1930s. Part of this struggle for the WILPF was its goal of an investigation of the munitions industry. One of the reasons for the women's interest in such an investigation stemmed from yet another failure of their national leaders, the failure to utilize the peacekeeping machinery constructed in the 1920s to resolve the Far Eastern crisis of the early 1930s.

On 18 September 1931, less than a month before the WILPF disarmament caravan motored triumphantly to the door of the White

House, the Japanese army invaded Manchuria. According to historian David Burner, "Japan's leaders claimed that their attacks were intended only to protect the lives and rights of their own citizens, harassed by nationalistic Chinese in a traditionally Japanese sphere of influence." Yet as events would subsequently indicate, "the Japanese objective was in fact the complete occupation of Manchuria."[1] Universal disarmament was more important than ever, but less likely to be achieved now that the uneasy postwar peace had been violated by a major world power, one that would soon join in disarmament negotiations after what appeared to all concerned to be a rather clear-cut case of hostile aggression against a neighbor.

As far as the WILPF was concerned, Japanese military action in China was a clear violation of the Kellogg-Briand Pact as well as the Nine Power Pact that safeguarded the rights and interests of China, and to which China, Japan, and the United States were signatories. The WILPF had long been aware of the Far East as a potential trouble spot; as far back as its annual meeting in April 1925 historian and WILPF member Mary Beard had addressed the group on "The Japanese-American Crisis," pointing out the arrogance with which whites had historically treated the Japanese, and noting that trade rivalry in China was the fundamental cause of the present crisis. "Let us watch for the incident that may set fire to the tinder," she had warned.[2] Now, apparently, it was here.

Within a few hours of learning of the outbreak of hostilities in the Far East, the WILPF sent a telegram to the White House urging President Hoover to invoke the terms of the Nine Power Pact. Two days later Detzer went to the Far Eastern division of the State Department where she was told that although the situation was indeed of concern, no action on the part of the United States was yet contemplated. When asked why the Department did not act on Article 7 of the Nine Power treaty, which provided for consultation regarding suitable joint action among the signatories, the official responded that the article stipulated consultation only if it was deemed "desirable," and at this point, it was not considered desirable.[3]

The WILPF deemed it most desirable and as the days passed with the crisis deepening and still no action on the part of the United States, a deputation from the WILPF called on the Secretary of State. Henry Stimson was obviously deeply concerned over the situation "but just as deeply annoyed by the concern of a disturbed public."[4] As he would again on 6 October when confronted by a delegation from the Emergency Peace Committee (organized in April to mobilize left-wing pacifist opinion), Stimson now told the women he could make no commitment as to the future action of this country concerning the crisis in Manchuria. Unaware at the time that the secretary was trying to convince the president to invoke the Nine Power Pact, WILPF leaders, disturbed over Stimson's apparent lack of decisiveness, urged their members to wire Hoover at once, calling for U.S. adherence to the terms of the treaty. The final leg of the disarmament caravan to Washington was fast becoming anticlimactic.

Telegrams pleading for the WILPF's intercession on behalf of China from the Chinese legation and a group of Chinese citizens prompted WILPF leaders to visit the State Department once again. The women spoke with Stanley Hornbeck, Chief of the Far Eastern division, who stressed the need for "easing along the civilian government in Japan." Then, much to the pacifists' amazement, he "dogmatically stated that treaties were to be used only as a last resort, and not as a prevention for war, . . . that if they were invoked and were not successful then a war would have to be indulged in." Detzer was not convinced that this "new attitude toward peace treaties" was shared by other State Department officials, and although lengthy interviews with Assistant Secretary of State James Rogers and other officials in mid-November did not particularly clarify the issue, they did shed some light on related questions.[5]

Since the Manchurian crisis had begun, Detzer was only one among many concerned over the paucity of reliable information about the true state of affairs in the Far East. She was disturbed as well as frustrated by the apparent unwillingness of the State Department to keep the American public informed as to the state of negotiations, if indeed any negotiations were actually taking place. Reinforcing her concern on this score was an article that appeared in the *Japan Times* of 19 October stating "that the United States Government is very favorably inclined toward Japan."[6]

Aware that the American public did not reflect this sentiment but on the contrary was sympathetic to the Chinese, Detzer could not help but wonder what her government was saying behind the scenes to give the Japanese such an impression. With echoes of the secret diplomacy of World War I reverberating through her head, Detzer wrote Stimson on 11 November urging the government to publish its communications with regard to the negotiations as Japan and the League of Nations were doing. The shroud of secrecy was giving "a false and inaccurate impression of the United States' position." The WILPF, she continued, considered it of the utmost importance that Japanese citizens "should know how the people of the United States view the refusal of their government to submit the Manchurian questions to impartial investigation."[7] To persist in secret diplomacy, she concluded, was all the more reprehensible given the failure of the United States to demand observance of the Kellogg Treaty and the Nine Power Pact.

One of the more interesting things the WILPF learned from Detzer's interviews with Rogers was that diplomats within the State Department were divided on the issue, and the president was the one advocating the policy of secret diplomacy. This disturbed the women all the more. The WILPF did not believe that any man, regardless of his sincerity or honesty, was "wise enough or good enough to hold this enormous power which directly involves the peace of the world without the searching light of public opinion on it."[8] The women believed that public opinion should be formed on the basis of accurate information, not ignorance. That was the essence of a functioning democracy. The U.S. citizen, insisted the WILPF, had not only the need but the right to know what the government was doing and why: "It is very difficult to know just how to proceed, as we have so little information as to what has already been done by the Department of State."[9] Pacifists' attempts to obtain information were politely but firmly rebuffed by a State Department unwilling to divulge its action.

Yet with all of this, there were some encouraging signs. By October 1931 the United States was cooperating with the League of Nations; Hoover sent two diplomats to sit in on the meetings of the council, a move that the WILPF heartily applauded. Stimson urged the president to go one step further by joining the League in imposing economic sanctions against Japan as a violator of the Kellogg-Briand Pact, a position toward which the WILPF had mixed feelings, but Hoover was adamant in his conviction that sanctions would lead to war. The WILPF was concerned that such a policy would block action that might be taken by the League. As events were to prove, the women were correct in this assessment, for the League eventually chose to dispatch the Lytton Commission to the area as a fact-finding body rather than to impose sanctions without the support of the United States.

A second WILPF concern was that the outbreak of hostilities in the Far East would result in a postponement, if not a cancellation, of the upcoming Geneva Disarmament Conference. In early November one of the vice-chairs of the WILPF office in Geneva alluded to "groups of people" (bankers and arms manufacturers) who, unable to obtain a postponement of the conference by more overt means, had decided upon the more indirect method of provoking a war somewhere remote

from Europe and thus had "influenced" Japan to "protect" her interests in Manchuria. She suggested that this covert effort to subvert the
conference was experiencing some success. Incited by the press, public
opinion in Europe was that it would be "absurd and inconsistent to
have a Disarmament Conference while one of the Big Five is engaged
in a war. And," she concluded, "this is exactly what groups interested in
the postponement of the Conference want to bring about."[10] When
questioned about this possibility by the U.S. Section, however, the State
Department assured the women that the conference would proceed as
planned.

The WILPF was also unhappy that the clear violation of both the
Kellogg-Briand and Nine Power pacts by the Japanese spoke to the
apparent weakness, if not meaninglessness, of such treaties generally
and would be so construed by other nations that might be toying with
the idea of similar aggression. The issue here, contended the women,
was not the treaties' weakness but rather "that the peace machinery to
which the United States is a party has not yet been used." The WILPF
understood the position of the State Department to be that because
Japan was being overwhelmed internally by its militarist faction, patience and forbearance on the part of the United States and other
powers would help strengthen its civilian government. It was a position
with which the WILPF disagreed. "Peace machinery," it admonished,
"exists to be used, not forgotten and neglected."[11] A prompt, sharp
note to the Japanese with reference to the treaties by all the other
signatories, believed the women, would have a sobering effect on Japanese militarists.

In mid-November 1931 WILPF leaders again urged members to
write the president, requesting that if he did not intend to invoke either treaty, the least he could do was assure U.S. cooperation with the
League of Nations in declaring Japan an "outlaw nation" if it continued
to refuse to submit the dispute to impartial investigation.[12] On 24 November Detzer and Hannah Hull sent yet another letter to Hoover,
pleading for "some strong public message" to Japan.[13] By the end of
December the WILPF was also urging its members to ask the president
to prohibit loans to either belligerent because this action would increase the difficulty of obtaining munitions, and to write their senators
and representatives, asking them to support measures in Congress to
forbid the shipment of arms to both Japan and China.

Casting about for some way to deal more constructively and directly with such a potentially volatile situation, the WILPF seized upon
the idea of an arms embargo. The problem was that the only embargo

legislation in force was the 1922 statute that applied to China and Latin America. In the WILPF's opinion, the present situation in Manchuria could not wait on new legislation, so Detzer inquired of Rogers about the possibility of executive action on an embargo that would include Japan. She was not particularly surprised to hear that such action was not possible. She was told further that "all hell broke loose" when the peace organizations of the recently formed Inter-organizational Council on Disarmament not only made this suggestion, but also supported the WILPF's position that the president should declare loans to the belligerents "contrary to public policy."[14]

Peace groups were not alone in their frustration over State Department policy. By December 1931 a contingent in Congress thought the time had come to take the situation more firmly in hand. In discussions with Hoover and Stimson in the fall, Borah had suggested that the three of them talk with the Japanese ambassador, explaining that they understood Japan's critical need for raw materials and markets and would attempt to help solve this problem. And because the United States had closed its doors to Japanese immigration, Hoover and Stimson in the administration and Borah in the Senate would try to alter this policy to allow Japanese immigration on a quota system.

Hoover rejected this proposal saying that the situation was so difficult that "he wanted to put this baby on the doorstep of the League." Borah was most unhappy with Hoover's subsequent failure to cooperate with the League as the president apparently had promised to do. "The truth is," Borah told the WILPF ln late January 1932, "Japan is our neighbor and we have the greatest influence with her. . . . By our complete bungling of the situation, we have encouraged Japan to do what she has done."[15]

Members of the House were as discouraged with administration policy as Borah was, yet none of the bills introduced in Congress that winter really covered the situation as far as the WILPF was concerned. Hamilton Fish's bill forbade the shipment of arms to nations at war when the president decided a state of war existed. But Hoover had not declared a war to exist and did not intend to do so, as neither of the belligerents had yet declared war. A second bill, to forbid the shipment of arms to a nation breaking the Kellogg Pact, was also inadequate because Hoover had yet to declare Japan a violator of either the Kellogg-Briand or the Nine Power Pact. The third bill would amend the Constitution to prohibit loans to nations engaged in armed conflict and thus was seen as "somewhat remote" by the WILPF.[16]

The women thought that the Fish bill would be workable if modified, so Detzer approached him to see about rewording it and to press for hearings. Fish declined to accept her version, "It is the policy of the United States of America to prohibit the exportation of arms, munitions, and implements of war to any nation which is engaged in armed conflict,"[17] but was willing to amend the bill in committee to more adequately cover the present situation once the hearings, scheduled for 13 January, were over. On 12 January, however, the House Foreign Affairs Committee canceled the hearings on the grounds that they might interfere with the Far Eastern situation. The six members (five men, one woman) who voted against the hearings as well as Committee Chair J. Charles Linthicum quickly became the main targets of WILPF pressure to obtain a future hearing.

Yet unanimity did not prevail among WILPF leaders regarding policy in the Manchurian crisis any more than it did in official circles. Detzer was eager to urge withdrawal of U.S. ambassadors, a move supported by at least one of the WILPF's International Joint Chairs, but Balch, among others, saw this as "a sterile and dangerous line of policy," although she favored some sort of international economic pressure.[18] A compromise was ultimately reached and a letter incorporating the WILPF position was sent to Hoover on 18 January 1932 urging the United States:

1. To secure from a suitable international tribunal an authoritative pronouncement on the question of treaty violation in Manchuria.
2. To continue and make more complete the collaboration of the United States with the Council of the League of Nations regarding Manchuria and at the same time to call a special conference of the signatories of the Nine Power Pact for consultation as to what action they should take, as such.
3. To publish at once the notes which have passed between the Government of Japan and the United States as a recognition of the primary principle of open diplomacy.
4. To give executive support to Congressional action to forbid the shipment of arms to Japan.[19]

Although finding no serious fault with the Fish resolution, Stimson, like Detzer, preferred to see it reworded so as to amend the 1922 law, which authorized the president to embargo arms to China and Latin America. Fish did so and hearings were once again scheduled for 9 February. The situation in the Far East had taken a serious turn for the worse in January; further extension of the Japanese army into China early in the month brought an angry response from Stimson that the United States would not recognize as legal the Japanese seizure of any part of Manchuria, a policy the WILPF had been urging for weeks. Japan ignored this warning and continued to advance, moving troops into Shanghai on 28 January. In light of these events a decision on the proposed arms embargo took on added significance.

The WILPF was informed of the hearings on Friday 5 February and Detzer immediately called for a meeting of the Interorganizational Council. It met on Monday to choose representatives to appear in favor of the bill the following day. Thirty-two witnesses, including Jeannette Rankin of the NCPW, as well as numerous spectators and reporters, filled the hearing room on Tuesday morning, thanks particularly to the efforts of the WILPF's executive secretary. Fish was amazed and delighted at this impressive showing on such short notice. Other members of the Foreign Affairs Committee were equally surprised but far less pleased.

Linthicum immediately called an executive session of the committee and hastened to advise the State Department of this unexpected turn of events. Following a hurried conference between Stimson and Rogers, Linthicum was told to cancel the hearings. Shortly before noon the committee emerged from the hearing room and informed the waiting crowd that hearings would not be held because "additional information was wanted on this question."[20] Fish, embarrassed and angry because so many people had traveled to Washington on a moment's notice to appear, told the disgruntled and somewhat perplexed group that he had in good faith requested Detzer to obtain witnesses and in good faith she had produced them. He was, he assured them, as astonished and disappointed as they that the hearings would not take place.

When queried as to the reason for the sudden cancellation, one committee member responded that hearings at the present time might irritate the Japanese; another answered that hearings might irritate the Chinese. Were munitions interests in some of the Congressional districts behind the cancellation? "I resent that insinuation," said a third member.[21] Whatever the reason, the pacifists refused to give up. Detzer immediately contacted the groups represented on the Interorganizational Council, urging them to ask their members to write or wire their Congressmen, asking for immediate hearings. The response was overwhelming.

Nor did Hamilton Fish sit idly by. On 9 February he introduced a new resolution "to instruct the American delegates to the General Disarmament Conference then meeting in Geneva to propose a multilateral treaty banning the export of arms and munitions to any foreign nation." As historian Robert Divine notes, "Fish cleverly suggested that since the Kellogg Pact banned war, it was only logical to end the international arms trade. This proposal, innocuous enough to prevent State Department interference yet liberal enough to attract the supporters of collective security, was a parliamentary work of art."[22] The State Department approved and a hearing was set for 8 March.

In the meantime, Detzer learned that the real culprit behind the canceled February hearing was the State Department, which considered such hearings "inadvisable." After all, she was told, the issue was merely "academic" because the United States was not shipping arms to either belligerent.[23] Somewhat skeptical, Detzer began to wonder if she had been guilty of overreaction. Then she spotted a small article in the newspaper that reported that large quantities of nitrates were being shipped from the Atmospheric Nitrogen Company in Virginia, presumably headed for the Sino-Japanese war.

Four ships—one each from Japan, Britain, Germany, and France—were ready to sail with their cargoes of war materiél from Hopewell, Virginia. Detzer quickly did her homework and made an interesting discovery. "The Atmospheric Nitrogen Company," she noted, "was a subsidiary of the Allied Chemical and Dye Company. The latter was closely interlocked with several other industries, and was a heavy stockholder in U.S. Steel and the Texas and Gulf Oil companies. The Gulf Oil Company was Mellon-owned. And Andrew Mellon was the Secretary of the Treasury."[24] Detzer realized that it was highly unlikely that Mellon knew of the ships loaded with nitrates at Hopewell, yet now the cancellation of the hearings on the Fish bill began to make more sense.

A few days later Detzer attended a day-long conference on the Manchurian situation in Philadelphia that was sponsored by the Pennsylvania branch of the WILPF. When it was her turn to speak she told her story of canceled hearings, State Department assurances that the United States was not shipping munitions, the newspaper article concerning nitrates shipments, and the connection between Hopewell and the administration. Reporters raced to the phones to get the story in the evening papers; only a brief article appeared in one paper and then not until the following day. The story had been killed.

When Detzer confronted Rogers with the evidence that the United States was indeed shipping war materiél to the Far East, he responded lamely that the United States was not shipping "many" munitions.[25] Rarely receiving the same explanation twice from State Department officials, the WILPF was becoming frustrated at the run-around. An interview with Stanley Hornbeck on 4 February had only compounded the problem.

Hornbeck admitted that the department was wrong in its failure to adopt a more rigid policy in the beginning. He even intimated that the course of action advocated by the WILPF might have been the wisest position. The crux of the situation now, however, was this: The Japanese were so certain that the United States would not now go to war that they were "defiant." Continuing to send notes would be an exercise in futility. Some action had to be taken soon and at present the State Department was attempting to find ways of frightening the Japanese. Continued declarations insisting on peace by the United States were less than useless, but the threat of an economic boycott might have some impact and he suggested that the WILPF press for one.

"You realize, of course," he said, "that the whole thing could be stopped in twenty-four hours if the United States did not insist on following the new method of treaties. In twenty-four hours the sweep of our guns could stop the whole Shanghai affair."[26] Resort to arms, always this resort to arms, thought Detzer. With administrative officials like this, so quick to conclude that a military solution was the way out of a complicated international situation, disarmament, let alone world peace, had precious little possibility of ever being realized. The WILPF's frustration and impatience with what it considered a narrow and dangerous point of view was exceeded only by its resolve to thwart its implications.

As was the case with the aborted February hearing, peace organizations were given short notice for the March hearing on Fish's new resolution. Nevertheless, on the eighth the committee room was filled to overflowing. Linthicum and Fish offered many telegrams that they had received favoring the bill, and read a few of them aloud. After the testimony from the representative of the Interorganizational Council, Detzer spoke, indicating support for the bill by the WILPF's International Office as well as the British, German, and Canadian sections. When committee members insisted that the United States was not selling munitions, she responded that the bill called for a multilateral agreement and that this country ought to be just as interested in stopping the Czech or French munitions industries from fomenting wars by shipping to nations engaged in armed conflict. The committee appeared interested with the most attentive members being those who had received numerous telegrams supporting the bill from their constituents. Certainly the pro-embargo witnesses were accorded more respect by the committee than had been true in the past, and the WILPF concluded that it was a good start.

The Fish bill was reported out of committee favorably on 15 March by a vote of fifteen to two, and it then went to the House Rules Committee. WILPF leaders sent each branch a list of committee members, urging them to write and request that the bill be given immediate precedent so that it could be considered at once on the House floor. This was imperative because Arthur Henderson, president of the Geneva Disarmament Conference, asked that each delegation that advocated the suppression of private munitions manufacture spend the three weeks of Easter vacation drawing up specific proposals. It was of paramount importance that the House consider the Fish bill so that such proposals at Geneva would have U.S. support.

The WILPF was not content to wait on events. On 19 March Detzer visited once more with the assistant secretary of state. She pointed out to Rogers that the favorable vote on the Fish bill by the Foreign Affairs Committee indicated a conversion of sentiment on the issue. It seemed significant that there were only two dissenting votes, considering the hostility shown in early February when it bowed to State Department pressure by refusing to consider the bill. Noting that the department's objection to the first bill ostensibly had been on the grounds that it might violate U.S. commercial treaties, Detzer remarked that certainly this objection was now removed because the new resolution merely called upon U.S. delegates to the Geneva conference to support a multilateral agreement. Considering Henderson's recent request, she was frank in telling Rogers of the WILPF's dislike for the kind of pressure his department was putting on the elected representatives of the American people to suppress discussion of the issue.

> "Miss Detzer, I like to think I have an open mind on this issue," Rogers responded, "but in all honesty, I do not consider it very practical or even advisable. I voted for the prohibition amendment and I believed in prohibition. Now I am in a tangle about it. I don't see that prohibition has solved the problem and, therefore, I believe that we would have the same question, the same ugly deceit, the same bootleg traffic. I think it is wiser to have it aboveboard."
>
> "I agree with you, Mr. Rogers, on the issue of prohibition, but I don't feel that prohibition and the munitions issue are comparable. Consider, for example, the purpose of the product we wish to prohibit."

Detzer pointed out that liquor was for social pleasure but the purpose of munitions was that of destruction. Though liquor could indeed become a vice, the purpose behind its manufacture was very different from that of armaments.

"Are you willing," she asked, leaning forward intently, "are you willing and ready to advocate the withdrawal of all laws for the suppression of the traffic in opium because there is bootlegging in opium and dishonesty on the part of the powers or because we have not yet managed to have perfect control?"

"Of course not," he responded immediately, "but opium and drink are two different things."

"We know the opium problem is not solved," she continued, "we know further that as decent people we must solve it—it is a problem to be confronted and dealt with head-on rather than give up in despair because of the possibility of boot-legging. Some day we will succeed in educating people to a new attitude, just as we have done with slavery. It still exists, but not for much longer because people have been educated to its evils. It is my feeling, Mr. Rogers, that the government and decent people the world over should bracket the traffic in both opium and munitions because both are destructive to the human species."

Rogers was silent for a moment, and then remarked that this was a fresh idea to him and most interesting. "Be that as it may, Miss Detzer, there is so much to be discussed at the Disarmament Conference, I don't see how a practical solution to the question can be worked out right at this moment." "The Fish bill does not ask for a practical solution," Detzer explained patiently, "it does not call for a method; it does nothing more than call upon our delegation to support the idea. A plan of implementation will evolve later."[27]

As the discussion continued, Rogers acknowledged Detzer's point that such a multilateral agreement would have the advantageous effect of breaking the control of the larger nations over the foreign policy of smaller ones because of the dependence of the latter on the former for armaments. But before the talk moved on to other matters, Detzer again pressured Rogers for a commitment to support the Fish bill. Once again Rogers demurred, saying that although he would not oppose it, he could not support it until he had given the matter further study.

Three days later Detzer looked across a massive desk piled high with papers as she tried to persuade Borah to introduce a bill in the Senate to the same effect as the Fish bill. The Senator's attitude was not unlike that which she had encountered elsewhere on Capitol Hill, namely, that there was no point in taking any action as the delegates to the disarmament conference were not going to do anything anyway. The conference, it was widely believed, was nothing more than an exercise in futility. Detzer left Borah's office discouraged but undaunted. How can anything be accomplished, she thought to herself as she headed back to her office to write Mary Woolley in Geneva, so long as the delegation in Geneva says we must work at obtaining Senate approval for the idea of a multilateral arms embargo, and the Senate says we must work at obtaining the support of the delegation in Geneva?

While the WILPF and other peace organizations pushed for the Fish bill, a much more powerful group worked quietly behind the scenes to ensure that the bill would progress no further. Spokesmen for the munitions industry visited the State Department on at least three occasions in March alone and apparently not without effect, for the Fish resolution died quietly shortly thereafter.

To compound the arms embargo situation, less than two months later in June 1932, an undeclared war broke out between the Latin American countries of Bolivia and Paraguay. Although less globally threatening than the Manchurian crisis, this territorial dispute did raise the issue of traffic in arms, for as the conflict progressed, U.S. munitions manufacturers eagerly sold their wares to both sides. The United States cooperated with other American nations to effect a negotiated settlement, but their efforts were unsuccessful. The knowledge that U.S. arms manufacturers had a vested interest in the conflict's continuation finally prompted Stimson in mid-December to propose to Hoover that he request from Congress the authority to embargo munitions shipments to nations at war or to nations in which war appeared imminent. According to one historian, this recommendation, "drafted in the form of an amendment to the 1922 Embargo Act, implied a far-reaching change in American policy. The legislation Stimson requested would permit the United States to embargo arms to any nation, even before the outbreak of war, and would allow the president discretion to act against an aggressor."[28]

When Hoover, although without enthusiasm, approved Stimson's recommendation, the WILPF immediately notified him of its "deep satisfaction and gratification."[29] At the same time Undersecretary of State William R. Castle informed Stimson of his opposition. Such a bill, he argued, would only arouse the ire of the arms industry and create an unpleasant controversy for the administration. When through a press leak, the proposal became public knowledge, Castle's prediction was realized. By the end of December the flood of protests from munitions manufacturers caused Hoover to back down. He would not send the message to Congress. The WILPF initiated a campaign directed toward the president to counter the "tremendous drive" of the arms industry.[30] It pledged its full support in the effort to obtain such legislation, "trusting that adequate measures would eventually be enacted to prevent the traffic in munitions at any time."[31]

The campaign was not without effect. When Stimson brought up the proposal again in early January 1933, Castle now backed him, fearing that "a reversal would lead to charges that the Hoover administration was under the influence of the munitions industry."[32] Hoover finally agreed to a compromise and on 10 January a revised draft, "requesting the Senate to ratify the 1925 Geneva convention for control of the arms trade, and then proposing the arms embargo as an alternative," was sent to Congress. Hoover's letter of explanation clearly indicated his hesitancy to go too far, for he suggested that the recommendation of an arms embargo be limited to "cases where special undertakings of cooperation can be secured with the principal arms manufacturing nations."[33] Arms control would be a cooperative venture for the United States or not at all.

Congress was quick to respond. The president's message was incorporated into a resolution sponsored by Borah that "empowered the president to lay an embargo on the shipment of arms or munitions of war to any country he might designate, provided that he secured the cooperation of other arms-producing nations."[34] The Senate Foreign Relations Committee passed the resolution unanimously within twenty-four hours and Borah brought it up for full Senate consideration on the nineteenth. Approval without debate seemed secure.

But Senator Hiram Bingham of Connecticut, president of the National Aeronautic Association, insisted on full debate, threatening a filibuster. The WILPF concluded that this move was probably prompted by pressure from the arms industry, which was centered in Bingham's home state. Industry representatives had continued their efforts to block the entire issue by pressuring the State Department, Congress, and the Departments of War, Navy, and Commerce. With Bingham blocking the bill in the Senate, Representative Sam D. McReynolds, chair of the House Foreign Affairs Committee, introduced a duplicate bill in the House. As one historian has recorded, "nearly every major peace organization in the country went on record in favor of arms embargo legislation. The House Foreign Affairs Committee received a large volume of letters, telegrams, and petitions from pacifist groups, all urging adoption of the Borah resolution as a means of implementing the Kellogg Pact. Miss Detzer lobbied constantly in Congress and kept the State Department fully informed of the situation."[35]

When the McReynolds bill came up for hearings, representatives of the peace organizations consulted as to whether or not to press for public hearings. They concluded unanimously that inasmuch as the State Department and the president were now asking for this legislation, the best strategy lay in showing support, but not to appear in a hearing where the munitions people could create "a kind of 'pacifist-militarist' row" and thus divert attention away from the main objective.[36] The wisest course of action, pacifists decided, was to try to keep committee members focused on the bill and arouse as little opposition to it as possible.

Unfortunately, Helen Hoy Greeley of the Women's Disarmament Committee appeared before the committee without consulting the other peace groups. WILPF leaders thought that this incident stirred up the opposition unnecessarily. State Department officials believed likewise that it was Greeley's unexpected appearance that caused committee members to insist on hearing the other side, which in all probability would not have happened otherwise.

As it was, representatives from the Winchester Repeating Arms Company and the Colt and Remington companies appeared before the committee on 14 February. As she listened to their arguments against the bill, Detzer acknowledged that at least they were honest about their desire not to have their business interfered with by munitions makers of other countries. They made no effort to straddle the issue or to pretend that they were interested in anything except the question of profit. Yet indications were that the bill would be favorably voted out of the House committee on the fifteenth, though it was doubtful that it would pass the House before the end of the current session unless tremendous pressure was exerted by the public.

When the Foreign Affairs Committee met on the fifteenth, the situation in the Far East had once again reached critical proportions. Compounding the problem was a report issued on the previous day by the League of Nations. Based on the Lytton Commission's findings, the League condemned Japan as an aggressor. Fish, among others, was thus convinced that the pending legislation was directed at Japan and to him this meant war between the United States and Japan should the bill pass. As a compromise move, therefore, the Foreign Affairs Committee voted out the arms embargo bill to apply only to Latin American countries, a solution that the WILPF felt was almost worse than no bill at all. It again exhorted members to write their Congressmen to amend the bill on the floor to apply to all countries engaged in armed conflict, but to no avail. The committee reported favorably on the compromise measure, and although Hoover urged its passage, Congress adjourned without taking action on it.

Decrying the isolationist sentiment in Congress as keenly as Stimson, the WILPF vowed to keep the issue alive. In late March 1933, when under the new Democratic administration a resolution almost identical to that originally recommended by Stimson was introduced in Congress, the WILPF gave it whole-hearted support; another vigorous letter-writing campaign was underway. The House Foreign Affairs Committee passed the bill and, anticipating a "good fight" in House debates in early April, the campaign to persuade Congressmen to vote in its favor was stepped up.[37]

The women were correct in their expectation. When the McReynolds bill reached the floor of the House on 13 April, an emotional debate ensued with Democrats speaking for it and Republicans vehemently against. The main bone of contention was the degree of leeway given to the president in determining an aggressor nation. Opponents were convinced that Roosevelt would use that power to embroil the United States in foreign conflicts, and thus they demanded an impartial embargo that would apply equally to all belligerents. Supporters of the bill evinced faith in the president's wisdom to employ the discretionary clause in the best interests of the country. Fish's amendment for an impartial embargo was rejected, and the McReynolds resolution passed, 254 to 109.

The Senate Foreign Relations Committee began consideration of the measure in early May 1933. By mid-month it was clear that it would not receive committee approval without an amendment making the embargo impartial rather than discretionary. With Roosevelt's assent, an amendment to that effect by Hiram Johnson was attached and by the end of the month, the bill was reported out favorably. Yet Secretary of State Cordell Hull, strongly opposed to an impartial embargo, persuaded the president to drop the entire subject for the time being and there the matter remained for the rest of the year.

This failure of Congress to pass a discretionary arms embargo in spring 1933 has been attributed by diplomatic historians to "isolationist sentiment" in the Senate, but not all advocates of an impartial embargo were motivated by such considerations.[38] The WILPF, for example, was strongly committed to the impartial embargo on the grounds that it more nearly represented true neutrality, but went on record in March in full support of the Borah resolution for a discretionary measure. The women adamantly supported international rather than unilateral action to abolish the munitions trade and to restrict loans or credits for military purposes or to an aggressor nation. Only if international cooperation failed to materialize would the WILPF advocate unilateral action on the part of the United States. "Isolationism" was not the issue for the WILPF; world peace was, and for the women a unilateral embargo, albeit discretionary, was preferable to no embargo at all.

While FDR and the State Department continued their holding pattern on embargo legislation until Congress reconvened in January 1934, the WILPF, supported by the NCCCW, NCPW, FOR, and the recently formed National Peace Conference (NPC), pursued its goal of an investigation of the munitions industry.[39]

The WILPF was unable to find a senator willing or able to sponsor the desired legislation in 1932, so it temporarily pursued another avenue to the same end when the country's great banking institutions became the target of a Congressional investigation in the early summer of 1933. The women submitted a number of questions to the investigating committee, which they requested be addressed to the financiers under scrutiny. The WILPF was told, however, that although the information desired was indeed important—it concerned possible connections between bankers and munitions makers—it was not relevant to the inquiry at hand. Hence, the committee declined the WILPF's request.

The women then tried another angle. By this time National Recovery Administration (NRA) codes were being effected all across the nation and the WILPF thought perhaps that through the NRA's "code authority, . . . some check might be made on the munitions makers." So the WILPF requested that Roosevelt appoint "a special representative whose sole responsibility shall be to watch the munitions code," as it related to the domestic sale of fire arms and to the manufacture of and trade in munitions for the purpose of war.[40] According to Detzer, the executive branch found the idea valuable but Hugh Johnson, NRA director, was strongly opposed; another avenue was blocked off. The WILPF had to resume its search for a senator to sponsor a Congressional investigation.

Encouraged by the election results of the previous year as "half a dozen of the most military senators [had] been retired to private life,"[41]

Detzer approached George Norris in the fall of 1933 and together they
went through a new list of senators one by one:

> With his pencil poised, he began the process of elimination.
> "He could do it," Norris would say, pointing to a name. "That
> man has great intellectual gifts. But I am afraid he is a moral coward."
> And the red pencil, with a swift, heavy stroke, would discard that
> name. Then, perhaps hesitating for a moment, Norris would reject
> the next on the list.
> "You had better not ask him," Norris would explain. "You see you
> might persuade him to do it," he would add with a smile, "and that
> would be unfortunate; for he's too close to the Army." And the red
> pencil struck out another name. . . . The red pencil went on eliminat-
> ing, eliminating.

Finally they reached the end of the list. Every name but one had a big
red slash through it. That remaining name stood out in bold black
letters: Gerald P. Nye, North Dakota. Norris's reasons for believing that
Senator Nye was the WILPF's man were sound:

> "Nye's young, he has inexhaustible energy, and he has cour-
> age. . . . Those are all important assets. He may be rash in his judg-
> ments at times, but it's the rashness of enthusiasm. I think he would
> do a first-class job with an investigation. Besides," Norris added, "Nye
> doesn't come up for election again for another four years; by that
> time the investigation would be over. If it reveals what I am certain it
> will, such an investigation would help him politically, not harm him.
> And that would not be the case with many senators. For you see, there
> isn't a major industry in North Dakota closely allied to the munitions
> business."[42]

Backed by a vote of the WILPF National Board at its December
1933 meeting, Detzer began to concentrate her time and energy on
obtaining the munitions investigation. She approached Nye immediately following the Christmas recess. He had been among the original group of twenty senators approached by Detzer in the spring of
1932—and he had turned her down. This time, however, Nye found
himself unable to resist. "I'm afraid my conscience won't let me refuse
you again," he said, "I'll do it."[43]

On 8 February 1934 the senator from North Dakota introduced his
bill calling for an investigation of the munitions industry. Thanks to
Nye's superb sense of timing, the resolution was accepted without a

murmur and sent to the Senate Foreign Relations Committee. But Key Pittman, committee chair, wanted no part of the bill and managed to gain Senate consent to transfer it to the Military Affairs Committee, composed primarily of "military-minded men."[44]

This turn of events was a major blow to the peace groups. They feared that "one of two courses seemed inevitable—either they [members of the Military Affairs Committee] would kill the resolution outright by refusing to report it favorably to the Senate or, by assuming responsibility for the investigation themselves, they would whitewash the most important facts."[45] The WILPF went to work immediately to prevent either course of action. It proposed to the committee that the Nye resolution be combined with one previously submitted by Senator Arthur Vandenberg, which called for a Congressional review of the War Policies Commission's report.

Because the Vandenberg resolution was supported by the American Legion, one bill combining both resolutions would give it "double-barreled support from two diametrically opposed wings of public opinion—the peace movement and the Legion." The second part of the women's strategy involved the proposal that a "select committee" undertake the combined investigation.[46] The plan worked. The Military Affairs Committee reported favorably on the combined resolutions and recommended to the Senate that it appoint a seven-member committee with subpoena power and a $50,000 appropriation to begin work.

The appropriation was subsequently reduced to $15,000, insufficient for a full-scale investigation but enough for an adequate start. Then came the task of winning full Senate approval for the resolution. State Department backing soon followed from Cordell Hull, an important factor in persuading staunch New Deal senators to support the bill. It was hoped that a national campaign by the peace movement would convince enough uncommitted senators to fall into line.

While the usual barrage of letters, telegrams, and visits to the Senate from its peace-minded constituents commenced, supplemented by mass meetings and demonstrations, the arms embargo issue resurfaced. Much to the surprise of Roosevelt and the State Department, on the last day of February the Senate unanimously adopted the resolution that the Foreign Relations Committee had passed the previous spring, Johnson amendment and all. It permitted the United States to embargo arms to any nation on an impartial basis rather than at the president's discretion. The WILPF, also caught off-guard, concluded (mistakenly as it turned out) that Roosevelt felt compelled to make some kind of peace move because of pressure from pacifists, and so had called upon Senate leaders to push through the embargo measure.

In point of fact, the impartial embargo was just as undesirable in administration circles in the early spring of 1934 as it had been in the late spring of 1933. Thus the State Department exacted a promise from McReynolds, Chair of the House Foreign Affairs Committee, to block the measure when it reached the House. At the same time, however, the Chaco War between Bolivia and Paraguay dragged on with munitions from U.S. companies going to both sides.

The WILPF all but ignored the embargo issue as it devoted its attention to other concerns. The organization was immersed in the unfolding drama leading to the Nye Committee investigation and it vigorously worked against the Vinson Naval bill, which called for an expenditure of between $500 and $800 million on an updated navy. There was little point in wasting energy on what appeared to be a lost cause when Nye needed all the help he could get. Every effort on his part to bring the munitions investigation bill up for a vote was blocked by the forces of the opposition. At long last, however, on 12 April 1934, through an adroit series of maneuvers by the Nye-Vandenberg forces, the Senate, "without a dissenting vote . . . authorized an investigation of the munitions industry."[47]

While rejoicing over its success, the WILPF kept an eye on the progress of the arms embargo measure. Detzer reported at the annual meeting in early May that final action on the bill would be taken only when McReynolds called for it. What she did not know, of course, was that McReynolds had no intention of doing so. The State Department's procrastination was explained to the peace groups as a desire to hold off on the bill until the results of the disarmament conference were known.

At the same time, a League of Nations committee studying the Chaco conflict now recommended an arms embargo on shipments to both belligerents. The State Department, eager to cooperate, persuaded Congressional leaders to introduce legislation to that effect and at the end of May, Congress passed a bill that "authorized the President to prohibit the sale of arms to both Paraguay and Bolivia, if, in his judgment, such action would contribute to the restoration of peace between the two nations."[48] Peace groups were momentarily satisfied and with the adjournment of Congress shortly thereafter, they turned their full attention to preparations for the September opening of the investigation of the munitions industry, hoping to extend such an inquiry internationally.

The select committee, appointed by the vice president in the spring, included Nye as Chair, and Senators Vandenberg (Michigan), Bennett Champ Clark (Missouri), Homer T. Bone (Washington), James

P. Pope (Idaho), Walter George (Georgia), and Warren Barbour (New Jersey). The WILPF was quite satisfied with those selected, but there was still the question of who would be appointed to the key position of chief investigator. "It seemed essential," thought the WILPF, "that the committee appoint to its staff no one even remotely connected with the government or, for that matter, with the munitions industry or the peace movement either. For however conscientious or incorruptible a man might be it was obvious that a connection with the munitions industry would automatically warp his judgment; that a connection with the peace movement could easily prejudice his attitude, and a government connection, at least subconsciously, temper his detachment."[49]

After consultation, peace activists decided to push for the appointment of Steve Raushenbush, Dartmouth College economics instructor. A rather shy, quiet young man with what Detzer described as a "first-class intellect," Raushenbush possessed "the proficiency of an experienced investigator."[50] From the point of view of leading peace advocates, he was the perfect man for the job. He was not a wild-eyed radical but rather a man of seemingly real courage and love for humanity. Would he be willing to serve as chief investigator? More importantly, would the committee be willing to *ask* him to serve?

Not only was Raushenbush willing, but within eight hours of being contacted by peace people, he put together a plan outlining his thoughts as to how the committee might best proceed with its work. Within twenty-four hours he was named chief investigator, and not long thereafter a three-member staff, equally as acceptable to peace supporters, was appointed: Alger Hiss, later to become (in)famous in the Whittaker Chambers case; Robert Wolforth; and Josephine Burns, who subsequently married Raushenbush. They spent the summer of 1934 busily collecting data in preparation for the scheduled opening of formal hearings on 4 September.

Detzer was in Zurich, Switzerland, attending the International Congress of the WILPF when the munitions investigation opened that September. Much to her surprise, she found herself acclaimed by the European peace community for her part in bringing about the Senate inquiry. Back home Washington columnists Drew Pearson and Robert S. Allen devoted their "Washington Merry-Go-Round" on 4 September to the opening of hearings in the Senate, giving "chief credit . . . to a young lady who initiated the idea long before anyone else but quietly remained in the background. She is Miss Dorothy Detzer of the Women's International League."[51]

In point of fact, Detzer *was* the key figure behind the two-year investigation. Given the temper of the times it is probable that had she not pushed for the Congressional inquiry, someone else from among the peace organizations would have. But this probability notwithstanding, credit for bringing the investigation about belonged to the WILPF's executive secretary. This was acknowledged by her contemporaries and by historians of the subject, even those like John Wiltz, who tended to belittle the committee's findings and the entire investigation.[52]

Despite Wiltz's effort to discredit the Nye Committee's findings as well as the two major studies of munitions manufacturers' tactics published at the time—H. C. Engelbrecht and F. C. Hanighen's *Merchants of Death* and George Seldes's *Iron, Blood, and Profits*—by intimating that these men saw conspiracy where none existed, the evidence from the ninety-three hearings showed that there was excellent cause for concern. As historian Charles Chatfield notes in his study of the interwar peace movement,

> It [the committee] charged that private armament interests circumvented national policies as defined in arms embargoes and treaties, sold weapons to both sides in time of war, bribed government officials, lobbied for military appropriations and against embargoes, stimulated arms races between friendly nations, and thrived on excess profits and favoritism from the government. The committee concluded, too, that American arms companies had arrangements with British firms to exchange patents and to divide profits and sales territories. It held that the international armaments industry influenced defense and foreign policies of the government, but that the United States was powerless to prevent or regulate shipments of weapons to warring nations in violation of embargoes.[53]

Wiltz apparently missed the point of pacifists' concern over the tactics, power, and exorbitant profits of the world's munitions makers, for as William T. Stone of the Foreign Policy Association noted at the time, there was a

> dual character of the munitions industry. . . . Munitions firms are private corporations responsible to shareholders, whose chief concern is the prompt payment of dividends. Dividends can be paid only out of profits, and profits depend on the sale of war materials in the world market regardless of political or social consequences. At the same time munitions firms receive government aid in time of peace in recognition of the part they are expected to play in the mobilization of

industry for war. Yet governments, when they encourage the development of the domestic munitions industry, are not only involved in the
abuses of the industry but are forced to effect compromises with their
own policies.[54]

In this same vein, Chatfield notes that "peace seemed to be threatened
by the association of profit-making and semi-public functions in the
same industry. In this limited respect, at least, many people were convinced that capitalism was a cause of war."[55]

Perhaps there was some validity to this conclusion. Writing in *The
Christian Century* in fall 1934, Russell J. Clinchy put his finger on the
key issue:

> The simple fact begins to dawn on the observer [of the munitions
> hearings] that these are not men who seek blood, but only a group of
> successful business men who are using much of the same business
> methods the other members of their club use. . . . It will do no good
> to think of these men as fiends who rejoice dealing in blood and
> death, for they are not. . . . [T]he only difference between these mu-
> nitions men and many of the business men of the world is not in
> ethics or business technique, but simply the commodity in which they
> deal. Every one of the techniques with which they deal—exploitation;
> appeals to fear, prejudice, and vanity; allocation of territory; pitting
> buyers against each other in competitive markets—all of them are the
> general techniques of what is called "good business" today.[56]

Detzer's conclusions were in accord with these observations. Commenting on the testimony of the U.S. giants in arms manufacturing,
the four DuPont brothers, she remarked that for them, "the corporation's profits of 400 percent during the First World War seemed only
the good fruit of sound business. And they seemed not the least embarrassed by the disclosure that during one of the war's most crucial periods, they had refused to build a powder plant—deemed essential by
the government—until their corporation could be guaranteed what
they stipulated as an adequate 'margin of profit'."[57]

The solution to the problem as Clinchy saw it in 1934 was not
necessarily to "punish or erase the DuPonts" because "four others will
take their places."[58] As historian John K. Nelson has observed, here is
where the ideology of the interwar pacifists, an ideology based on the
Progressive faith in the system, served them ill.[59] For Clinchy's two-part
recommended solution was no solution at all. Unwilling or unable to
face the implications of his own analysis and thus to call for the aboli-

tion of the capitalistic system, his recommendations dealt with *effect* rather than *cause*.

He first called for Christian businessmen to "throw the weight of their influence and power against these practices. Christian laymen must begin to demand that Christians be as incorruptible and ethical in business as they now demand their ministers must be in their profession."[60] Second, he echoed Detzer's statement before the War Policies Commission some few years earlier when she had advocated nationalization of the munitions industry, an almost meaningless suggestion whatever its merit as an abstraction, in a society so thoroughly committed to the sanctity of so-called "private enterprise" as the United States.

By this time even Detzer was forced to acknowledge that although the ultimate goal for the WILPF with regard to the armaments industry was total abolition, "this goal would appear to be impossible without a change in the whole basis of society."[61] Yet she dodged the question of what this change implied, for she admitted at the same time that "complete nationalization of the industry is not possible under our present economic system."[62]

Despite efforts on the part of munitions makers to bring a quick and early end to the investigation, and despite efforts of some of the nation's larger and more influential newspapers to downplay the more damning revelations brought forth in testimony, the committee continued the hearings throughout the fall and winter of 1934. Then in early December, to everyone's amazement Roosevelt announced a cabinet meeting to consider a plan to "take the profits out of war."[63] Peace advocates had been expecting a move by the administration to prevent further appropriations for the committee, but this sudden decision came as a complete surprise, all the more so because no one from the Nye Committee was included.

The WILPF quickly sized up the situation and was probably correct in its assessment, details of which were contained in a letter sent to all members within twenty-four hours of the president's announcement. It noted that the Nye Committee was already considering implementation of "as large an amount of nationalization of the munitions industry as is practical and possible," and this, it thought, was the key to explaining Roosevelt's action. It was widely believed in Washington that the administration felt that even a limited degree of nationalization was "too socialistic," and so it would preempt any such recommendation by the Nye Committee with its own, more "moderate" plan. Second, the WILPF surmised, the investigation was "getting very close to the present Administration," and this fact coupled with the strong opposition of "banking interests" to a continuation of the hearings had thus prompted the president's unexpected proposal.[64]

There was a military factor operative here, too, for it was suspected on good authority that the secretaries of War and Navy had been prodding Roosevelt to call a halt to "further disclosures on the tie-up between those two Branches of the Government and the Munitions Industry."[65] Last was the factor of party politics. Nye and Vandenberg, the two most prominent committee members, were also prominent Republicans and were enthusiastically supported in their investigation by a third Republican heavyweight, William Borah. And coincidentally, Roosevelt's announcement came on the eve of a large Republican rally scheduled in New York at which Nye and Borah were to be the keynote speakers. Tickets for the rally had been sold out for days.

The conclusion for the WILPF was inescapable. It urged its members to "pressure" the president "until he declares that it is not his intention to stop the Hearings."[66] A letter to that effect from Hannah Hull and Detzer went out to the White House that same day. The WILPF hoped that peace groups would raise "such a storm" of protest that additional funds for the Nye Committee would have to be appropriated by the administration, however reluctantly.[67] When Congress reconvened in January 1935 following the holiday recess, the money was forthcoming and the Nye Committee continued its investigation throughout 1935 into 1936.

But Roosevelt still went ahead with his plan to produce an administration proposal for taking the profits out of war. By early March 1935 it was embodied in the McSwain bill, which the WILPF opposed with some vigor. By the resolution that created it, the Nye Committee was empowered to make recommendations regarding the munitions industry; hence, thought the WILPF, any legislation dealing with that subject ought to come from the committee. The women would not support any legislation sponsored by another source.

Second, as Detzer pointed out to WILPF members, nowhere in the McSwain bill was there a proposal for "taking the profit out of war." Third, there *were* provisions calling for the "freezing of prices," which the WILPF opposed as the Nye Committee had already brought forth evidence that such a freeze could make for *greater* profit rather than less.[68] There were two or three additional provisions in the bill to which the WILPF was opposed and so the women were relieved when the Senate referred it immediately to the Nye Committee.

In the meantime, although the revelations emerging from the Nye Committee's investigations "helped stimulate a vociferous demand for the absolute prohibition of arms exports as a way of curbing the 'merchants of death',[69] other forces were also at work in the mid-1930s, moving the American people and their representatives in Washington toward a comprehensive arms embargo law, or so-called "neutrality" legislation. By 1935 the international scene looked threatening indeed, and a growing number of Americans were becoming alarmed over the possibility of another general European war. With the revelations of the Nye Committee's investigation fresh in their minds, they vowed that *this* time munitions makers and Wall Street financiers would not drag the United States into the maelstrom.

11

The Search for Neutrality

BY 1935 THE PROPEACE EFFORTS of the previous decade gave way completely to efforts to prevent another world war. Japan continued its belligerence in the Far East, and although the United States re-established diplomatic relations with the Soviet Union in the fall of 1933, at the same time Germany withdrew from the League of Nations and the Disarmament Conference. By the summer of 1934 that conference, nominally still in existence through the retention of committees, had for all practical purposes dissolved in failure. The Hitler terror continued in Europe; and in December 1934 the first clash occurred between Italy and Ethiopia. Although Mussolini agreed to arbitration in January 1935, it was soon apparent that this was merely subterfuge while he stalled for time.

It was against this backdrop of ugly rumblings abroad that Roosevelt went to Congress in January 1935 to ask for U.S. adherence to the World Court. Although the WILPF had never made this issue a priority, it advocated U.S. participation all along and enthusiastically backed Roosevelt. It seemed highly probable that Congress would accede to the president's request, but a strong last-minute anti-court campaign by the Hearst press, Senator Huey Long of Louisiana, and Father Charles Coughlin, the "Radio Priest," won the day. On 29 January the vote in the Senate fell seven short of the necessary two-thirds required for U.S. membership. Keenly disappointed by this latest demonstration of isolationism, the WILPF was convinced that the result would have been otherwise had the president appealed directly to the American people.

As for new legislation on the arms embargo, the State Department was still at loggerheads over whether such a measure should be impartial or discretionary. This problem, coupled with strong Navy opposition to any renunciation of traditional neutral rights, kept Roosevelt from submitting a proposal to Congress. Instead he approached Senator Nye, requesting that his committee consider the issue. Agreeing, on 9 April 1935 Nye and Champ Clark introduced two neutrality measures in the Senate. The first would give the president the power to forbid U.S. citizens from traveling on belligerent ships or in war zones, and the second banned loans and credits to nations for the purpose of purchasing war matériel. At the same time, Maury Maverick of Texas and Frank Kloeb of Ohio introduced similar measures in the House. Less than a month later, Nye and Clark introduced a third measure, an embargo on the shipment of arms to all belligerents with the stipulation that shipments of other contraband goods to belligerents would be at the risk of the shipper. While the State Department vacillated, peace groups quickly mobilized in support of these measures.

Contrary to the assertion of most diplomatic historians, the peace movement did not support strict neutrality measures out of isolationist sentiment or because it was "torn between a belief in collective security and the desire to avoid American involvement in war."[1] Peace groups did not believe that collective security and noninvolvement in war were mutually exclusive. They were, rather, simply two sides to the same coin. The WILPF, for example, had worked from its inception for the creation of an internationally organized world through various treaties and tribunals while simultaneously endeavoring to eradicate the basic economic causes of war.

Yet as the Manchurian crisis so clearly demonstrated, the "collective security" arrangements of such treaties as the Nine Power and Kellogg-Briand pacts were meaningless if their signatories chose to ignore them. Treaties, like other laws, insisted the WILPF, were destroyed not when they were broken but when there was a failure to enforce them. In the Manchurian crisis, the United States, the League, and Japan were all guilty for the breakdown of the treaty system then in existence. If anyone had abandoned internationalism or the idea of collective security, it was not the peace groups but the Great Powers. Thus continued efforts by pacifists to stimulate collective international action for peace appeared not only futile but almost ludicrous.

Therefore, concluded WILPF pacifists, it seemed wisest "to make a strategic retreat—or rather, deliberately and frankly to be peace opportunists" by supporting a policy of U.S. neutrality. But, they declared, "this does not mean that the WILPF repudiates its efforts for an internationally organized world—that must come—and we do not feel that the neutrality legislation is inconsistent with this policy. But we do have the opportunity now—immediately—to secure strong domestic peace legislation." The women were under no illusion that such legislation would provide a "water-tight guarantee against the United States being drawn into another war," but they did view such laws as an important step in that direction. And if war *did* break out, affirmed the WILPF, "probably the greatest contribution that the United States can make is to remain out of that war, and refuse in any way to help or support it."[2] Hence, the group decided at its annual meeting in May 1935 to concentrate on obtaining passage of the strongest neutrality legislation possible, and delegates used the occasion of their meeting, which also happened to be the twentieth anniversary of the WILPF, to garner as much publicity for the cause as they could.

The meeting was held in the nation's capital, where the publicity given a White House reception on 2 May with Addams and Eleanor Roosevelt in the receiving line certainly did the WILPF's public image no harm. A dinner for over 1,200 people at the Willard Hotel that night included Oswald G. Villard, Gerald Swope, Sidney Hillman, Harold Ickes, and Eleanor Roosevelt among its speakers as well as Dr. Alice Hamilton and Addams of the WILPF. The following day WILPF members escorted a delegation of students to Capitol Hill, where they met Key Pittman, chairman of the Senate Foreign Relations Committee; then it was on to the White House and later, a dinner at which both Nye and Kloeb spoke. A mass peace demonstration in McPherson Square under the WILPF's direction included an international radio hook-up. The huge crowd, orchestra, and a grandstand of international and American notables listened to peace messages from Tokyo, Paris, Moscow, and London.

Some Americans, however, criticized the WILPF for being prejudiced against Germany in this gala anniversary celebration. Wilbur K. Thomas of the Carl Schurz Memorial Foundation chided the women for their failure to include German representation. "Some are saying," wrote Thomas, "that there was no invitation extended" to the German Embassy although all other major foreign officials were approached. Noting that the German Embassy did indeed receive an invitation (to which there was no response), the WILPF also informed Thomas that it "would never have invited the representatives of the Hitler Government to share our platform" as it had with other nations for its international broadcast. "To have done so," the WILPF made clear, "would have been to betray our brave and devoted German comrades who are now suffering in exile outside of Germany as refugees, or who are in prison camps, or who are dead as the result of Nazi policies. . . . If our failure to invite the Hitler Government to participate in our world-wide broadcast has in any way indicated to their [*sic*] representatives here the moral indignation which we feel with an increasing intensity," wrote Detzer without equivocation, "our Celebration rendered an extra service, which had not been intended, but for which we can now feel well gratified."³

At the same time it was taking it on the chin for supposedly being anti-German, the WILPF was also accused again of being communist. Not only were branch meetings interrupted with such allegations by ordinary citizens, the government once more did its part. In mid-1935 Commander S. A. Clement of Naval Intelligence circulated an official memorandum that the WILPF, NCPW, ACLU, and the Federal Council of Churches were all "organizations which while not *openly* advocating the 'force and violence' principles of the communists, give aid and comfort to the communist movement and party." Among "a long string of communist-minded intellectuals" who were described as "fringe revolutionists" were Roger Baldwin, Clarence Darrow, Frederick J. Libby, Kirby Page, and Jane Addams.⁴

Certainly the WILPF's continued affiliation with the communist-backed ALAWF did nothing to counter such charges, but it was a risk the women felt compelled to take in the interest of peace. They had decided to remain in the ALAWF's "united front" so long as it took no action to "compromise" the noncommunist affiliates on the premise that pacifist participation might help "steer" the new organization's policies in a more peaceful direction. In response to WILPF members who found it difficult to "square the W.I.L. stand against violence with the Communist propaganda," Detzer, speaking for the majority that voted to continue in the ALAWF at the 1934 Annual Meeting, observed that the WILPF "has never hesitated to cooperate with the Chamber of Commerce, the Rotary Club, the General Federation of Women's Clubs, and all those right-wing groups, which would never take our position against war." But, she pointed out,

These people believe just as much in violence and dictatorship as do the Communists, only it is a different type of violence and dictatorship by a different group which they support. The Communist openly declares that in a struggle for power, overt violence is inevitable, and that the Communist will be ready to use it. Present big industrialists as represented in the Chamber of Commerce do not only advocate violence, but use violence in the use of company police in strike situations, and surely are guilty of the covert types of violence, such as the paying of starvation wages, which violate health and the right to decent living conditions for the workers. You and I do not feel this violence. Therefore we are repelled by the use of the word violence in

the connection . . . [but] to the ten million unemployed, the United
States must represent a dictatorship of the owners of industry.[5]

As for "communist propaganda," Detzer had commented some
months earlier that "it is not what they say, but what they do that is
important."[6] By fall 1935 what the communists did was becoming more
important, not so much in the United States but on the international
scene. As Detzer indicated at a meeting of the WILPF's International
Executive in Geneva, it was in the best interest of the Soviet Union to
have her allies "heavily armed." Thus the signing of a mutual aid pact
between the Russians and the French that year might help deter potential German aggression, but it would also "split the united front between pacifists and Communists," as Russia would undoubtedly ask
communists in France and other countries to support arms increases
for defense against possible fascist attacks.[7] This eventuality, she
thought, would only make the possibility of war more likely. A strong
unified peace movement was thus imperative.

Such unity characterized the American peace movement in 1935
as it began its drive for a strict neutrality law. Representing twenty-eight
organizations of which the WILPF was one of the more active members, the NPC met regularly throughout May to plan strategy to push
the neutrality legislation through Congress before adjournment. It appointed a committee, headed by James T. Shotwell of Columbia University, to study the issue and make recommendations; sponsored a mass
meeting in Carnegie Hall at which senators Nye and Clark and representative Maverick delivered impassioned speeches to a large and supportive crowd; and secured a hearing before the House Foreign Affairs
Committee in mid-June. Its position on neutrality—that the policy of
this country "should be revised in order that the risk of entanglement
in foreign wars may be reduced and in order that the United States
may not obstruct the world community in its efforts to maintain
peace"—did not go nearly far enough to suit the WILPF, but in the
interest of a united front, the women accepted it.[8]

Phillip Bradley, Amherst College political science professor, represented the NPC at the hearings and made a "brilliant" showing as he
"urged adoption of a four-point program designed to keep American
arms, contraband goods, money, and travelers away from belligerent
countries."[9] When the hearings ended, however, Sam McReynolds kept
his promise made to the administration in spring 1934; the committee
took no action. While the State Department thus stalled, the WILPF
swung into action: "In June and July of 1935, telegrams and letters

began arriving in Washington from local branches of the Women's International League. . . . The writers referred to the policy of neutral rights that led to American entry into World War I and appealed for a new program before war came again in Europe. Letter after letter mentioned the tense Ethiopian situation, describing it as the prelude to a great war."[10] A series of peace-oriented radio broadcasts sponsored by the NPC accompanied the writing campaign.

In late July the State Department and Roosevelt reached consensus in support of a discretionary arms embargo to allow the president some leeway in cooperating with other powers against an aggressor. Conferences between the State Department and Senator Pittman's committee produced a draft satisfactory to the administration, but a long way from the more rigid measures already on the Congressional calendar. And by this time—1 August 1935—the peace movement was becoming increasingly impatient with the procrastination. "For some reason . . . all this legislation is being held up, either by the President or the State Department. Whether the Navy Department or the munitions interests, or both, are behind this administrative hedging, we do not know, but the time has come to divert all our energies to demanding neutrality legislation from the President and Secretary Hull at this session, before it is too late. . . . Unless our neutrality policy is revised before the first loan is made to Italy or Ethiopia, the stopping of such loans, in even a few weeks, could be considered as a hostile act."[11]

Time was indeed running out—Mussolini had rejected the latest offers of the French and British to effect a peaceful settlement of the Ethiopian situation, and all-out war in Africa appeared imminent. Perhaps for this reason on 20 August, Senators Nye, Clark, Bone, and Vandenberg began a filibuster to force Senate action. It was quickly forthcoming. With the filibuster only a few hours old, Pittman introduced a bill approved only twenty-four hours earlier by the Foreign Relations Committee, and requested action on it the next day. Stunned by this about-face on the Senate's part, peace forces quickly recovered and spent virtually every waking hour of the next few days on Capitol Hill. "The atmosphere was so tense," wrote one WILPF member, "that people who remembered 1917 felt an almost terrifying resemblance between this Congress and that one, in the feverish days before the Declaration of War. Even the doormen in the House galleries remarked on the similarity."[12]

On the following day the Senate passed the bill virtually within minutes and sent it to the House. Amended to include a six-month time limit, the House passed the compromise version on 23 August;

the next day the Senate did likewise. On 31 August 1935 Roosevelt signed the first American Neutrality Act into law. Once the president declared a war to exist between two or more foreign nations, a mandatory embargo on arms to the belligerents would go into effect. The president was given discretion in defining "arms" and in applying the embargo to other countries should they enter a war in progress. The act further prohibited arms shipments in U.S. ships either directly to belligerents or indirectly to neutrals for trans-shipment to belligerents. The president could also declare that Americans who sailed on belligerent ships did so at their own risk.

Not exactly what the peace movement had hoped for, it nevertheless represented a workable compromise between the mandatory and discretionary positions. From the WILPF's perspective, the act's major defect was its time limitation. The mandatory arms embargo would automatically expire on 29 February 1936, a mere six months away.

Only a little over a month later in early October 1935, Detzer was on her way home from a three-months' sojourn in the WILPF's Geneva office when she heard the news that Italy, without formally declaring war, had launched a full-scale attack on Ethiopia. Having kept a close eye on the situation from her vantage point in Switzerland where she attended the League of Nations Council meetings, Detzer was not particularly surprised to hear of the invasion. Her concern that this conflict involving a major European power could easily escalate into a more generalized war was reflected in the many messages the WILPF had sent to the White House and Congress for over six months. Now the question was, how would Roosevelt respond to this latest act of hostile aggression?

Detzer did not have long to wait, for on 5 October the president invoked the recently passed arms embargo, warned Americans against traveling on belligerent ships, and proclaimed to U.S. businessmen that he who traded with either belligerent did so at his own risk. Because Ethiopia had neither ships upon which Americans would be traveling nor strong economic ties to the American business community, these warnings clearly indicated U.S. disapproval of Italian aggression. The WILPF fired off a letter, praising Roosevelt for his prompt action.

Following quickly was the League of Nations' condemnation of Italy for violating the Covenant. This announcement was of even greater import, for now the way was open for economic sanctions against Italy. Shortly thereafter, the League placed an embargo on the shipment of arms to Italy and recommended that League members halt their imports of Italian goods. But the most decisive sanction of all—an embargo on strategic raw materials, particularly oil—was not applied. The one measure that undoubtedly would have rendered the Italian war machine impotent in a matter of weeks was the one measure that France and England would not agree to.

The WILPF also gave serious thought to the issue of sanctions, and it quickly became inextricably bound up with its views on neutrality. The subject first emerged during the Manchurian crisis, and at the WILPF's National Board meeting in March 1933 Balch presented a policy statement for consideration. The board agreed that the group's position should be one of friendliness to all nations and that each individual case of conflict should be judged on its own merit. The WILPF should not hesitate to note disapproval of "recognized" aggression. The women also condemned the traffic in arms to any nation at any time and opposed loans and credits for war purposes to all nations equally. In a case where one nation was clearly the "victim," however, and would be "injured by a prohibition affecting both sides," the women favored nonmilitary aid.

On these points board members were of one mind; this was not the case when it came to stronger sanctions. The issue of private boycotts by Americans of an aggressor nation's products was tabled, and discussion over withdrawal of U.S. ambassadors produced no consensus. As for "other economic pressure" that might be applied, the women could agree only on their opposition to a food blockade.[13]

Renewed concern over the issue of sanctions came in the wake of the Italo-Ethiopian conflict. At its October 1935 board meeting, the WILPF resolved to continue its opposition to arms shipments and loans to all belligerents. It now reached consensus on boycotts as well, for the women urged the "acceptance of exports from any of the belligerents."[14]

As for the neutrality law, the crux of the issue as the women saw it by the end of the year was whether Congress "should substitute for the present inadequate law new neutrality legislation which will give the President the power to cooperate with the League in imposing sanctions on an aggressor, or whether the legislation should be mandatory upon the President to apply embargoes on both sides." Noting that the present law was not really neutrality legislation at all but merely embargo legislation, the WILPF concluded that to invoke it against an aggressor only—in this case, Italy—was "to risk the United States being drawn into a League war." Thus the women wanted the law revised so rigidly that the United States could not be drawn into any conflict "through the gate of economic sanctions." The WILPF believed that economic sanctions led to military sanctions, and military sanctions meant war. This point was of particular concern, for the women viewed the Italo-Ethiopian conflict as "only a curtain-raiser for what may come when Germany breaks loose, or when Japan goes too far in the Far East."[15]

With an eye on 23 February 1936 when the Neutrality Act would expire, peace organizations as well as the State Department worked feverishly in late 1935 to come up with an acceptable replacement law. In December Shotwell's NPC committee produced a bill that recommended "the continuation of the arms embargo, a ban on loans to belligerents, and a discriminatory embargo on raw materials whereby the President could prohibit the export of strategic items which he considered essential to any war in progress. The embargoes were to apply impartially to all belligerents, but if the President found that any nation went to war in violation of the Kellogg-Briand Pact, with the consent of Congress he could lift all embargoes on the countries that had been attacked."[16]

This last provision was supported by peace advocates such as the CEIP and the League of Nations Association, which believed that collective security was the top priority, but was vigorously opposed by the more militant pacifist groups such as the WILPF, FOR, and NCPW, all of which thought that keeping the United States out of war should come first, a position that appeared to push them into the isolationist camp. In order to clarify the pacifist view, the WILPF pointed out that these organizations were not isolationist "in the accepted sense of the word." Rather, "they stand for an internationally organized world, but an internationally organized world divorced from any military obligations."[17] Here was the distinction the more radical peace societies would make again and again, that of the difference between a rigid isolationist policy and a "non-military" policy. The former was represented by a small bloc in Congress and was a continual source of frustration to pacifists who adhered to the latter view.

At the same time as the NPC bill, the State Department proposed its measure, outlined by Roosevelt in his annual message to Congress on 3 January. Earlier that same day Pittman in the Senate and McReynolds in the House introduced two identical bills with the provisions requested by the administration, thus diverting attention from that proposed by the NPC. Then three days later Nye and Clark brought up yet another resolution in the Senate identical to one introduced by Maverick in the House.

Rejecting the NPC draft, the WILPF supported the Nye-Clark measure rather than Pittman's administration bill. Both measures were mandatory in their embargo on the shipment of arms, ammunition, and implements of war, and both forbade loans to belligerents and travel by Americans on belligerent ships except at their own risk. The section on loans in the Nye-Clark bill was preferred by the WILPF because the administration measure gave the president the power to exempt, at his discretion, commercial credits and short-term obligations.

The bills differed most sharply on the question of raw materials essential for war purposes. The Nye-Clark bill provided for a mandatory embargo on the shipment of such materials over and above a certain quota, the normal trading average of the five preceding years. The trading allowed would be on a "cash-and-carry" basis with all goods shipped on the purchasing nation's vessels with transfer of title made before such goods left U.S. ports. The Pittman bill gave the president the power to decide whether or not trade in such materials could be carried on without restriction or not at all. The significant difference between the two measures thus came down to one basic issue. Should the president have discretionary power to invoke the provisions as he saw fit?

While Congress held hearings, a third measure was introduced that would extend the 1935 Neutrality Act until 1 May 1937, adding only a ban on loans to belligerents. Proposed by Senator Elbert D. Thomas, the bill represented what Thomas hoped would be a satisfactory compromise between the other two.

Congressional support for the stronger resolutions began to waver under heavy pressure from the business community opposed to the trade restrictions in the Pittman and Nye-Clark measures, and from the Italian-American community, which thought that the bills discriminated against Italy, plus the pressure of an election year and the threat of a filibuster by isolationist Hiram Johnson. With the deadline only a few weeks away, the Thomas compromise measure began to look more and more like a way out. Ignoring the protests of pacifists and the administration, Congress accepted the extension proposal on 18 February 1936.

In his explanation for the failure of Congress to pass a more rigid neutrality law, diplomatic historian Robert Divine asserts that the Roosevelt administration "still sought for ways to co-operate passively with the League in its efforts to restrain aggressors. The Nye group was equally determined to adopt a policy aimed solely at insulating the United States from contact with European wars." This assertion may be correct as far as it goes, but to then conclude that "the real issue in 1936 differed little from that of 1935—it was isolation versus collective security," is to over-simplify and dichotomize a more complex reality.[18]

There was indeed that small bloc in Congress combined with like-minded Americans who were "isolationist" in the strictest sense of the word. They wished as little political intercourse with the Old World as possible, even to the extent of curtailing commercial relations, if necessary. Then there were those Americans, well represented in the administration by Cordell Hull and Henry Stimson before him, who firmly adhered to a position of collective security, that is, of cooperation with European nations even to the point of war.

But there was also a third group of Americans who did not fit neatly into either the "isolationist" or "collective security" camps. Included here were a substantial number of the peace organizations, particularly those founded during or after World War I, which diplomatic historians have lost in the shuffle, preferring to lump them together with the isolationists. Although this group desired to insulate the United States from European wars, as did the isolationists, they also advocated cooperation with the European nations, considered anathema to isolationists. And here is where these organizations, the WILPF among them, begin to defy simplistic categorization.

Internationalist in both philosophy and policy, the WILPF was less interested in the concept of collective security as a deterrent to would-be aggression—essentially a negative policy—than it was in cooperative ventures with other nations to remove the inequities and injustices that lead certain countries to believe that aggression is the only viable alternative for redress of grievance. This positive conception of "collective security" did not, however, include cooperation for war or even preparation for war. This is a distinction that historians of U.S. foreign relations have failed to make clear. It has, apparently, been too easy to equate "antiwar" with "isolationism," however erroneous in point of fact that equation may be.

Such antiwar groups were disappointed that the Nye-Clark bill was passed over in favor of the Thomas compromise, but the latter was still deemed preferable to the Pittman measure. The neutrality legislation debate was by no means over, however, for the Thomas compromise would expire on 1 May 1937 and in the interim, the arms embargo issue took on added significance when in July 1936 the Spanish Civil War broke out. The Thomas measure was ominously silent with respect to civil wars and the Spanish conflict had critical ideological as well as political and military ramifications, for both Hitler and Mussolini used it as a military "testing ground" in their support of the fascist attempt to topple Spain's republican government.

In the meantime, with the neutrality issue temporarily settled by mid-February 1936, pacifists turned to other matters, organizational as well as political. The party conventions looking ahead to the national election in the fall were right around the corner, and in order to influence both candidates and platforms, pacifists needed to solidify their newly created organization, the Emergency Peace Campaign (EPC).

Disturbed by the lack of militancy among the thirty-one groups of the NPC,[19] approximately 100 pacifists from the WILPF, FOR, NCPW, AFSC, and various religions, labor, student, and farm groups met in early December 1935 at Buck Hill Falls, Pennsylvania, to discuss how they might take a more active role in the peace movement.[20] As Detzer pointed out, pacifists were a minority in both the NPC and NCPW, and "three-quarters" of NPC members "were not clear regarding the point at which they would separate themselves from any war undertaken by the United States." Moreover, the NPC would not "tackle" issues like lynching, but a "left-wing" group like the EPC "could and should." Jeannette Rankin, representing the NCPW, also reflected the conference's more militant tone when she declared there was "no time to educate" people to a more pacifistic point of view as the NPC, NCPW, and NCCCW were prone to do. Pacifists must "make present peace sentiment effective" in what she termed the current "crisis situation."[21]

That situation included "the increasing number and frequency of serious international situations" in Europe and the Far East. It also involved "universal rearmament," which included the United States with its "billion dollar program for 1935, announcement of high increases above this for 1936, [and] expansion of 'defenses' far into the Pacific," and the failure of disarmament negotiations. As disturbing as anything else was "the clash of rival systems" wherein communism, fascism, socialism, and capitalism were all "struggling . . . for supremacy in the years ahead." What made this ideological conflict all the more ominous was that "not one of these systems . . . is completely pacifist, although the third is approximately so." When these factors were combined with "the probability of revolutionary violence" and the pervasive "depression weariness," the conclusion was inescapable: "The rush toward war is under way with tremendously accelerated speed. If this continues unchecked, war on a world scale will result within the next few years."[22]

Agreeing to embark upon a vigorous two-year campaign to "keep the United States from going to war and to promote world peace," the radical pacifists of the EPC vowed to "strengthen the pacific alternatives to armed conflict, bring about the political and economic changes essential to a just and warless world, and build up a dynamic movement of people who have determined not to approve of or participate in war."[23]

Granted affiliation with the NPC as its "action arm" in March 1936,

Ray Newton of the AFSC was named executive director of the EPC and Detzer, Olmsted, and Emily Cooper Johnson of the WILPF became three of the executive committee's twenty-two members.[24] The NPC officially launched the Emergency Peace Campaign at a meeting in Washington, D.C., on 21 April that included a national radio broadcast with Eleanor Roosevelt as one of the featured speakers. Kirby Page, head of the EPC Speakers Bureau, organized meetings, lectures, and conferences from one end of the country to the other. In Washington the group's Legislative Committee, chaired by Detzer, worked with other pacifist organizations pressuring both the president and Congress to limit the nation's military to "the minimum needed to defend [the] continental United States from an aggressor," and to pass the Frazier Amendment to the Constitution, which called for a war referendum vote of the people.[25]

At the same time the WILPF, maintaining its customary nonpartisan political stance, continued to work closely with the nonpacifist peace groups in pressuring both major political parties to incorporate into their platforms an eleven-point program adopted by the NPC in May. This was not an isolationist program to keep the United States aloof from world affairs, but rather one that stressed active U.S. participation in international efforts to stabilize currencies, reduce tariff barriers to trade, control the munitions industry, take the profit out of war and preparation for war, and reduce national military establishments. Additional planks urged continued U.S. activity in the International Labor Organization, continued American cooperation with the League of Nations in its "social, economic and humanitarian activities," and an extension of the neutrality law "to include an embargo on supplementary war material."[26]

The peace movement was unable, however, to persuade the Republicans to act positively on this program. Registering its "intense chagrin" at the party's foreign policy planks, which said nothing about embargoes, arms reduction, or control of the munitions industry, the NPC called them "the most isolationist in the party's history" and "utterly unrealistic." Although the Democratic platform stressed domestic over foreign policy matters, peace advocates agreed that it was not only "much more international in its outlook," but also more in line with NPC recommendations.[27]

As for the WILPF, its 1936 program echoed that of the NPC but its statement of policies went much beyond what many NPC organizations would have found acceptable. "The danger of a fascist development places a serious responsibility upon those who believe in peace and freedom," the women declared. They therefore made it WILPF policy "to demonstrate the basic relationship between war and fascism," to preserve civil rights for all, to fight against racial prejudice and discrimination, "to stand for political and economic justice to aliens," to oppose the use of violence against labor unions and in breaking strikes, and to "recognize that covert forms of violence inherent in the inequalities of our present economic system, and are unethical and cruel as overt types of violence."[28]

Such strong statements apparently smacked of "un-Americanism" for those who still viewed pacifists with suspicion. In March Hannah Hull, in response to a Connecticut man who wanted to know how many socialists were connected with the WILPF in an "official capacity," patiently told him that after looking over a list of board members, she could not honestly say to what political party they belonged. She explained that she herself was a member of the Republican Party but was "far from proud of it." Congresswoman Caroline O'Day of New York and WILPF vice president, on the other hand, was a Democrat. "I do not doubt that we have Socialists," Hull commented, "but we never make a point of asking each other to what parties we belong,"[29] perhaps her way of trying to tell the gentleman that the WILPF had more pressing issues about which to be concerned.

The Salem, Massachusetts, branch was threatened with the resignation of some of its more faint-hearted members after a retired army officer "attacked the League" in the local press, based on a damning but unsubstantiated indictment of peace organizations in a book entitled *The Red Network* by one Elizabeth Dilling. "It is so utterly ridiculous that it is hard to believe that anyone takes 'The Red Network' seriously," exclaimed Olmsted. What disturbed Martha Elliott of the Boston WILPF was that while all the hysteria over "reds" was resurfacing, more important—and more menacing—was the "increased antipathy and animosity against the Jewish people" and the declaration of an officer in the conservative and "patriotic" Sentinels of the Republic that "what we need in this country is another Hitler."[30]

The attacks against the WILPF continued through that summer, including a full-page diatribe in the Hearst-owned *Philadelphia Inquirer* entitled "Red Pacifism." While stressing in rebuttal that "pacifism does not 'march with Marxism' or any other 'ism'," Hannah Hull *did* emphasize that the WILPF "opposes Fascism, which is directly contrary to every principle of Freedom and of American Democracy."[31] As Detzer remarked a few weeks later, "people are always asking us why we don't fight against Communism as much as Fascism." The answer was simple:

the WILPF had first-hand knowledge of the fascist threat to life and liberty whereas it "did not consider . . . Communism [to be] a menace at this time."[32]

And by fall 1936 fascism was indeed the "menace," for during that summer just as the U.S. political campaign was heating up, the Spanish Civil War erupted. This conflict was more than just an effort on the part of General Francisco Franco's fascist rebels to overthrow the republican government. It was also symbolic of the ideological struggle of which the EPC had spoken only six months earlier, and it very quickly posed a problem for the Roosevelt administration. By August Germany and Italy were aiding the rebels while the Soviet Union rallied behind the Loyalists. Not particularly enamored of the idea of supporting either the fascists or the communists, England and France attempted to prevent war materiél from going to either side, and Roosevelt concurred. Because the 1936 neutrality law was silent with respect to civil wars, all the administration could do was verbally discourage traffic in arms.

The war also posed a problem for the WILPF. No one was more fervently antifascist than these women pacifists who already had lost a number of their prominent European members to the repression and violence of Hitler. A victory by Franco's forces was the last thing they wanted in a Europe already stricken with hatred, fear, and despair. Yet in their conviction that nothing of worth can result from war and determined to keep the United States from being embroiled through aid to either side, they insisted that an embargo not only on arms but also on essential raw materials be invoked against both belligerents, with the full knowledge that it would do far more harm to the Loyalists' cause than to Franco's fascists. The women also urged a truce "so that reason could have a chance to make itself heard," and persistently called for mediation by the United States.[33]

In the meantime, Roosevelt won re-election in a landslide victory that was "marvelous," thought Detzer, "when one realizes that on the Landon side was the entire Hearst press . . . also the Rockefellers, Morgans, Mellons, etc." With the exception of one New York candidate for Congress, she noted, "all of our friends were re-elected,"[34] an outcome that pleased the International WILPF leaders in Geneva as well. With the campaign and election behind them, the WILPF and other organizations of the EPC under the guidance of Charles P. Taft II, prepared for a renewal of the struggle over neutrality legislation as Congress reassembled in January 1937. In December Roosevelt announced his intentions of asking for permanent neutrality legislation.

By the beginning of the new year four points of view emerged in the debate, two representing the discretionary position and two advocating a mandatory stance. Those who favored discretion wanted the president to have the power when war erupted anywhere to decide himself what embargoes, if any, would be placed on which belligerent. One group of "discretionists," part of the nonpacifist wing of the peace movement, desired to see the U.S. aid the League of Nations in applying sanctions against an aggressor; the other group, believing that "the dictators are mad-dog nations [*sic*] about to strike and that the way must be left clear" to support England, France, and the Soviet Union, would give the president power to choose which side to support. Among the advocates of this collective security, or interventionist, position were the Foreign Policy Association, a number of leading newspapers, and those who preferred to "fight again to make the world safe for democracy" rather that "see a Hitlerized Europe."

Favoring the mandatory view—that the president must declare embargoes on all belligerents "in advance of an outbreak of war"—were isolationists like Senator Hiram Johnson and newspaper magnate William Randolph Hearst who were "fed up with Europe's bloody mess" and quite willing to let it "go merrily to hell." Ironically, also advocating the mandatory view was the majority of peace societies, particularly in the EPC, which were "aware of the blood on our hands for present world conditions and know that we are bound up with the world, but who absolutely repudiate war as a means of changing the situation."[35] Thus the 1937 neutrality debate promised to be no less acrimonious than that of the previous year, now compounded by the Spanish Civil War.

When Congress reconvened in January, upon the recommendation of Roosevelt, it quickly passed an embargo law specific to the Spanish situation. Under a suspension of the rules, only fifty minutes for debate was allowed with no right to amend. Representative Maury Maverick was later praised by the WILPF for his outstanding presentation of the inequities of the measure as it did not forbid shipments of war supplies to Germany, Italy, and Portugal where they could be reshipped to Franco's fascist rebels. But with the immediate issue of the Spanish Civil War resolved, however unsatisfactorily from the pacifists' perspective, the government turned to the more complex problem of permanent neutrality legislation.

As was the case a year earlier, the most intensely debated issue was whether an arms embargo should be mandatory or imposed at the president's discretion. WILPF pacifists were becoming increasingly concerned with this issue because it brought up the question of war-making power in a supposedly democratic society. The WILPF had for some time advocated placing this power directly in the hands of the people through a war referendum measure and supported the WPU's effort to amend the Constitution accordingly. It seemed a "dangerous departure," thought the women, "for democratic government to transfer this power to the Executive, even through the indirect medium of permissive neutrality legislation."[36] A sufficient number of Congressional representatives agreeing with the WILPF stymied discretionary legislation and by the end of March, all proposed neutrality laws were in the hands of a Congressional conference committee where they remained for the next six weeks.

While peace activists awaited the committee's decision, the EPC embarked upon its No-Foreign-War Crusade, an intensive effort under the direction of Admiral Richard E. Byrd in April and May to "make articulate and effective the widespread determination to keep the United States out of a world war through the adoption of an adequate program of neutrality legislation, a basic change in our military and naval policy, the easing of economic tensions through reciprocal trade agreements and cooperation with international agencies of justice."[37] The campaign opened on 6 April, the twentieth anniversary of U.S. entry into World War I, with a radio broadcast by Byrd, not a pacifist himself but a military figure "whose strong will for peace was an outgrowth of his experience at the Advance Base in the Antarctic" where he reflected "upon the madness of a civilization so periodically swept with war." Joining in the broadcast were the Rev. Harry Emerson Fosdick, EPC Chair, and Eleanor Roosevelt, with over 7,000 "listening-in" meetings among farm groups alone.[38] Immediately after its beginning, "volunteer workers and local committees spread the Crusade's message through some 2,000 towns and cities and on 500 college campuses." As DeBenedetti notes, the campaign "raised pacifist influence in the antiwar movement of the thirties to its highest level."[39]

Yet that influence had little impact on the neutrality issue. With just two days to go before the expiration of the 1936 law, the Congressional committee broke its deadlock and reported out a compromise measure. The Senate conferees had given way to the discretionary features of a bill earlier approved by the House, a move that pleased the administration while disappointing the peace forces. Compounding this discouragement was the "disgraceful way in which the . . . bill was rushed through Congress at the very last minute, after months of stalling." According to Detzer, House opponents of the measure were denied the opportunity to speak against it, and only twenty minutes was devoted to discussion before the final vote. Foreign Affairs Committee Chair McReynolds, whose behavior was "dictatorial, . . . conducted himself disgracefully for a public servant;" at least one representative did not have the opportunity to vote "no" and a voice vote was called for "so indistinctly" that few knew what was happening.

The situation in the Senate was less conducive to "railroading" legislation; here, five hours' debate was allowed.[40] Senators Bone, Nye, Vandenberg, and Clark all protested vehemently against the discretionary features of the bill, but despite this angry opposition, the Senate passed it. The House quickly followed suit and Roosevelt signed the 1937 Neutrality Act on 1 May.

The WILPF applauded the act's mandatory features, which included an embargo on the shipment of arms, ammunition, implements of war, and on loans and credits to belligerent nations or those involved in civil war. But the women strongly opposed the provision giving the president authority to lay down rules and regulations governing the solicitation of funds for the relief of human suffering in war-torn nations, for this meant that Americans could be prohibited from raising money for food, clothing, and medicine for civilian populations.

The act also stipulated a "cash-and-carry" policy for the shipment of war materials that the WILPF endorsed. But it did *not* approve of the provision that such a policy was to be invoked at the president's discretion, because the women were leery of conferring that degree of power upon any one individual. "Those who argue so consistently for permissive powers," wrote Detzer when it was all over, "appear to have much more faith in the Executive Departments of the Government than it would seem that past history should warrant. However much faith we might have in the peace aims of the present Administration . . . I should never be sure that a future President would be on the 'right side'."[41]

In addition, the act prohibited the arming of U.S. merchant ships and the carrying of arms to belligerent nations in American vessels as well as the travel of U.S. citizens on belligerent ships. Here again the WILPF protested, for the president was given the power to make exceptions as he saw fit. "Having severely curbed munitions makers and bankers, Congress chose not to impair foreign trade by imposing drastic limitations on the export of contraband goods other than arms, despite the revelations of the Nye committee which indicated that general trade in wartime was far more likely to lead to involvement than the export of munitions. . . . The legislators decided to limit risks while preserving profits." No one seemed particularly happy with the new law. As Robert Divine notes, it was a "haphazard compromise which failed to establish a clear-cut neutrality policy for the nation,"[42] and as armed aggression became more blatant in the months ahead, this failure became increasingly evident.

The division within the peace movement between pacifist and nonpacifist that emerged in the 1937 neutrality debates demonstrated how fragile the peace coalition was when the potential of global conflict threatened. Signs of strain began to surface even among pacifists. When the ALAWF approached the other peace societies to join in an appeal to the administration to embargo arms shipments to Italy and Germany on the grounds that both were participating in the Spanish conflict, Eleanor Fowler, legislative assistant in the WILPF's National Office, eagerly sought Board approval. Quickly denying her request, Hannah Hull explained that there was no direct evidence that Hitler and Mussolini were shipping arms to Franco: "The only *proof* that we have of participation by these countries . . . is the participation of volunteers in the armies; of which, of course, other countries are also guilty." Moreover, said Hull, the United States could not embargo arms to Italy and Germany alone "without the implication that they are definitely guilty and they alone,—and we would therefore be taking sides."[43]

For Fowler, "taking sides" was precisely the point and it would become *the* issue in the next few years dividing the peace movement right down the middle. It was not just that there was ample evidence as far as Fowler was concerned that Italy's and Germany's participation in the Spanish war went far beyond that of individual volunteers. It was, more importantly, that "the fight in Spain is the battle between fascism and democracy. . . . We in the WILPF recognize that peace is tied up with democracy, and war with fascism, that a victory for fascism is a victory for war."[44] The WILPF's insistence on a policy of strict neutrality, while ideologically pure, had the effect of aiding the spread of fascism and was, therefore, a capitulation to a war mentality.

Fowler was not alone among pacifists in desiring a stronger antifascist stance. In early winter 1936 the American Friends of Spanish Democracy, dominated by nationally known figures in the peace movement, urged the administration "to make no endeavor to prevent the shipment of arms to the beleaguered and betrayed democracy of Madrid while continuing in full force its present stand against traffic with the fascist insurgents." Incensed at this instance of "taking sides," Detzer, a member of the organization's executive board, immediately declared to Executive Committee member Roger Baldwin that if the group did not retract that statement, she would resign.[45]

About six months later, many of the same pacifists came out in support of a Congressional resolution proclaiming Germany, Italy, and Portugal nations at war as defined in the Neutrality Act and thus automatically subject to an embargo on war materials. When asked for its backing of this resolution, again the WILPF was divided and for the same reasons. Not until spring 1938 did it take the stronger stand earlier advocated by Fowler calling for application of an embargo to Germany and Italy "whose governments have sent invading armies into Spain and therefore are among the belligerents."[46]

This division within the WILPF over the issue of acknowledging the distinction between victim and aggressor did not immediately result in organizational rupture. It did, however, anticipate the growing outrage and indignation of many within the WILPF and the peace movement as a whole as fascist aggression accelerated unchallenged throughout the remainder of the decade, compelling pacifist and nonpacifist alike to join those Americans who desired stronger U.S. action in response.

While the debate over American response to the Spanish Civil War continued until Franco's forces were ultimately triumphant in 1939, the 1937 neutrality law was given its first serious test in the summer when hostilities again erupted between China and Japan. In early July the military forces of both countries clashed near Peking and such encounters continued sporadically throughout the remainder of that month. Neither side declared war, even after Japan launched a full-scale attack in mid-August.

Hoping that this latest clash in the Far East would not escalate into all-out war, the Roosevelt administration stalled. It was hesitant to invoke the embargo law that it felt would work to the detriment of the Chinese. The president refused to proclaim that a state of war existed. He would invoke the neutrality law only when one side or the other declared war, or if and when the likelihood of U.S. involvement appeared imminent.

Gravely concerned that this fresh outbreak of hostilities would precipitate a more widespread conflict, the WILPF urged Roosevelt to consult with other nations as to how this threat to world peace might best be met. When in August the U.S. ship *Augusta* was fired upon, killing one seaman and injuring seventeen others, and the administration still continued in its procrastination, the women's demands for action became more insistent. Press releases, letters, and telegrams poured out of the national office on an almost daily basis as the WILPF strove feverishly to move public opinion behind its demands.

On 5 October 1937 the president finally responded. While in Chicago on a tour of the Midwest, he made a major foreign policy address that quickly became known as the "Quarantine" speech. On the surface, it seemed to signal an impending shift in U.S. policy toward aggressors abroad for Roosevelt declared that "when a epidemic of physical disease starts to spread, the community approves and joins in a quarantine of the patients in order to protect the health of the community against the spread of the disease."[47] Although he did not elaborate on the form this "quarantine" might take, he left the distinct impression that the United States could not, and would not, remain aloof from such a "community" effort.

Pacifists were appalled. Six peace organizations, the WILPF among them, "condemned the President's Chicago speech as rousing a war spirit." Highly distressed that Roosevelt could condemn other nations for breaking international law while at the same time ignoring a U.S. statute designed to meet a crisis just like the present one, these pacifists concluded that global conflict was no longer the only threat. Now it appeared that democracy at home was also under siege.

> We agree with the President that the disease of war should be quarantined. But the only protective quarantine for the people of this country is the invocation of the neutrality law. . . . If the democracies are going to unite for the protection of democracy it is essential that democratic processes be preserved. The usurpation of that power by the Executive is the foundation of dictatorship. The reasons advanced by the President for refusal to apply the neutrality law are so inadequate as to indicate that the real reason is the intention of asserting executive power as over and above any right of Congress to limit that power. Unless the neutrality law is applied the President has in his hands a blank check on which he can write whatever foreign policy he sees fit at whatever cost to the American people.[48]

The WILPF was particularly disturbed by what the "Quarantine" speech seemed to represent as a portend of American fascism. "We believe that in a world in which Fascism is rising, in which democratic methods are falling by the wayside, it is imperative for the head of a great democratic country to carry out the law." When such a leader fails to do this, the women warned, "it is a most dangerous precedent." They were not convinced by Roosevelt's assertion that the Western Hemisphere would not escape attack should war "come to pass in other parts of the world." The president, they alleged, "knows as well as we do that Continental America will not be attacked." His only purpose for making such a statement was to throw fear into the American people, a fear that would bring public support for his "two billion dollar armament program," a program unnecessary for national defense, the WILPF believed, but one which the administration would use to deal with the unsolved unemployment problem at home."[49] If there was any enemy that the United States should fear, thought the WILPF, it was not Japan nor Germany nor any other foreign power, however warlike in behavior. "Though we have a formidable foe," asserted Detzer in November, "that foe is the twin evil of militarism and poverty. . . . They are part and parcel of the same war system under which we live."[50]

At about the same time as Roosevelt's speech, the League of Nations condemned Japan for violating the Nine Power and Kellogg-Briand pacts. The State Department quickly supported this move. It also accepted a League invitation to a November conference in Brussels to discuss the Far Eastern situation, but Japan refused to participate and by Thanksgiving, the conference ended, an abysmal failure. Still Roosevelt refused to invoke the Neutrality Act, and by this time the WILPF was unequivocal in charging the administration with "manifesting a definite fascist tendency. One of the first ways in which that occurs," Detzer told her audience, "is when the central government takes up power which belongs to a parliament or, in other words, defies the law. The President . . . refuses to carry out the intent and purpose of the neutrality act and we therefore have, to my mind, the first dangerous manifestation of fascism."[51]

The Japanese bombing of the U.S. gunboat *Panay* on 12 December 1937 infuriated pacifists. Had the United States withdrawn its military forces from the area of the Yangtze River in the beginning, protested the WILPF, such an incident could not have occurred. The government's handling of the incident only corroborated the WILPF's distrust of the administration, for Cordell Hull's reply to a letter of protest from the women was "the first official admission in America, so far as we know, that our gunboats were actually protecting Standard Oil ships (and no doubt convoying them to the Chinese troops)." For the WILPF, there was only one conclusion to be drawn: "Administration policy is not based on high moral grounds, or on any interest in the 'victims of aggression,' but primarily on the protection of American interests and property."[52]

The *Panay* incident only served to increase American sympathy and support for China, and thus the administration finally acknowledged openly the policy it had been following for months. Because application of the neutrality law would operate in Japan's favor, the administration declared it had no intention of putting the law into effect. This announcement, as the administration had anticipated, caused hardly a stir, except, of course, in pacifist circles where those who had fought against presidential discretionary power felt confirmed in the legitimacy of their fears.

In the middle of all the furor over events in the Far East came congressional consideration of the war referendum issue. On 10 January 1938 members of the House gathered to consider a motion to compel the Rules Committee to allow debate on Louis Ludlow's bill, which would amend the Constitution to provide for a referendum vote of the people before Congress could declare war. William Bankhead, speaker of the House, opposed Congressional consideration of the bill and so, too, did Roosevelt. According to Balch, the administration and its "collective security" supporters were against the measure "because they believe this will weaken their hands in a diplomatic game of bluff with Japan—they are afraid to have Japan think that America would not fight or that the government would be hampered by a plebiscite before it could act."[53] As she saw it, using such a threat of war as an instrument of national policy was every bit as much a violation of the Kellogg-Briand Pact as war itself.

A spirited debate followed the speaker's remarks but the administration won the day. The vote, after only twenty minutes, remarked Detzer, was not only "a victory for gag rule," but involved the "basic question of democracy" as well. The issue was not so much one of "war and peace," asserted the WILPF, but "whether or not the representatives of the people should respond to the demand from the country and debate the measure" that for three years had been "pigeon-holed in committee." As the women pointed out, a poll taken by the Institute of Public Opinion in October showed that 73 percent of those polled favored the referendum. Here, then, was "a clear case in which the majority of the House responded not to the will of their [sic] constituents, but to the will of the President." From the WILPF's perspective, the House vote not to debate the bill "shows clearly that in a crisis, representative government cannot be trusted with the issue of war and peace."[54]

Supporters of the war referendum refused to let it die, and in mid-March 1938 a similar resolution was introduced in the Senate. Events in Europe, however, quickly overshadowed the issue, for in that month Hitler again violated the Treaty of Versailles by forcing *Anschluss* on Austria, adding that country to his Third Reich.

The WILPF was "horrified by this march of German fascism against Austria" and with other pacifist groups, renewed its efforts to strengthen the Neutrality Act. They wanted a mandatory embargo on war materials other than munitions and subsidization of the industries and labor that might suffer economically under such an embargo. The choice, they maintained, was not between collective security and isolation. The former belonged in "the realm of fantasy and wishful thinking;" the latter was "impossible." But "non-intervention and non-cooperation with war are possible" and, thought the WILPF, imperative. "Our first duty," it asserted, "is to keep America out of war. When that can be fully assured, the United States can then be in a position to lend its greater power, *through peaceful means*, in dealing with the problems now wrecking the world."[55]

When France and England made no more than verbal protest against *Anschluss*, Hitler immediately began making demands that Czechoslovakia turn over the Sudetenland to Germany, populated as it was by primarily German-speaking peoples. As spring 1938 became summer these demands became increasingly strident, but Czechoslovakia adamantly refused to give in, even mobilizing her military in the event that Germany tried to take the region by force. This new crisis had even greater potential for war because France and the Soviet Union had mutual aid treaties with the beleaguered democracy. Moreover, loss of the Sudetenland would leave Czechoslovakia vulnerable to further aggression for not only did it contain key industry, it also housed practically all of the country's defensive fortifications.

At the WILPF's International Executive Committee meeting in Geneva in early September, Clara Ragaz, one of the three joint chairs, reported that despite their commitment to pacifism a growing number of WILPF members in Czechoslovakia "were in the very strange position" of supporting the "military measures" taken by the government to defend the country. Lola Hanouskova of the Czechoslovakian WILPF corroborated Ragaz's observation. "After the annexation of Austria," she noted, "the Czechoslovak people felt only too well that Hitler does not want and will not allow any rapprochement between the nations of Central Europe. Czechoslovakia waited for the reaction of the other countries to the annexation and when it failed, it realized that its own turn had come. It also realized that it had to depend on its own strength and could not rely on support from outside. . . . The Czechoslovak people," she concluded emphatically, "are determined to defend their independence and not to allow Germany to triumph over them."[56]

By the end of the month, the Czechs were given a graphic demonstration of just how little "support from outside" they could expect. At a conference with Hitler in Munich to which neither Czechoslovakia nor the Soviet Union was invited, England and France agreed to persuade the Czechs to accede to German claims on the Sudetenland in the interest of "peace in our time," as British Prime Minister Neville Chamberlain put it.

But "is this PEACE?" asked the outraged joint chairs of the WILPF. "There is undoubtedly a widespread feeling of relief in all countries that the bloodshed of WAR with all its horrors . . . has been avoided," acknowledged the three women, but it was not the kind of peace for which the WILPF was striving. "It is a sham peace based on the violation of law, justice, and right. . . . The leaders of the [so-]called Democracies have given way to shameless lying and brute force." Reminding WILPF members everywhere that "pacifism is *not* quietistic acceptance of betrayal and lies for the sake of 'peace' " nor the "weak acceptance of 'faits accomplis' achieved by brute force," the joint chairs urged their national sections to support a four-point program of aid to the Czech people and an effort "to destroy the net of insinuations, calumnies and lies about Czechoslovakia" that Hitler had used as the pretext for his aggression.[57]

Given its distance from events in Europe psychologically as well as geographically, the U.S. Section of the WILPF responded to the Munich conference with less passion. If nothing else, noted the Americans, the outcome showed once again that collective security was "an illusion and a myth. For the fact remains that empires always put self-interest first. . . . When Democracy and Imperialism clash, Democracy goes down." Yet the American women were grateful that "however unjust and tragic" was the Munich decision, the world "was not plunged into war" for that would have been "worse than anything else." Whatever happened in the next few months, they stressed, "our task is clear:"[58] to prevent the United States from any military commitments that could draw her into war.

As for the administration in the wake of the Munich conference, Roosevelt "embarked on a new phase of his political career. Quietly abandoning his New Deal reforms . . . he set out to unite both conservatives and liberals behind a program of national preparedness designed to meet the dangers facing the United States in the international arena."[59] Thus in October he announced an increase of $300 million for national defense. The WILPF, among others, maintained that such massive military spending was more a matter of "domestic recovery" from the depression than one of national defense, and therefore would only "open the door to American fascism at home." As William Stone pointed out in his "Economic Consequences of Rearmament," recent history showed that huge arms expenditures "leads almost inevitably to dictatorship or government intervention . . . in the operations of the national economy" and the suppression of civil liberties.[60]

But if another reason for the military increase was to "offset Nazi economic penetration" of the Western Hemisphere, as the WILPF alleged, then it was possible that "psychologically, the threat of force may give the Germans pause." The price, however, was too high: "The danger to our own . . . democracy and liberties in building up a war machine large enough to 'protect' us from fascism abroad," warned the WILPF, "may prove to be the most fertile soil for breeding fascism at home."[61]

The growing number of such warnings by radical pacifists as the end of the decade drew near was neither specious nor a form of demagoguery. Spain, Italy, Germany—all former democracies now threatened or controlled by fascist dictatorship. What had been the catalyst? As the WILPF saw it, the major culprit was the pervasive economic dislocation throughout Europe following World War I. The lesson learned by the women pacifists was clear: No nation where economic inequity prevailed was immune to the fascist contagion, not even the United States.

Although the gap between rich and poor had widened alarmingly in the United States during the so-called "prosperity decade" of the 1920s, it took the Crash of 1929 and the onset of the Great Depression to call attention to the lack of economic democracy here at home. As Eleanor Fowler pointed out, "In 1935 the *net* income of [General Motors] was $167,226,510. Ten of its executives got more than $200,000 a year. Five more got between one and two hundred thousand. Twelve more, from $50,000 to $100,000. The wage of the average worker for the same period," she stressed, "was about $900."[62] And although Congress had appointed a committee in 1934 to investigate "Nazi propaganda activities" and Roosevelt ordered the Federal Bureau of Investigation (FBI) to look into the Nazi movement in the United States, growing repression of labor activity despite—or perhaps because of—the Wagner Act seemed to indicate to the WILPF that by 1937 there was a "fascist development in America."[63]

The 1934 cotton textile strike involving some 400,000 workers; the ongoing strikes of agricultural workers throughout the decade, particularly in California where over 88,000 laborers were involved between 1933 and 1936; the San Francisco General Strike and the Minneapolis truckers' strike in 1934; an Idaho loggers' strike in 1936—all were attended by one kind of violence or another as corporation police, vigilantes, and law enforcement officials assaulted strikers with fire hoses, beatings, tear gas bombs, and machine guns. As Fowler reported in early 1937, "the testimony so far given before the LaFollette [Civil Liberties] Committee makes it clear that the General Motors Corporation has had a consistent anti-union policy, and has spent large sums of money on labor spy work throughout its plants. . . . Clearly the great corporations have done everything in their power to nullify . . . the rights of the workers to organize into unions of their own choosing and to bargain collectively with their employers."[64]

Given the alarming growth of government-sanctioned antilabor violence, in fall 1936 the WILPF appointed Elisabeth Christman, secretary of the Women's Trade Union League, chair of a newly organized Labor Committee with Fowler as a half-time labor secretary. In February 1937 the committee published the first issue of its new labor news bulletin, the "W.I.L. Labor Front."[65] Shortly thereafter, "in order to live up in fact to our labor pronouncements," Detzer reported that the WILPF was in the process of "completely unionizing" its National Office and hoped that the branches would soon follow suit. Based on the group's recognition "that there is a close connection between peace and a decent standard of living," the purpose of its new labor program was twofold; on the one hand, to gain labor's cooperation on certain peace issues, and on the other, to cooperate with labor "in its efforts to gain the economic and social conditions which we recognize to be fundamental to peace."[66]

In her 30 April report, Fowler documented the extensive cooperation between the WILPF and organized labor in just the first six months of the new committee's existence. Some branches engaged in education work or lobbied Congress for a child labor amendment. Others concentrated their efforts among agricultural workers or raised money and collected food and clothing for striking laborers. A "splendid spirit of cooperation" developed between the WILPF and the Women's Trade Union League, a group that represented over a million women industrial workers. As Fowler stressed, "it is of the utmost importance that we, who are working for permanent peace and freedom, should have a mutually friendly and helpful relationship with that large group of industrial women."[67] One of the more encouraging examples of this new partnership was the mass meeting on "Labor and the Menace of War" held in Washington that April under the joint auspices of the District Women's Trade Union League, the District WILPF branch, the Ladies' Auxiliaries of the Bankers and Typographical Unions, and the Hotel and Restaurant Employees Union.

Most of the labor picture in 1937 and 1938, however, did not reflect such peaceful cooperative endeavor as severe recession wiped out the New Deal's economic gains. The Berkshire Hosiery strike in Reading, Pennsylvania; the Seaman's Strike on the West Coast; the anti-union activity of coal mine owners in Harlan County, Kentucky; the Memorial Day Massacre at Republic Steel in Chicago; the pecan-shellers strike in San Antonio—these were just the tip of the iceberg from early 1937 through early 1938 as almost two million workers went out in over 4,500 strikes. And whether success or failure, most involved violence and bloodshed. At the Berkshire Mills, for example, young workers on strike since October 1936 and influenced by Richard Gregg's *The Power of Non-Violence*, attempted to put Gandhi's philosophy into practice with their "lie-down strike." As Fowler reported, "they lay in front of the main gate of the plant and forced the strike-breakers to walk over their prostrate bodies to get in. They could not be dislodged by tear or vomit gas thrown by the police, and were finally only removed by wholesale arrests, which they did not resist."[68]

Delegates to the WILPF's annual meeting in May 1937 attended the hearings of the LaFollette Civil Liberties Committee and listened to miners from Harlan County, Kentucky, "tell of organized anti-union activity by the company and the local authorities, in the shape of intimidation, eviction of the miners from their homes for joining the union, hiring by the companies of gangs of thugs, deputized as sheriffs, who broke up union meetings, hunted union organizers, beat up, shot and killed workers." In early March 1937 pecan-shellers went back to work in San Antonio, Texas, after a strike of only five weeks. "They won union recognition, a six months contract, and an impartial commission to arbitrate the question of wages," exclaimed Fowler jubilantly. But they paid a stiff price: "continuous police brutality, beating and tear gassing of workers, and . . . virtual starvation of many of the workers."[69]

It did not have to be that way, as delegates to the annual meeting learned at a banquet devoted to "techniques in industrial disputes." After A. J. Muste, FOR Labor Secretary, "gave a tempered and intelligent picture" of current labor problems, Josephine Roche, Colorado owner of the Rocky Mountain Coal Company, spoke from the employer's perspective. She told her listeners how shocked she was when she took over the company to learn that prior management had spent $500,000 in nineteen months to break a miners strike. "That sum," she declared, "would have paid the increased wages the men were asking for 8 years." After the company negotiated an agreement with the miners that provided for a 25 percent wage increase, it discovered that "increased efficiency of work and lowering of operating costs actually brought added profit . . . in spite of the increased wages."

Following Roche was the evening's principal speaker, Michigan Governor Frank Murphy, "whose fine judgement and great patience resulted in the peaceful solution of the General Motors and Chrysler strikes." Stressing repeatedly that violence was self-defeating, Murphy "condemned" those who had pressured him to use force against sit-down strikers. He insisted that workers had a right to "decent conditions in their jobs" and suggested that employers must change their "worn-out philosophy . . . that workmen must be kept in their places" if industrial disputes were to be settled peacefully.[70]

Yet less than a year later the LaFollette Committee, in its investigation of the National Association of Manufacturers, learned that although the organization had over 4,000 members, only 207 "were responsible for 60% of the industrial purchases of tear gas"; that the Bethlehem Steel Company not only provided the money "used by the Johnstown Citizens Committee in strikebreaking activities," but also supplied the tear gas used by city police against pickets. Committee members also witnessed the violence and bloodshed at the Ford plant in Dearborn where union organizers, "with permits from the Dearborn authorities for leaflet distribution," were attacked and "systematically beaten up" by men suspected of being part of Ford's private security force.[71]

But it was not just the employer who used violence against labor; law enforcement officials did as well. Even before the 30 May 1937 clash between the Republic Steel Company and striking workers in Chicago, a committee of the National Lawyers Guild investigated the relationship between the company and city police and found that the police were "actively cooperating with the Republic Steel Corporation to break the strike." As a result, ten strikers were dead and as many injured. A news film made of the strike, suppressed at the time for fear that it might incite a riot, showed "not the story of a riot but of a massacre." It took over two weeks for the truth to come out, but when it did, the WILPF immediately sent a letter of shocked protest to Chicago's mayor. "The firing of the police on a completely unarmed line of marchers seeking only to establish a picket line in accordance with their rights," proclaimed the women, "is to us an almost unbelievable violation of the most elementary human rights. The brutality exhibited by the police in hunting down and beating up the fleeing strikers is a sad commentary on the training which these men have received."[72]

As Detzer commented after reading a detailed description of the news film, "it is a ghastly story and one which should fill every American with the deepest shame. The hideous brutality of the Chicago police makes one think of Nazi Germany." Attempts by Congress to vitiate the success of the Pacific Coast Seaman's Strike also smacked of fascist methods, thought the WILPF. Two new bills, Fowler pointed out, "provide for compulsory arbitration and outlawing of strikes in the maritime industry," both of which characterized fascist Italy and Germany.[73]

When in late summer 1937 Senator Arthur Vandenberg proposed a series of amendments to the Wagner Act, not only did the AFL suggest that they were fascist, so, too, did Senator Wagner. According to the union, Vandenberg's desire to increase the number of "unfair practices" in the Wagner Act would "provide for an extent of regulation of unions by the Government that falls little short of the example set by Fascist Germany." Wagner's reaction was no less condemnatory. The Michigan senator, he declared, was "expressing the view of those employers who do not believe in unionization, who do not believe in collective bargaining. But that is a Fascist state," and he intended to do all he could to prevent the emasculation of the law that bore his name.[74]

As important to the WILPF as was the creation of true economic democracy in turning away the threat of fascism at home was the preservation of what its members perceived to be an American political democracy. But so long as the Congress, Constitutionally charged with representing the interests of the people, fulfilled that obligation responsibly and consistently, political democracy was safe from the threat of totalitarianism. Should the elected spokesmen for the people ever abrogate that responsibility, however, a fascist dictator was sure to step into the void, particularly if the problem of economic inequity persisted. By 1938 the WILPF was concerned on both scores.

The president's 1937 attempt to pack the Supreme Court with pro-New Deal justices to counter the Court's reactionary make-up did not sit well with the WILPF, and the women's support of Congress's May 1938 creation of the House Committee on Un-American Activities (HUAC, also known as the Dies Committee) quickly dissipated. Understanding that the committee would focus on the activities of Nazi-front organizations and other right-wing groups, the WILPF watched with trepidation as HUAC began to direct its attention against the Left with its "continual and irresponsible charges of widespread subversion."[75]

Not surprisingly, the WILPF did not escape the negative effects of this xenophobic atmosphere, the most serious coming from the American Legion. In spring 1938, for example, an adjutant-general of the Legion advised its post in Altoona, Pennsylvania, to prevent Detzer from speaking at a local church because she was an "absolute Communist." The Legion warned the WILPF that if Detzer showed up, she would be "ridden out of town on a rail," and when her train arrived, a police escort was necessary for her to reach the church safely.[76] Even then, her speech had to be canceled for fear of violence.

For months thereafter, legion harassment was a constant thorn in the WILPF's side despite the women's efforts to persuade the group that they were not "stooges and fronts" for the communists, and had even severed their connection to the ALAWF as far back as October 1937. But as Dorothy Hommel reported grimly to the joint chairs in March 1939, "the attacks against us mount up. I am really alarmed by the fascist trends."[77]

By early 1939, however, the WILPF had more important concerns than the futile effort to ward off the ridiculous charges of communism. Roosevelt's January message to Congress in which he declared that his administration would use any and all methods "short of war" in the attempt to stem the tide of aggression abroad, which threatened the security of the United States, was a clarion call to action for pacifists. Not only did Roosevelt demand a stronger military force, he urged Congress to revise the Neutrality Act by giving the president greater power with respect to U.S. response to foreign wars. Arguing that such modification of the neutrality law coupled with an increased armament program would only take this nation closer to involvement in such conflicts, the WILPF feared for American democracy. As Detzer had said about a year before, "We must recognize the fact that Fascism will hold us just as soon as the United States goes to war."[78]

The WILPF, FOR, NCPW, and the Keep America Out of War Congress (KAOWC), organized in spring 1938 by pacifists and socialists, protested Roosevelt's request as a means of "taking us on the same road" to war down which Wilson had some years earlier. "We begin by being an arsenal for our future Allies," asserted pacifists. "We build a false prosperity on armaments paid for with cash at first, perhaps with the lives of American boys later on. . . . We oppose this whole fantastic scheme and the deliberate incitement to fear on which it is built. The danger to democracy is from within and not from without."[79]

And this was the country's fundamental problem, declared the WILPF in response to Roosevelt's Congressional address—to save democracy at home. "This cannot be done with a continuance of 13 millions unemployed. It cannot be done if we solve the unemployment problem with an armament economy and the armament economy is inevitable if we take measures 'short of war'." Fascism, the women emphasized, "cannot possibly get a foot-hold where democracy is made to work." Roosevelt's proposals meant that "one man—the President—is given extraordinary powers—powers which certainly the whole tradition of America has not intended one man to have. . . . It means that the two branches of our government which are dictators, namely, the army and the navy—have the greatest control of taxpayers money— this is not in line with democratic principles. It means again the dominance of the munitions interests and the vested interests in war. This is definitely," exclaimed the WILPF, "what measures 'short of war' actually would mean in terms of public policy."[80]

Thus on 13 February when Senator Thomas introduced an amendment to the neutrality law, which would give the president the power, with the consent of Congress, to lift all embargoes on belligerents as well as impose them, pacifists vehemently opposed it. Other bills to revise the Neutrality Act followed quickly, and by early April when hearings began in both houses, the issue took on added urgency. Just a few weeks earlier, Hitler's troops marched into Prague and the remainder of a now-defenseless Czechoslovakia was swallowed up. More determined than ever to keep the neutrality law from being emasculated, pacifists sent Detzer to testify at the Senate hearings in early May.

Weary of constantly being accused of isolationism, Detzer began her remarks by pointing out the international affiliation of two of the organizations she represented, the FOR and the WILPF. "It is impossible for us to be isolationist either in feeling or in spirit," she noted, "or to be disinterested in the fate of Europe or Asia." She acknowledged that public opinion polls indicated a great deal of American sympathy for the victims of aggression, but those same polls showed that Americans were determined to stay out of war. This determination, she maintained, "should be the basis and foundation of American foreign policy," and therefore, the organizations for which she spoke opposed the Thomas bill for they perceived it as but one more way of involving the United States in a foreign war.

The Thomas amendment meant that the United States would lend material support to such nations as England and France to help them stave off further aggression by such nations as Germany and Japan, and thus implied, Detzer remarked, that the "good countries" were pitted against the "bad countries." At the very least, this was a "naive oversimplification," thought the WILPF's executive secretary. "During the 20 years of the League of Nations' existence, there was no evidence at all that the great powers were prepared to call into effect Article 19 of the Covenant . . . or to reduce the 7000 miles of tariff barrier in Europe, or to take the first essential steps to adjust currencies or in any way to prevent the inevitable struggle which we are now witnessing."

These were the countries that the United States would assist through the Thomas amendment. "It may be true," Detzer acknowledged, "that the status quo countries are democracies at home, but in their foreign policies they are empires and they function as Empires. We are witnessing once more in Europe the old struggle to control Europe, the Mediterranean, and the Near East. . . . Before the Congress passes a bill like the Thomas amendment, surely the American people have the right to know just what the Empire Democracies are prepared to do so that the United States would not be called on every 20 years to help settle the age-old struggle for power in Europe."

As for other proposed bills, the groups she represented opposed all that allowed the shipment of arms. Reminding her listeners of the Nye Committee's evidence that the traffic in arms was "an important factor" in U.S. entry into World War I, Detzer chastised those speakers who argued that the current neutrality law was a blatant failure. "Am I wrong in my contention," she asked, "that the Neutrality Act has never been fully applied in any situation? . . . It is not the law that has failed, but the Administration that has failed to carry out [that law]."[81]

According to the reports that came back to the WILPF's annual meeting held in Washington at the same time as the hearings, Detzer did an excellent job of presenting the mandatory position. But there was not such easy unanimity among the women concerning the issue. Organizational consensus reached a year earlier behind "extension of present mandatory neutrality legislation to include embargoes on the shipment of raw materials essential for war purposes to all belligerents in international war" broke down in May 1939.[82] Reflecting Fowler's more militant position, the Wisconsin state branch requested an organizational referendum on the neutrality question. Somewhat taken aback, national leaders nevertheless agreed, but persuaded members to accept an opinion poll instead due to inadequate finances at the national level.

Of the 958 women voting from forty-five branches, 714 supported the mandatory position while 244 were in favor of a collective security, or discretionary, policy. The Los Angeles branch added a third alternative, a combination of the other two giving the president and Congress joint power to name an aggressor and give nonmilitary aid to all belligerents. Thus the vote from Los Angeles was twenty-seven for a mandatory policy, seven for the discretionary position, and six for the combination alternative. The fact that only about 7 percent of the group's 13,622 members participated in the poll suggests that the vast majority was satisfied with organizational policy as it stood.

The poll's results were decisive in confirming that policy. Although it was one with which Balch, honorary International WILPF president, personally disagreed, she was gratified that the organization arrived at this position through the democratic process. Balch believed that mandatory neutrality was "a mistake," but she added that it was "not important enough to make any difference in my feeling toward the people with whom I have worked so closely for so many years and for whom I have such a genuine regard."[83]

With Balch's statement setting a conciliatory tone for the remarks to follow, Elsie Elfenbein noted that part of the difficulty in the present situation lay in the "terrific attack of public opinion" against the peace movement "systematically nurtured" by pro-war propagandists. "We are said to be selfish, unconcerned, negative," she commented, "participating in a betrayal of our own people." But now was not the time to waver, she cautioned: "We must stand steadfast by those fundamental principles which called the W.I.L.P.F. into being. To do otherwise would be a betrayal of peace, and therefore, the greatest betrayal of the people." The WILPF's neutrality policy was not negative, Elfenbein continued; it left the door open for any international cooperation that did not call for armed force or its threat. "Let everyone count on our aid for peaceful construction," she concluded, "and let no one count on it for war."

A third speaker disagreed. She could not in good conscience accept a neutrality policy that "aids the aggressor and ties the hands of our government." Therefore, she supported the Thomas amendment for she thought it imperative to distinguish between "treaty-respecting" and "treaty-breaking" nations. "I oppose the sale of arms to any nation at any time," said this Virginia women, "but realizing that this country has always done so and will continue to do so I want that sale to be on the side of Great Britain or France."

After a St. Louis member expressed support for the mandatory position, warning of the dangers of this country allying itself with the "so-called democracies" of Europe, Olmsted shared a letter from Clara Ragaz outlining the position of the joint chairs. With respect to economic sanctions, Ragaz acknowledged that they were indeed a form of warfare. But, she contended, they were certainly "less cruel" than war itself and, if applied in time, would prevent war and threats of war. It was true, however, that in order to apply them, concerted action was necessary on the part of the "less guilty" nations against the "more guilty," and this was a distinction she knew the U.S. Section did not accept.

Ragaz disagreed with those of the U.S. Section who asserted that taking sides between two warring nations would make it impossible for the United States to act as mediator. She, too, thought that the most important service the United States could render at this critical time was to keep itself democratic, which it could not do if it became involved in war, but she still insisted that "taking sides" in the form of economic sanctions would not lead to war but would actually shorten the duration of any war already in progress.

It may very well be, as Balch's opening remark suggested, that the discussion involved some personal as well as policy clashes, for as the meeting came to a close, Detzer moved on behalf of herself and Olmsted, that "Whereas the policy of the United States Section has been clearly affirmed as supporting strict mandatory neutrality, the Women's International League for Peace and Freedom reaffirms also its deep belief in the importance of individual conscience, and as always welcomes as members those who sincerely accept its fundamental principles even when they do not concur in this or other particular policies."[84] The group voted its approval.

The WILPF's annual meeting ended on 6 May 1939. The Congressional hearings on neutrality legislation ended on 8 May. Where the women had resolved their differences on the issue, even if only for the moment, neither committee in Congress, in spite of subsequent executive sessions, reached any decision whatsoever. It was generally conceded that the next move depended on events in Europe and on any decisions that the administration might make. At present, the "hands-off" policy of Roosevelt and the State Department regarding the neutrality debate left all sides up in the air.

Events in Europe were not encouraging. After swallowing up the remainder of Czechoslovakia in violation of his pledge at Munich, Hitler turned to Poland, demanding among other things that the free city of Danzig be returned to Germany. Poland refused and when Hitler did not back down, France warned him that it would fulfill its treaty obligations to aid Poland. England, too, indicated its willingness to come to Poland's assistance in the event of overt German aggression. Although England, France, and the Soviet Union had been negotiating secretly since April, no agreement had been reached.

Finally, after months of procrastination, vacillation, and frustrating delay, the administration acted. On 27 May, five days after Hitler and Mussolini signed their "Pact of Steel" promising mutual aid in the event of war, Secretary of State Hull released to the press a statement embodying a neutrality program which the Administration then asked Congress to approve:

> Pointing out that in modern warfare there was no valid distinction between munitions and raw materials, Hull called for a return to traditional international law through repeal of the arms embargo. The great danger of involvement in war, Hull maintained, came not from exports but from the movement of American ships and citizens into war zones. Therefore, Hull suggested a six-point neutrality program which would remove the arms embargo, ban American ships and travelers from combat zones, provide for the transfer of title on all exports to belligerents, and continue both the existing prohibitions on loans and credits and the licensing of arms exports by the National Munitions Control Board.[85]

Two days later Sol Bloom, chair of the Foreign Affairs Committee, introduced a bill in the House incorporating the administration's proposal. Within a week the committee reported it out favorably. Thoroughly disheartened, WILPF leaders nevertheless mustered up the energy for one more letter-writing campaign, pleading with the branches to wire their Congressmen immediately to keep the mandatory embargo. If this section was stricken, warned Detzer, "our fight is lost to keep America out of war."[86]

The debate in the House began on 27 June and it proved to be an emotional one, with short tempers and hot exchanges on both sides. Neutrality advocates expressed their horror over the vast amount of discretionary power given the president, for the Bloom bill allowed the chief executive to invoke an embargo if and when he saw fit; to decide if and when to apply the title transfer provision and to select the commodities covered by this section; and to choose the war zones forbidden to American travelers and ships. "Speaker after speaker warned against surrendering the power to declare war to the President."[87]

A surprise move came during the debate on amendments. John M. Vorys of Ohio put forward an amendment for a limited arms embargo that would prohibit arms shipments, but no other implements of war. To everyone's amazement, it squeaked through, 159 to 157. Efforts by Democratic leaders supporting the original bill to rescind this action got nowhere, and much to the relief of peace forces, the Bloom resolution with the Vorys amendment attached, passed the House. A modified arms embargo was not exactly what the WILPF had in mind, but after what the peace movement had just been through, the women accepted it gratefully.

The administration was unwilling to accept the House decision. In early July the president called upon the Senate to reject the amended Bloom bill and repeal the arms embargo altogether. The Senate, however, was no more unified behind the administration's proposal than the House had been. Embargo supporters began immediately to line up a solid bloc of pro-embargo votes, threatening to filibuster if the Foreign Relations Committee reported favorably on the bill. But, as in the House, a surprise was again in store. The committee chose a third course of action, voting to postpone consideration of the issue until the next session. Roosevelt was livid. Subsequent attempts to get the Senate to override that decision failed—the Neutrality Act of 1938, although bruised and battered, remained intact by mid-July 1939.

A little over a month later Germany and the Soviet Union stunned an unsuspecting world by signing the Nazi-Soviet Nonaggression Pact. By this agreement Hitler not only prevented the possible rerun of the World War I alliance of England, France, and Russia against Germany, he was also given a green light for his planned invasion of Poland. It came at dawn on 1 September 1939 when, using blitzkrieg tactics, German troops swept across the frontier. When Germany did not respond to their demand to halt the invasion, England and France declared war. World War II was underway.

12

Keep America Out of War!

Once more the shadow of war and confusion envelopes the world. . . .
In this world crisis we of the Women's International League for Peace
and Freedom call upon the people of the United States to remember
that dictators are not imposed upon a nation only by foreign conquest: in these days they rise to despotic power within a nation's bor-
ders by promises made to the bewildered and the desperate, and our
democracy is threatened so long as mass misery and mass unemployment exist. . . . We . . . must strive more devotedly than ever to make
democracy succeed at home. We must free our people from poverty
and unemployment, from unjust discrimination against race, religion,
or sex: above all, we must maintain our civil rights. . . . We call upon
our citizens to accept the sacred duty to remain at peace that we may
preserve the democratic ideal not only for the 130,000,000 people of
this country but for all mankind.[1]

UNTIL THE JAPANESE ATTACK on Pearl Harbor, the WILPF's message
did not change: Fascism will come to the United States when war does.
To save democracy not just for Americans but for the world, the United
States must stay out of war. The women said it again and again: Fascist
totalitarianism was not the exclusive product of the German people,
but will "appear inside democratic frontiers when a democratic state
fails to solve its basic economic problems . . . *Only a nation at peace* can
create a synthesis of political and industrial democracy."[2]

The thirty-nine organizations of the National Peace Conference
voiced the same sentiments. "We are determined to keep out of war,"
declared NPC Director Walter VanKirk, "not because we want to save
our own skins; not because we are afraid; not because we shrink from
sacrifice; not because we want to profit from the war. . . . We desire

peace because we are devoted to our democratic form of government, because we hate regimentation and dictatorship, . . . because war sows the seeds of revenge, hatred, retaliation and persecution; because in fighting we lose that for which we fight."[3]

The WILPF was instrumental in drafting the NPC's six-point program "to meet the world crisis," which began with the declaration that the United States must be kept out of the war. Second, it recommended that this country "initiate [a] continuous conference of neutral nations to procure a just peace." Calls to "prevent exploitation of the war for private gain" and to resist the "subtle appeal of propaganda" were the next two points, and fifth, it called for strengthening American democracy "through solving pressing domestic problems and vigorously safeguarding civil liberties." Last, Americans were urged to "work for permanent world government as the basis of peace and security."[4]

The president's response to the war's outbreak on 3 September 1939 encouraged the NPC, for Roosevelt told Americans that he hoped the country would stay out of the war. "I believe that it will," he said, "and I give you assurances that every effort of your government will be directed toward that end." Reminding the branches that Woodrow Wilson was re-elected in 1916 on the slogan, "He kept us out of war," Detzer admonished WILPF members that "we must not count too strongly on words."[5]

Concerned that the administration would now "urge a revision" of the Neutrality Act to aid England and France, the WILPF's executive secretary declared, "I do not want America to become an arsenal for Europe." Given the conclusion of the Nye munitions investigation that the shipment of arms was a significant factor behind U.S. involvement in World War I, there was "little doubt" in Detzer's mind "that if we ever get involved in a war trade, sooner or later we will be sending not only munitions but men." The present neutrality law must, therefore, not only be retained, the WILPF insisted, but strengthened by a restriction on the sale of raw materials to a "cash-and-carry" basis with limits put on the amount sold.

Should the United States enter the war, thought the women, "we shall probably be under some type of military dictatorship. Our greatest hope is to get as much democratic control now of foreign policy as possible." Thus they urged the creation of "a permanent joint committee of the Senate and House foreign affairs committees, to advise and consult with the State Department and the President on all major decisions on foreign policy, before any final steps are taken."[6]

Keep America Out of War Congress (KAOWC) organizations concurred. "Our supporters in Congress," declared Jesse MacKnight of the NCPW, "want to fight to the last ditch against repeal of the arms embargo." A KAOWC petition embodied the WILPF's position on U.S. neutrality: "We, the citizens of the United States of America, hereby earnestly petition the President and the Congress . . . *to keep the United States out of war*," it began.[7] It also called for a policy of strict neutrality, a prohibition on the sale of arms to either side, neutral mediation, and a stronger neutrality law. KAOWC groups then endorsed a WILPF plan for a mass antiwar mobilization in Washington on 29 September, shortly after Congress was to convene in a special session called by Roosevelt.

Within two days of the declaration of war by England and France Roosevelt announced that he wanted the arms embargo repealed, saying that this was essential for national security. The way the president presented the issue was "absolutely inexcusable" as far as the WILPF was concerned. The struggle over the neutrality law, exclaimed the women, "should be fought on the real issue—to help England and France and not on the phoney [sic] one that to lift the embargo would be 'neutral'."[8]

To bolster grass-roots support for a whole host of antiwar activities, the NPC appointed Olmsted chair of its Committee on Field Work. So while Detzer led the pacifist fight to save the Neutrality Act in Congress, Olmsted focused on the local level to counter prowar sentiment. Suggesting that Americans establish classes in propaganda analysis, circulate relevant books and articles, hold "great numbers of neighborhood meetings to consider what war would mean to the people living there," and organize training schools and courses for peace workers, Olmsted reported that within three weeks of the war's outbreak, Minnesota WILPF women had already secured 40,000 signatures on a petition to keep the United States from becoming involved. The Pennsylvania branch ran a newspaper ad calling for peace volunteers and circularized the subscriber lists of *The Nation* and *The New Republic* for the same reason. Noting that in this effort, "we have unusual supporters, such as the Nat'l Assn [sic] of Manufacturers, the Veterans' organizations, Father Coughlin, etc.," Olmsted urged WILPF women to "make the most of this opportunity to educate their members to the deeper implications of what is required to stop war."[9]

The KAOWC also kept up its pressure. On 23 September it requested the Inter-American Conference, then opening in Panama, "to implement the Declaration of Lima by maintaining strict hemispheric neutrality including an embargo on arms and implements of war" based on the belief that "the struggle for democracy in Latin America . . . will be endangered by any policy tending to involve the nations of this hemisphere in the European conflict."

A week later the nine organizations of the KAOWC called upon Roosevelt to extend the arms embargo to the Soviet Union, given that country's "military occupation of a large portion of Poland." Two weeks later when it was learned that a number of French and British citizens and government officials were arriving in the United States to make lecture tours, the KAOWC inquired of Secretary of State Hull "if the State Department would compel them to register as propaganda agents for foreign powers" as required by U.S. law.[10] The NPC, although less able to reach consensus as quickly as the KAOWC, continued its efforts to influence the administration as well, and the NCCCW issued a statement on 10 October agreeing with the more radical peace organizations that the United States' first priority should be to stay out of war.

Told that one of the reasons for the continued "phony war" was that the British and the French were waiting to see what the United States would do on the neutrality issue, the WILPF thought that even if the peace groups lost their fight in Congress, with enough public pressure the vote would probably be a close one, and that would be "significant" in itself. It would send an antiwar message to the president and it "might indicate to the British and the French that America is not going into this war."[11]

Business interests supported Roosevelt in his drive for repeal of the arms embargo, but when Congress and the White House were inundated with protests from the peace bloc, administrative spokesmen, having discreetly kept silent on the issue, worked covertly to sway public opinion behind neutrality revision. Clark Eichelberger, director of the American Union for Concerted Peace Efforts and an important figure of the collective security wing of the peace movement, received State Department backing for his recommendation that a committee be formed to do just that.

By early October, such a group—the Non-Partisan Committee for Peace Through Revision of the Neutrality Act under the leadership of Kansas newspaper editor William Allen White—began its work. A formidable opponent for the peace bloc, the new group, soon to be renamed the Committee to Defend America by Aiding the Allies, was backed financially by Pittsburgh industrialist Frederick McKee and by Henry Luce, wealthy publisher of both *Life* and *Time* magazines. With local branches in thirty states and a national office under Eichelberger's direction, the White committee quickly embarked upon a media campaign, saturating newspapers and radio with the administration's position. Slowly the opponents of neutrality revision began to lose ground.

In late September the Senate Foreign Relations Committee approved a bill that repealed the arms embargo. Yet "in every other respect it embodied the philosophy of mandatory neutrality," and for this reason business interests worked diligently to amend certain of its more stringent features. Within a month they were successful, for after lengthy and intense debate, the Senate accepted two amendments "which in effect confined the cash-and-carry restrictions solely to the North Atlantic area."[12]

WILPF leaders were "pretty depressed" by this turn of events; "12 years work just out of the window!" lamented Detzer to Gertrude Baer. "But," she continued, "I don't feel that we are 'licked' yet because it [the repeal of the arms embargo] must be confirmed by the House and it at least will be very close whichever way it goes there."[13] By no stretch of the imagination could it be argued that the final vote on the repeal was "very close" in either the House or Senate. To be sure, "the House engaged in a fierce debate marked by brief, sharply worded speeches, frequent emotional outbursts, and a brutal frankness that laid bare the central issues," but when it was all over, peace forces were dealt a stunning defeat.[14] The arms embargo was repealed. The antiwar message that the WILPF hoped a close vote would send to Roosevelt and the Allies had not materialized.

Although some further minor revision of the Neutrality Act would follow in November 1941 when Congress amended the law to allow "American merchant ships to cross the Atlantic, enter a war zone where German submarines were taking a daily toll of shipping, and travel to British ports,"[15] the revised Neutrality Act of November 1939 essentially spelled out U.S. policy vis-à-vis World War II prior to U.S. involvement. On 4 November Roosevelt signed the new law into effect, and immediately followed it with a proclamation defining an extensive war zone through which no U.S. ship could enter even if destined for a neutral port. U.S. ships could not stop at any belligerent port in either the Mediterranean or Black seas. U.S. ships could go to all belligerent ports in the Indian, Pacific, and South Atlantic oceans, but not if they carried arms, ammunition, or implements of war. The restrictions on loans and passenger travel in the earlier law remained unchanged. But now Americans could sell arms, ammunition, and implements of war to belligerents even though all such trade had to be conducted in foreign ships with transfer of title to purchaser prior to departure from the United States.

As disturbing to the WILPF as was the successful presidential attempt to revise the Neutrality Act was the immediate effort to get around it. In early November, the women reported, "an attempt was made . . . to evade the purpose of the Bill when both the Maritime Commission and the shipbuilding industries urged the transference of American ships to Panamanian registry." The understanding in Washington was that Roosevelt was "in full agreement with this action, and . . . knew that this effort would be made before the Neutrality Act was signed." The plan was scuttled, apparently because of "determined opposition" of cabinet officials like Hull and Attorney General Frank Murphy who feared a "terrific public reaction."[16]

But as the WILPF knew, this behind-the-scenes attempt by the administration to evade the law was by no means the first such incident. Back in late January 1939, a California plane crash that cost several lives subsequently revealed the heretofore well-kept secret that the French "were being permitted to fly United States Army aircraft and acquaint themselves with highly secret equipment." The revelation that Roosevelt and the War Department made private assurances to the French in 1938 that they could expect to share generously in the increased output of fighter planes from U.S. production facilities now clarified the president's request of Congress earlier that January for a "vastly increased appropriation" to expand the military's air power. The "suspicion that the objective was to build a reserve of planes on which the British and French might draw" was borne out sooner than anyone might have anticipated.[17] For the WILPF, Roosevelt's brand of neutrality was disturbingly reminiscent of Woodrow Wilson's and was "destroying the confidence of many."[18]

Detzer was concerned that some WILPF members might "resent" the suggestion that "the Administration wants to get this country into war." Speaking for herself, she assured those women that she was not now nor ever had "attributed a Machiavellian motive to the President. I do feel, however, that the desire on the part of the Administration to help the British and the French is so great, that it is ready to risk the most dangerous steps which may involve this country in war." She reminded Americans that the conflict was not a simple case of "bad dictatorship on the one hand and good democracy on the other." After all, the "good democracies" allowed the subjugation of Czechoslovakian democracy while they rallied to the defense of autocratic Poland. And if Hitler personified a "Machiavellian glorification of bad faith," it needed to be recalled that the victorious democracies at the end of the last war "did not carry out the pledge to disarm down to Germany's level."[19]

What was this war all about, then? As Cor Ramondt-Hirschmann in the Geneva Office put it, "we are told . . . that the Third Reich is fighting to secure the necessary 'Lebensraum' for her people and that the Western powers are defending the freedom of their peoples, of all nations in fact. There is no doubt, however," she continued, "that the real aims and purposes of this war, which the official slogans are meant to hide from the people, are not nearly so clear and unambiguous as they appear."[20] For Detzer, the war was "fundamentally a struggle of rival empires for power," and this, she said, was "Europe's problem—not ours." Yet she admitted, "American responsibility is enormous." The WILPF was not "disinterested" in Europe's fate nor did it believe that the United States would be unaffected by events there. If nothing else, Hitler's treatment of the Jews was appalling to all fair-minded Americans, but, asked Detzer pointedly, "Can we effectively fight Hitlerism by the war method and keep our own democracy? I do not believe we can."[21] And if the United States ceased to be democratic, then the prospects for a postwar world of peace, freedom, and justice were slim indeed.

The debate over neutrality revision did not bode well for keeping democracy. "It has become impossible to get to the President," wrote Dorothy Hommel to Baer in late October, "and there is no doubt that he is not speaking with the consent either of the people or Congress."[22] Detzer had stressed this point in the fall of 1938 when she commented on "the pressures which are brought to bear on any President." There was, first, the pressure of political party. "We do not suggest that large campaign contributions consciously influence officials, but the sub-conscious effect. . . ." And in a crisis situation, she noted, the average citizen "will discover that it is not difficult for prominent industrialists, admirals, bankers to get the ear of the President," but almost impossible for anyone without such power and "terribly difficult for liberal or peace groups."[23]

This situation did not improve by 1939. From what peace groups gleaned from sources in Washington, the British and French enjoyed greater access to Roosevelt than his own constituents. With respect to the peace movement's call for neutral mediation by the United States, Americans were being told that "a neutral conference was out of the question because the little neutral nations were too afraid to ask for it and would not welcome it." Not true, said the WILPF: "The real reason for the Administration's not doing so is because the British and the French were opposed to it," a view with which Frederick Libby of the NCPW concurred.[24] And according to John Nevin Sayre of the FOR, officials high up in both the Belgian and Dutch governments indicated that "the people in the neutral countries of Europe are apparently distressed to see America doing nothing to prevent the war from starting up in earnest."[25] The WILPF corroborated these observations in January when the women visited the embassies of the Netherlands, Sweden, Belgium, Denmark, Norway, and Switzerland, for only the latter two were unfavorably inclined toward the idea of neutral mediation.

When Roosevelt sent Undersecretary of State Sumner Welles on a peace initiative trip to the belligerent nations in February 1940, peace forces were encouraged because Welles was seen not only as an astute diplomat, he was understood to be the key figure in the State Department desirous of keeping the United States out of the war. Nothing came of the Welles mission, however, and no efforts at neutral mediation were forthcoming from Roosevelt. Not only did the president frustrate peace advocates on this score, he also alienated them with respect to domestic policy. Despite warnings from advisors in early 1940 that the economy was taking a nose-dive, Roosevelt continued his policy of budget-cutting initiated in late 1939. The only area of government spending left untouched was that of the military. While social programs declined drastically, military appropriations increased, and the unemployed still numbered between seven and ten million.

While the peace bloc struggled valiantly to save social welfare programs and prevent military build-up, it was compelled at the same time to deal with its own internal divisions imposed by the circumstance of war. Creating confusion in the public's mind was the shifting position of the Communist-backed American League for Peace and Democracy, earlier the American League Against War and Fascism from which the WILPF resigned in 1937.

Prior to the Nazi-Soviet Nonaggression Pact, the American League supported the collective security position, urging the democracies to stop Hitler by economic and other measures, and endorsed FDR's "quarantine" proposal and armament program. After the pact, the Communist party did an about-face and so did the American League. Now it took the position that the war was between "rival imperialist groups" rather than a conflict between fascism and democracy, a radical switch that created an untenable situation for its noncommunist organizations. That, coupled with pressure from the Dies Committee, resulted in its dissolution by late February 1940.

At that point the Communist party began to cause problems for the KAOWC by forming committees of the same name and demanding that the United States stay out of the war, thereby creating confusion in the public mind. The FOR, KAOWC, and the WILPF all felt compelled to publicly disavow any connection with the Communist party, communist ideology, and the newly formed communist-inspired "Keep America Out of War" committees, while continuing their repudiation of fascist ideology and associations.

Within six months the KAOWC made an even stronger statement of disavowal in connection with publicity over the "Emergency Peace Mobilization." The press linked pacifist groups with the newly created "Committee to Defend America by Keeping Out of War," which sponsored a mass antiwar demonstration in Chicago at the end of August. Pointing out that this new organization was founded and dominated by communists, and that the KAOWC, comprising the "Non-Interventionist Bloc" of the peace movement, did not "cooperate with Communists under any circumstances," pacifists emphasized that they were "in no way taking part in the 'Emergency Peace Mobilization'." Not only had the communists proved themselves to be "shifty allies" of the other peace societies, said KAOWC members, "we believe that supporters of the Soviet regime obviously are not against war or for democracy no matter what their verbal commitments. We are not only against war," they stressed again, "but also against every expression of totalitarianism."[26]

It was an awkward situation all the way around. First, in rejecting communist cooperation, however reasonable that rejection may have been, pacifists contributed to the growing division within the peace movement. Second, with socialist Norman Thomas, a 1940 presidential candidate, still an important spokesman for the KAOWC, Americans who associated "communism" with "socialism" were bewildered by the latter's repudiation of the former. To compound this perplexing situation, antifascist pacifists now found themselves opposing U.S. involvement in the war in concert with fascist sympathizers in industry, veterans' organizations, government, the "America First" Committee, and among certain racist and religious groups. As John T. Flynn, KAOWC National Chair, remarked, "since our movement started, we've had some pretty strange bedfellows."[27]

By early 1940 the NPC could also be characterized as a case of strange bedfellows. Pacifists were always a minority in the group and that was the primary reason for forming a temporary partnership with socialists in February 1938 to create the KAOWC. Although a charter member of the new coalition, initially the WILPF was quite concerned when in May the KAOWC decided to continue indefinitely. WILPF pacifists felt that the new organization in combination with the recession, which put their group in serious financial straits by 1938, represented "serious problems which now threaten the very life and continued existence of the WIL."[28] Yet at the same time, growing division in the NPC between minority pacifists and majority "intervenationalists"[29] threatened to weaken even more the fragile unity of the peace movement precisely at a time when such unified effort was most sorely needed.

At about the same time that NPC pacifists helped to organize the KAOWC, NPC member Clark Eichelberger of the League of Nations Association formed the Concerted Peace Efforts and began to frustrate pacifists in the NPC by advocating repeal of the arms embargo and repudiation of the war referendum. Despite the threat to its very existence, which the WILPF believed the KAOWC represented, the women felt that they had no choice but to remain an active part of the more radical group if Eichelberger's efforts were to be successfully countered. After the war broke out and Eichelberger put his new organization behind the administration's efforts to revise the Neutrality Act by helping to form the William Allen White Committee, he was obviously working at cross-purposes with the WILPF, yet both remained active in the NPC.

The relationship between the WILPF and the NCCCW provides another example of the growing division in the peace movement between the pacifists and nonpacifists after the war began. Although there was still some WILPF participation in the NCCCW as late as 1936, it decreased steadily and all but disappeared by 1939. Throughout the late 1930s, the National Committee of Church Women asked Detzer to be one of its delegates to the NCCCW, but until the conference of January 1940, she declined. Although in the fall the NCCCW had joined with the more radical peace groups in insisting that the United States be kept out of the war, it also supported Roosevelt's efforts to revise the Neutrality Act. Detzer's decision to attend the January conference as a delegate of the church women was in part based on her desire to move the organization in a direction more in line with the WILPF's position, particularly with respect to the issue of neutral mediation.

The NCCCW's October statement said nothing about neutral mediation, but by its January conference, leaders presented a rather weak statement that Detzer characterized as "wishy-washy:" "We would support the government of the United States in offers to mediate in the

European war when the opportunity arises."[30] According to Detzer, she then introduced a stronger statement that called for the administration to initiate a conference of neutrals to offer mediation terms to all belligerents. Conference leaders opposed this modification rather strenuously, but when the vote was taken, 107 approved it while only 69 were against.

While continuing on its own and as part of the KAOWC to garner grass-roots support for its antiwar program from late 1939 into early spring 1940, the WILPF focused on lobbying Congress against both increased military appropriations and legislation that would curtail civil liberties and on the growing refugee problem, a matter of grave concern to the women from the first days of the Hitler regime. Nazi anti-Semitism was no secret and the German government's early discriminatory policies against Jews had been followed by the repressive Nuremberg Laws of 1935, and then on 10 November 1938, by the violence and terror of the "Night of the Broken Glass." Expressing its "deep sense of grief and despair" at the systematic destruction of Jewish businesses and synagogues all across Germany by Nazi thugs, the U.S. Section of the WILPF was determined that American "outrage . . . not be wasted in futile protests."

The women urged Roosevelt to call a special session of Congress immediately "for the purposes of widening our quotas as they apply to the victims of European pogroms." They acknowledged the "difficulties" that such an influx of people would raise "because of the labor situation," but were "confident" that "all wings of the labor movement would raise no serious objections if assurances were given that the refugees would be handled as a special problem." As the WILPF had observed earlier, "it would be possible to open our doors to all the Jewish refugees from Germany under a special law limiting the visas for 5 years and carrying a clause which would forbid their obtaining jobs, so that they would in no sense constitute a threat to the labor movement." Americans were generous enough, the WILPF asserted, "to support all these victims of Nazi persecution on a wide-scale relief plan" such as the one Herbert Hoover had directed in post-World War I Russia.[31]

While waiting for a response from the White House or Congress, the WILPF persisted in its own efforts to find sponsors for the numerous refugees applying to its Geneva office for help. The process was so frustratingly complex and time-consuming that occasionally, those with the most urgent need to escape did not receive help in time. The U.S. Section feared that this would be the case with Gertrude Baer if something was not done quickly. Part of the problem was Baer herself;

as one of the International WILPF's joint chairs, she had been living in exile in Geneva since spring 1933, and refused to give up her post there so long as her help was needed. But after the Night of the Broken Glass, even she acknowledged that it might be time to accept the U.S. invitation to relocate in Washington. It would not be easy. Not only was there growing xenophobia in the United States, there was the frustrating intransigence of U.S. officials to see that the refugee issue, particularly as it applied to Jews, represented an extraordinary situation calling for extraordinary measures. Balch and Olmsted visited the State Department after the Night of the Broken Glass, for example, to see about the possibility of classifying religious and political emigrés seeking asylum differently from ordinary immigrants falling under the established quota. The official in charge of such matters "would not even consider such a thing." Saying that "America was quite as generous as any other country in her attitude toward immigrants," he nevertheless could see no reason for making the United States responsible "for more of these people," and was "opposed to any plan for developing special settlements for refugees."[32]

Acknowledging the fact that "our work as an organization is and should be the promotion of peace and freedom and not relief of the victims of war and tyranny, we nevertheless recognize that we must do everything in our power for our refugee members and their relatives without lessening our efforts for peace."[33] So declared the U.S. Section in October when it created a Committee on Refugees, unique in the group's history because neither its composition nor its beneficiaries were limited to WILPF members. A few months later, another new committee was formed to report on anti-Semitic trends.

Hitler's march into Prague in March 1939 intensified the refugee situation, and despite the best efforts of the WILPF in the United States and in Europe, many of its Czechoslovakian members vanished into concentration camps as was the case earlier in Austria and Germany. In the United States the WILPF's Committee on Refugees stepped up its efforts accordingly as its chair, Margaret Jones, designed a program of action for the branches so as to expedite as many cases as possible. At its annual meeting in May, the WILPF made extension of the quota system one of its primary objectives for the coming year, and Jones reported that her committee was working closely with other organizations, among them the Non-Sectarian Committee for Aid to German Refugee Children, a group sponsoring legislation to permit 20,000 children under fourteen to enter the United States during the next two years. Using her talent as a riveting public speaker to aid the cause, in a radio address in mid-May Detzer pleaded with Americans to "open [their] doors to the tragic victims of aggression abroad." She called attention to studies from Holland and England that showed that refugees, "instead of being a burden" to the host country, "actually helped to stimulate" the economy by "bringing in new work and new talents."[34]

With the outbreak of war, all refugee work in Europe was "more or less in abeyance" as U.S. Consulates gave priority to American citizens stranded overseas. The National Refugee Service reported at the same time that affidavits were still "desperately needed" by German refugees in border countries. Jones also reminded WILPF members that "sympathetic help" for refugees already in the United States was needed.[35] By way of example, she cited the case of a Polish man whose wife and son were still in Warsaw. He had been in this country for almost six months but could not find a teaching position and was nearly desperate.

In Europe, the Swedish and English sections of the WILPF took into their homes more than one hundred Czechoslovakian refugees, and the Danish section placed three hundred Jewish children from Berlin, Prague, and Vienna into homes of farming families. Efforts to obtain information about WILPF members and their families in Poland were unsuccessful. Joint chairs Baer, Ragaz, and Kathleen Innes sent a letter to Roosevelt "begging" him to "uphold the standards of civilization by opening the doors to freedom in his country as widely as possible" to victims of political, racial, and religious persecution.[36] They also thanked the U.S. Section for offering to have the International Office, Baer, and two staff members brought to this country. They chose, however, to remain in Geneva until that moment when their work there would be "completely paralyzed by coming events."[37]

By mid-December Jones sailed for Europe to work more directly with refugees under the auspices of the AFSC, and Eva Wiegelmesser, herself a German refugee who arrived a year earlier with her two sons, took over as chair of the WILPF's Refugee Committee. The situation was not encouraging, she reported. With the WILPF already hard-pressed financially, it learned that ship passage for refugees now must be paid in U.S. dollars, ranging from $152 to $225 for each person, and that refugees were "no longer able to pay for their passages themselves." To make matters worse, she noted, "non-Aryans are still forced to leave Germany; if they have no chance to immigrate to another country, they are forced to go to Poland. They are permitted to leave Germany for another country except Poland only if their papers are in order, and that includes the paid passage ticket. Also," she pointed out despondently, Consuls in countries outside Germany, where refugees were temporarily permitted to stay until their quota number for the U.S. was called, "do not grant a visa *unless the passage money is paid.*"[38]

Reporting to the KAOWC on the European situation after her trip there in December for the WILPF's International Executive meeting, Detzer indicated that the refugee situation was "acute." Switzerland was "cluttered" with refugees, the Swiss people were "desperate," and the U.S. Consulate was less than helpful. The situation was almost as critical at home; as Wiegelmesser reported, "3,500 refugees arrived in New York City in November" and just in the first week of December alone, another 3,000 landed.[39]

In Geneva, Baer anticipated a growing number of appeals in the near future, a problem that concerned Wiegelmesser because WILPF members were not responding to the need for the affidavits to the degree she anticipated. Part of the problem, she knew, was financial, and part was due to the fact that a sponsor thereby accepted responsibility for the refugee for the next five years. In trying to arouse greater interest and overcome these obstacles, she began including in her branch letters personal histories of individuals so as to personalize the process and, hopefully, strike a responsive chord among members.

In late February 1940 peace forces were somewhat encouraged by information from War Department sources who anticipated that Hitler would "threaten" the Netherlands and Belgium to put pressure on Britain "to stop fighting," but would not actually invade either country. Nor was it expected that Hitler would attack France if he could avoid it. These department sources concluded that "Germany has only enough oil for a defensive war."[40]

The War Department was wrong. With sudden fury, on the morning of 9 April 1940 the Germans invaded Denmark and Norway. The long months of uneasy silence, of apprehensive waiting and watching were over. It was in the shadow of this latest horror that the U.S. Section of the WILPF held its annual meeting in Pittsburgh. In her address to those gathered at the banquet to celebrate the group's twenty-fifth birthday, Detzer gave eloquent voice to the feelings of fear and despair shared by all assembled there:

> Our people in Europe are nearly all trapped and tonight we remember that this is not only our birthday but theirs. Some way, all through this weekend, we have wanted to identify ourselves with them. Where are they tonight? We know that most of our Leagues are broken—we know that one of our leaders in Poland is dead and that

fiery, brilliant leader of Czechoslovakia lies tonight in the ghastly concentration camp at Dachau. What must this birthday be to them—
those who have cared so passionately for the freedom of the human
spirit? . . . Their courage has forced them to give up freedom—comfort—perhaps their lives. They are paying the supreme price for
peace.[41]

Yet the nightmare for their comrades in Europe had barely begun.
Less than two weeks after the women pacifists at Pittsburgh had "eaten
a delicious and expensive dinner" to emerge afterwards on that "beautiful spring night to lighted streets," knowing that there would be "no
death raining down" upon them from the sky—on 10 May, the Germans stormed into the Netherlands and Belgium.[42] Eighteen days later
the Belgians surrendered; shortly thereafter Italy entered the war on
the side of the Germans; and on 24 June, the French capitulated to a
triumphant Adolf Hitler. As was the case with most Americans, the
women of the WILPF were stunned, comprehending only with great
difficulty not just the magnitude of the Nazi victory, but also the rapidity and apparent ease with which that victory had been achieved.

Although demoralized by this abrupt end to the "phony war," pacifists were at the same time galvanized into action, knowing now that
"there will be a tremendous campaign to have the United States go in
to save the British Empire." Analyzing the military as well as the political situation, they concluded that Japan would probably take advantage
of the desperate situation for the British and continue her advance in
the Pacific, "raising the spectre of our involvement in war with Japan."
Reiterating their basic program of keeping the United States out of war
through a war referendum, neutral mediation, full application of the
neutrality law, and Congressional checks on the war-making power of
the president, KAOWC pacifists began immediately to plan "an intensive, dramatic, nation-wide campaign."[43]

It began with an Anti-War Mobilization in Washington on 7 June,
which was accompanied by letters to congressmen, the White House,
and newspapers; the distribution of antiwar literature, drawing upon
the talents of the Writers Anti-War Bureau and its weekly newsletter,
Uncensored; and special radio broadcasts. Among the speakers at the
rally were Montana Senator Burton K. Wheeler, "outstanding in his
opposition to an interventionist program"; O. K. Armstrong, national
leader from the American Legion who declared that "regardless of
what small groups of the Legion might say, the official position of the
Legion was absolutely against letting the government take us into war

abroad"; and Detzer, whose basic theme was borrowed from assassinated Senator Huey Long: "When fascism comes to America, it will be
called *anti*-Fascism."[44]

Three hundred delegates from the seven sponsoring organizations
in nineteen states drafted six "peace planks" to be presented that summer to both major political conventions:

1. An *unequivocal* declaration for keeping the United States out of the
   wars of Europe and Asia.
2. The creation of a congressional commission to determine what the
   American people want to defend and a rational defense program
   limited to the carrying out of that policy.
3. The utilization of the strength of the United States for peace instead of for war by pressing for the earliest possible armistice and
   mediation.
4. The extension of democracy by providing for a popular referendum on war.
5. Support of a generous policy for the relief of victims of war.
6. The preservation of democracy at home by opposing all attempts to
   curtail civil liberties and by using our enormous resources to extend economic security more widely.[45]

If, as Olmsted noted, public opinion polls showed that 90 percent
of the American people opposed U.S. involvement in the war, then that
sentiment had to be made clear to candidates of both major parties.
The Socialist party needed no prodding to adopt peace planks or candidates; nominating Norman Thomas as its presidential candidate, it
simply took the KAOWC program as its 1940 platform, thereby inspiring the FOR, if no other peace group, to support Thomas. "We have
the gravest doubt," said the FOR, "that any candidate who may represent either the Democratic or Republican party is likely to pursue a
course calculated to keep us out of war."[46]

When the Republican convention opened in Philadelphia on 24
June, peace forces were ready. Centrally located in their headquarters
at the Walton Hotel, WILPF members under Detzer's direction conducted a "lobby school" on the first morning, "giving people advice as
to how to button-hole delegates" and present the peace planks to them.
With the NCPW's assistance, the WILPF also printed a newspaper to
ensure publicity, and participated with other KAOWC organizations in
extensive lobbying, distribution of 5,000 "Keep-America-Out-of-War"
buttons, and an "impressive" parade. A girls' drum and bugle corps led
the parade "to all the newspaper offices and then to the headquarters

of all the candidates. In the parade, beside the drum and bugle corps, were young people from the Youth Committee Against War who carried sandwich boards and placards with interesting and appropriate slogans, and bringing up the rear were others distributing our newspaper," reported Detzer. "We then secured a bus and sent them out to the Convention Hall where they did the same thing."[47] In one role or another, approximately seventy-five WILPF members participated in the peace activities of the convention.

The same strategy was employed at the Democratic Convention, which opened in Chicago on 12 July. Urging members to inundate Senator Robert Wagner, Resolutions Committee Chair, with telegrams demanding the party's adoption of the peace planks, the KAOWC and WILPF felt strongly that the "enormous pressure" building for the presidential candidacy of Senator Wheeler was a good sign whichever way the convention finally went. Speaking for thirteen of the forty organizations of the NPC representing more than 4,000,000 members, Walter Van Kirk presented five peace planks to the resolutions committee as he had earlier at the Republican gathering.

The most important of the planks called for keeping the country at peace. The remaining four urged support for neutral mediation, creation of world government, strengthening the Good Neighbor policy toward Latin America, and global economic cooperation. Because of the "extreme points of view" within the NPC, not only was this the strongest statement its members would agree to, it was also decided that NPC activity at the conventions would be limited to VanKirk's presentation of it.[48]

When the conventions were all over, Wendell Willkie, a utilities magnate, emerged a sixth-ballot winner over Republican stalwarts Robert Taft and Thomas Dewey, and Roosevelt, although presumably with no desire for a third term, won renomination by the Democrats on the first ballot. Willkie's initial strategy of attacking Roosevelt for "seeking dictatorial power [and] preventing the return of real prosperity" could have had its appeal to pacifists, but his accusation that the president had failed "to rearm the country fast enough in the face of foreign threat" vitiated this appeal completely. As for Roosevelt, he was committed to support his party's platform, one that stipulated that, if elected, the Democrats would "not participate in foreign wars" nor "send our Army, naval, or air forces to fight in foreign lands outside the Americas, *except in case of attack.*"[49]

With the campaigns underway, pacifists turned their attention to the issue of civil liberties, the major thrust of Detzer's speech at the

June Anti-War Mobilization. With Hitler's advance through Belgium into France, a "war hysteria" swept the country, "paving the way for the inevitable corollary," declared Detzer, "the shutting off of the people's liberties—the silencing of opposition. . . . We are being told," she said, "that . . . the Government does not intend to jeopardize the institutions of Democracy." But "let us look at the record of just this week;" it included the "shocking decision" of the Supreme Court in *Minersville School District v. Gobitis* that school children could legally be expelled for refusing to salute the American flag. "And this country was founded for religious liberty!" Detzer exclaimed in disbelief. Then there was the "struggle . . . behind closed doors in Congress" over whether to allow the President, after Congressional adjournment, "to move the National Guard and American troops not only any place in this hemisphere but *any place in the world.*"[50]

A month later after the Smith bill became "the first peacetime sedition law in American history since 1798," the WILPF, noting that Congress had previously refused to pass bills "of this type," observed that it was now "evident that the war hysteria is . . . making heavy inroads on our cherished liberties." As the ACLU commented, the Smith Act "presents so astounding a violation of the first amendment to the Constitution as to justify widespread protest. It makes criminal any utterance or publication held to incite disaffection in the armed forces. 'Military disaffection' thus becomes a major crime, opening the door to all sorts of prosecutions of pacifist and anti-war literature." Most dangerous of all, however, warned the WILPF, was the Burke-Wadsworth bill calling for the conscription "of all male citizens wherever resident between the ages of 18 and 65," introduced in the Senate in late June.[51]

Never before in the United States had a peacetime draft for the military been passed by Congress, but by late spring 1940, military leaders were calling for a "trained army of one million men" and at that time, only 375,000 men were authorized by law to serve in the regular U.S. Army.[52] Hearings on the conscription bill before the Senate Military Affairs Committee were quickly called for 3 July, and a week later, the WILPF's Finance Secretary Catherine FitzGibbon testified against it.

After protesting the proposed law as both undemocratic and a "complete reversal of American tradition," FitzGibbon focused on the same point that Detzer would stress even more strongly in her testimony before the House Military Affairs Committee later that month. The essence of both statements was fascism. "We protest this Act," said FitzGibbon, "because it approximates Hitlerism. Under cover of protecting democracy, its provisions are totalitarian in essence. This Act calmly assumes that citizens of the United States are mere vassals of the State and, as such, are entitled to no occupational activity independent of the State. The same assumption made by Germany, Italy, and Russia not only deified the State; it also raised the symbols of those States, Hitler, Mussolini, and Stalin, to the rank of gods who can do no wrong, whose word is absolute, whose slightest whim is law."[53]

Detzer was even more acid in her remarks before the House:

Section #2 of the measure states that the integrity and institutions of the United States are being threatened. Mr. Chairman, it seems to me that in a Democracy, it is reasonable to ask what institutions are threatened, how they are threatened, and by whom. We are not given this information in the Bill. May I submit, gentlemen, most respectfully, that the only institution which seems immediately threatened is the institution of Democracy—threatened by this Bill.

In this same Section, declaring the purpose of the Bill, we are told that to insure the independence and freedom of the people, it is imperative to destroy the independence and freedom of the people by conscription. May I again suggest what I know must have been said over and over again before this Committee—that there is a large bloc of public opinion which does not believe that you can fight Hitlerism with Hitlerism—Fascism with Fascist measures.[54]

Also testifying against the bill were Norman Thomas and Libby, and many witnesses, including those from the WILPF, urged Congress to try a "volunteer measure" with more attractive remuneration for at least six months before conscription was considered. But as Olmsted reported later, "it was admitted at the hearings that they [military leaders] were turning to conscription because military service has become so unpopular that people will not volunteer for it."[55] As other pacifists pointed out, military experts agreed that a "large standing army" was unnecessary for adequate national defense. Thus "enactment of peacetime conscription can only mean either the laying of groundwork for fascism at home or preparation for military adventure abroad, or both."[56]

Balch, however, saw the issue in a different light. Although firmly opposed to conscription and to "most of the provisions in the Burke bill," she also pointed out that "if we are dealing, not with what we think best, but with the question of the actual situation and its possibilities, and all that the government has committed us to, it seems inconsistent to say that we have the armaments, but we will not prepare men to use them." Unlike others in the peace movement, she was not as sure that just because "Hitler could not land enough troops to occupy all the continental U.S." that Americans need not fear being dragged into the war through "attack."

What about the possibility, she mused, of civil war in Mexico with one side or the other inviting Hitler to intervene? "What if Martinique is fortified as an air base? Or Iceland? Or Greenland? Or Canada bombed? What then?" she asked. "I think we must reckon with the possibility of war." And that being the case, she thought, "there is a serious responsibility . . . both for the sake of the men and for the sake of the country" to have those men adequately trained. "If it is true that it is impossible to secure enough 'trainees' freely, then it is involved in the whole set-up that they be required to train. I think there is a real difference," she asserted, "between people being compelled to learn how to use a weapon and compelling them to use it." She reiterated her hatred of "any and all conscription," but considering "the point we are at, I feel hesitation in agitating against requiring men of military age to undergo training."[57]

Balch's was the minority view among pacifists, however, and as July 1940 became August, the fight over conscription intensified. The press, newsreels, and the William Allen White Committee—all stepped up their proconscription propaganda while pacifists struggled valiantly against such formidable odds to prevent implementation of what they believed was simply another form of involuntary servitude. KAOWC organizations sponsored an anticonscription mass mobilization in Washington on 1 August. Despite oppressively hot weather and only five days' notice, 300 people from twenty-three states turned out, and an evening meeting attracted about 1,000 more who listened to speeches by Norman Thomas and senators Wheeler and Nye, among others. The Committee on Militarism in Education obtained the signatures of 300 prominent men and women in academia, social work, and related professions on a petition opposing the Burke bill on the grounds that peacetime conscription negated democracy, violated American tradition, disrupted economic and social life, and would be the "opening wedge for the totalitarian dogma that individual citizens are pawns of the state from birth until death, without any rights which those in positions of power are bound to respect."[58]

In early August Roosevelt, having carefully avoided a public stance on the issue, finally acknowledged his support and two weeks later when Willkie followed suit, that apparently settled it. On 14 September Congress approved the bill and two days later Roosevelt signed it into

law. For pacifists, it was another major step down the road to involvement in the war, and from the WILPF's perspective, the circumstances
of the debate indicated that the "ugly sinister atmosphere of war is
already here."

It was not just the lack of evidence "to show that volunteer enlist-
ments had failed," nor the fact that "the Army had deliberately broken
the law," which provided that a man, upon enlisting, could choose between a one-year "hitch" and service for three years. "The Army chiefs,"
Detzer commented, "acknowledged that they did not carry out the law
[for they] had never permitted anyone to volunteer for 12 months'
time." Of even greater concern was the behavior of law enforcement
officers who responded overzealously to the increased tension and activity on Capitol Hill during the final week of debate.

As the WILPF pointed out, the heat and humidity of a Washington
August was "enough to be a great strain on even the most valiant
spirits." Couple this debilitating weather with the pressure of an upcoming congressional election campaign and the long hours involved
in the debate with intense lobbying on both sides by the "thousands of
people [who] poured into Washington," and the result was inevitably a
tense and potentially volatile situation. Early in the week there was a
fist fight on the floor of the House, and in the lobbies the police,
"puffed up with a 'little brief authority,' became provocative and inso-
lent." Acknowledging that the police had a difficult job, nevertheless,
observed Detzer soberly, "the pushing and shoving, the sneering comments about the crowd, the inciting actions—such as fingering a re-
volver while taunting people with the observation that 'this would be a
swell bunch of communists on which to do some target practice,' all
gave me great concern for the future."[59]

Norman Thomas expressed much the same sentiment at an antiwar rally in New York City on 4 October. More than 1,000 people determined to fight for repeal of conscription listened as he voiced
pacifists' opinion that "every effort to repeal this law, no matter how
unsuccessful at first, will act as a brake upon America's rapid descent to
fascism."[60] On 16 October, registration day for conscription, the Youth
Committee Against War along with eight other organizations held a
"'Day of National Mourning' for the loss of democratic rights through
the conscription law" on college campuses.[61] Labor, however, would be
the "chief victim" of the new law, argued Pauli Murray of the KAOWC.
"Industry has insisted upon a 'reasonable' compensation for its share in
the defense program," she noted, "and yet a worker's only property, his
income, is to be taken away without any compensation for the loss,"

since a man employed in private industry at $1,200 annually would be paid only $328 as a soldier.[62]

The conscription law created many problems for the peace movement, not just concerning the situation for labor, but also in regard to conscientious objectors, deferments, and related issues. Thus pacifists formed a special advisory committee chaired by Edwin C. Johnson of the Committee on Militarism in Education to prepare an analysis of the new law, "push for liberalization of its administration and for its eventual repeal, and . . . act as a clearinghouse on advice to conscientious objectors, trade unionists, and others, in order to safeguard their rights and to prevent discriminations."[63] The FOR was already working with the Quakers on the issue of conscientious objectors; others indicated their desire to test the constitutionality of conscription. New peace groups sprang up in at least seventeen cities and the ACLU planned to hold a conference to discuss all of the relevant issues.

The WILPF was concerned on all scores, and when A. J. Muste asked Detzer to serve on a National Board for Conscientious Objectors being established by the United Pacifist Committee, she accepted with enthusiasm. But the WILPF, like Libby of the NCPW, was more disturbed for the moment over Roosevelt's Destroyers-For-Bases deal with England, which was arranged in August through executive agreement so as to circumvent anticipated opposition in Congress.

The air war between the Luftwaffe and the Royal Air Force known as the Battle of Britain had begun on 8 August, anticipated in mid-June by Winston Churchill who had turned to Roosevelt for help in repelling Hitler's planned invasion of the island. "As Americans heard radio commentators tell of Britain's ordeal, saw pictures of London burning, of women and children huddling in subways," writes one historian, "a wave of sympathy for Britain swept the country. White's Committee, . . . now boasting of six hundred chapters, built up a huge agitation on the destroyer issue. Millions signed petitions."[64]

As Detzer pointed out, however, a 1917 law prohibited the United States, if neutral, to transfer any vessels of war to a belligerent country. Yet Roosevelt, "who has sworn to uphold the Constitution and the laws of the land," declared Detzer angrily, "deliberately broke the 1917 law." By so doing, she continued, "he establishes a precedent which . . . has dangers far beyond the immediate question of 50 destroyers." The issue was not the sanctity of law, for she acknowledged that "the finest citizens" sometimes feel conscience-bound to disobey a law they believe to be wrong. "But those people," she stressed, "are prepared to accept the penalty for such action. As long as we live by a system of law, this is essential." This executive agreement, however, had nothing to do with conscience, and Roosevelt knew when he made it that "he was protected against paying the penalty" because impeachment proceedings, by law, must begin in the House of Representatives where prevailing opinion supported the administration. This kind of "Government by 'decree'," she warned, "is a terrifying manifestation of a disintegrating democracy." Libby's response was no less condemnatory. He called the arrangement a "grave threat to our democracy," indicative of a country "sinking into dictatorship."[65]

The upcoming election was the key, said Libby. Because Roosevelt's interventionist foreign policy seemed to be supported by his Republican opponent, peace groups *"must concentrate on electing an anti-war, anti-dictatorship House of Representatives.* If President Roosevelt should win re-election," Libby reasoned, "a Republican anti-war House would be the only possible check on his foreign policy. If Mr. Willkie should win, a Senate that will be Democratic for four years anyway will be a check on any war tendencies that he might develop."[66]

On election day fifty million Americans, more than ever before, made their decision: "a decisive victory for Roosevelt, . . . [but] largely a personal one; the Democrats gained only six seats in the House . . . and lost three in the Senate."[67] From pacifists' perspective, political party was not the major issue. Using the earlier vote on conscription as a yardstick with which to measure results in the House, those who were defeated were evenly distributed: twenty-seven favoring conscription and twenty-five opposed to it lost their seats. Re-elected, however, were 132 who voted against conscription. In the Senate, "all the anti-interventionists were re-elected," Libby reported. If this Congress could be "fearless" enough to refuse to "rubber stamp" presidential foreign policy, he thought, the United States had a fighting chance to "preserve and strengthen" democracy by staving off "dictatorship and war."[68]

While waiting to see what Roosevelt's next move would be and how the new Congress would respond, pacifists concentrated on a three-point program: Keep the country out of the war, assist conscientious objectors, and feed Europe. The third issue was particularly important to many WILPF women who still had vivid memories of World War I. Thus they invited Herbert Hoover, head of the post-World War I relief program, to an early November board meeting where he presented a relief plan contemplated by the government. A discussion of several hours followed during which Gertrude Baer's comments had the greatest impact.

Probably no one there was more concerned with the hunger problem in Europe than Baer, who had finally arrived in the United States in mid-June. Although she understood the humanitarian desire of "religious people who wanted to feed equally friend and foe," she reminded her listeners that the WILPF was not a religious society. Neither was it a humanitarian nor a philanthropic organization, but was, rather, a body of women "independent of other organizations neither religious or political," and its mission was "to educate women all over the world for the big international issues and objects" for which the WILPF stood. She suggested, therefore, that those women concerned with relief might best contribute to the cause by working with the Quakers or the Red Cross, already well-organized to handle the problem. Perhaps on the basis of Baer's observations, the board finally voted to "reaffirm its principle of feeding the victims of war" by urging its members "to support whatever plans they believe to be practical to carry that out."[69]

As for further efforts to keep the United States out of war, as the end of 1940 approached, pacifists agreed that "a much more vigorous and broad campaign must be carried on . . . with more sponsorship and more money."[70] But this was precisely the problem. Recognizing that they had little chance of effectively countering the "tremendous propaganda campaign" of the White Committee with its command of "influential and socially-prominent sponsors" and almost unlimited financial resources when, in the words of KAOWC secretary Alice Dodge, "we have absolutely no money and . . . very little activity," pacifists were becoming "dissatisfied" and discouraged.[71]

Although the FOR and the WRL reported an increase in members and financial contributions, the KAOWC's financial situation was "acute" and "lack of money" was a "serious problem" for the plans of the Youth Committee Against War to sponsor a "Christmas Congress."[72] The NPC lost seven local affiliated peace councils and rumor had it that the AAUW and the Federation of Women's Clubs would shortly withdraw. For the first time in fifteen years Catt canceled the annual NCCCW due to financial problems and, in all likelihood, to lack of unity among member organizations as well. As for the WILPF, its situation was not much better.

Despite Olmsted's cheery reassurance to an Illinois branch, depressed over the influence of the White Committee, that the Springfield, Massachusetts, branch had doubled its membership in the past year in response to the committee's work, Springfield was the exception. At the spring annual meeting, Olmsted reported that the group lost 626 more members than it gained in the past year. In 1935 the

WILPF counted approximately 9,000 members and it had grown steadily until reaching its peak in 1938 at 14,084. By April 1940, however, it was just four members shy of 13,000 and in her report to other KAOWC members at the end of the year, Olmsted commented ruefully that the WILPF's most notable achievement in 1940 was that it had kept going, trying to forestall further resignations.

A loss of 1,000 dues-paying members in just two years did not help the WILPF's always-shaky financial picture. But at $1.00 per member annually, dues did not represent the organization's primary source of funding. Small contributions from members throughout the year; large gifts from wealthy members, sympathetic nonmembers, and legacies; and foundation or other grants made up most of the WILPF's income. The group was hard hit by the 1937 recession; although membership peaked in April 1938, January's financial statement showed an operating deficit of $7,200 and by June, National Chair Dorothy Hommel noted worriedly, "we are faced with the danger of dissolving the U.S. Section for lack of financial support."[73]

An effort to raise dues to $2.00 at the annual meeting failed to win approval, and appeal letters were disappointing in their meager results. As of January 1939, the deficit had been reduced slightly, but staff had been slashed to the bone and a customary contribution of $1,500 from the Christian Social Justice Fund was lost, as were other smaller contributions, because of WILPF's radical stance on neutrality and aid to the Allies.

By February 1941 the group's financial picture began to improve. The latest appeal for funds brought a better response than in previous months, but as the national office reminded members, "while we are paying off the last of the debt, we must not forget our current expenses."[74] Because Americans would be paying a 10 percent surcharge on their income tax for "defense" in 1941, national leaders suggested that members offset that tax by a comparable donation to the WILPF. It may be that the increasing number and amount of contributions already coming in reflected such an "antitax" donation from WILPF members indignant at being compelled to support a policy with which they disagreed.

Although the FOR made plans for a payment protest demonstration against the tax and the WILPF sent out protest stamps to be affixed to tax returns, the main issue pacifists confronted as 1941 opened revolved around that plank in the Democratic platform that called for "material aid to liberty-loving peoples wantonly attacked" restricted by the condition that such aid be "consistent with law and not inconsistent with the interests of our own national self-defense." In his 6 January message to Congress, Roosevelt, in keeping with this plank, submitted his Lend-Lease proposal. He wanted the U.S. government, rather than private business enterprise, to provide the Allied Powers— which in reality meant Great Britain—with arms, munitions, and other implements of war through "loan, lease, or otherwise . . . to be paid for, temporarily, by American taxpayers, not by the foreign belligerents who received them." As Charles Beard has pointed out, notwithstanding FDR's assertions to the contrary, "under international law . . . it was an act of war for a neutral government to supply munitions, arms, and implements of war to one of the belligerents engaged in a war."[75]

Speaking for the KAOWC, John T. Flynn said as much at the time. "What the President now proposes is war, undeclared war. It is not merely a question whether Hitler will construe [it] as an act of war. It *is* an act of war." The WILPF opposed Lend-Lease not only because the women agreed with Flynn, but also because in its opinion the proposal conferred upon the Chief Executive "enormous powers . . . [which] were to be effective 'not withstanding the provisions of any other law'."[76] Roosevelt, however, reassured Americans that Lend-Lease would not violate either the Johnson Act, which prohibited loans to belligerents, or the Neutrality Act.

A third issue of concern to pacifists with respect to Lend-Lease was that of transportation: "It would seem strange," wrote Beard in 1948, "for the United States to manufacture huge quantities of supplies for Great Britain, turn them over to British ships in American harbors, and then quietly allow German submarines to send them all to the bottom of the sea, instead of assuring delivery by convoying supply ships into British waters or to Iceland." But convoying, too, was an act of war under international law, and Roosevelt himself had said back in October that "convoys mean shooting and shooting means war."[77] The president declared, therefore, that the U.S. government had no intention of convoying Lend-Lease supplies to Britain.

Pacifists quickly mobilized to defeat the Lend-Lease proposal as hearings began before the Senate Foreign Relations Committee in late January. Calling it "the war dictatorship bill," the WILPF asserted that its "basic purpose is to give the President what amounts to almost absolute power."[78] Acknowledging that situations occasionally arise that call for "a free hand on the part of the Executive so that red tape may be cut in order to get things done," and that in a crisis situation "the parliamentary method is clumsy and slow," the WILPF did not consider this such a situation. "This bill," asserted the women, "is a clear abdication of political democracy itself."[79] The KAOWC took its opposition one step further, maintaining in its program of action adopted at a national demonstration against the bill in Washington on 21 February, that Lend-Lease was a new and dangerous example of "Anglo-American imperialism."[80]

Hearings continued in the House and the Senate through February into early March when both houses finally approved the measure. On the eleventh, Lend-Lease—"An Act to Promote the Defense of the United States"—became law with Roosevelt's signature. "The fateful significance of the passage of this bill," said A. J. Muste somberly, "can hardly be exaggerated. It may well be that March 11, 1941, will go down in history as the date of America's entry into World War II."[81]

For pacifists, it was one discouraging defeat after another: revision of the Neutrality Act, conscription, Lend-Lease. And from the WILPF's perspective, the press was now rubbing salt in its wounds. During the debate over Lend-Lease, Drew Pearson and Robert Allen in their syndicated "Washington Merry-Go-Round" column reported that Balch had resigned from the WILPF's Executive Board, thereby "cracking" the "isolationist front" of the group. According to these journalists, Balch, who "strongly" favored aid to England, disapproved of "the anti-British stand" of Detzer, and was only one of a number of WILPF leaders "up in arms over Miss Detzer's views." Rumor had it "that a showdown on foreign policy will soon be forced within the organization."[82]

Although some WILPF leaders, Balch among them, did indeed disagree with Detzer's views, as WILPF President Gertrude Bussey pointed out, Detzer did not control organizational policy but simply administered the policy "agreed upon by members at our Annual Meeting." Moreover, Balch had not resigned nor did she intend to, and in her letter asking for a retraction, she observed that "as regards a showdown within the organization, we have fortunately a continuous series of them in the shape of votes on controversial issues."[83] Pearson and Allen quickly printed a corrected version, but without apology.

The pacifist "front" of the WILPF may not have been "cracking," but there were problems within the KAOWC, not so much with respect to policy as ideology. At the end of January 1941 the FOR voted to withdraw from the pacifist bloc while still continuing its cooperation with pacifist activities. The key issue, said Muste, was that of military defense. FOR members, as absolute nonresistants, found it ideologically incompatible to remain affiliated with the KAOWC so long as it continued to cooperate with the America First Committee, which advocated an "impregnable military defense" for the United States. Further, asserted Muste, "there are representatives of reactionary economic trends in these 'defend America' organizations, perhaps even persons of dubious international ties, identification with which even in indirect fashion would seriously discredit us."[84]

The KAOWC had waxed and waned over cooperation with the America First Committee since its inception in September 1940. By January 1941 pacifists concluded that the committee was a "sincere conservative American committee of business men, interested in keeping America out of war. Henry Ford and others objectionable to us have been removed from the committee, and it has definitely repudiated anti-semitism." Although not entirely in agreement with its program, said KAOWC members, "we cannot but welcome its presence, since it seems to be able to attract the moral and financial support of elements we have been unable to reach effectively."[85] Giving further credibility to the new organization was its publicity director Sidney Hertzberg, former director of the Writers Anti-War Bureau and editor of *Uncensored,* and the presence of John Flynn on its national committee.

It may be that the FOR's withdrawal combined with the "smear campaign" of journalists who equated KAOWC pacifists with "fascists" and "appeasers" compelled the organization to re-evaluate its structure and function, for in early March it did just that. It ceased to be a federated group of pacifist organizations and became one with individual dues-paying members who signed a statement "declaring themselves in agreement with our program and opposed to all forms of totalitarianism, here and abroad." Its basic program did not change: "opposition to involvement in war, making democracy work at home, opposition to armament economics and imperialism, [and] opposition to permanent peace-time military conscription."[86] There is no indication of how many rank-and-file WILPF members subsequently joined the KAOWC, but Detzer and Olmsted were soon elected to its governing committee.

The KAOWC's first major undertaking after its restructuring was a three-day National Anti-War Congress held over Memorial Day weekend in Washington. With 600 delegates from twenty-five states participating, pacifists considered it a great success. It opened on Friday evening with a mass meeting chaired by John T. Flynn, KAOWC National Chair. An audience of about 3,000 listened to speeches by Senator Wheeler, Norman Thomas, and Rabbi Sidney E. Goldstein. Six roundtable discussions took place on Saturday: "Guns or Butter," "Civil Liberties, Labor, Pressure Groups," "Peace Aims and World Federation," "Conscription and Conscientious Objectors," "America Looks South," and "United States Foreign Policy-On the Pacific-In Europe," chaired by the WILPF's Gertrude Bussey with Olmsted as secretary. Detzer chaired the plenary session Saturday night with another round of speakers, and Jeannette Rankin presided at a Memorial Service on Sunday afternoon. Cooperating organizations included the WILPF, NCPW, FOR, WRL, Youth Committee Against War, and the Washington chapter of the America First Committee.

Participants passed a resolution supporting a war referendum as well as resolutions concerning each roundtable discussion topic. All were precisely what one would expect from an antiwar gathering dominated by pacifists, but one was decidedly more radical than the rest. That delegates approved the "Guns or Butter" resolution at all is a measure of how disillusioned pacifists had become by mid-1941.

"An armaments economy is one which gives up the attempt to expand the economic activities which produce the life of the people, and turns to the expansion of those designed to produce death," the resolution began. An economy based on armaments, whether for war or simply preparation for war, demanded maximum production for the military with minimum production for the welfare of people. The resulting decline in the standard of living, therefore, was not "a by-product or a mistake in administration," but was, rather, "an essential and fundamental feature which the armaments economy deliberately attempts to achieve. . . . This deadly perversion of economic activity is one of the major aspects of fascism, which this Congress heartily condemns."

Noting the "inadequacy" of the "present economic system" in the United States, delegates asserted that the impossibility of "patching up" this system was clear from the expenditure of billions of dollars "to bolster . . . our private economy by deficit financing. The present hysterical armaments program is only a larger and more wasteful outlay." Delegates thus called for the immediate public takeover of "all defense industries, all natural resources and basic industries and the banking and credit system. They must be operated to meet the need of our people instead of for profit, and they must be operated under democratic control." As strong as this statement was, there was more:

> An economic system built on the private corporate basis is at odds with a political system based on democratic equality. The fascist answer to that contradiction is to scrap political democracy and get a totalitarian system which unites economics and politics in the worst of

all possible ways. The democratic answer to that contradiction is to scrap corporate economic dictatorship for a cooperative and socialized economic order which can live in the same house with political democracy. (Only thus can we avoid being impaled on the horns of the dilemma of guns or butter).[87]

The press immediately reported that the Anti-War Congress voted to "confiscate all private property in the U.S." When printing up the resolutions for distribution, the KAOWC added an explanation designed to "clear up any misapprehensions which may have arisen as a result of distorted statements which appeared in some newspapers." First, the KAOWC reminded everyone that none of the resolutions were binding on participating individuals, organizations, or the KAOWC. Second, at the time the "Guns or Butter" resolution was adopted, the chair of that roundtable "specifically stated" that it did not imply confiscation of private property. Last, it was noted that delegates unanimously voted when adopting that resolution that their action "should not be interpreted as endorsement of the Socialist platform."[88]

These disclaimers notwithstanding, the resolution went too far for Frederick Libby of the NCPW. Although acknowledging his "sincere conviction that the KAOWC can do things which neither America First nor the National Council for Prevention of War can accomplish in educating public opinion towards a more democratic way of life here," he thought it best to resign from the KAOWC in the interests of both the NCPW and KAOWC. As a member of the KAOWC, he noted, he was helping America First, a group whose "nationalism" and "impregnable defense" position he disagreed with.[89] Second, in light of the Anti-War Congress resolutions, it was clear that the KAOWC was moving in a more socialist direction and this would reduce his effectiveness among liberal middle class people if he remained a member.

Libby was not the only pacifist to react negatively to the radical stance of the KAOWC Congress. If Alice Thacher Post's response was indicative of any substantial number of WILPF members, then it, too, must have had defections accordingly. When informed that the board had elected her an honorary vice-president, Post declined the position due to personal "inadequacies" (she was eighty-seven years old), to what she saw as the "close collaboration" between the WILPF and isolationists, and to the WILPF's "nonresistant" character.[90]

Although Libby and Post were uncomfortable with the more radical aspects of the pacifist bloc, Norman Thomas and the WRL were becoming increasingly disturbed by its continued cooperation with the America First Committee. In late July the WRL submitted a resolution to the KAOWC that it did "not favor future cooperation" with America First, given that group's "nationalist and isolationist philosophy." For Thomas, the issue was the anti-Semitism that persistently surfaced among America First spokesmen. The WILPF, too, felt compelled to deny any connection "whatever" with America First that summer, and A. J. Muste affirmed his belief that "it is better to appear politically ineffective at a given moment than actually to be or to give the appearance of being intellectually confused or spiritually compromised" by too close an association with those of dubious character who might also oppose U.S. involvement in war.[91]

Muste's statement, although reflecting the FOR's attitude toward America First, may also have been precipitated by the emergence of a new organization, the Union for Democratic Action, headed by former pacifist Reinhold Niebuhr. Composed of "liberals and ex-socialists," the new group was just as concerned as pacifists that democracy not become a victim of the war. But the way to ensure this, said the Union, was not by remaining aloof from the war, but rather by defeating the Axis powers through "full military participation" if necessary. It must have been difficult for KAOWC pacifists to repudiate this position because they had "often fought side by side with members of this new group in behalf of liberal social and economic causes," but repudiate it they did. "There is certainly no more reason today than there was twenty-five years ago," declared thirty-seven pacifist leaders, "to hope that liberalism can be injected into the conduct of war or advanced after it."[92] Drew Pearson and Robert Allen may have been wrong in January by asserting that Balch's alleged resignation from the WILPF's Executive Board was a sign that the peace front was "cracking," but by summer's end that observation was correct.

The role of the NPC provides another example of such disintegration. Increasingly ineffective because of its own internal divisions, the NPC simply removed itself from the ongoing struggle over the war issue and focused instead on planning for the postwar world. A reasonable enough direction to take under the circumstances and an important one as well, the NPC did not contribute in any meaningful way to the effort to keep the United States at peace, even after the KAOWC became a member in the fall.

The NPC was not alone in its concern that summer of 1941 with the issue of the postwar world; so, too, were Roosevelt and British Prime Minister Winston Churchill. On 14 August the press reported that a secret meeting between the two men had taken place aboard ship somewhere in the Atlantic earlier that month. They discussed, said administration spokesmen vaguely, "the problem of supply of munitions as provided by the Lend-Lease Act," but more important from a long-range perspective was their declaration of "common principles" upon which they wished the postwar world to be organized.[93] Subsequently referred to as the Atlantic Charter, its eight points affirmed the right of peoples everywhere to decide upon their own form of government and territorial alterations, called for equity among all nations with respect to trade and access to the world's natural resources, and stressed the desirability of international peace free from the use of force.

From the WILPF's perspective it was hardly anything to get excited about. Calling it "a sterile document" and "disappointing in its vague generalities and lack of realism," the WILPF pointed out that it had the familiar ring of an earlier president's "Fourteen Points" —and it had not required any great effort on the part of world leaders two decades earlier to violate the spirit if not the letter of those equally noble concepts. And as Olmsted noted, the very existence of Atlantic Charter now attested to a fresh violation:

> The President now states that this meeting has been planned since last February, yet Congress was not consulted, and everyone who attended sneaked away pretending to be somewhere else. President Roosevelt has certainly rejected President Wilson's great objective of "no more secret diplomacy, open covenants, openly arrived at" for he has sent more "personal" representatives everywhere and carried on more secret diplomacy than any of his predecessors that I can recall, even though Congress has been steadily in session with a large Democratic majority, so that these momentous *one-man* decisions have not been necessary.[94]

Moreover, as Balch pointed out, this joint declaration omitted any reference to disposition of colonies, individual rights and liberties, reparations, or the creation of an international organization in "any specific shape, whether through a League of Nations, Federal Union, United States of Europe or otherwise." For Bussey and Detzer, the major problem with the charter was that in its reference to "the destruction of the Nazi tyranny" combined with its call for unilateral German disarmament, it repeated the mistake of "the sole guilt clause" of the Versailles Treaty and, therefore, was likely to "stiffen German resistance and to sow the seeds of future wars."[95]

When the Atlantic Charter was made public, Roosevelt assured Congress and the American people that "no new commitments for the United States" were made at his meeting with the Prime Minister. Even though the situation in the Far East had become more ominous, the president declared that he and Churchill "had reached no understandings that brought the United States nearer to war." Yet no one argued that the European war was going well for the Allied powers. Hitler's violation of the Nazi-Soviet Nonaggression Pact in June had sent the Soviets reeling. Harry Hopkins had just returned from his "mission to Moscow" where Stalin told him that U.S. aid was necessary to stave off further German advances, and on the other side of the globe, Japan continued to progress toward creation of the Greater East Asia Co-Prosperity Sphere. If war for the United States did not loom on the European horizon, the continuing inability of U.S. and Japanese diplomats in their ongoing negotiations to find a common ground of understanding increased the chances almost daily for military confrontation in the Land of the Rising Sun.

Although Democratic leaders in Congress "hailed the Atlantic Charter as a magnificent statement of war aims," and the American people seemed to support it as well, most Americans were undoubtedly relieved by the president's reassurance that the meeting did not mean war. An opinion poll taken "immediately after the conference showed that 74 percent of the country still opposed involvement in the war."[96] The Democrats' commitment in 1940 to keep the United States at peace "except in case of attack" apparently remained unaltered by the Atlantic Conference of August 1941.

Within less than a month came that "attack." "On September 4, the Navy Department announced that a submarine of undetermined nationality had attacked the American destroyer *Greer* that morning in the Atlantic on its way to Iceland; that torpedoes had been fired at the vessel; that the *Greer* had counterattacked by dropping depth charges, with unknown results. The destroyer, the department explained, was operating as a part of the Atlantic patrol established during the summer by President Roosevelt and was carrying mail."[97] The KAOWC was "greatly disturbed" over this report and others of a similar nature, and within a few days asked Secretary of the Navy Frank Knox to make "a full and detailed report on exactly what happened."[98]

Not until 11 September did Roosevelt issue an official response. The *Greer* was merely carrying mail to Iceland, he maintained, flying the U.S. flag, when she was deliberately attacked by a German submarine with the intent of sinking her. "The aggression is not ours," he continued, "ours is solely defense. But let this warning be clear. From now on, if German or Italian vessels of war enter the waters, the protection of which is necessary for American defense, they do so at their own peril. The orders which I have given as Commander in Chief to the United States Army and Navy are to carry out that policy—at once. . . . There will be no shooting unless Germany continues to seek it." But for all of his strong words, Roosevelt "did not invoke the escape clause of the Democratic antiwar plank and call upon Congress to authorize war."[99]

For the WILPF, the president's speech "was a startling statement of war policy." Although any president of the United States by virtue of his role as commander-in-chief "is clearly within his constitutional right in giving instructions to the Navy," the women acknowledged, they were nevertheless appalled that he would so blatantly go against public opinion that was still opposed to a "shooting" foreign policy. Speaking for the KAOWC, Executive Director Mary Hillyer echoed the same sentiment: "While the American people through Congress have approved the policy of aid to Britain, they have given no sanction to the President's newly announced policy of shooting our way through belligerent waters to get the supplies to Britain," she declared emphatically.

This executive decision brought up the issue of democracy yet again. "If it were possible under our constitution for a President to declare war," Hillyer continued, "Mr. Roosevelt's instructions to our armed forces at sea . . . would constitute such an act. . . . If we are to preserve our constitutional democracy, we must see to it that this power remains with the people's representatives." The KAOWC and the WILPF demanded that Congress "be asked now whether it approves the President's action."[100] The Senate chose instead to investigate the *Greer* affair because journalists and others in Washington were making allegations that the official version of the incident did not represent the truth.

In the meantime on 9 October, Roosevelt asked Congress to repeal the provision in the Neutrality Act that prohibited the arming of U.S. merchant ships. The House Foreign Affairs Committee immediately called for hearings but announced that they would be closed. The decision was rescinded after protest from Republicans and the peace bloc, but it made little difference. House action in support of the president was quickly forthcoming and the revised Neutrality Act went to the Senate.

At its National Board meeting in mid-October, the first resolution the WILPF passed was directed at the Senate Foreign Relations Committee, urging it to reject any further revision of the Neutrality Act. "It

is an historic fact," the women reminded the committee, "that the arming of merchant ships was a direct factor in American entrance into the
last war."[101] Pacifists, however, were fighting a losing battle. Just one day
prior to their meeting, the Navy Department announced another German submarine attack. This time the USS *Kearny* had been torpedoed
while on patrol; eleven American men were missing, several more had
been injured.

Thus the debate in the Senate over the revised Neutrality Act was,
from the WILPF's view, extremely discouraging. The arming of merchant ships and other provisions were discussed. By 7 November when
the vote come in the Senate, it was fifty in favor and thirty-seven against
a revised act that not only repealed those sections that forbade the
arming of merchant ships, but also repealed "the sections relative to
commerce with states engaged in armed conflict and to the exclusion
of American ships from combat areas."[102]

On 13 November the House concurred, 212 to 194. Albeit a narrow margin of victory for the administration, a victory it was nonetheless and for the WILPF it represented an "abdication of powers by the
Congress." The elected representatives of the American people were
simply rubber-stamping policies already implemented by the president,
thus allowing their important decision-making power "to pass by de-
fault to the executive branch of the government. The result," noted
this concerned group of pacifists, "is a growing habit of the executive
to act without consultation of Congressional leaders and sometimes
even in contradiction to the expressed views of the Congress."[103] This
was not the WILPF's concept of a democracy.

Despite the incidents of "attack" against the *Greer* and the *Kearny*,
as well as other "shootings and sinkings" in the Atlantic in late October,[104] they were not used by the Roosevelt administration to call for a
declaration of war. Clearly the American people were no more unified
in support of such a drastic move by November 1941 than they had
been a year earlier when such antiwar sentiment had forced both political parties to base their election campaigns on the promise to keep
the United States out of foreign wars. If Roosevelt wanted to unify
Americans behind U.S. involvement in the Allies' struggle with Germany, it was going to require something more momentous than a few
isolated incidents of shooting in the Atlantic.

On 7 December 1941 the Japanese provided that momentous
event with their surprise attack on the U.S. Pacific Fleet stationed at
Pearl Harbor in the Hawaiian Islands. Numbly glued to her radio that
Sunday afternoon, Detzer listened with a growing sense of desolation

and grief as the magnitude of the catastrophe at Pearl Harbor became increasingly clear. War had come to her beloved United States. In the months to come, she would frequently be asked, "What would you peace people have done, had you been running the government at the time of Pearl Harbor?" For Detzer, there was only one answer. "War," she replied, "was perhaps the only logical method for our government to use. . . . No other method . . . had been developed to take its place."[105]

13

World War II

WHEN CONGRESS DECLARED WAR in December 1941 in adherence to Constitutional law, American pacifists were compelled to accept the reality that for the second time in less than twenty-five years, the United States would militarily decide the political fate of Europe and perhaps of the entire world. Convinced that fascism would come to the United States when war did, pacifists labored diligently throughout the war years and beyond to prevent militarism from becoming entrenched in American society. If democracy was a casualty of this war, they believed, there would be no hope for a democratically organized postwar world of peace, freedom, and justice.

Within three days of Pearl Harbor, the National Board of the U.S. Section of the WILPF voted unanimously its "reasserted unshaken faith in the goal of a warless world and determination to work toward it," its unswerving commitment to the "enduring ideals of democracy," and its condemnation of "the attack of Japan as a resort to violence." Despite the women's prior criticism of the administration's handling of the uneasy situation in the Atlantic, the policies of the president and the State Department in the Pacific did not warrant similar castigation: "We are profoundly grateful," declared the WILPF, "that our government during the last two months has made such genuine and serious efforts to resolve the conflict with Japan."[1]

Although the WILPF'S official response to U.S. entry into World War II indicated an apparent consensus, the women were no more unanimous in their initial reaction to the attack at Pearl Harbor than was the country at large. As Detzer observed, "there is a difference of opinion both in Washington and among our members about the part played by our government during these past difficult months."[2] Evidently some WILPF members were among those Americans suspicious that there must be more here than met the eye. Senator Tom Connally put it this way in his question to Roosevelt the very day of the attack: "How did they catch us with our pants down, Mr. President?"[3] Journalists and others who had opposed FDR's "war-mongering" foreign policy joined the chorus of voices from Congress who felt that they had not been given all of the facts surrounding the events of 7 December 1941.

There was good reason for skepticism. The incidents involved in the "shooting war" in the Atlantic in the fall, for example, had not been honestly explained to the American people. An investigation by the Senate Committee on Naval Affairs of the attack on the *Greer* brought a written response on 20 September from Admiral Harold R. Stark, chief of Naval Operations. Although a few members of Congress were immediately made privy to the admiral's explanation, it was not disclosed to the general public until late October. As Beard pointed out in 1948, had Roosevelt asked for a declaration of war based on the *Greer* attack, he undoubtedly would have encountered stiff congressional opposition, for the gist of Stark's account "made the President's statement of the case . . . appear in some respects inadequate, and, in others incorrect."[4]

Then there was the *Kearny*, allegedly torpedoed by a German submarine during the Congressional debate on the arming of U.S. merchant ships. Roosevelt's response appeared to be an attempt to invoke the "escape clause" of the Democratic platform with regard to U.S. involvement in a foreign war, for he had declared, "America has been attacked." Yet two days later Secretary of the Navy Frank Knox issued a report that did not corroborate the president's statement. Members of the Senate Committee on Naval Affairs learned "that the *Kearny* was actually on convoy duty at the time of the shooting and had been engaged at length in fighting a pack of German submarines before she was hit by a torpedo."[5] Not made public until early December, this information in the hands of Congress would have made it virtually impossible for the administration to get a declaration of war by way of German "attacks" in the Atlantic.

The revelation that the *Kearny* was on convoy duty suggested that opponents of Lend-Lease had been right in their earlier prediction that in order to fulfill the act's purpose of aiding Britain, U.S. ships would have to convoy British ships into British waters or, at the very least, patrol the North and South Atlantic to protect against German or Italian submarine attacks. At the time, the administration and its Congressional supporters reiterated the president's earlier pledge that no such plan was contemplated. Within a few months, however, Cabinet members began to comment on the need to expedite shipment of supplies to England, despite opinion polls showing that the American people opposed U.S. naval escorts for such a purpose.

At a 25 April press conference Roosevelt "denied that the Government was considering naval escorts for convoys and stated that warships and airplanes were engaging in 'patrol' work." He did not, however, adequately explain the distinction between a "convoy" and a "patrol," and if that fact did not sound a warning knell to the average citizen, it did to the KAOWC. "The President," said these pacifists, "has ordered patrol of the Atlantic 1,000 to 3,000 miles from our coast to watch for enemy vessels and warn the British. PATROLS," they declared emphatically, "ARE JUST 'SHORT OF' CONVOYS," reminding the American people of Roosevelt's earlier statement that "convoys mean shooting [and] shooting means war."[6]

As spring 1941 became summer, Roosevelt continued his public declarations that the United States was engaging in—and extending— only its patrol in the Atlantic, while his critics charged that these patrols were in reality convoys regardless of what the president chose to call them. Events soon proved these critics right, and since the convey issue was only one of a number of examples where Roosevelt's forthrightness could legitimately be questioned, it would seem that those women of the WILPF who suspected a similar degree of dissimulation on the administration's part with respect to its Far Eastern policies may have been justifiably dubious.

Events were moving too fast in those hectic first few days following Pearl Harbor for the women to pause for any in-depth analysis of the situation, however, and such a critical situation called for an immediate organizational response. Because a majority of WILPF leaders did not share the skepticism of the minority, the group issued its public statement of 10 December supporting administration policy in the Far East. The women apparently were willing to live with the inconsistency of their position, that is, a Roosevelt foreign policy designed to *involve* the United States in World War II through deceit and manipulation in the Atlantic, a Roosevelt foreign policy of openness and honesty in the Pacific designed to *prevent* U.S. involvement in the war.

The possibility that the president and his advisers might have manipulated their diplomacy in the Pacific to leave the Japanese with but one course of action—war with the United States—and had known of the coming attack on Pearl Harbor in time to have diverted it or, at the very least, to have responded militarily was a possibility so unthinkable that few people at the time *did* think it.[7] That included the KAOWC as well as the WILPF, despite the fact that just six days prior to the attack in a lengthy telegram to the president, its distrust was clearly evident:

> We are relieved that negotiations between the United States and Japan will continue and we ask that these negotiations be open. Have you delivered an ultimatum to Japan and if so what does that ultimatum contain? For weeks the American people have been kept in the dark and we have a right to demand an answer to that question. Have you forgotten that no president has the power to deliver an ultimatum to any foreign government which would involve this country in war without the consent of Congress?
>
> If you now force the nation into an Asiatic war through secret diplomacy you will be faced by such a division in national sentiment that men's faith in democratic institutions will be destroyed. . . .
>
> *The people do not want war with Japan and if they are tricked into it by manufactured incidents . . .* they will not know what they are fighting for.[8]

Neither in its official response to the attack at Pearl Harbor nor in the meeting where that response was formulated was there the slightest indication that any member of the KAOWC suspected a "manufactured or provoked incident."

Both the FOR and WRL were "shocked . . . by the manner" in which the Japanese forced belligerency status upon the United States, but they, too, apparently did not suspect deceit. They would not, however, "accept the too common notion that the sole guilt for this war rests upon Japan. The guilt rests also," declared the FOR unequivocally,

> upon the United States and other nations. The invasion of Asia and the subjugation of its people by western Powers, including ourselves; the insistence of these nations on keeping their armed forces in the Orient in order to maintain their control over strategic raw materials; their tariff policies; our Oriental Exclusion Act branding the Japanese as an inferior people . . . ; our devious course in recent years of selling war materials to Japan and at the same time making loans to China— these and similar policies were factors in bringing the Japanese military clique into power and bringing the present awful tragedy upon the peoples of Japan, America and other lands.[9]

Believing as they did that such policies of imperialism, militarism, racism, and profit-before-people had once again brought the scourge of war, it would have been understandable if American pacifists had joined with the "old-line peace societies" like the Church Peace Union and the APS in "suspending peace efforts 'for the duration'." Pacifists could not have followed the example of the League of Nations Association or the "more moderate groups associated in the National Peace Conference" by pledging support for the war, but after two decades of unstinting effort to truly "make the world safe for democracy," it would be difficult to fault them had they given up in defeat, discouragement, and just plain exhaustion.[10] But they did not, and the energy and determination they displayed after Pearl Harbor is testimony to the passionate intensity of their faith in the righteousness of their cause and its eventual triumph.

"Under no circumstances, regardless of the cost to ourselves," declared the WRL in mid-December, "can we abandon our principles or our faith in methods that are the opposite of those demanded by war."[11] Those principles were peace, freedom, and justice, and the methods were democratic, and the FOR, KAOWC, and WILPF expressed the same sentiment in much the same language. "War remains the final infamy," said the WILPF. "Mankind must some day be released from the violence and suffering and waste of this recurring tragedy. We base our faith and our action on the enduring ideals of democracy."[12]

Because war had come to the United States through the democratic process, believed the women, they would not interfere with, obstruct, or attempt to sabotage "civil or military officials in carrying out the will of the government." They would welcome into their ranks all who opposed war and violence, and cooperate "in community affairs" with those who did not insofar as conscience would allow. They would work for the "equal distribution of the economic burden of war, [and] the earliest possible attainment of a just and lasting peace" through a world government "based on the principles of justice and good will." They would "encourage" their own members to "assist in non-partisan relief" for the homeless and hungry victims of war, and continue and extend their efforts on behalf of fair treatment for conscientious objectors. And with World War I fresh in their minds, they would strive "with particular vigilance for the protection of freedom of speech, press, and assembly, and the maintenance of racial and religious tolerance."[13]

The first step for the KAOWC came on 16 December when it formally dissolved and then reconstituted itself under a new name with a new purpose. Fourteen of the eighteen members of the KAOWC governing committee present, including Detzer and Olmsted, formed themselves into a Provisional Committee Toward a Democratic Peace, and adopted a three-point program of action to prevent war profiteering and maintain civil liberties and democracy while striving for a just and peaceful postwar world. In early January 1942 Mary Hillyer, KAOWC Executive Director, was elected to that position for the new organization and in February, the committee became the Post War World Council (PWWC). It remained in existence until December 1967.

While the WRL and FOR concentrated on aid to conscientious objectors (COs) and problems related to the Selective Service and Espionage Acts, the NPC continued its pre-Pearl Harbor focus on the postwar settlement. "The coming of war to the U.S.A. does not change the purpose and function of the National Peace Conference," it stated in January 1942. "It is a clearing-house council of thirty-eight national organizations, and of affiliated state and community councils, holding varied points of view but sharing a common desire to seek and work for the things that will make for a just and enduring postwar peace."

The "cooperative agencies" of the Allied Powers created for war, continued the NPC, "should be extended into the immediate post-war period" to provide the foundation for relief and reconstruction. Olmsted took exception to the way this statement was worded for it implied a repeat of the post-World War I period, a peace imposed by the victors on the vanquished, which in this case would mean a postwar world dominated by Britain and the United States. She suggested a change in wording which "envisaged [that] from the beginning the [postwar] agencies should be international and include equally both conquering and conquered in the machinery of nations," but her proposal was voted down.[14]

This concern with the possibility of a postwar "Anglo-American imperialism" was not Olmsted's alone. In early March the PWWC took exception to the Secretary of Navy's remark that "the combined British and American fleets will rule the oceans 'for a hundred years'," echoing one of the WILPF's nine "future policies" formulated in late December 1941, which opposed any effort to create such "an unhealthy and dangerous" partnership.[15] While the peace movement remained vigilant for any indication that the Allies planned to dictate peace terms in the war's aftermath, of more immediate concern was a 1942 legislative measure that appeared to affect peace organizations directly, threatening to sharply reduce their influence should it be decided that they fell within the parameters of its provisions.

Six months after U.S. entry into the war an amended form of the Foreign Agents Registration Act of June 1938 went into effect. As Frederick Libby pointed out, although originally designed to ferret out "front" organizations of the Nazis, "a cursory examination convinces us that the net will not only ensnare the groups for which it is intended but that it will lay a heavy burden on all of the peace organizations." According to the amended act, the NCPW would have to register as a "foreign agent" for simply reprinting in its newsletter a speech made by a member of Parliament. Not only that, but "if the W.I.L. or F.O.R. or A.F.S.C. should register under this act," he noted, "no other organization or individual would be permitted to circulate or display its publications without registering also!"[16]

It was Detzer's understanding that the amended version was not intended for "groups like ours," and so inquired of Roger Baldwin if an ACLU attorney could "take up this matter" for all of the "poverty-stricken" peace groups involved. A mid-July meeting of Detzer and Libby with the bill's sponsor was not encouraging; as John Nevin Sayre reported to James Vail of the AFSC, the two came away from that meeting with the feeling that "there was real danger that the Department of Justice would insist" upon peace groups complying with the Act's requirements to register as "Agents of a Foreign Principal."[17]

Olmsted was outraged and agreed with Baer "that under no circumstances" should the WILPF allow itself to be so classified. "I also think," she wrote to Detzer, "that we should not in any way commit ourselves to submitting everything we issue, . . . such as Branch and Organization Letters, voluntarily to any government agency. If we do, we thereby give tacit consent to the principle to which we are opposed that the government has the right to censor our attitudes. That," we declared, "would establish the Nazi philosophy in this country in one step."

To Olmsted, it was "inconceivable" that "respectable peace organizations" could possibly be included in such legislation, a position that Detzer felt was "much too sanguine." Although she disagreed with Olmsted about "voluntarily sending our material to the government," saying that she was "delighted to have them [sic] see anything that we put out," Detzer noted that "the situation is very serious." If the WILPF was required to register and refused, "every member of the Board is liable to a five-year jail sentence and a ten thousand dollar fine." Although Olmsted was convinced that if the WILPF was "brought under the act, it will be to shut us up for political reasons," she still preferred to fight the case in court "even to the point of being completely extinguished" rather than submit to such a ruling.[18]

By the 28 July deadline, Detzer managed to secure an extension for the WILPF until 1 October. Baldwin did not think that the government would begin criminal proceedings against the other peace groups in the meantime if they chose not to register, and told all peace leaders that they must not be "cajoled or scared into registering at this stage." In mid-August the ACLU petitioned the Justice Department for exemption of the peace organizations, suggesting that a statement be added to the act that "no organization is required to register whose policies in the United States are determined solely by its United States membership or officers, and whose international connections are only those of cooperation with like organizations of similar purposes in other countries."[19] Whether or not this memorandum was responsible for the eventual outcome is not clear, but 1 October came and went and the WILPF did not register as a "foreign agent" nor, so far as the record shows, did any of the other peace organizations.

If U.S. pacifists were thus able to finish out the war years unmolested by the government, such was not the case for thousands of Americans on the West Coast. Where the civil liberties of these Japanese-Americans were concerned, the peace movement's vow to ensure that the excesses of World War I not repeat themselves had no impact.

Despite controversy among historians as to whom in the Roosevelt administration should bear responsibility for "the uprooting of tens of thousands of Japanese-Americans from their homes on the West Coast and their incarceration in concentration camps hundreds of miles away," ultimately the decision was the president's. On 19 February 1942, Roosevelt signed an executive order of relocation and a month later, Congress passed a law supporting it. Described later by the ACLU as "the worst single wholesale violation of civil rights of American citizens in our history," the relocation of 110,000 Americans of Japanese descent was inspired more by racism than political or military necessity, regardless of what the government said. As one historian has noted, "the supreme irony of the evacuation was that while Germans and Italians offered the same alleged threats to military security as the Nisei and Issei, their guilt was established on an individual basis, not a racial basis. Roosevelt was quite aware of this distinction and supported it."[20]

Pacifists were appalled. The PWWC and FOR issued strong statements of protest, emphasizing their shock at such blatant racism and violation of "true standards of democracy and humanity." Writing to Roosevelt at the end of April, the PWWC, while acknowledging the "difficulties of the situation," stressed the uncomfortable parallel it perceived in such action: "Enforcing this on the Japanese alone approximates the totalitarian theory of justice practiced by the Nazis in their treatment of the Jews."[21] Roosevelt sent the letter, signed by 200 "distin-

guished citizens," to Stimson for reply, but the PWWC was not persuaded by the Secretary's assertion of "overwhelming necessity."[22]

Representatives from thirty-three organizations, the WILPF among
them, met at a special conference on 18 June called by the PWWC to
address the "Japanese situation." After hearing detailed reports of the
appalling conditions in the camps and the circumstances under which
the evacuees were forced to leave their homes and businesses,[23] conference participants released a strongly worded statement to the press.
Echoing a similar statement adopted by the WILPF at its annual meeting in May, it recommended that "evacuation be held within its present
geographical bounds"; that civilian control replace military authority
over the entire process; that "wholesale detention" be dispensed with
and instead, hearings be set up to consider individual cases; and that
the "temporary shelters . . . in which life can scarcely be maintained at
a human level, shall not through any cause be permitted to become
even semi-permanent."[24]

While acting through the PWWC in the persons of Detzer and
Olmsted on the evacuation issue, the WILPF was also working to obtain
repeal of the Oriental Exclusion Act, and through its West Coast
branches to provide assistance to Japanese-American detainees. A
group of WILPF women from Seattle visited the camp at Puyallup,
Washington, taking food and other items requested by inmates, such as
rugs to cover up the "large cracks" in the floor, curtains, wash tubs and
boards, books, and magazines. "I almost dread going down to the
camp," wrote Mrs. Fred W. Ring, Regional Chair of the Northwest. "I
keep thinking 'this is a nightmare'. It can't be that my country has put
children and women behind barbed wires."[25]

The fact that two-thirds of the detainees were U.S. citizens while
some 5,000 more offered to sacrifice their lives in the U.S. armed
forces was, for the WILPF, "a great wrong." Gladys Walser, chair of the
WILPF's Committee on Japanese in America organized in early 1943,
saw the implications clearly. "The evacuation has impaired the value of
citizenship," she wrote in January 1944, "has caused the suspension of
full constitutional rights for law-abiding citizens and aliens of one race,
thus jeopardizing those rights for people of all races, [and] has set
aside the Bill of Rights."[26]

When the War Relocation Authority (WRA) adopted regulations
enabling "qualified evacuees" to leave the camps for resettlement in
communities farther inland, the WILPF worked closely with the AFSC,
the Committee on Resettlement of Japanese Americans, and other organizations to find homes and jobs for them. Because some Japanese-

American students were also allowed to leave the relocation centers to pursue their education, the WILPF endeavored to place as many of these young people as possible in schools where sympathetic WILPF members could take them under their wing. Walser, whose knowledge of Japanese culture was without parallel among WILPF leaders—she had just returned to the United States after living for twenty-five years in Japan—surveyed WILPF members in spring 1943 to determine the extent to which they were willing to help in the resettlement effort.

Encouraged by the response, Walser recommended that the WILPF undertake as a special project "the establishment and maintenance of a hostel for Japanese Americans who are leaving the Relocation Centers." It was unanimously approved. She suggested that the most likely cities for this hostel were Cleveland, Detroit, New York, and Boston, and asked WILPF members in those areas "to send any information which will facilitate the work of this committee" in choosing the best location. By mid-summer, however, the WILPF abandoned the idea due to expense—"$4,000 is considered necessary as an initial investment"—and decided instead to work with other organizations and churches toward the same end.[27]

Irate at the "delight" with which the press, movies, radio, and "some of the agencies of our own government" portrayed the Japanese throughout the war as "bloodthirsty, crafty brutes," the WILPF did not ignore the more prevalent antiblack and anti-Semitic racism already rampant in U.S. society. It condemned the whole notion of "superior and inferior races" as well as the "discrimination" and "injustice" that resulted from such an assumption, and it continued efforts to obtain congressional passage of a national antilynching law and abolition of the poll tax.[28]

By the beginning of 1943, Detzer was reporting that several antilynching bills and over half a dozen antipoll tax bills had been introduced in Congress, and in mid-May the House voted 265 to 110 in favor of one of the antipoll tax measures. But House approval was no guarantee of like action by the Senate, she noted, especially because that body killed similar legislation in 1942 through a filibuster. Despite the best efforts of the National Committee to Abolish the Poll Tax and other groups like the WILPF, Congress did not act favorably on either the antipoll tax or the antilynching bills during the war years.

Although discouraged on this score, the WILPF had every reason to believe that economically the war years might help ameliorate the black American's bleak situation. For Mercedes Randall, Roosevelt's June 1941 executive order banning discrimination in war industries and creating the Fair Employment Practices Commission (FEPC) as an enforcement agency was a giant step in this direction. "Of all the ostracisms, exclusions and double standards which have beset the Negro," wrote Randall in April 1943, "the most disastrous has been the discrimination against him in the field of employment. For on this has depended his entire existence."

But "from the first," she observed indignantly, the FEPC faced opposition "from Northern industrialists, Southern Democrats, reactionaries in Congress, and 'lily-white' unions. This resistance mounted in spite of the fact that winning the war depended on utilizing *every source* of man-power, and that we were fighting for the equality of all peoples in a free world." In July 1942 when the FEPC was merged with the War Manpower Commission, those who heralded its creation were even more discouraged, and the "final blow" came in January 1943 when Paul McNutt of the commission "postponed indefinitely the widely heralded hearings on discrimination against Negro workers on American railroads." Randall urged WILPF members to send letters and telegrams to Roosevelt and McNutt to reschedule the hearings; to restore the FEPC to its former independent status under the president "with powers of enforcement; to keep it a *voluntary* committee"; to increase its members from seven to nine with the appointment of two women, one white and one black; and to provide it with "an adequate budget and staff."[29]

The country's tense racial situation exploded only a couple of months after Randall's call to action on behalf of the FEPC. In early summer 1943 "a series of race riots," reported Detzer, erupted in "different parts of the country within a fortnight. In Beaumont, Texas, hoodlums destroyed practically all the Negro section. . . . In Detroit and Los Angeles the situations were even worse. The local police [were] . . . in some cases too weak to handle the problem and there is evidence that . . . [they] even helped the rioters" in these rascist outbursts of violence. In Washington Detzer joined a committee of concerned citizens, one of many similar groups quickly organized all across the country "to anticipate race difficulties and to try to prevent any repetition" of the riots.[30] Because one of Detzer's primary concerns was the treatment accorded COs, she also kept tabs on the racial situation in the Civilian Public Service (CPS) camps. In the Danbury camp that fall the men began a work strike to protest the segregated status of the camp's occupants, but segregation was the rule for all CPS camps as it was for the armed forces.

WILPF members who attended the Bryn Mawr Institute on International Relations at the end of June heard Pearl Buck's opening address dealing with the country's racial situation. Her "brilliant analysis" was prophetic, for she spoke of the "tremendous consequences which it will have on the whole world" for decades to come, reported Olmsted, and stressed that "something must be done with great rapidity in this country, or we are in for constant wars between white and dark races until this thing is fought out."[31]

Other WILPF members were impressed by Bayard Rustin's remarks at the Institute, and when the Pennsylvania branch began planning its fall series of meetings on the theme, "The Home Front," Olmsted invited him to participate in the one devoted to the racial situation. The issue was important to her because, among other reasons, she believed that Philadelphia was ripe for racial violence. She was not far wrong, for exactly one year later, in August 1944, the city was crippled by a transportation strike triggered by race discrimination. Once the strike was over, the Pennsylvania WILPF sponsored an all-day meeting in early October for all of the city's organizations interested in "Equal Opportunity For All—What are the Facts?" Among the speakers were those who had participated in a special session devoted to "Racial Problems" at the WILPF's annual meeting earlier in the spring.

Organized on the theme of "Tomorrow's World," the 1944 annual meeting included an all-day institute concerned with "Tension Areas in America Today." While the session on "Racial Problems" focused on black America, there were three others on "The Japanese American," "The Conscientious Objector," and "Anti-Semitism." If racism against blacks aroused Mercedes Randall's indignation, no less so did anti-Semitism, both here and abroad. In her April 1943 letter of appeal on behalf of the world's Jews, she described in graphic detail why there was such a desperate need for U.S. action:

> The butchery of something like two million Jews is a crime that staggers the imagination— . . . and the remaining four million living in the shadow of an impending doom. . . . Thousands upon thousands of Jews have been packed into sealed, lime-strewn cattle cars, with no food, water, or elementary conveniences, and shunted off to die, standing. Records tell of "scientific" extermination centers, asphyxiation trucks, gas-chambers, machine-gunning into self-dug graves, introduction of air bubbles into veins. . . .
>
> In this welter of blood and fury, two things stand out as unbelievable. The first is the crime itself. In this too we bear an awful guilt. You and I and the President and the Congress and the State Department are accessories to the crime and share Hitler's guilt. If we had behaved like humane and generous people, instead of complacent,

cowardly ones, the two million Jews lying today in the earth of Poland
and Hitler's other crowded graveyards would be alive and safe. We
had it in our power to rescue this doomed people and we did not lift
a hand to do it—or perhaps it would be fairer to say that we lifted just
one cautious hand, encased in a tight-fitting glove of quotas and visas
and affidavits, and a thick layer of prejudice.

The second unbelievable thing is the apathy of the civilized
world—of ourselves—to the crime. Have we, like the Germans, lost
the power or will to protest? They had at least the excuse of the Ge-
stapo whips at their backs. How shall we face the verdict of the future
with the record of our inhumanity and inaction?[32]

Observing that "the democracies have so far made no concerted
efforts to save" European Jews, Randall noted that as she wrote, the
Anglo-American Conference on Refugees was beginning "its belated
efforts" in Bermuda. As citizens of a "free state," she declared, "it is our
clear duty to bring the utmost pressure to bear" on the government to
intervene in every possible way "to rescue the Jews remaining in Europe
from the fate prepared for them." She urged all Americans to deluge
the three U.S. delegates to the conference, as well as the president and
other officials with letters to that effect: "Do you think it is worth sitting
down in your comfortable homes tonight and writing these . . . letters?
You are public opinion. *You* are disinterested pressure. It is the least
that you can do. Alas, it is also the most that you can do."[33]

With respect to the Holocaust, Randall was right; there was little
else that could be done. There was greater opportunity to act in behalf
of the conscientious objector, and the women, many of whom remembered the inhumane treatment accorded COs in World War I, worked
diligently to ensure that history not repeat itself. The WILPF's list of
"Volunteer Civilian Services for Women" included a number of activities directed toward COs. Those interested in learning more about
"the history and theory of the relation of the individual to the government" and the citizen's obligations under law were urged to contact
the WILPF's Literature Committee. A lengthy list of agencies to contact
for advice concerning the legal requirements for COs was also provided. Noting specifically the twenty-six CPS camps then established for
COs, the WILPF suggested that members in those locales visit the men
or "write to ask how you or your group can be helpful."[34] Members
could donate, for example, clothing, games, books, magazines, musical
instruments, and special food items that otherwise the men would do
without since they received no pay for their work and had to provide
$35 a month for board.

Cooperation among pacifists on behalf of CO at the local and national level was integral to the WILPF's wartime program. In Philadelphia, for example, as early as February 1942, a "Consultation Service for Conscientious Objectors," sponsored by the local WILPF, FOR, WRL, AFSC, and "several religious denominations," was held at the WILPF headquarters every Monday and Thursday evening.[35] Soon after U.S. entry into the war, Grace Rhoads, chair of the WILPF's Committee on Conscientious Objection, contacted Abe Kaufman of the WRL "to work in the closest possible cooperation with other groups having the same interests, and to avoid duplication."[36]

Kaufman and Jessie Wallace Hughan observed in their May 1942 report that "'Pearl Harbor' brought with it a tightening up in the Selective Service Administration's dealings with conscientious objectors" that was already "evident" in numerous ways, thereby increasing the need for intervention on their behalf. Local draft boards were interpreting more narrowly "religious training and belief" and were increasingly reluctant to classify men as COs.[37] Thus the number of appeals was growing while at the same time more appeals were being refused by the Justice Department, and more men were being imprisoned for failing to report for induction after losing an appeal.

The National Service Board for Religious Objectors (NSBRO), formed in fall 1940 by the Friends, Mennonites, and Brethren, quickly came to include participation by other pacifists, including Detzer of the WILPF. Throughout the war NSBRO was the "official representative of all the cooperating agencies in dealing with varous branches of the U.S. government." It handled complaints, appeals, establishment of CPS camps and camp assignments, and attempted "to interpret the position and philosophy of the religious pacifist to the Government and general public."[38]

A second group organized in 1940, the National Council for Conscientious Objectors with A. J. Muste as executive secretary, was a "coordinating effort" of the United Pacifist Committee that included the WRL, FOR, NCPW, AFSC, and WILPF. "Its main effort," noted Hughan and Kaufman, "has been the setting up of advisers in various parts of the country . . . [who] are kept informed of the latest developments in connection with regulations and interpretations" and advised COs accordingly.[39]

In late fall 1942, problems within NSBRO compelled pacifists R. Boland Brooks and George Reeves to resign from its staff. They were unhappy over Director Paul French's failure "to protest vigorously" against a new Selective Service ruling concerning paroles for COs who were refused IV-E classification and were then imprisoned for refusing

induction. The government began to rule that such men were "insin-
cere" COs and should be "punished" and thus could not be paroled to
CPS camps. There were also the issues of too few COs achieving a
favorable verdict upon appeal, "maintenance and pay" for COs, and
"much too limited opportunity for real public service" by COs who engaged in essentially frivolous activity like raking leaves.

Moreover, as A. J. Muste pointed out, "in carrying on anything in
the nature of pressure activities the N.S.B.R.O. is limited by the fact
that the Mennonites are an important factor in the N.S.B.R.O. and
they simply will not participate in any such activities[,] but conscien-
tiously believe in an almost completely passive attitude toward government." Thus, a group of pacifists who thought it necessary to form a
separate committee "willing and eager to 'go to bat with the government on issues affecting C.O.s'" came together in mid-December and
organized the Legal Service to Conscientious Objectors (LSCO) with
Brooks as director and Reeves as associate director.[40]

The FOR's Committee for Legal Aid to Conscientious Objectors
was subsumed under the new organization which was designed to focus
on the problems of "parole and prison conditions;" the "development
of special projects" for COs on parole; "representation, upon request"
for men in CPS camps concerning "camp life, Selective Service classification, legal questions, dependency and related matters"; "counsel
and legal aid . . . for Conscientious Objectors whose claims have not
been recognized and those who have refused to conform with existing
laws and regulations"; and provision of bail. All services were available
"without fee [and] . . . without regard to . . . race, religion or Selective
Service status." Detzer was unanimously agreed to be "the ideal person
to be in charge of the Washington work" of the committee.[41]

To confuse the issue, however, was the formation at approximately
the same time of the National Committee on Conscientious Objectors
(NCOO) of the ACLU involving many of the same people, including
Detzer. Although the LSCO was to concentrate on "individual cases"
and the NCCO was to focus on matters of "broad policy," as Albert
Hamilton observed, such a division was "arbitrary" and "almost impossible. Individual cases and policy simply are not mutually exclusive," he
argued, suggesting instead that "an effort be made to almalgamate the
Washington work of both Committees under one staff."[42] While those
involved pondered the suggestion, the WILPF's executive committee
agreed to release Detzer to contribute one-third of her time to the
NCCO for three months at $100 a month.

In Mid-January 1943 the LSCO and NCCO agreed to adopt Hamilton's proposal, and the newly consolidated committee was known thereafter simply as the NCCO. Reeves and Brooks directed its "action arm" in Washington with Detzer as part-time coordinator whose responsibilities included obtaining the removal of military men from boards reviewing CO cases; working for the assignment of COs to "detached service under civilian control direct from draft boards and prisons without going through CPS camps"; lobbying for pay to men on detached service; and obtaining the release of COs from prison. Functioning in an advisory capacity to the new NCCO was its National Committee in New York, composed essentially of the original group in the LSCO. NSBRO was kept fully informed of all proceedings and "agreed that these additional efforts are desirable in principle," and NCCO members promised to work in close cooperation with NSBRO.[43]

Given their understanding that there was "a serious manpower problem in the country," NCCO activists approached Paul McNutt, director of the War Manpower Commission, to see about making "more effective use" of COs in "socially useful projects through detached service." McNutt was not receptive. COs, he reportedly said, "were lucky to be even in prison and that from the point of view of manpower, 'they were a drop in the bucket' and 'not important.' His apparent scorn of the COs," Detzer continued, "distinctly implied that he saw them as cowards and fortunate to be living in a country which refrained from shooting its conscientious objectors."[44]

A dinner conference of pacifists with Major General Lewis B. Hershey of Selective Service in early April went no better, so shortly thereafter Detzer sent a lengthy letter to Fowler Harper, Deputy Chair of the Office of Emergency Management in the War Manpower Commission. Protesting that "120 men beautifying a highway drive which nobody now has gasoline enough to drive on" was not, as the Selective Service law stipulated, "work of national importance," she called it just one of many examples of "boondoggling." Grateful that some COs had been released from CPS camps "to do such significant work as serving as human guinea pigs in medical research projects, working in mental hospitals, on dairy farms, [and] training for work in China," Detzer noted that these examples were the exception, not the rule.

"As a matter of fact," she went on, "it is very puzzling to us that in a time of great crisis we should have to plead with our government for the effective use of men in constructive and creative jobs when they are so eager to serve and when the need is, obviously, so great." Referring to the Danbury prison hunger strike of COs Stanley Murphy and Louis Taylor, she could not help but comment on "the fact that two normal, able-bodied men are now in the 70th day of a hunger fast because they have felt so seriously about men dying on the battlefields in Europe while they and their fellow objectors were given useless work. . . . [S]urely," she said, this was "proof that there is something amiss."[45]

Three months later the NCCO's Washington Committee concluded that "since our dinner with General Hershey last April we [have] gained almost nothing." Convinced that Hershey was the "key to the problem," the situation by summer's end had actually "deteriorated appreciably" as the government "has become more hard-boiled and punitive in its policies with respect to conscientious objectors."[46]

The issue of the conscription of women appeared as though it, too, might become a matter of conscientious objection. Early in 1942 a bill providing for a volunteer army of women was introduced in Congress. Although its sponsor apparently did not intend it as a conscription measure, the WILPF understood that the government soon planned to introduce a bill calling for the registration of women with a measure providing for their conscription to follow. Detzer was not particularly concerned with the registration issue and believed that the WILPF should save its energy for opposing conscription if the need arose. Olmsted, however, was appalled on both counts and was determined to fight the entire issue.

In order to clarify organizational policy, the Executive Committee of the WILPF's National Board discussed the issue at great length in mid-February. Those who agreed with Detzer pointed out that because the government required birth certificates, marriage and automobile licenses, and similar limitations of individual freedom, registration of women should not be opposed because it fell into this same category. Because registration did not involve a question of conscience, they argued, and because the WILPF would be more effective from a psychological perspective if it made a fight at the point of conscription where conscience *was* involved, proponents of this view saw no point in opposing registration.

Agreeing with Olmsted were those women who argued that because this registration was for "the express and definite purpose of preparing for conscription for war, it was part of the whole war system" and should be vigorously and immediately opposed.[47] About equally divided between these two views, the Executive Committee took no official position but left the decision up to individual conscience. Not long thereafter, the WILPF's Committee on Conscientious Objectors voted unanimously to oppose both the registration and the conscription of women, and so, too, did the FOR and WRL.

On 18 March the Baldwin bill was introduced in the House. It called for the registration of all female citizens and aliens between the ages of eighteen and sixty-five with the express purpose of providing for "complete information as to the capacity and availability of the registrant for service, civilian or military, in connection with the prosecution of war." As a member of NSBRO, Detzer attended an all-day meeting of the group in late March to discuss the matter. Although against the bill, participants admitted that it would be difficult to rouse opposition to it in Congress because "a woman is not going to be required to kill," and thus the issue of conscience was not directly involved. They finally decided to attempt amendment of the bill to exempt from registration all women "who because of religious training or belief cannot participate in war in any form."[48]

Pacifists were also concerned about other measures before Congress, such as the Biddle bill, which would make it a criminal offense to divulge the contents of "so-called 'secret' or 'confidential' government documents." WILPF leaders called upon members to oppose this measure "with all vigor" because it was "clear that if such a bill was made law, . . . any government document could be marked 'confidential and secret'. . . . [I]t would completely jeopardize all public criticism of government action," warned the National Office.[49] But most frightening was the Total Mobilization Bill introduced in the Senate on 23 March 1942 and, like the conscription of women, supported by Eleanor Roosevelt.

Designed as an amendment to the Selective Training and Service Act, the WILPF explained, its purpose was to mobilize "all men, women, property and labor in the United States, 'during the continuance of any wars in which the United States is engaged'." Under this amendment Section 1 of the act would conscript Americans "to perform so long as may be deemed necessary any type of work or duties which those persons are capable of performing." Section 2 would require all citizens eighteen years of age and older to register with the government, and added to Section 3 would be a provision calling for "a total mobilization of the labor of all persons in the United States, both men and women, who are not soldiers. Penalty for refusal is five years imprisonment or a $10,000 fine or both. Section 4 authorizes the President to draft any and all property he deems necessary for the prosecution of the war."[50]

As the WILPF warned, here was "totalitarianism in its purest form." So much so, in fact, that when the bill was first introduced, Detzer simply discounted it as being "too extreme to be dangerous." When she learned from "reliable authority" that there was a good chance of its passage, there was only one conclusion she could reach: "If these . . . amendments do become a part of the Selective Training and Service Act, then certainly our work in the Women's International League is over, and as individuals we no longer exist as free citizens. Though here in America we should not have to face the tortures which obtained in German concentration camps, nevertheless, *legally* we shall be as enslaved and regimented as though in a Nazi state."[51]

Viewed in light of the increasingly repressive atmosphere already part of the home front, the Total Mobilization Bill compelled Olmsted to conclude sharply that "totalitarianism, which we pretend to despise, is coming upon us stealthily but swiftly,—not imposed by victorious armies from overseas, but from within our midst; not through Russian communists or German Bundists, as we have been told to fear, but through 'patriotic' Americans."[52]

The issues of manpower mobilization and the conscription of women continued to hold pacifists' attention throughout the remainder of 1942. Action on both was postponed prior to November, in all likelihood to forestall any negative effect on Congressional re-election campaigns, but such inaction did not lull the peace movement into thinking that the measures were no longer of interest to Congress. Olmsted's opposition only intensified; by December she was "determined" to go to prison "rather than register, should such a law pass." In explaining her intransigence to WILPF members, she did not attempt to proselytize her position. "This is, of course," she noted, "my personal decision and in no sense represents the position or advice of the W.I.L. which never urges anyone to disobey a law or even to be a C.O." Nor had she reached this decision "lightly or quickly, but only after long, long thought as to how I could best serve my fellow woman beings in a world of engulfing totalitarian ideas." With the WILPF's Executive Committee willing and eager for her "to devote as much time as possible" to the issue, by 10 December the Committee to Oppose the Conscription of Women was organized under her leadership.[53] It was formally launched on 7 January 1943 with the WILPF's Grace Rhoads as secretary and A. J. Muste, treasurer. Becoming the Women's Committee to Oppose Conscription (WCOC) in 1944, it endured until 1950.

Within a month, the government provided Olmsted's new committee with a fresh focus. In early February 1943 Senator Warren Austin of New York and Congressman James Wadsworth of Vermont introduced a joint bill that called for the conscription of labor, male and female.

Although pregnant women would be exempted, as would "any woman who has living with her and under her care a child or children under 18 years of age or other persons who, because of illness or advanced age, need her care," all other women between the ages of eighteen and fifty would "be liable to contribute by personal service to the war effort in a *non-combatant* capacity."⁵⁴ It also included every man between eighteen and sixty-five; had no provision for conscientious objectors; and penalized failure to comply with a $100 fine or six months in prison.

The WILPF argued that there was no need for this "National War Service Act." With approximately "three million Spanish Americans, five million aliens (of whom at least 98 to 99% can be considered loyal to the United Nations), seventy-one thousand Japanese Americans in concentration camps, some 6,000 conscientious objectors in C.P.S. camps and about 1400 in jail, [and] . . . 600,000 Negroes not yet employed at their highest level of skill," there was an abundance of manpower for war industry without resorting to conscription.⁵⁵ While the FOR and NCPW went to work mobilizing their members against this example of "totalitarianism in kid gloves," as Detzer called the Austin-Wadsworth bill, the WCOC not only began mobilizing "500 women in 23 different states," but immediately began "to lobby quietly" against it in Congress.⁵⁶

From Olmsted's perspective, the Austin-Wadsworth bill was another example of "the tightening grip of the military upon every element of the population, in every phase of life." In asking, "Shall the military or civilian mind dominate the country?" she saw this growing militarism at home as "the great menace to democracy" against which all Americans must struggle incessantly. "It is curious," she commented, "how easily we copy the patterns which we think we hate and are fighting to escape and never notice that only the labels are different. In one column our noblest orators denounce 'the enslavement of labor' or 'forced labor' or 'labor serfs' in fascist countries and in the next we are told that our own workers must be 'frozen' or 'ordered' or drafted to work in this or that war industry."⁵⁷

Hearings began before the Senate Military Affairs Committee in March. While Detzer arranged for speakers to represent the WILPF, PWWC, and ACLU, arguing that "a general attack on fascism and the whole bill rather than on details" was the proper strategy, Olmsted lined up six women, including herself, to speak against the bill for the WCOC.⁵⁸ By the time that hearings began in the House in April, "indications in Washington" were that the bill would not pass, but was "being used to measure public reaction to such a proposal and to accustom us to the idea so that when the administration is ready to introduce its own total conscription bill, opposition will have died down." This meant, declared Olmsted, that "we must show now such sharp opposition" to the whole idea that "with a presidential election in the offing, political leaders of both parties in Congress will hesitate to take responsibility for it."[59]

But there were problems. First was lack of money. As Olmsted succinctly reported to Muste in mid-March, "We are out of money again." In a plea to WCOC supporters for funds, it was more important than ever, she exhorted, to keep the new committee "going full steam ahead." The American Legion was demanding passage of the War Service Act, which "has already resulted in a change of opinion favorable to the bill," and all signs pointed to the Congressional introduction of an administration bill incorporating "the same objectionable features" of the Austin-Wadsworth measure and "an attempt made to push it through Congress with a great deal of speed." A second problem also loomed. The House hearings were closed, and only after three attempts to reach the Chair of the Military Affairs Committee did Olmsted finally receive a reply. The WCOC could not testify at the hearings, but it could "send a statement for the record."[60]

Olmsted did. The whole idea of the conscription of labor, she wrote, "would create forced labor, which is in direct contradiction to the Thirteenth Amendment of the Constitution." Further, the wording of certain sections of the measure "would make possible the extension of many dangerous and discriminatory economic patterns" as well as "break up homes, increase divorce and promote greater juvenile delinquency." Last, it would "put all civilian life under military control, which even in wartime is contrary to the basic principles of our democracy."[61]

Congress did not act on any manpower bill that spring. The WILPF reported in early August, however, that the issue was still current and probably would surface again later in the fall. Thus, pacifists kept up their pressure. Oswald Garrison Villard joined the struggle with an August article in *The Christian Century* in which he echoed the WCOC's assertion that the essence of the issue was democracy. "The truth is," he wrote, "that any such regimenting of women will carry us another long step toward the totalitarian state. The very arguments advanced [for it] —that by it women will be made the tools of government and feel themselves cogs in the governmental machine—are fascist arguments. What the United Nations pretend to be fighting for is freedom for the individual from the domination of the state, or of any group of men who assume the powers of government, legally or illegally."[62] Villard's view reflected that of an attorney and fellow train passenger of Olmsted's that summer who turned to her after reading his evening newspaper and remarked, "Well, everything is going just the way you people said it would if we got into war. We apparently *can't* fight a war against fascism without acquiring it."[63]

Pacifists held a six-day seminar on the conscription issue in October 1943 at the Quaker retreat in Pendle Hill, Pennsylvania. Given the fact that as early as March a bill to establish permanent peace-time conscription had been introduced in Congress, participants were concerned about the "threat of permanent conscription and militarization throughout the world in the post-war period."[64] They discussed disarmament, nonmilitary sanctions, peace proposals, federalism, military coercion, the conscientious objector, and democracy. Each topic was examined in an international context as well as from an historical perspective, and participants reached a general consensus on most issues. This was particularly true of the topic given the most attention: conscription and its implications for the future of democratic government.

Noting that the Austin-Wadsworth bill was temporarily "in abeyance," Pendle Hill pacifists pointed with equal alarm to the Gurney-Wadsworth bill, which called for permanent military conscription. This measure, particularly when viewed in the context of other antidemocratic trends, did not bode well for the postwar world. First, there was the "attempt to develop a cleavage between organized labor and the men in the armed services," which pacifists saw as part of the pattern "out of which fascism grows. The unemployed veterans after the war will blame labor for all of their ills, and the unions can be broken."

Another disquieting trend bringing the nation "closer to totalitarianism," thought the group, was "our treatment of minorities. . . . Increasingly we are seeking scapegoats in these groups," and even more disturbing was that this trend was "ahead of schedule" when compared to World War I. With respect to U.S. democracy, participants noted "a growing tendency of the Attorney General and the Post Office to suppress publications," and concluded that in the FBI, "we have an agency which has developed many of the techniques used by European secret police . . . which might become a real threat to democracy if administered by men with the wrong motives." One commentator remarked that when it came to press censorship, "the government has followed the policy of cutting off news at the source," and Detzer observed that probably the greatest threat to political democracy "lay in the complete freedom of the executive in handling foreign policy, largely through appointive officials, with no check by the elected representatives of the people."

As the fall of 1943 became winter, pacifists continued their efforts to arouse public opinion against conscription. Around Thanksgiving they organized a "Town Hall" debate on the Austin-Wadsworth bill in New York with Grenville Clark arguing in support of the measure, and Victor Reuther, against. Although pacifists agreed that "the debate itself was splendid" and press coverage "excellent," they were greatly disappointed in the small attendance, "not only because it left us with a deficit in meeting finances, but because it showed an appalling public apathy toward total conscription."[65]

Paralleling pacifists' concern over "this willingness of the people to accept . . . complete civilian regimentation" was their "even deeper concern over the ominous signs of a well organized plan to make military conscription a permanent part of American life." Thirty-five people from twenty-two organizations met on 17 December to consider "the implications such as peace-time conscription holds for democracy and future peace." They created a continuing committee under PWWC auspices "to initiate and coordinate an educational and action campaign" on the subject, and they named Dr. Broadus Mitchell, NYU economics professor and research director for the International Ladies Garment Workers Union (ILGWU), its chair.[66]

In January 1944 Mitchell wrote the foreword to Norman Thomas' pamphlet, "Conscription: The Test of Peace," which was particularly relevant given Roosevelt's 11 January message to Congress calling for passage of a National Service Act. There were rumors in Washington that the president's speech was part of a War Department plan to obtain "an enormous post war army and peace time conscription for both boys and girls," and if this was true, asked Thomas, "against what and whom will this conscript force be employed?" As he warned, those "special classes and interests" with "much to gain from enormous conscript armies and immense armaments—the officer class, the armament makers, and other manufacturers and sellers of supplies" would ensure that there *was* an enemy against whom the country must arm itself. And these vested interests, Thomas claimed, "will be supported . . . by the conservative interests which oppose government spending to end unemployment on any other terms than militarism."[67]

In a "Town Meeting of the Air" address in early February, Olmsted hammered away at the undemocratic aspects of conscripting women. "To draft women for the armed forces," she argued, "would be to admit to all the world that however complete our victories over fascism abroad might be, the vicious plant has sown its deadly seed in our own soil. . . . Our most precious American tradition is that government must be the *servant* of the people, not the people the servant of the government." After noting five reasons why women had not enthusiastically volunteered for the military, almost as an afterthought she commented, "women are naturally and rightly the home makers, producers, and conservers of life. There is something bold and shocking to both men and women about women's taking an active part in what is intended to *destroy* life."[68] If the old argument that women-as-mothers were instinctively more pacifistic than men was not yet dead, it was not the central argument in World War II that it was in World War I. The survival of democracy was the crucial issue now.

No other issue commanded as much of the peace movement's attention in 1944 as that of conscription. In March the WCTU denounced female and peacetime conscription and shortly thereafter, a group of religious leaders from all denominations registered their opposition. William Green, AFL president; Philip Murray, CIO president; A. Philip Randolph, international president of the Brotherhood of Sleeping Car Porters; and James B. Patton, president of the National Farmers Union, all followed suit.

By fall, "after many months of carefully laid groundwork in important newspapers, the campaign for compulsory peacetime military training is now fully under way," warned pacifists. COs in CPS camps volunteered their services in the fight against it and other groups, such as the National Education Association, the Congress of Parents and Teachers, the NAACP, the Workers Defense League, PWWC, and sixteen NPC organizations, "all declared they disapprove a decision on postwar conscription until after the war." Convinced that the issue would not come up for discussion in Congress before the November election, pacifists called a national conference for the sixteenth and seventeenth of November in Washington to consider the "most effective ways of combatting" the proposal, declaring that they were "prepared to cooperate with non-pacifist bodies to the fullest extent."[69]

The WCOC issued a strongly worded seven-page document against peacetime conscription in December, and on the understanding that the War Department advocated such a move "because we are arming against Russia, and/or some other specific foe," Detzer met with Undersecretary of State Edward Stettinius to determine if this was indeed the case. She reminded him "that the Soviet government alone among the nations had offered a real plan for total disarmament at Geneva in 1932," and urged the United States to appeal to the Soviets to jointly sponsor an international conference for the abolition of conscription. Detzer left Stettinius discouraged and disheartened, for what she learned led her to conclude that the "administration's plan for a permanent conscript army revolves in part around the desire of the government to hold the most powerful bargaining position" in peacetime negotiations, particularly with respect to the Soviet Union.[70]

Pacifists continued the fight against conscription into 1945 with remarkable zeal and activity given both their depleted numbers and financial resources, especially after Roosevelt's January message to Congress "asking for conscription of nurses, of men classified as 4-F, of all men and women of working age, and for permanent peace-time conscription."[71] But for the peace movement, the conscription issue was only part of the whole question of the kind of peace the victorious United Nations would effect once the war was over. The first few months of 1944 had been fairly encouraging for as the WILPF noted, certain "positive achievements" had occurred, one of which was the creation of the United Nations Relief Association. The women were aware, however, of the potential for political blackmail involved in relief work, for they recalled "the use of food as a political weapon in certain countries following the last war."[72]

A second "gratifying" achievement was the creation of a War Refugee Board, "set up to find ways and means of bringing out [of Europe] religious and political victims of the Hitler terror." This agency, observed the WILPF, "has proceeded with such imagination, energy and dispatch that it is one of the great tragedies of this tragic period that the Board was not set up at the very outset of the war. Thousands are now being rescued who otherwise would have been slaughtered. Thousands more could have been saved had America acted in time." A third accomplishment noted by the women—"perhaps the biggest job we have done this year and the one for which we can take the widest amount of credit"—was the Senate's unanimous passage of the Gillette-Taft Resolution for the feeding of Europe.[73]

Introduced in Congress in February 1943, the Gillette-Taft bill was designed to "prevent the impending tragedy of mass starvation abroad" in countries like Belgium, Norway, and Czechoslovakia by working in cooperation with England, Sweden, Switzerland, and the "accredited representatives of other governments concerned." The WILPF had urged immediate hearings, but "found little interest" on the Hill; even Senators Taft and Gillette seemed unconcerned "about pressing for action." By early October when hearings still had not been scheduled, the WILPF could take the procrastination no longer. Detzer went to

Gillette's office and told him she was "staging a one-man sit-down strike
. . . —that there I intended to stay until I got time definitely slated for
the hearings."

The ploy worked. Hearings were scheduled for early November,
but Gillette, saying that he did not have time, "tossed the organization
of the hearing back into my lap," reported Detzer. Through incredible
effort by the WILPF but with no cooperation from, and even the active
hostility of the subcommittee's chair, Elbert Thomas, hearings were finally held in mid-November 1943. With Senate action not forthcoming
until February 1944, Detzer remarked that "it is tragic that it took a
whole year to secure passage." By April of that year when Roosevelt still
had not acted, she could not help but comment that it was "still more
tragic that now three months after this unanimous action the Administration has failed to carry out the united will of the Senate."[74]

"D-Day," the massive Allied invasion of Western Europe on 6 June,
as Detzer put it, "has, of course, jeopardized all chances for a feeding
program in occupied Europe now."[75] Here, too, the WILPF had attempted to sway administration policy and with about the same degree
of success. When plans for such an invasion were first made public, the
WILPF tried to persuade Roosevelt "to postpone the plan of invasion
until every possible appeal for an Armistice has been made to the German people, over the heads of the Nazi government."

Part of this appeal involved the issue of "unconditional surrender,"
opposed by the WILPF and other peace organizations. As a CPS newsletter explained, "conditional surrender is an agreement which imposes restrictions first and obligations second upon victim and victor
alike. On the other hand *un*conditional surrender imposes no limitations on the victor and he is free to do as he wishes. In an unconditional surrender, the defeated people assume no obligation to work
either singly or jointly with the occupation force toward the recreation
of their own country or of world order. Unconditional surrender means
that the victor accepts without reservation total responsibility for what
comes out of the state of affairs after hostilities cease."[76]

The WILPF proposed instead that the United States offer the German people "generous armistice terms." These "should not be vindic-
tive," but "offered in the spirit of the Atlantic Charter," opening the
way for cooperation between victor and vanquished. As "preliminary
conditions," the women proposed an eight-point program that included evacuation of all territory conquered by the Axis or occupied
"against the will of its inhabitants"; demobilization of all armed forces;
the immediate lifting of all blockades; liberation of all prisoners of war

including political prisoners, internees, and concentration camp inmates; freedom with full legal and political rights for all refugees and other displaced persons; "immediate cessation of all persecution and discrimination on grounds of race, religion, or nationality"; the return of all stolen art treasures and industrial equipment; and last, "restoration of the rights of labor."[77]

The WILPF sent these proposals to Roosevelt in February 1944, and during a lengthy discussion with Stettinius a month later, Detzer presented him with a copy since the President had yet to respond. Reiterating the WILPF's concern "that before the scheduled invasion of occupied Europe starts . . . the people of this country have the right to know that their government has exhausted every available means to prevent that disaster," Detzer exacted from Stettinius his promise to bring the issue to the attention of Roosevelt and the secretary of state.[78]

On the very day of the invasion that the WILPF had tried to prevent, Detzer once again met with Stettinius, specifically to learn "whether anything was 'moving' on the question of feeding . . . [and] what he had been able to do in regard to peace terms." He told her that there were "enormous stocks of food . . . available and ready to go . . . and that they would follow in immediately on the heels of the army." As for peace terms, he acknowledged that "he had gotten no where," pointing to British opposition as the stumbling block.[79] When she pressed him for Roosevelt's and Hull's opinion on the matter, he confessed that they, too, favored unconditional surrender.

Given the implications of what unconditional surrender meant for the distribution of power in the postwar world, the peace movement attempted to influence both political conventions that summer to adopt foreign policy planks that would "establish a just and lasting peace so that the United States and other nations may live together in prosperity, confidence and security." The NPC called for "the immediate establishment of a United Nations Council which shall as its first task further define on the basis of the Atlantic Charter the principles in accordance with which present and future political decisions are to be made." Second, it recommended that this council establish "a general international organization" with full U.S. participation to create a viable means for peacefully altering unjust conditions that might lead to war; a world court; "a law-making body and institutions to facilitate the settlement of international disputes by peaceful means"; an international police force "under codified legal controls"; and last, provide for world-wide "limitation and reduction of armaments." The NPC also proposed a system of "reciprocal trade policies, control of international cartels and adequate efforts to raise living standards in areas with which we exchange goods and services."[80]

As always with the NPC, there was considerable difference of opinion; pacifist organizations not only wanted a stronger statement of economic justice, but also found it difficult to accept the idea of an international police force. Such dissension brought a plea for unity from Dr. John Paul Jones, steering committee chair: "Everybody knows that no political convention is going to adopt a statement as we present it, but," he maintained, "the crucial issue . . . is whether the United States is going to participate in world affairs in any wholesome and hopeful manner. The cards are daily being stacked against us."[81] Jones' pessimistic assessment, pacifists knew, was not unwarranted.

Only a short time earlier, for example, delegates to the WILPF's annual meeting heard their executive secretary assert that "the old sinister balance of power is once more the dominating factor in British and Russian policy," and this "resurgence of power politics," she thought, "will once again jeopardize any stable and genuine international organization for peace in Europe." While perceiving "a fundamental cleavage in the political sphere with Britain and Russia in one camp, and the United States in the other," Detzer was admittedly puzzled by "American policy." It had not "always been clear, consistent, or understandable," and in Italy and North Africa, where the United States was collaborating with antidemocratic forces, she observed, "there has seemed to be a diplomatic ineptitude impossible to comprehend."[82]

It was a "bewildering" and discouraging situation as the WILPF saw it, all the more so when at the political conventions pacifists' appeal to the platform committees for implementation of a feeding program for Europe and repudiation of unconditional surrender fell on deaf ears. The Dumbarton Oaks Conference that opened shortly thereafter to formulate proposals for a postwar international organization did not seem promising, either, as it was "veiled in complete secrecy."[83] When these proposals were finally revealed to the public, the peace movement was as one in its condemnation. As the WRL put it, the plan's "reactionary character" was deplorable.[84]

Although the structure of the proposed organization was similar to that of the League of Nations, noted the WILPF, its functions "are far less democratic and frankly more militaristic."[85] Because all power would reside in the Security Council with its five permanent members —England, France, the United States, Soviet Union, China—and six rotating members and "virtually no power at all" given to the General

Assembly of remaining smaller nations, this was "no true international arrangement," declared the WRL, "but the domination of the world by the five most heavily armed powers. It is a step back to the Triple Alliance, with special privilege for certain nations based on the old and dangerous principle that might makes right."[86] The FOR agreed: "This is not an advance over the League of Nations, but a retreat to the vicious and undemocratic Holy Alliance of armed nationalistic states following the Napoleonic Wars."[87]

As Edith Wynner pointed out, membership would be open to "all *peace-loving* states," but the "definition of what constitutes a *peace-loving* nation is 'still being studied' and is the 'subject of negotiation'." Membership was also affected, she commented, "by the fact that nations may be *suspended* as well as *expelled* . . . as a means of enforcement." The conclusion, she thought, was obvious: "The United Nations plan is potentially universal but actually ideological."[88]

The WILPF stressed the fact that there was "no provision for disarmament in the entire draft. In fact," wrote Detzer in amazement, "disarmament is not even mentioned among 'the general purposes,' [and] . . . any recommendations in regard to it are left to the whim of a military staff committee. This," she noted dryly, "is about as reasonable and will no doubt prove to be about as effective as would the recommendations of pacifists on the strategy of battle."[89] Moreover, nowhere did the proposal define "aggression," yet as Muste observed, the emphasis throughout was "on the use of force in order to prevent resort to force in international disputes."

That situation, thought Muste, was "hopelessly aggravated" by the fact that the reliance on force to keep the peace was "unrelated to any explicitly agreed upon principles of justice."[90] The WRL, too, had problems in this respect: "No specific instruments," it commented caustically, "are proposed to do away with the underlying causes of war in race tensions, economic inequalities and territorial irredentas, except that economic and social welfare is handed over to a council without power." And imperialism, commonly recognized as a major cause of international conflict, said the WRL flatly, "is here completely disregarded."[91]

As Muste concluded, the Dumbarton Oaks proposals "constitute the ratification of an existing power structure," or as Wynner put it, "offers the form of international government without the reality. . . . Its assembly cannot legislate, its Court is a shadow, and its Council of great powers can act only against the weak. . . . It is limited to enforcement of peace by means of war."[92] For the FOR, Dumbarton Oaks had only "served to deepen the feelings of uneasiness and doubt, even of disillusionment and cynicism, which fill the hearts of multitudes of Americans today as they think of the peace and the post-war world."[93]

The situation looked no more hopeful in early 1945 when the results of the Yalta Conference were announced in mid-February. While applauded for their reaffirmation of the Atlantic Charter, Roosevelt, Churchill, and Stalin then turned around and violated those principles by their continued denial of "democratic processes" in Italy, Greece, and the Balkans, remarked the PWWC. Apparently solidifying an earlier agreement made at Teheran in winter 1943 "whereby Russia was to be permitted a free hand in Eastern Europe," it was understood that the United States and the Soviet Union agreed at Yalta not to disturb "British imperial interests . . . in the Mediterranean, in Greece, in the Near and Middle East."[94]

For the peace movement, the Yalta decisions only confirmed Olmsted's earlier observation of January that "a little of the veil has been torn away and exposed the nationalistic jockeying for spheres of influence that has been going on secretly among 'the big three'," a situation according to the British press, reported Detzer just prior to Yalta, for which the United States bore equal responsibility. In light of those arrangements, the PWWC called upon Americans to "awake and insist on at least four proposals basic to any lasting peace."[95]

First, "the self-government granted to liberated European states must be genuine," not a fig-leaf to cover the power politics of "London and Moscow." Second, "independence within a framework of regional and world-wide federation must be promised to all peoples," and third, "enemy peoples, disarmed, stripped of conquest and purged of marauding leadership," must be included in a cooperative effort for post-war planning. Last, universal disarmament and abolition of military conscription must follow immediately as "an essential condition of collective security."[96] Muste agreed, calling also for Congressional repudiation of all Yalta decisions that violated the Atlantic Charter and U.S. refusal to accept the Dumbarton Oaks proposals. And all agreed now with the WILPF that "the importance of the San Francisco Conference," scheduled to open on 25 April 1945, "cannot be exaggerated."[97]

The United Nations Conference on International Organization where big and small countries gathered to decide on the post-World War II form of a league of nations "will set the pattern and tone for the future," thought the WILPF. "If the Big Three completely dominate San Francisco, so that the future world organization is merely the perpetuation of a military alliance with all the middle and small nations as mere satellites and 'yes men' to one of the bigger powers, then the Conference may turn out merely an empty gesture. But if all the nations gathered at San Francisco assert their right to make decisions now in regard to the peace, the chances are that the Dumbarton Oaks agreement could be whipped into a workable organization for peace."[98] Other NPC members, although more supportive of Dumbarton Oaks than pacifists, agreed.

As plans for the conference solidified that spring, the State Department asked "some forty organizations" to send consultants to San Francisco and, according to the WILPF, "chose groups representing various opinions in their different fields." The conservative American Bar Association, for example, as well as the liberal National Lawyers' Guild were asked to send consultants. With respect to business, labor, church, and farm groups as well as veterans organizations, both the "Right and Left Wings" were "carefully" included. "Only with the peace movement," observed the WILPF, was this not the case; "not one of the old, established peace groups were [sic] invited. . . . [I]t was obvious that in the case of the Peace Movement only those so-called peace organizations which have slavishly followed Administration policy were invited."[99]

It appeared that the WILPF was right, for the NPC and CEIP were approached, as were the recently formed Americans United for World Organization and the Women's Action Committee for Victory and Lasting Peace, the NCCCW in new form. Pacifist groups were not included. Senators from both parties with whom the WILPF discussed this problem were, Detzer reported, "incensed . . . and prepared to act against such procedure," but, politically, the timing could not have been worse.[100] Just at that juncture, Roosevelt died.

When the conference opened, the WILPF was there unofficially with Detzer heading up "an excellent working team" of Mary Farquharson, Ruth Gage Colby, and Hannah Clothier Hull's daughter, Mary Hull O'Fallon. All were hard at work attempting to persuade delegates to include clauses providing for racial equality and a "minimum international Bill of Rights" in the new organization's charter, when the news reached them of Mussolini's downfall and then shortly thereafter, of V-E Day itself.[101]

The war in Europe was over, and the FOR undoubtedly spoke for all pacifists when it declared, "We have to live in 'one world' with those who were our 'enemies' in war; they have to live in 'one world' with us. Peace means learning to work with them in healing the wounded, feeding the hungry, clothing the naked, building homes for the homeless, putting men back to work at all sorts of useful tasks which will minister to their material needs and bring self-respect and the sense of security back into their hearts." But, it went on, "We shall be unable to give ourselves single-mindedly to this colossal task in Europe so long as we are at war in the Orient." Thus the FOR called upon the president, "in the name of common sense and humanity . . . to state publicly specific terms of settlement with Japan which will provide a worthy place for the Japanese and all other Oriental peoples in an orderly, democratic world society and on this basis to call for the immediate cessation of hostilities."[102]

But the war continued in the Pacific and in San Francisco, pacifists labored against mounting odds to move delegates in a more democratic direction. No agreement was reached "with respect to a trusteeship plan under which 'dependent countries' might be enabled 'as soon as possible to take the path of national independence'," something which pacifists "deeply" regretted. It was "clear" to such groups "that the United States in the desire to secure control over bases in the Pacific, and Great Britain in its determination to hold on to Empire," were the major obstacles.[103]

Detzer's analysis of the proceedings was strikingly at odds with the consistently cheerful reports sent back by Jane Evans for the NPC. "I have never seen such a low state of depression as exists here among those who are not perpetual optimists," she wrote. "I talked the other day to Kingsley Martin, editor of the 'Statesmen and Nation,' of Brittain [sic] and he said that he had not been as low in his mind since the War was declared in 1939." Nor was he alone in his disillusionment. "This same attitude," Detzer observed, "is reflected by all the newspapermen with any experience and understanding of the issues, who are not mere cynics, and by practically everyone who sees behind the glittering facade. My only hope," she concluded, trying not to despair, "is that we have reached the bottom and that things may begin to be brighter as the document is finally whipped into shape."[104]

Detzer's discouragement may not have stemmed entirely from her observations at San Francisco. She and other pacifists had for some time been concerned "that the perpetuation of the balance of power in Europe, plus the old urge of empire abroad" might result in the "emergence of an American drive for empire." Events at San Francisco gave credence to these fears, but equally as disturbing were "certain current revelations" with respect to secret diplomacy that were "so startling that we are naturally alarmed regarding other commitments which may already have been made but not yet revealed." Her reference here was to the Yalta agreement, "which would have granted three votes to the United States in the new United Nations organization." The specific issue was not the problem; the fact that it was part of a secret agreement was.

But, she went on, "of far greater and more profound significance, and one having consequences which cannot be measured, was the state secret which has now come to public knowledge through the publication of Ambassador Grew's book 'Ten Years in Japan.' In this book Mr. Grew records the efforts of the Japanese Government to arrange a meeting between Mr. Roosevelt and the Premier of Japan in the late summer of 1941." The details of this effort outlined by Grew were of such importance in Detzer's view that she quoted from them at some length, observing that whether or not such a conference would have avoided the Pacific war could, of course, never be established. What she found most alarming was "the fact that the American people were never informed of Japan's offer and hence, were never given the opportunity to express their united will."[105]

On 26 June 1945 the fifty nations at San Francisco signed the charter creating the United Nations. Presented to the Senate for ratification by President Harry Truman on 2 July, it was almost identical to the Dumbarton Oaks plan, but was endorsed by the NPC two weeks later. Calling for the support of the Senate and the American people, in a "fervent plea" to the United States and the other "Great Powers" the NPC urged that "in the use of the new machinery, they think constantly in terms of mutual responsibility and interdependence, rather than of unilateral power and authority. . . . We join with supporters of peace throughout the world in urging that governments and peoples bend every effort to build, through the Charter, a world of justice and security."[106]

Of more immediate concern to pacifists was the continuing war in the Pacific. At its annual meeting in May, the WILPF called upon the U.S. government to "take the initiative in exploring any possibility of bringing about peace with Japan so that wholesale destruction of life and property may cease."[107] The PWWC elaborated upon this theme at the end of the month in a letter to the president that repeatedly asked for clarification of reports that secret agreements had been made assuring Stalin's "trusteeship over Korea and overlordship" in Manchuria; that Southeast Asia "will be returned to masters, French, Dutch and British," thus re-establishing "white imperialism"; and that "the Japanese seek peace," having already "offered terms of surrender of empire which approach the demands made by Roosevelt and Churchill in their Cairo statement. . . . We ought to know the facts," declared the PWWC emphatically.[108]

Olmsted was particularly outraged at the continuation of the destruction, writing in early June about "the way in which we Americans are literally burning alive in their homes thousands upon thousands of women and children and old people, leveling universities and schools, destroying places of worship." Foreshadowing the incensed protest of Americans some twenty-five later over U.S. military operations in Vietnam, Olmsted observed indignantly that "this new 'jelly bomb' of ours with its shriveling and spreading and unextinguishable heat, if invented and used by Germans or Japanese would have raised an outcry in this country. Invented and used by us, not against military objectives alone but against helpless civilians, we hear only voices of praise for the cleverness of our scientists and the strategy of our military leaders. . . . What a reservoir of hate and fear we must be now piling up against us with our destruction of both Europe and Asia!"[109]

Worse was yet to come. On 6 August and again on 9 August 1945, the United States dropped atomic bombs on the Japanese cities of Hiroshima and Nagasaki. On 10 August Frank Olmstead of the WRL wrote to that organization's members that "the radio has just said that Japan accepts the Potsdam terms [for a modified unconditional surrender]. . . . World War II is over."[110] As the WILPF put it three days later, "It is now 'Peace or Perish'."[111]

"We have known from the beginning," wrote Olmsted in early 1945, "that we could not support this war because good does not come out of evil, and a better world for humanity cannot be created by teaching hatred and the use of violence but only out of spreading understanding and 'goodwill to men,' the realization that what injures one people injures all."[112] If Olmsted was right, then the dropping of the atomic bombs, while ending the most destructive war in human history, was also frighteningly symbolic of what might portend for the postwar world. American pacifists realized this possibility and their response to the bomb's use and its future deployment reflected that concern, politically and morally.

In its 12 August telegram to Truman calling for public hearings "before any decisions are made on future plans for the control and use of the atomic bomb," the PWWC stressed the political nature of the issue with its emphasis on the democratic process. But the more common reaction was a moral one. No peace group expressed this sentiment better than Hanson W. Baldwin in his *New York Times* column of 12 September when he wrote, "the truth is that the United States has sacrificed its moral leadership of the world."[113]

Forty-nine "religious and educational leaders," including Dr. John Paul Jones, Muste, Balch, and Oswald Garrison Villard, echoed Baldwin. In dropping the atomic bombs, they declared, the United States "committed an atrocity of a new magnitude; and though technically it may not contravene the recognized rules of 'civilized' warfare, in essence it violates every instinct of humanity. . . . This 'cosmic disturbance' . . . has dragged the war and all of us with it, to a new low of inhumanity. . . . It has our unmitigated condemnation."[114]

The WILPF expressed its "sense of misery and shame" that it was the United States that first employed "this 'atomic atrocity,'" suggesting that its "tragic significance . . . does not lie alone in the charred bodies and rubble of pulverized cities, but in the shattered moral authority of the United States." In a letter to Truman, Muste observed, "We are all aware of what would have been said if the Germans or the Japanese had resorted to atomic bombing. I cannot understand why the same things should not be said, now that it was the government of the United States which resorted to this crowning atrocity." George Hartmann of the WRL probably best summed up the collective response of pacifists when he declared that the atomic bombing "demonstrates finally (assuming that such evidence were needed) that the 'morality' of America at war is not one bit above that of the late enemy nations."[115]

A few voices in the peace movement tried to sound a positive note by arguing that the bomb "destroyed not only the city of Hiroshima but the whole purpose of conscription. It certainly will give an impetus to disarmament," thought Detzer, "as nothing else has ever done." Both Detzer and Frank Olmstead believed that "the possibility of using this new discovery for creative purposes is great. If it is true," Detzer wrote, "that it can take the place of oil and coal, it will shatter the whole basis of our present economic system. Moreover it can destroy the advantage of large countries over small."[116] Such optimistic expressions, however, were all but drowned out by the chorus of voices reflecting pessimism and discouragement.

In the weeks following the war's end, Muste probably best expressed this sense of foreboding, writing letter after letter in which he quoted from a statement of 9 August by Bishop G. Bromley Oxnam, president of the Federal Council of Churches, and John Foster Dulles, chair of the Council's Commission on a Just and Durable Peace: "If we, a professedly Christian nation feel morally free to use atomic energy in that way men elsewhere will accept that verdict. Atomic weapons will be looked upon as a normal part of the arsenal of war and the stage will be set for the sudden and final destruction of mankind." As Muste commented, Oxnam and Dulles were men "of exceedingly high standing in the church and in the nation and were consistent and useful supporters of the nation's war effort." They were not pacifists, in other words, from whom one might expect such sentiment and, therefore, "what they have said certainly cannot be lightly dismissed."

Acknowledging that it was the U.S. government "that took the responsibility for launching upon the world the moral and material terror to which Bishop Oxnam and Mr. Dulles refer, . . . it seems clear," he concluded, "that upon the government and the people of this country squarely rests the responsibility for taking the initiative in removing this terror from the earth." To do this, Muste asserted, two things were required. First, "the moral atmosphere has to be changed" to restore the people's "confidence" necessary for a "genuine and lasting peace." This could be accomplished if the U.S. government ceased manufacture of atomic bombs "and similar instruments of destruction immediately," followed by a pledge "that it would under no circumstances resort to the use of such instrumentalities in the future." Second, the United States must "take the initiative in securing immediate drastic reduction of armaments (and presently complete disarmament) and abolition of conscription by international agreement."[117]

The WRL concurred. Jessie Wallace Hughan even suggested that the "formula" for the bomb's construction be destroyed. As she and Frances Witherspoon pointed out, "though the United States has—or believes she alone possesses—the dreadful secret, it is naive to think we shall long possess it alone among nations. . . . This being so, *all* nations must outlaw this abomination *together* at the earliest moment."[118]

To those who suggested that "men may now be frightened into peace," William Jaffe responded that "what is important is to point out . . . why the atomic bomb or any other terrible invention is by itself unlikely to save mankind from the scourge of war. . . . The problem in warfare," he observed almost prophetically, "is to be the first with some terrifying lethal instrument." No, thought Jaffe, people will not be frightened into abolishing war—"it requires a collective human will . . . by ferreting out the complex causes of war and eliminating them."[119]

Throughout the remainder of 1945, Muste led the pacifists' fight to abolish the bomb, conscription, and war, but to no avail. Events seemed to be substantiating the observation made by a discouraged Reinhold Niebuhr in August, that "nations do not deprive themselves of new sources of power and prestige, once it [*sic*] has been placed in their hands. This is a terrible fact but it is so."[120] This situation prompted the PWWC just before Christmas to call upon the president and Congress to "act at once to stop the further manufacture of atomic bombs and further experiments with them." In no uncertain terms the seventy-member PWWC Board of Governors condemned U.S. atomic policy:

> The Post War World Council believes that it speaks for the American people when it expresses indignation and consternation at the report that the United States is continuing the manufacture of atomic bombs. This is an action for which we can see no conceivable excuse. It invites universal suspicion of our sincerity in seeking renunciation of the use of atomic energy for war. It goes far toward justifying the almost pathological concern of the Soviet Government for its security. It creates weapons capable of unimaginable destruction whose mere physical existence is a peril to mankind.
>
> The report that the Army and more especially the Navy are considering experiments in the use of atomic bombs to destroy ships in some lonely place in the ocean adds to our concern. At the very least no such experiments should be undertaken without the unanimous assurance of all competent scientists that it may not be fraught with danger of loosing uncontrolled and uncontrollable forces.[121]

What neither the peace movement nor the general public knew, of course, was that when it came to U.S. "atomic diplomacy," the government was operating according to a hidden agenda. Although some within the peace movement suspected that there was more to the Hiroshima and Nagasaki bombings than the president's claim of "military necessity" to save thousands of American lives that an invasion of Japan would have cost, they did not have the evidence available later to historians that confirmed these suspicions. As Charles Mee has pointed out in recent years, "after the war, the United States Strategic Bombing Command issued a study confirming the advice Truman had been getting before he gave the order to drop the atomic bomb: 'Japan would have surrendered even if the atomic bombs had not been dropped, even if Russia had not entered the war, and even if no invasion had been planned or contemplated.'"

Why, then, were the bombs dropped? First, "because of the vast sums that had been spent on the project"; second, "in order to end the war against Japan without Russian help" since Stalin had agreed to join that effort three months after the war in Europe was over; third, and most damning of all, was the reason given by Secretary of State James Byrnes, that the bombs were dropped "to make Russia more manageable in Europe."[122]

A second aspect of the government's hidden agenda revolved around the "War-Peace Studies" put together by the State Department and Council on Foreign Relations during the war. As Noam Chomsky explained in 1981, U.S. leaders knew by 1941–1942 that the United States would emerge from World War II as it did, by far and away *the* dominant global power. Thus they asked the all-important question: "What are the areas that are strategically necessary for world control?" or, in the words of another government document, control over what areas internationally would "give the U.S. the elbow-room necessary to ensure the health of the American economy *without any internal adjustments?*" After intensive analysis of all pertinent economic and political factors, American leaders had their answer: It would be necessary to control at a minimum the "entire Western Hemisphere, the Far East, and the former British Empire," referred to as "the Grand Area."[123]

In late summer 1945 Olmsted remarked that "in the present dividing up of Europe and in the proposed dividing up of Asia which is beginning to emerge, we see the exact reverse of the kind of world which so many believed they were helping to create. I recall that Frederick Libby was scoffed at when he stated back in early 1941 . . . that the war in Europe was being fought just to determine who should dictate the terms of peace." Had she and others in the peace movement been aware of the War-Peace Studies and the extent to which the United States was willing to go to ensure U.S. domination of the "Grand Area," Olmsted would have understood, although not have sanctioned, the "incredibly horrible and stupid peace" that her country had "dictated. Most of the things which we objected to the Nazis doing in Europe," she declared indignantly, "we are now doing—or our allies are—even to stripping the countries of food and machinery and all the means of making a decent honest living."[124]

U.S. global domination in the postwar world meant, of course, that neither atomic weapons nor a peacetime military would be abandoned. Because pacifists, like the American people, were unaware of their government's plans, accepting instead at face value the rhetoric of democratic goals and aspirations, they continued into 1946 and beyond to press for abolition of both. They struggled as well to influence the United Nations in a truly democratic direction, to establish a permanent FEPC, to create real social, political, and economic equality for women, minorities, and refugees, and called for amnesty for conscientious objectors. They opposed the formation of NATO and the Truman Doctrine as divisive and militaristic, and deplored the upsurge of virulent anti-Soviet propaganda by the government and the media.

As had Addams some fifteen years before, Balch won the Nobel Peace Prize in 1946,[125] and in a speech at a luncheon in her honor during the WILPF's 1947 annual meeting, Balch, still strong in body and mind despite her eighty years, assessed the world situation that pacifists now confronted. In spite of the "widespread pain and confusion" in Europe, she declared, "I see no reason for cynicism or inertia. . . . Men are consciously masters of their fate as they have never been before." Always concerned with the prospect of an internationally organized world, Balch saw "no reason why there should not be a gradual and natural growth of internationalism," pointing to the work of UN agencies as a step in the right direction.

As for the role of the United States, first, she thought, "it must refuse to be militarized. Key positions should be held by ordinary citizens, not by soldiers. We should have no peace time conscription, least of all conscription of our young men by subjecting them to military training by soldiers." Second, the United States "must not be tempted into imperialism, either dollar diplomacy with underground control of other peoples through economic pressure or colonial imperialism." Third, she addressed the emergent hostility of the Cold War between the United States and the Soviet Union: "We must not be anti-Russian nor anti any people. All proper . . . international means should be used to prevent the employment of violence, terror or chicanery to oppress any people or make any people the satellite of any other against its will."

Echoing the basic philosophical premise of the WILPF for over thirty years, Balch asserted that "the basic thing" needed for post-war peace and justice was education—"education of ourselves and others." And because education was a "two-way street," she concluded, "we must learn as well as help others to learn."[126] With Balch's speech setting the tone for the postwar WILPF, it continued to struggle for peace and freedom in the aftermath of World World II with the same commitment to brotherly love, education and rational persuasion, legality, and democracy it had shown in the wake of World War I.

Despite vastly depleted numbers—there were fewer than 5,000 American members in 1947—the U.S. Section of the WILPF survived the war and the early onslought of anticommunist hysteria of the Cold War. Although Detzer resigned as executive secretary in 1946 and serious financial difficulties compelled a complete reorganization of the group's national structure, the WILPF was cohesive and strong enough to hold its first postwar international congress in Luxembourg in 1946, attended by twenty-seven national sections. Balch remained honorary international president throughout the 1950s, and Olmsted continued as an active national leader in one capacity or another into the last decade of the century with undaunted spirit and remarkable physical energy despite her ninety-plus years of age.

When there were calls for an early armistice in the Korean conflict; when Americans protested the growing arms race; when antiwar sentiment began to build in response to increased U.S. involvement in the Vietnam conflict; when nuclear freeze advocates marched in Washington; when Americans called for a halt to U.S. intervention in Latin America; when black Americans demanded their Constitutional rights in the late 1950s and early 1960s; wherever and whenever militarism, war, injustice, and repression reared their ugly heads, the WILPF was there. It is still there today, and it is so in no small measure because of the commitment, determination, and faith of those World War I and World War II era women who created an enduring organizational framework for the political activism of members of their own gender who refused to accept the "is" as the "ought."

14

Conclusion

THE INTERWAR WILPF brought together three important strands of American political, economic, and social activism: the reform ideology of Progressivism, the radical strategy of pacifism, and the egalitarian philosophy of feminism. In this sense it was unique, for it was the only sizeable political action organization of the time, single-sex or mixed, to embrace all three movements. Although its influence and visibility was out of all proportion to its peak membership of only 15,000, the measure of its significance lies not so much in a list of its successes or failures, but rather in what those efforts can tell us about reform in U.S. society.

As feminists, the women of the WILPF, like those of the NWP, advocated complete equality of the sexes in all spheres of human activity. But unlike the more militant NWP, the WILPF believed that economic equity for women could only be assured through the unequal means of protective legislation for women workers. And where the NWP was single-issue oriented, the cause of equal rights for women, however defined, was for the WILPF only part of the larger issue of equal rights for all people in a peaceful and democratically-organized world. Although the women of the WILPF did not put it this way, it was clear to them that equality for women could be achieved automatically if they succeeded in reaching their larger goals of peace, freedom, and justice for all people everywhere.

Pacifism, more than women's rights, was the primary issue motivating the WILPF's political activism. To be sure, only a minority of WILPF women, although an important minority as it included most of its leadership, was committed to this radical means of nonviolent change. Yet pacifism had a critical impact upon the WILPF's assessment of the social order, particularly when viewed in conjunction with its Progressive outlook. When all is said and done, however important the WILPF was in attracting thousands of women into the political realm, providing this newly enfranchised group with the opportunity to participate in the political process, and by so doing to develop a sense of self-confidence and self-worth beyond the narrow confines of home and family—and this was no mean achievement—it nevertheless failed to reach its goals of peace, freedom, and justice. Ironically, however, it is in this very failure that the WILPF may yet enjoy its greatest success, for if today's peace advocates understand the reasons for that failure, they may yet turn it around and thereby provide tangible evidence that these determined and farsighted women did not labor in vain. To understand that failure it is necessary to understand the interaction of the WILPF's pacifism with its Progressivism.

The starting point of such an analysis must necessarily begin with the WILPF's faith in the American system as a democracy, at least a political democracy. The system in which they lived and strove to influence, the women believed, was one of laws, not men. That their government was the servant of the whole people was simply accepted without question, and this was true of the entire interwar peace movement. "Sovereignty," asserted the NPC in 1945, "resides in the people. It is a mistake to assume that sovereignty belongs to the state. The people assign to the state sovereignty over certain matters when it is convenient to have those matters dealt with by the state. . . . The people assign sovereignty over certain matters to the municipal government, over others to the States, over others to the national government."[1] There was, in other words, nothing wrong with the system itself. Any failure of the people to have their will translated into law was due primarily to the machinations of a few self-serving and immoral men, men who twisted the essential democratic nature of the system by enacting laws to serve their own personal ends, or by interpreting, implementing, or ignoring other laws in ways that subverted democracy as both process and goal.

Not only was political democracy threatened by such men active in private business and government; economic democracy and peace at home and abroad were also vulnerable. The threats were visible everywhere: Addams' experience in losing an election bid in Chicago's Nineteenth Ward to the political machine in 1898 is a case in point, and Madeleine Doty's experience as an attorney with "society's misfits" in pre-World War I New York, recounted in her 1914 book of that title, attests eloquently to her knowledge of the injustice and inequities suffered by the people when the reins of government fall into the hands of such men.[2]

It took Detzer a little longer to come to the same understanding, particularly with respect to the connection that the older women perceived between a self-serving ruling elite and the possibility of war. In her early twenties when Wilson declared that the United States must support the Allied powers in World War I to ensure that this would be "the war to end war," a naive and innocent Dorothy Detzer was quickly caught up in the wave of idealistic patriotism that swept over so many Americans in those days. In the summer of 1918 when her beloved twin brother, Don, responding with the same idealistic war fervor as his sister, enlisted in the army, Dorothy, bursting with pride, exclaimed to Addams how "wonderful" it was that he could now participate directly in such a noble enterprise.[3]

Not until the Nye investigation of the mid-1930s would the WILPF or the American public learn that the reason for U.S. entry into that conflict had less to do with "making the world safe for democracy" than with protecting the rather large investment of U.S. financiers. Because Detzer was the person most responsible for bringing about the Nye Munitions Investigation, the WILPF was especially interested in keeping abreast of the ongoing testimony of such reluctant witnesses as those representing the House of Morgan. While the general public received a distorted perspective on the revelations of the hearings, thanks to a national press dominated by the interests of big business and bankers,[4] members of the WILPF—Detzer in particular—attended the committee's sessions regularly, thus obtaining first-hand knowledge of such damning indictments of the collusion between the Morgan financial interests and the Wilson administration. "The Munitions Investigation Committee, under the chairmanship of Senator Nye," she noted, "has, during the past year, shown the country how the United States was drawn into the last war. As this is being written, Mr. J. P. Morgan and his partners are giving evidence to the Munitions Committee regarding the part that great financial House played in involving the United States in the World War."[5]

Yet despite the evidence that the United States entered the European war within a month of Ambassador Walter Hines Page's cable suggesting ominously that economic collapse threatened this country unless we assured an Allied victory, the American people were told that "'the United States went to war because German submarines sank United States ships without warning, killing United States citizens,' pretending," wrote journalist George Seldes in 1947, "that this childish statement was real history."[6] Profit for U.S. bankers and munitions man-ufacturers? Only an unavoidable indirect consequence of war, despite the fact that such profits, as Detzer noted in 1935, were "not niggardly. The capital assets of the DuPont Company, for example, rose from 61 millions in 1913 to 288 millions in 1918, and their earnings from 5 to 43 millions. That," she said flatly, "is a tidy profit in blood money."[7] The WILPF had learned a valuable lesson about wealth and power.

As pointed out in Chapter Five, the most important issue for the WILPF as the world reverted to peacetime in the early 1920s was that of economic imperialism. The women were quite conscious of the con-nection between capital investment abroad, and the resultant demand of those investors for a military force strong enough and large enough to protect that investment from the always-present threat of nationalis-tic revolution on the part of the exploited peoples who saw their politi-cal system, as well as their economy being manipulated for the gain of profit-seeking foreigners. As Doty observed from her vantage point at the abortive London Naval Conference in early 1930, "What . . . is at bottom of Navies? Let us be frank. It is trade and commerce, colonial imperialism, investments abroad. . . . As long as the flag and the battle-ships follow the investor, the situation is hopeless. . . . If it could be established as law that no flag and no battleship was to follow the dol-lar, the pound, the franc, the lire, and the yen a new day would dawn."[8]

The links between business and government were no secret. The capitalist's drive for new markets, new and cheaper sources of raw ma-terials, a cheaper and more docile labor force, and new areas for in-vestment meant imperialism; and imperialism meant the necessity, as the WILPF pointed out time and again, of public (i.e., government) protection (i.e., military might) of private business endeavor abroad. Even if the world's industrial-creditor nations were to work together in concert to exploit the resources of the other regions of the globe and thereby reduce the risk of war between or among themselves, imple-ments of war might still be used to suppress domestic conflicts should an exploited people either at home or abroad decide to rise up in protest. This, too, the WILPF understood, for the women witnessed some of the most blatant examples of this type of violence in numerous instances of state-supported repression against striking workers during the World War I era and later during the Depression.

The men of wealth and power, understandably enough, had no de-sire to relinquish even one iota of their privileged position. Hence, they consistently sought to maintain, extend, and consolidate that wealth and power. To be sure, some of these men were more venal than others, more unscrupulous, more willing to violate law and moral precept in the process, but the evidence that such men were perverting and distorting the American democratic system was clear. The women of the WILPF spoke of it, wrote of it, and persistently fought against it. The method they chose to utilize in this fight, however, was one that could not succeed, given the disproportionate degree of power in the hands of the opposition. For peace was not only the goal, said the WILPF again and again, it was the process as well. These Progressive reformers who never doubted the democratic character of the system, quickly saw their way clear to the basic strategy of restoring the purity, the integrity of an essentially moral, just, and equitable system—"new men, new laws" (generically speaking, of course). The election of "new men" and the passage of "new laws" would be accomplished through the peaceful legal process of democracy in action. Democracy as means would bring about peace and freedom and thus would result in restoring democracy as the end. It was a fundamentally sound system that called only for new people in power and new laws to restore it to health. These tenets for the WILPF were articles of faith.

And that was a crucial part of the problem. They *were* articles of faith, of a secular religious faith that rested on the Christian precept that we are all children of God, that repudiated artificial manmade distinctions such as national boundaries, that assumed as given that the ultimate interests of all people everywhere are the same. It was, in short, a curious blend of their entire national history: an amalgam of Enlightenment secularism, Romantic transcendentalism, Progressive rationalism, and Christian brotherly love.

So completely were the women given over to this secular religion and so thoroughly were they the products of their own time and place, that they literally could not liberate themselves from their own confining ideology to see the enormous chasm between the "is" and the "ought." They could not transcend the limitations and restrictions imposed by their vision of the ends, the "ought"—peace, freedom, justice —more accurately to identify the reality in which they sought to implement these goals, the reality that must necessarily dictate *means* of implementation. They began the process of analysis in the wrong place; they approached the issue of means from the perspective of the ends rather than from the perspective of the means available, and *possible*, if not necessary, in their own day-to-day reality. If peace was the goal, then working backwards, peace must necessarily be the means, for they had been persuaded that moral ends cannot be achieved by immoral means, that a nonviolent world cannot be realized through violent tactics.

Regardless of what Wilson said, a war to end war was a contradiction in terms, for war invariably results in winners and losers and thus breeds fear, animosity, and a desire for revenge, paving the way for future wars. Nor could there be a war to make the world safe for democracy, for war involves violence and coercion, and democracy is predicated upon the free choice of the individual and the voluntary consent of the people. War, in other words, was a methodological failure. It could not resolve problems or disputes between and among nations; it merely created new problems and gave rise to new disputes and, hence, new wars.

Given that generation's disillusionment with the results of World War I as well as its revulsion over the unprecedented extent of human and material destruction wrought by supposedly enlightened and civilized peoples in that struggle, it is not surprising that all wars—and by extrapolation, all overt violence between and among peoples—would be so thoroughly and unhesitatingly regarded in the same light. Yet to reach this conclusion was to misread the historical evidence to the contrary. A fundamental objective of the American Revolutionary war was independence from England—success. The goal of the American Civil War, said Abraham Lincoln, was preservation of the Union—achieved. The basic desire of U.S. imperialists in the more recent Spanish-American War was U.S. acquisition of the Philippines—done.

Not that every war ever fought achieved its objective, of course. In the American Civil War, the Southern Confederacy failed to achieve its goal of secession precisely because the North succeeded in attaining its goal of preventing that secession. Nor can it be validly argued that every war has been fought for some noble and worthy cause. Human history is replete with examples of military aggression solely for reasons of greed and power. Outbreak of war may indeed represent a failure of statesmanship or a repudiation of the concept that human life is sacred and inviolable, but that is not the same as alleging that war is a methodological failure, that it never achieves its objectives.

Convinced, however, that a "good" end cannot be achieved through utilization of a "bad" means, the WILPF condemned all war and violence. Such a repudiation did not involve, however, a concomitant rejection of conflict. Although frequently accused of being naive in this respect, the WILPF was realistic enough to know that conflicts between and among people will inevitably occur in an imperfect world inhabited by imperfect human beings. Conflict was simply an unavoidable part of life and the women concluded that the best method of reconciling opposing points of view was through the application of "sweet reason," through compromise, calm persuasion, accommodation, or, as Balch so adeptly practiced, the effort to bring about the "pooled intelligence" of a "third way." In other words, everyday conflicts could best be pacified through implementation of democratic principles, for democracy meant "consent of the people," an informed consent based on the relevant information available equally to all with all participating in the resolution process.

The WILPF's understanding of violence meant more than simply the brute force of imposing one's will on another through threat of bodily harm, however. Violence could also be covert in the form of economic injustice, and the WILPF rejected both types of violence. Yet the women never blinded themselves to the fact that the power structure did not necessarily share their abhorrence of either type of violence. The use of overt and covert violence by the men of wealth and power, in fact, indicated that if the system was a *political* democracy, however imperfect, it was not yet an *economic* democracy. For the power structure utilized overt violence to suppress those who protested against the covert violence, and both posed a threat to the continued existence of political democracy.

The WILPF concluded, therefore, that because the "present economic order" was unequal, unjust, and based on violence, peace could never be achieved within the system. In an attempt to explain the leadership's position in early 1935 to a disgruntled member, Hannah Clothier Hull indicated her understanding of this basic fact as she lamented the resurgence of international economic and political competition in the wake of world-wide depression:

> Peace is impossible under the present economic order. . . . The economic competition of the present order is one of the direct causes of international conflict. Many of our members, both here and abroad, are convinced that it is impossible to develop a cooperative world with nations whose economic systems are based on competition. . . . Some of our members feel that violence is inherent in the present social order, in the use of troops to put down strikes, in the third degree method in our prisons, in the use of Federal troops against unarmed, hungry men seeking the bonus, and there are more and more of our members who believe that the covert types of violence are as unethical and as much a denial of peace, as the overt types of violence. That is, they feel that a system which permits workers to be starved by low wages, or forced to live in frightful places by their economic conditions, is, in itself, a violation of life quite as cruel, though not as dramatic, as the obvious types of violence, such as shooting, etc.[9]

In other words, the *creation* of economic democracy was no less important for the WILPF than was the *preservation* of political democracy. The two went hand-in-glove for as the women warned throughout the 1930s, persistent economic inequity would result in fascism, and fascism meant totalitarianism and the disappearance of democracy.

The WILPF's economic radicalism was not born of the Great Depression, however. As far back as the organization's international Congress in 1921, a similar assessment of the social order prompted the following resolution:

> Since the Women's International League for Peace and Freedom aims at the peaceful solution of conflicts between social classes as between nations, it is the duty of its National Sections and of its individual members to initiate and support laws looking to the gradual abolition of property privileges (for instance, by means of taxation, death duties, and land reform laws) and to the development of economic independence and individual freedom, and to work to awaken and strengthen among members of the possessing classes the earnest will to transform the economic system in the direction of social justice.[10]

Here is the point at which we begin to discern a fundamental reason for the WILPF's limited success as a reform organization. For the women genuinely to have believed that "the possessing classes" could be persuaded to relinquish even a small portion of their wealth and power in the interest of social justice reflected their inability to recognize, or their unwillingness to accept, the reality of self-interest in their society. The women had abjured self-interest in behalf of the common good and this was only right, just, and proper. For in the world of the "ought" the interest of the self and the interest of the whole are one and the same. Hence, all people in a democracy are morally obligated to do likewise. That some men, however, did not share this vision of the "ought" was abundantly clear, and the women saw this, but only with their eyes, not their minds. They never integrated this knowledge into their assessment of reality. The question is why?

The women of the WILPF fell prey to the same error that plagued so many reformers of the Progressive generation. Convinced that ignorance rather than self-interest was the root cause of social conflict, they concluded that employing reason in the accumulation of the facts was the first step in the process of defusing conflict by replacing ignorance with knowledge. This would then be followed by reasonable presentation of the facts to those whose ignorance gave them an erroneous point of view. Because the interests of all people were basically the same and because all people are rational, once informed by accurate facts they would modify their position accordingly and the conflict would dissolve.

Part of the problem with this approach, as Reinhold Niebuhr noted in his 1932 publication of *Moral Man and Immoral Society*, was an overly enthusiastic reliance on the scientific method and education, and the danger of becoming "too enamored of the function of reason in life." The social injustice that gives rise to such conflict, argued Niebuhr, a former pacifist himself, "cannot be resolved by moral and rational suasion alone" because the cause of that injustice was not ignorance so much as it was self-interest, that is, power. "An adjustment of a social conflict, caused by the disproportion of power in society," he maintained, "will hardly result in justice as long as the disproportion of power remains." And this unequal distribution of power resulted from the unequal distribution of wealth which was a matter of self-interest, not ignorance. Thus, he concluded, "conflict is inevitable and in this conflict power must be challenged by power."[11]

Given their moral vision and their commitment to reason and education, the women of the WILPF rejected this notion of power and self-interest, both on an individual and a collective basis. Frequently, therefore, they were dismissed as being naive and unrealistic by the very power structure they sought to influence. It was probably this charge of being "unrealistic" that annoyed Detzer more than any other criticism leveled at the pacifist. Why? Primarily because she saw it as a ploy to avoid dealing openly and honestly with an awkward or perhaps embarrassing issue or situation. "The words 'realistic' and 'unrealistic' were employed," she argued, "chiefly as verbal tourniquets to staunch the flow of argument which, for one reason or another, appeared unanswerable, unorthodox, or distasteful. . . . In the political sphere 'realism' when stripped of its silky, diplomatic draperies is usually nothing more than that ugly sow's ear, *Realpolitik*."[12]

Realpolitik, power politics—Clearly to the WILPF an undesirable and wrong-headed approach to deal with conflict. Power politics was part of the problem, not, to be sure, a way to *solve* the problem. The following exchange between Detzer and an official of the State Department when the news of Japan's 1931 invasion of Manchuria was received is instructive in this regard:

> The State Department, he told me, was "studying the situation," and though it regarded "the Sino-Japanese conflict as serious," it did not hold it to be "critical."
> "Do you mean that the United States isn't even going to consult

with the other powers as they are pledged to do in Article 7 of the Nine Power Pact?" I asked with concern.

"There is no such commitment in the pact," he informed me.

"There isn't?" I said. "Then, what is the interpretation of Article 7?"

"That Article merely provides that the powers *may* consult with each other should circumstances appear to warrant such a step," he replied.

"Good heavens," I exclaimed, "what kind of circumstances could governments conceive which would warrant consultation more? Asia's aflame."

"You peace people always get so excited over every little local conflict," he complained. "How would you like it if Japan protested every time the United States sent marines to Nicaragua?"

"I think that would be just dandy," I replied. "Unfortunately, there is no Nine Power Pact guaranteeing the integrity of Nicaragua."

"Well," the young official interrupted, "you must remember that the government must always use discretion when invoking a treaty."

"Discretion?" I repeated. "Discretion? What would happen to domestic law, do you think, if federal officials used discretion in applying it to lawbreakers?"

"I don't see any logical connection," he answered shortly.

"Well, the connection as I see it is this," I explained. "If a person commits a murder, he breaks the law against murder but he does not destroy the law. Law is not destroyed when it is broken; it is only destroyed when it is not enforced. It seems to us that this applies to international law as well as domestic law."

The young man waved this argument aside. Such a contention, he said, might be valid theoretically, but unsound practically. "For after all," he pontificated, "you have to be realistic."[13]

For this State Department official the issue was one of power politics, of national self-interest, however that might be defined. But for Detzer the issue was one of legality in the interests of an ethical norm. As a committed democrat who believed that she operated within a democracy, she was acting out the philosophical position of her revolutionary forebears. Democracy was not merely a system of laws designed by the whole for the good of the whole; it was the promulgation in form and structure and statute of the wishes and needs of a virtuous people, not just in political terms but economically and socially as well. As such, it was a system of ethical truths and moral absolutes, *not* one of crass, self-interested *Realpolitik*.

Detzer's stress upon the law, and upon the government's and the citizen's obligation to obey that law, reflected the WILPF's commitment to democracy, to the right of the sovereign people to govern themselves through their chosen representatives and to expect that such decisions, once written into law, would be carried out to the letter of that law by those representatives and obeyed by the whole people. But this emphasis upon law was only part of the WILPF's ideological premise. Strict compliance with the law was critically important because it represented the "ought." It *was* the moral and ethical expression of the virtuous people and thus should be obeyed on moral as well as on legal grounds.

The WILPF did not accept the old cliché that rules are made to be broken. To "break a rule" in the sense of violating a democratically promulgated directive was not merely to violate the law in a strictly legal sense; it was to break faith with the people themselves. For those who composed the power structure to ignore or to break the law and hence violate the people's wishes meant that the system was not operating as a democracy, Constitutional rhetoric and institutional arrangements notwithstanding.

Although a reasonable conclusion given the evidence, it was one the women of the WILPF never came to, perhaps because it would have required a reassessment of their belief that in the struggle for peace and freedom, means and ends must be consistent. Tactics grounded in a democratic framework—petition, persuasion, political participation (i.e., "new men, new laws")—would be useless in a system where the power structure was dominated by men who operated according to self-interested power politics. If the system was not a political democracy, then it could never be an economic democracy; and without economic democracy there could be neither peace nor freedom.

Had the women acknowledged that this might be the way the system really worked, they would have had to acknowledge the element of power in the social situation, the *disproportionate* power in the hands of the few—power used for the benefit of the few through exploitation of the many, an exploitation that took the form of violence, overt and covert, at home and abroad. Such power could ignore the law or break the law, if necessary, to maintain or extend that power. It is at this point that Progressive reformers should have acknowledged their most crucial tactical dilemma: how to reconcile the logical inconsistency of expecting the man who has achieved wealth and power through coercion to relinquish that privileged position voluntarily and altruistically for the benefit of those very people against whom he has just directed his repressive measures. The WILPF apparently did not understand this dilemma, and thus for all of her protestations to the contrary, Detzer was wrong; the WILPF *was* unrealistic.

On the surface of it, the women of the WILPF—and all interwar peace advocates of a Progressive mentality—given the reality of the U.S. social, political, and economic system, needed to be revolutionaries to achieve their goal. But revolutionaries break laws, revolutionaries employ coercion, revolutionaries must often resort to violence and bloodshed. And if means and ends must be consistent, then true democrats can never be revolutionaries. Thus it would appear that the women of the WILPF could have been none other than what they were —reformers. Reformers doomed to failure because democratic tactics and democratic strategy cannot "re-form" an undemocratic system.

But things are not always as they appear. The WILPF had an option short of revolution, an option that was embodied in their pacifism: nonviolent direct action protest and demonstration. As the activists of the 1960s civil rights movement discovered, nonviolent confrontation with representatives of the power structure can bring about at least a certain degree of reform within the system. As Richard Gregg pointed out in his 1934 work, *The Power of Nonviolence,*

> In a struggle between a violent person and a non-violent resister, if there are any onlookers or a public that hears of the conflict, the nonviolent resister gains a strong advantage from their reaction. When the public sees the gentle person's courage and fortitude, notes his generosity and good will toward the attacker, and hears his repeated offers to settle the matter fairly, peaceably and openly, they are filled with surprise, curiosity and wonder. If they have been hostile to the victim before, they at least pause to think. His good humor, fairness and kindness arouse confidence. Sooner or later his conduct wins public sympathy, admiration and support, and also the respect of the violent opponent himself.[14]

The WILPF did not need the example of the civil rights movement to see the possibilities for change in nonviolent direct action. Not only were the women familiar with Gregg's book, they worked with him in the peace movement, and were very much aware of and supported whole-heartedly Gandhi's movement in India. Why, then, when Roosevelt refused to invoke the neutrality law, or when the government failed to act energetically on behalf of Europe's persecuted Jews, or when Japanese-American citizens were herded into concentration camps, or when delegates to the disarmament conferences failed to implement any meaningful degree of arms reduction—why, in all of these instances and others as well, why did the women not act on their pacifistic philosophy and engage in mass nonviolent direct action protest when their verbal and written protests achieved such limited and disappointing results?

At the risk of oversimplification, I would suggest that the WILPF never really gave serious consideration to such an option because they were Progressives first and pacifists second. As Progressives who believed they operated within a democracy, there was no need to resort to a methodology any more confrontational than that of "new men, new laws." The system would eventually right itself through the "purposeful" action, as Balch said in 1947, of people like WILPF members in educating themselves and others and passing laws progressively leading toward a more "beneficent" world unity. The injustices and violence of U.S. society were not seen as systemic, but rather as a matter of ignorance within a basically equitable system that could, and would, be eradicated by greater effort on the part of true democrats.

For the native peoples of India it was different. They knew they did not enjoy the rights and privileges of a democratic society, but suffered the inequities and injustices of domination by a foreign power for the interests of the foreign power. And for black Americans the situation was different. If they lived in a political democracy, they saw—and finally were compelled to accept what white middle class Progressives could not—that if it was a democracy, it was a "democracy for the few," as Michael Parenti entitled his 1988 study of the U.S. system, and that, of course, is a contradiction in terms.[15]

Where there has been no real democracy, people who desire freedom, justice, and equality have learned that nonviolent resistance to the power structure can result in a certain degree of change—India in the 1930s, black America in the 1960s, Eastern Europe in the late 1980s, just to note a few. But nonviolent resistance is a "last resort" methodology for those who do not wish to see the violence and bloodshed of revolution, and American pacifists did not view their interwar situation to be that critical.

And perhaps it was not. But we cannot simply brush aside the fact that the Progressives' strategy of "new men, new laws" did not work. It did not result in the abolition of war, the reduction of arms, or a decrease in violence against striking workers and minorities. In short, it failed to move humankind any closer to true peace, freedom, and justice. No one is eager to admit failure, whatever the endeavor. We can admire, respect, and empathize with the women of the WILPF for their vision, their determination, their energy, and we should. We can agree passionately with their commitment to peace, justice, freedom, and democracy for all people everywhere. But for all that we must admit at last their failure: failure to persuade the men of power to lay down their arms, to repudiate war as an instrument of international "diplomacy," to relinquish methods of force, coercion, and violence in their interaction with others—in short, their failure to convince these men to abjure self-interest, to trade their privileged position of wealth and power for greater social, economic, and political equality among all peoples everywhere.

It was, perhaps, an impossible task from the beginning. If the women's Progressive ideology blinded them to the possibility that they did not live in a functioning democracy where government is the servant of the whole people, their pacifism, grounded as it was in a vision of Christian brotherly love, may have gotten in the way of understanding that not all people everywhere are motivated by the same values. To be sure, the men of power have argued that they, too, wish for a world without war or violence, a world of peace and freedom for all people. Their words are replete with such noble sentiments. But unlike the WILPF, their actions tended all-too-frequently to belie their words, for such action, time and again, reflected little more than self-interest, whether for economic gain or greater political power. And their actions equally as often were colored by violence, physical and psychological, overt and covert.

It is undoubtedly true that some men (and some women, too) do not see war as inherently evil, negative, or undesirable. After all, did not Theodore Roosevelt supposedly find the Spanish-American conflict "a splendid little war," did he not assert with some vigor that war inculcated "manly virtues," whatever those are? Most men of power will excuse, even defend, violent acts such as war with reference to the goals of peace, liberty, and justice by the old adage that the end justifies the means. And perhaps for a small minority (one thinks of Thomas Paine, Fidel Castro, Ho Chi Minh), this will be the truth. But for others, such goals are viewed in a more restricted sense.

There are those who firmly believe, as one antebellum American slaveholder put it, that "some men are born with saddles on their backs, and others booted and spurred to ride them, and the riding does them good."[16] Such men—and women—do not believe that all people are, or should be, equal. Such men—and women—are unswervingly committed to social, political, and economic *inequality*, that a dominant "aristocratic" class *should* have power and control over the multitude, that certain people *should* have rights and privileges not accorded to the rest of us. One does not have to look very far in the historical record to discover that from the beginning of human history there have always been those who did not accept democracy as a good thing, who derisively and with horror equated democracy with "mobocracy."

The evidence suggests that the women of the WILPF, although perhaps recognizing an Adolf Hitler or a Benito Mussolini as belonging to such a category (and suspicious that perhaps Roosevelt, too, might share such a sentiment although most certainly in more benign fashion), were persuaded that adherence to such a value system was the result of ignorance. After all, as late as March 1940 Detzer was "not convinced that it is impossible to deal with Herr Hitler. I am not suggesting that it is easy. . . . He is a symbol of the psychic result of the defeat and humiliation of a nation . . . where the logic and realism of modern statesmen has failed but where *it is possible that patience and an intuitive understanding might yet win.*"[17] If Hitler was not seen as embracing an antithetical value system out of which he might be reasoned, then it is understandable that the WILPF would not have entertained the more farfetched notion that in a supposedly democratic society like the United States, there would be those who seek and hold political, economic, and social power not out of any commitment to democratic values, but rather because they desire to perpetuate a system of inequality.

Such people have no interest in altering the status quo in a more democratic direction and will respond to demands for such change only when they perceive, rightly or wrongly, that their privileged position is threatened by rebellion from below, or when they can implement such change with no serious modification of the existing distribution of power. To assume, as interwar pacifists did—and as most of us still do—that the "human traits of love, faith, courage, honesty and humility exist in greater or less strength in *every* person"[18] is to make the fatal mistake of believing that all people share the same value system in which these traits are deemed absolute moral goods. However much we might wish it to be so, the historical record is replete with examples of men and women for whom this was clearly not the case. We may characterize them as "immoral," "amoral," "irrational," or even "mad," but the appellation makes little difference. When such people hold the reins of power and speak of peace, freedom, and justice, their vision is diametrically opposed to that of the WILPF, and they willingly, even eagerly, utilize coercion, violence, and war to realize *their* vision of the ideal society.

The WILPF was important to the cause of feminism in the interwar period because despite its failure to endorse the ERA, its contribution to the politicization of the American woman was invaluable. It provided undeniable evidence that women every bit as much as men could intellectually grasp the complexities of the political system and organize quite as effectively to influence that system. And it did so without a concomitant "masculinization" of its members. That it failed to have any significant impact upon that system was not a matter of gender, for male activists experienced the same limited success. The WILPF also contributed to the cause of feminism in a more perverse fashion, through its internecine quarrels and conflicts, providing evidence that women, no less than men, are not biologically more prone to compromise, conciliation, and cooperation, and thus should not be elevated to some pedestal of unrealistic moral virtue.

Although a commitment to pacifism in practice was embraced only by a minority of WILPF members, that commitment showed that such a radical philosophy could attract supporters outside the religious community and was not, therefore, incompatible with political activism of a more traditional nature. But where the WILPF's pacifism and Progressivism came together was where it made its most important contribution to the ongoing effort of antiwar advocates to implement peaceful change for greater freedom and justice.

The WILPF's failure to push its pacifism to it limits by engaging in Gandhian nonviolent resistance stemmed from its acceptance of the U.S. system as a functioning democracy, and its assumption that all people basically shared its values and its vision of what our world ought to be. Its methodology of change was predicated upon that understanding. We have the advantage of historical hindsight some fifty years after World War II, based on a plethora of new evidence and our own experience, to realize that the women were wrong. We have the research of Ferdinand Lundberg and Jerry Fresia to add to Charles Beard to show us, if we are willing to see, that our Constitutional system was not and is not a functioning democracy nor was it intended as such, rhetoric notwithstanding.[19]

We have more evidence than we would like—the Central Intelligence Agency's subversion of democracy abroad and the Federal Bureau of Investigation's subversion of democracy at home; the CIA's experiments in mind control with human guinea pigs; the high-level conspiracy that assassinated John F. Kennedy, among others; the war in Vietnam; the Watergate and Iran-Contra scandals—to show that a value system grounded in democracy as both means and end is not necessarily shared by leaders and followers. And we have more than enough examples of the failure of "new men" and "new laws" to democratize the system— whether in tax reform or civil rights or equality for women—to tell us that continuing to adhere to the WILPF's strategy for change is a blueprint for continued failure.

If the WILPF failed to persuade the men of power to embrace its more egalitarian view of what the world should be, it was not only because the system was not the democracy the women believed it to be, it was also because not all people everywhere are motivated, as were the women, by a vision of love. In a very real sense, the men of power were too "tough-minded" while the women of the WILPF were, perhaps, too "tender-minded." They could not communicate with each other because there was no common ground of understanding, no shared values. Most important, it must be remembered that if the world was moved no closer to true peace, freedom, and justice as a result of the WILPF's tireless efforts, the failure was not the women's. It was the men of power who failed, for it was they who refused to lay down their arms, to repudiate war as an instrument of "diplomacy," to relinquish methods of force, coercion, and violence nationally and internationally.

The interwar WILPF's commitment to democracy as both process and goal was its greatest weakness while it was its greatest strength as well. Although it blurred the women's understanding of the system and the operative values of that system's "warriors," it also allowed them to assess more realistically that system's problems and defects. This, I would argue, is its most enduring legacy for us, one of supreme importance: that those who ignore history are doomed to repeat it.

Notes
Selected Bibliography
Index

Notes

Preface

1. Jane Addams, *Peace and Bread in Time of War* (Boston: G. K. Hall & Co., 1922; reprint, 1960), 140.
2. Ibid., 151.

1. Introduction

1. Charles DeBenedetti, *The Peace Reform in American History* (Bloomington: Univ. of Indiana Press, 1980), 109.
2. Bertram D. Wolfe, *A Life in Two Centuries: An Autobiography* (New York: Stein and Day, 1981), 22, 36.
3. DeBenedetti, *Peace Reform*, 108.
4. For a study of the pre-World War I peace movement and its lack of influence, see David S. Patterson, *Toward a Warless World: The Travail of the American Peace Movement 1887–1914* (Bloomington: Univ. of Indiana Press, 1976).
5. DeBenedetti, *Peace Reform*, 114.
6. Quoted in Marie Louise Degen, *The History of the Woman's Peace Party* (Baltimore: Johns Hopkins Univ. Press, 1939), 52.
7. Emily Greene Balch to Anna Garlin Spencer, 1 Apr. 1920, Women's International League for Peace and Freedom papers, series III, box 31, Univ. of Colorado, Boulder (hereafter cited as WILPF papers, Univ. of Colo.).
8. I have not included the World Woman's Party in my discussion of women's peace groups in the interwar period because Alice Paul did not found it until 1938.
9. Fanny Garrison Villard, Elinor Byrns, Katherine Devereaux Blake, Mary Ware Dennett, Lucy Watson, Rose Hicks, Edna Kearns, Caroline Lexow Babcock, Gratia Gollar to "Dear Member" [of the Executive Committee of the Women's International League of New York State], 12 Sept. 1919, Women's Peace Society papers, Swarthmore College Peace Collection, box 1, Swarthmore, Penn. (hereafter cited as the WPS papers, SCPC).
10. Addams, *Peace and Bread*, 3.
11. Sondra K. Herman, *Eleven against War: Studies in American Internationalist Thought, 1898–1921* (Palo Alto: Stanford Univ. Press, 1969).

12. Mercedes M. Randall, ed., *Beyond Nationalism: Social Thought of Emily Greene Balch* (New York: Twayne Publishers, 1972), 109, quoting Balch, "Our Call," *Bulletin* [WILPF], Feb. 1922, 3.

13. Dewey W. Grantham, Jr., "The Progressive Era and the Reform Tradition," in David M. Kennedy, ed., *Progressivism: The Critical Issues* (Boston: Little, Brown, 1971), 109–21.

14. Addams, *Peace and Bread*, 243–44.

15. Quoted in Randall, *Beyond Nationalism*, xvii.

16. Quoted in Ibid., Introduction.

17. Although Degen published her study of the WPP in 1939, since World War II there has been only one study of a woman's peace group, that of Harriet Hyman Alonso, *The Women's Peace Union and the Outlawry of War, 1921–1942* (Knoxville: Univ. of Tennessee Press, 1989).

2. Born of War

1. Degen, *Woman's Peace Party*, 74, quoting Jane Addams.

2. "Charter Members of the Woman's Peace Party," n.d., Woman's International League for Peace and Freedom Papers, Swarthmore College Peace Collection, series C1, box 4, Swarthmore, Penn. (hereafter cited as WILPF Papers, SCPC); Mildred Scott Olmsted, "50 Years Ago and the Road Ahead," Report of the Executive Director to 50th Anniversary Annual Meeting, 13–17 Oct. 1965, WILPF Papers, SCPC, 1, Series C1, box 6; Grace H. White to "Mabel," 21 Mar. 1925, Hannah Clothier Hull Papers, Swarthmore College Peace Collection, box 3, Swarthmore, Penn. (hereafter cited as Hannah Clothier Hull Papers, SCPC). Among the organizations represented at the conference were the American Peace Society, the American Peace and Arbitration League, the American Association for International Conciliation, the World Peace Foundation, the National American Woman's Suffrage Association, the Women's Christian Temperance Union, the National League of Teachers' Associations, the National Federation of Settlements, the National Women's Trade Union League, the National Council of Women, and the Daughters of the American Revolution. From Degen, *Woman's Peace Party*, 38.

3. William L. O'Neill, *Everyone Was Brave: The Rise and Fall of Feminism in America* (Chicago: Quadrangle Books, 1969), 175.

4. Degen, *Woman's Peace Party*, 41–42; Addams, *Peace and Bread*, 7.

5. Addams, *Peace and Bread*, 7.

6. Catt was a charter member of the WPP but was relatively inactive from the beginning because she wished to concentrate on the suffrage struggle and because she thought that passions among the belligerents ran too high for a conference of neutrals to have any meaningful impact. See O'Neill, *Everyone Was Brave*, 177–78.

7. Gertrude Bussey and Margaret Tims, *Pioneers for Peace: The Women's International League for Peace and Freedom 1915–1965* (1965; reprint, London: WILPF, British Section, 1980), 17–18.

8. "Is the Women's Peace Movement 'Silly and Base'?" *The Literary Digest* 50 (1 May 1915): 1022–23.

9. Addams, quoted in Paul Kellogg, editorial, *Survey* (15 Jan. 1916): 444, in series I, box 1, WILPF papers, Univ. of Colo.

10. National Peace Federation, "Points for an Address," vi of twelve-page untitled program of action, n.d. [probably late Oct. 1915], series III, box 31, WILPF papers, Univ. of Colo.

11. Arthur S. Link, "Wilson and the Struggle for Neutrality," in *The Impact of World War I*, ed. Arthur S. Link (New York: Harper and Row, 1969), 19.

12. WPP to Woodrow Wilson, 30 Oct. 1915, WILPF papers, Univ. of Colo., series I, box 6.

13. Lucia Ames Mead to Chrystal Macmillan, 7 Feb. 1916, WILPF papers, Univ. of Colo., series I, box 6.

14. Jane Addams to Woodrow Wilson, 3 Feb. 1917, WILPF papers, Univ. of Colo., series I, box 6.

15. WPP to Woodrow Wilson, 5 Feb. 1917, WILPF papers, Univ. of Colo., series I, box 6.

16. WPP, "Statement of Principles Formulated by a Conference of Members of the Executive Board and Representatives of Affiliated and Local Branches of the Woman's Peace Party," 21 Feb. 1917, WILPF papers, Univ. of Colo., series I, box 6.

17. John Louis Lucaites and Lawrance M. Bernabo, *Great Speakers and Speeches*, 2nd ed. (Dubuque: Kendall/Hunt, 1989, 1992), 187.

3. Struggle to Survive

1. DeBenedetti, *Peace Reform*, 102.

2. Allen F. Davis, *American Heroine: The Life and Legend of Jane Addams* (New York: Oxford Univ. Press, 1973), 245.

3. Pauline Angell, "Origins of *Four Lights*," WILPF papers, SCPC, series A2, box 3.

4. Addams, *Peace and Bread*, 127–28. As David Kennedy so succinctly put it in his work dealing with the "home front" during World War I, "Xenophobia was not new in America in 1917, but the war opened a wider field for its excesses." David Kennedy, *Over Here: The First World War and American Society* (New York: Oxford Univ. Press, 1980), 24.

5. Degen, *Woman's Peace Party*, 204–5.

6. Addams, *Peace and Bread*, 140.

7. Mercedes M. Randall, *Improper Bostonian: Emily Greene Balch* (New York: Twayne, 1964), 243; *Beyond Nationalism*, 80.

8. Addams, *Peace and Bread*, 151.

9. Ibid., 140.

10. Davis, *American Heroine*, 250.

11. WPP, "Annual Meeting: Report of the Secretary of the Woman's Peace Party, Philadelphia, Pennsylvania, December 6, 1917," WILPF papers, Univ. of Colo., series III, box 31, 2–3.

12. "Statement Adopted by the Executive Board, Woman's Peace Party, Section for the United States of the International Committee for Permanent Peace," n.d. [Jan. 1918], WILPF papers, Univ. of Colo., series III, box 31.

13. Lucia Ames Mead to State Chairman, n.d. [May 1919], WILPF papers, Univ. of Colo., series III, box 31.

14. Davis, *American Heroine*, 257.

15. International Congress of Women, Resolutions, 1, WILPF papers, Univ. of Colo., series I, box 13; Lucia Ames Mead to State Chairman, n.d. [May 1919], WILPF papers, Univ. of Colo., series III, box 31. Addams, *Peace and Bread*, 158–59.

16. International Congress of Women, Resolutions, WILPF papers, Univ. of Colo., series I, box 13, 1–2.

17. Ibid., 2–3. Louis Gannett to Jane Addams, 20 May 1919 and Louis Gannett to Emily Greene Balch, 1 June 1919, WILPF papers, Univ. of Colo., series II, box 1; Lucia

Ames Mead to State Chairman, n.d. [May 1919], WILPF papers, Univ. of Colo., series III, box 31; Degen, *Woman's Peace Party,* 228.

18. Jane Addams, opening address, International Congress of Women, Zurich, Switz., May 1919, WILPF papers, Univ. of Colo., series I, box 13, 3.

19. International Congress of Women, Resolutions, WILPF papers, Univ. of Colo., series I, box 13, 1–2; Lucia Ames Mead to State Chairman, n.d. [May 1919], WILPF papers, Univ. of Colo., series III, box 31.

20. "Copy of Report of Miss Jane Addams and Dr. Hamilton's Visit Into Germany," n.d. [Summer 1919], WILPF papers, Univ. of Colo., series I, box 6; WILPF News Sheet 4, 17 Sept. 1919, and News Sheet 5, 17 Nov. 1919, WILPF papers, Univ. of Colo., series V, box 2; "Malnutrition of Children in Germany," *Pax International* (17 Sept. 1919): 3, WILPF papers, Univ. of Colo., series V, box 3; Aletta Jacobs to Emily Greene Balch and Cor Ramondt-Hirschmann, 6 Aug. 1919, WILPF papers, Univ. of Colo., series II, box 1; Addams, *Peace and Bread,* 167–72.

21. Kennedy, *Over Here,* 234.

22. Oswald Garrison Villard to Emily Greene Balch, 4 Nov. 1919, WILPF papers, Univ. of Colo., 1–2, series III, box 31.

23. Jane Addams to Emily Greene Balch, 27 Nov. 1919, WILPF papers, Univ. of Colo., 1–2, series III, box 31.

24. Degen, *Woman's Peace Party,* 156, 206; Addams, *Peace and Bread,* 20.

25. Anna Garlin Spencer to Emily Greene Balch, n.d. [Summer 1919] and Anna Edinger to Emily Greene Balch, 28 June 1919, WILPF papers, Univ. of Colo., series III, box 31.

26. Emily Greene Balch to Anna Garlin Spencer, 31 Dec. 1919, WILPF papers, Univ. of Colo., series III, box 31.

4. Pacifism and Patriotism

1. Addams to Anna Garlin Spencer, 2 Dec. 1919, 1 and Anna Garlin Spencer to Jane Addams, 23 Feb. 1920, WILPF papers, SCPC, series C1, box 1, 3.

2. Gertrude Borchard, Clara S. Laddey, Alice B. Greene to "Members of the Women's International League," 5 May 1919, WILPF papers, Univ. of Colo., series III, box 31.

3. Mrs. Henry Villard, "A Real Peace Society," 21 Sept. 1914, Women's Peace Society papers, Swarthmore College Peace Collection 1, box 1, Swarthmore, Penn. (hereafter cited as WPS papers, SCPC).

4. Fanny Garrison Villard, Elinor Byrns, Katherine Devereaux Blake, Mary Ware Dennett, Lucy Watson, Rose Hicks, Edna Kearns, Caroline Lexow Babcock, Gratia Gollar to Dear Member [of New York state branch of the WILPF], 12 Sept. 1919, WPS papers, SCPC, box 1.

5. Statement and Pledge of the WPS, 1920–21, WPS papers, SCPC, box 1.

6. Ibid. In a letter to WPS members, Villard and Byrns noted that they had organized the WPS "not because of any friction with the Women's International League, but merely because the American Section of the League has not endorsed the principle of non-resistance." Fanny Garrison Villard and Elinor Byrns to "Dear Member" of the WPS, 30 June 1920, WPS papers, SCPC, box 1.

7. WILPF, U.S. Section, "Constitution (as revised at Annual Meeting, 1919)," WILPF Papers, SCPC, series A1, box 1.

8. Fanny Garrison Villard et al. to Dear Member [of the New York state branch of the WILPF], 12 Sept. 1919, WPS Papers, SCPC, box 1.

9. Elinor Byrns[?] to Miss White, 7 Dec. 1920, WPS Papers, SCPC, 1, box 1.

10. Mable Hyde Kittredge to Jane Addams, 31 Oct. 1920, WILPF Papers, SCPC, 2, series C1, box 1.

11. Anna Garlin Spencer to Jane Addams, 23 Feb. 1919, WILPF Papers, Univ. of Colo., series III, box 31.

12. Emily Greene Balch to Jane Addams, 4 Sept. 1919, WILPF Papers, Univ. of Colo., series III, box 31.

13. Emily Greene Balch to Florence Guertin Tuttle, 17 Dec. 1919, WILPF Papers, Univ. of Colo., series III, box 31.

14. Emily Greene Balch to Fanny Garrison Villard, 1 Apr. 1920, WILPF Papers, Univ. of Colo., 2, series III, box 31.

15. Emily Greene Balch to Anna Garlin Spencer, 31 Dec. 1919 and 1 Apr. 1920, WILPF Papers, Univ. of Colo., series III, box 31.

16. Anna Garlin Spencer, "To the Members of the Section for the U.S.A. of the W.I.L.P.F.," 15 Mar. 1920, WILPF Papers, Univ. of Colo., series III, box 31.

17. Ellen Winsor to Elinor Byrns, Apr. 1921, WPS Papers, SCPC, 1-2, box 1.

18. Elinor Byrns to Miss [Mary] Abbott, 11 Apr. 1921, WPS Papers, SCPC, 1-2, box 1.

19. Ibid., 1.

20. Elinor Byrns to Fanny Garrison Villard, 14 Apr. 1921, WPS Papers, SCPC, 1, box 1.

21. Fanny Garrison Villard to Elinor Byrns, Sept. 1920, WPS Papers, SCPC, 1, box 1.

22. Mabel Hyde Kittredge to Jane Addams, 24 Apr. 1921 and 27 Feb. 1921, WILPF Papers, SCPC, series C1, box 1.

23. WPS, "Report of the Business Committee of the Women's Peace Society, January 1–June 1, 1921," 2, June 1921, WPS Papers, SCPC, box 1; Elinor Byrns, "The Women's Peace Union," n.d., Women's Peace Union Papers, Swarthmore College Peace Collection, 1, reel 88.1, Swarthmore, Penn. (hereafter cited as WPU Papers, SCPC).

24. Elinor Byrns, "The Women's Peace Union," n.d., WPU Papers, SCPC, 1, reel 88.1.

25. Joan M. Jensen, "All Pink Sisters: The War Department and the Feminist Movement in the 1920s," in *Decades of Discontent: The Women's Movement, 1920–1940*, ed. Lois Scharf and Joan M. Jensen (Westport, Conn.: Greenwood Press, 1983), 209.

26. Ibid., 209.

27. Ibid., 210.

28. Lucia Ames Mead to John Weeks, 13 Nov. 1922, WILPF Papers, Univ. of Colo., 1-2, series III, box 31.

29. Jensen, "All Pink Sisters," 211. Lucia Ames Mead to John Weeks, 12 Apr. 1923; Dwight F. Davis (acting secretary of war) to Lucia Ames Mead, 1 May 1923, WILPF Papers, SCPC, series C1, box 1.

30. Jensen, "All Pink Sisters," 212.

31. Francis Ralston Welsh to Mrs. John L.C. Harvey, 24 Mar. 1924 and 31 Mar. 1924, WILPF Papers, SCPC, 1-3, series C1, box 1; Francis Ralston Welsh to Emily Greene Balch, 21 Nov. 1924, WILPF Papers, SCPC, 1-3, series C1, box 1.

32. Amy Woods to Eva Perry Moore, 24 Apr. 1924, WILPF Papers, SCPC, 1, series C1, box 3.

33. Maud Wood Park to John Weeks, 2 Apr. 1924, WILPF Papers, SCPC, series C1, box 1.

34. Amy Woods to Eva Perry Moore, 24 Apr. 1924, WILPF Papers, SCPC, 2, series

C1, box 3; Emily Greene Balch to Roger Baldwin, 19 May 1924; Emily Greene Balch to Anna Garlin Spencer, 20 May 1924; Emily Greene Balch to Susan L. Knapp (secretary, Women's Overseas Service League), 23 Oct. 1924, WILPF Papers, SCPC, 1–2, series C1, box 1; George L. Darte (adjutant-general, Military Order of the World War) to Elim A. E. Palmquist, 30 July 1924; DAR to Jane Addams, July 1924, WILPF Papers, SCPC, series C1, box 1.

35. Jane Addams to Fellow Member, 1 Mar. 1924, WILPF papers, SCPC, series E4, box 1.

36. Although Bussey and Tims, *Pioneers for Peace,* indicates that twenty-two countries sent delegates to the Congress, my sources show that twenty-five countries were represented: Holland, France, England, Belgium, Czechoslovakia, Bulgaria, Denmark, Germany, Hungary, Greece, Ireland, Austria, Italy, Norway, Poland, Sweden, Switzerland, Japan, the Ukraine, China, India, the Philippines, Canada, Mexico, and Uruguay.

37. Bussey and Tims, *Pioneers for Peace,* 45–46.

38. Roger Baldwin to Amy Woods, 30 Apr. 1924, WILPF Papers, SCPC, series C1, box 4.

39. Martha Trimble to Emily Kneubuhl, 22 Apr. 1924, 1–2 and Martha Trimble to Alma Sickler, 7 May 1924, WILPF papers, SCPC, series C1, box 4.

40. Martha Trimble to Jane Addams, 23 and 24 Apr. 1924, WILPF papers, SCPC, series C1, box 1.

41. Martha Trimble to Alma Sickler, 7 May 1924, WILPF papers, SCPC, 1, series C1, box 4.

42. Martha Trimble to Louisa Knox, 20 May 1924, WILPF papers, SCPC, 2, series C1, box 4.

43. Martha Trimble to Louise Atkinson, 20 May 1924, WILPF papers, SCPC, 2, series C1, box 4.

44. Bussey and Tims, *Pioneers For Peace,* 48.

45. "Report on Chicago Summer School," May 1924, WILPF papers, Univ. of Colo., series I, box 23.

46. Carrie Chapman Catt to Jane Addams, 27 May 1924, WILPF papers, SCPC, 1, series C1, box 1.

47. Hannah Clothier Hull to Eva Perry Moore, 16 Dec. 1924, Hannah Clothier Hull papers, SCPC, box 6.

48. Hannah Clothier Hull to Eva Perry Moore, 19 Jan. 1925 and 16 Dec. 1924, Hannah Clothier Hull Papers, SCPC, box 6.

49. Carrie Chapman Catt to Hannah Clothier Hull, 30 Jan. 1925, Hannah Clothier Hull papers SCPC, 2, box 6.

50. Program of the Third, Ninth, and Fifteenth Conference on the Cause and Cure of War, 15–19 Jan. 1928, 16–19 Jan. 1934, 22–25 Jan. 1940, National Conference on the Cause and Cure of War papers, Swarthmore College Peace Collection, box 3, Swarthmore, Penn (hereafter cited as NCCCW papers, SCPC).

51. Quoted in Jensen, "All Pink Sisters," 212.

52. Ibid., 199.

53. Ibid., 217.

5. Challenging Economic Imperialism

1. DeBenedetti, *Peace Reform,* 109.

2. William Appleman Williams, *The Tragedy of American Diplomacy* (1959; reprint, New York: Dell, 1962), 115.

3. Ibid., 126, 127.

4. "Woman Objects to U.S as Bill Collector," *The San Francisco Call* [?], 27 July 1923, WILPF papers, SCPC, 32, series C1, box 1.

5. Madeleine Z. Doty, "Editorial," WILPF, Section for the United States, *Bulletin* No. 13, Mar. 1925, WILPF papers, SCPC, 2, series E2, box 1.

6. Hannah Clothier Hull to Members of the National Board and Chairmen (or Secretaries) of State and Local Branches, 1 Dec. 1924, WILPF papers, SCPC, series E4, box 1. The exact wording of Concurrent Resolution No. 22 as introduced into the first session of the 68th Congress is as follows:

> Resolved by the Senate of the United States (the House of Representatives concurring), that the President be and he is hereby requested to direct the Department of State, Treasury, and Commerce, the Federal Reserve Board, and all other agencies of the Government which are or may be concerned thereunder, to refrain henceforth, without specific prior authorization of the Congress, from
>
> 1. directly or indirectly engaging in the responsibility of the Government of the United States, or otherwise on its behalf, to supervise the fulfillment of financial arrangements between citizens of the United States and sovereign foreign governments or political subdivisions thereof, whether or not recognized *de jure* or *de facto* by the United States Government or
>
> 2. in any manner whatsoever giving official recognition to any arrangement which may commit the Government of the United States to any form of military intervention in order to compel the observance of alleged obligations of sovereign or subordinate authority, or of any corporations or individuals, or to deal with any such arrangement except to secure the settlement of claims of the United States or of United States citizens through the ordinary channels of law provided therefor in the respective foreign jurisdictions, or through duly authorized and accepted arbitration agencies.

68th Congress, 1st session, S. Con. Res. In the Senate of the United States 1924, WILPF papers, SCPC, series E4, box 1.

7. "The Resolutions," 1915 International Congress of Women, WILPF papers, Univ. of Colo., series I, box 13.

8. Amy Woods to Zonia Baber, 13 Nov. 1924, WILPF papers, SCPC, 3, series C1, box 2. For an expression of this same sentiment by the NCCCW, see "Findings of the Conference on the Cause and Cure of War," *The Jewish Woman*, Mar. 1925, NCCCW papers, SCPC, 14–16, box 1 (95a).

9. Press release from the Publicity Department of the WILPF, 1 Dec. 1924, WILPF papers, SCPC, series E4, box 1.

10. As Scott Nearing and Joseph Freeman pointed out at the time, the fact that the Dawes plan did not specify the number of years Germany would be expected to make reparations payments amounted to "the most complete modern system of exploitation ever devised and applied in the relations between great powers" for, they concluded (not unreasonably in 1925), that "Germany will pay until the Reparations Commission decides that she has paid enough." Furthermore, the "outsiders" who were to control German financial policy were the seven members of a fourteen-member General Board that would exercise that control over a new bank established by the Dawes Plan "entirely free from Government control or interference." Thus, they noted, "the ultimate financial policy of Germany is directed by foreigners, and the central financial system of the Ger-

man Empire is a private and alien institution." See Scott Nearing and Joseph Freeman, *Dollar Diplomacy: A Study in American Imperialism* (New York: B. W. Huebsch and Viking Press, 1925), 299–31.

11. Williams, *Tragedy of American Diplomacy*, 149.

12. Quoted in "Congressional Hearing on W.I.L. Resolution," WILPF, Section for the United States, *Bulletin* 13 (Mar. 1925): 5; and WILPF, Section for the United States, "Should the Government Put Pressure on Foreign Countries on Behalf of Financial Claims of Private Citizens[?]," *The Pax Special*, 1, No. 3 (Oct.–Nov. 1925): 4, WILPF Papers, SCPC, series E2, box 1.

13. Quoted in WILPF, "Economic Imperialism," News of the United States Section, *Pax International*, June 1926, WILPF Papers, SCPC, series E2, box 1.

14. Ethan Ellis, *Republican Foreign Policy, 1921–1933* (New Brunswick, N.J.: Rutgers Univ. Press, 1968), 243.

15. WILPF, News of the United States Section, *Pax International*, Dec. 1926, WILPF Papers, SCPC, series E2, box 1.

16. Dorothy Detzer to Frank B. Kellogg, n.d., included in "Report of the Executive Secretary," Minutes, Exec, Comm. Mtg., 14 Dec. 1926, WILPF Papers, Univ. of Colo., 1, series III, box 31.

17. WILPF, News of the United States Section, *Pax International*, Vol. 2, No. 3 (Jan. 1927), WILPF Papers, SCPC, series E2, box 1.

18. Williams, *Tragedy of American Diplomacy*, 126.

19. Ellis, *Republican Foreign Policy*, 243.

20. Dorothy Detzer to Madeleine Z. Doty, 23 Dec. 1926, WILPF Papers, Univ. of Colo., 2, series III, box 31.

21. Jane Addams, "Impressions of Mexico," WILPF, U.S. Section, *Bulletin* No. 14, Apr.–May 1925, WILPF Papers, SCPC, series E2, box 1.

22. Dorothy Detzer to Madeleine Z. Doty, 23 Dec. 1926, WILPF Papers, Univ. of Colo., 2, series III, box 31.

23. Ellis, *Republican Foreign Policy*, 256.

24. Untitled three-page report on "Peace with Latin America" conference, 16 Jan. 1927, WILPF Papers, Univ. of Colo., 1, series III, box 31.

25. Ibid., 1–2.

26. Ferdinand Lundberg, *America's Sixty Families* (1937; reprint, New York: Halcyon House, 1939), 153.

27. Dorothy Detzer to Branches, 18 Jan. 1927, WILPF Papers, SCPC, series E4, box 1.

28. Dorothy Detzer, "Report of the Executive Secretary," Jan. 1927, WILPF Papers, SCPC, 2, series A2, box 1.

29. Ellis, *Republican Foreign Policy*, 244.

30. U.S. Section, WILPF, Minutes, National Board Mtg., 5–6 March 1927, WILPF Papers, SCPC, 4, series A2, box 1.

31. Ibid.

32. Dorothy Detzer to Emily Greene Balch, 17 Mar. 1927, WILPF Papers, SCPC, series C1, box 1.

33. DeBenedetti, *Peace Reform*, 118.

34. Ellis, *Republican Foreign Policy*, 257.

35. Elting E. Morison, *Turmoil and Tradition: A Study of the Life and Times of Henry L. Stimson* (New York: Atheneum, 1966), 225.

36. Ibid.

37. Dorothy Detzer to Calvin Coolidge, 21 July 1927, WILPF Papers, SCPC, series C7, box 8.

38. Ellis, *Republican Foreign Policy,* 245–46.

39. Ibid., 249–50.

40. Emily Greene Balch, "Proposal as to Policy, by the Director of Policies, Cleveland, 1927," Minutes, Annual Mtg., 29 Apr.–2 May 1927, WILPF Papers, SCPC, series A2, box 1.

41. Ibid. Dorothy Detzer, "Report of the Executive Secretary," May 1927, WILPF Papers, SCPC, 1, series A2, box 1.

6. Cruisers for "Crime"

1. According to Charles Chatfield, the Harmony Plan

would . . . [link] the basic ideas of outlawry with the entrance of the United States into the existing World Court. . . . It urged the United States to enter the Permanent Court of International Justice immediately . . . with the understanding that the nations of Europe should call an international conference to negotiate a general treaty outlawing war as a crime under the law of nations. Were no conference called in two years the United States might withdraw its adherence to the World Court; should no conference be called in five years the American government would be obligated to withdraw. The international conference should outlaw war and also create a code of international law based upon equality and justice between all nations. The plan did not challenge the right of national self-defense, and its signatories represented their personal, not organizations, view.

See Charles Chatfield, *For Peace and Justice: Pacifism in America 1914–1941* (Knoxville: Univ. of Tennessee Press, 1971) 104.

2. U.S. Section, WILPF, Minutes, National Board Mtg., 16–17 Sept. 1925, WILPF Papers, SCPC, 6–7, series A2, box 1.

3. Dorothy Detzer, Annual Report, 1925–1926, WILPF Papers, SCPC, series A2, box 1.

4. Ibid.

5. Emily Greene Balch, "Proposal as to Policy by the Director of Policies, Cleveland, 1927," 1, Minutes, Annual Mtg., 29 Apr.–1 May 1927, WILPF Papers, SCPC, series A2, box 1. According to Detzer, the WILPF was not the only peace organization to respond with enthusiasm to Briand's proposal: "every organization from Mrs. Catt's conservative groups [NCCCW] to the left wing have welcomed it." See Dorothy Detzer to Madeleine Z. Doty, 6 May 1927, WILPF Papers, Univ. of Colo., 2, series II, box 6.

6. Dorothy Detzer, "Report of the Executive Secretary," July 1927, WILPF Papers, SCPC, 1–2, series A2, box 1.

7. U.S. Section, WILPF, Minutes, National Board Mtg., 28 and 29 Nov. 1927, WILPF Papers, SCPC, series A2, box 1.

8. Robert James Maddox, *William E. Borah and American Foreign Policy* (Baton Rouge: Louisiana State Univ. Press, 1969), 178.

9. Dorothy Detzer, "News of the United States Section," *Pax International* (Apr. 1928), WILPF Papers, SCPC, series E2, box 1.

10. Dorothy Detzer to Vilma Glucklich, 29 May 1925, WILPF Papers, SCPC, 1–2, series C1, box 5.

11. U.S. Section, WILPF, Minutes, National Board Mtg., 28 and 29 Nov. 1927, WILPF Papers, SCPC, 10, series A2, box 1.

12. Dorothy Detzer to "Dear Friend," 1 Feb. 1928, WILPF Papers, Univ. of Colo., series IV, box 9.

13. "Pacifists Assailed at Naval Hearing," *Baltimore Sun* [?], 17 Feb. 1928, WILPF Papers, Univ. of Colo., series IV, box 9.

14. Dorothy Detzer, "Not For Publication" [re: Naval Affairs Committee hearings], n.d. [Feb. 1928], WILPF Papers, SCPC, series E4, box 1.

15. Dorothy Detzer, "News of the United States Section," *Pax International* (Mar. 1928), WILPF Papers, SCPC, series E2, box 1.

16. Dorothy Detzer to Emily Greene Balch, 23 Apr. 1928, WILPF Papers, SCPC, 1, series C1, box 5.

17. U.S. Section, WILPF, Minutes, Annual Mtg., 3–5 May 1928, WILPF Papers, Univ. of Colo., 9, 12, series III, box 32.

18. Dorothy Detzer to Branches, 31 May 1928, WILPF Papers, SCPC, series E4, box 1.

19. Ellis, *Republican Foreign Policy,* 226.

20. Charles DeBenedetti, "Borah and the Kellogg-Briand Pact," *Pacific Northwest Quarterly,* 63 (Jan. 1972): 22.

21. Dorothy Detzer to Emily Greene Balch, 23 June 1928, WILPF Papers, SCPC, 1, series C1, box 5.

22. Dorothy Detzer, "News of the United States Section," *Pax International* (Aug. 1928), WILPF Papers, SCPC, series E2, box 1.

23. Eleanor S. Patterson, "News of the United States Section," *Pax International* (June 1928), WILPF Papers, SCPC, series E2, box 1.

24. Mary Sheepshanks, "The Kellogg Peace Pact and After," *Pax International* (Aug. 1928), WILPF Papers, Univ. of Colo., series V, box 3.

25. Dorothy Detzer quoting Borchard in "News of the United States Section," *Pax International* (Sept. 1928), WILPF Papers, SCPC, series E2, box 1. In response to an inquiry from the WPU regarding the loopholes in the Pact, Roger Baldwin of the ACLU noted shortly after it was ratified that he did not take it "seriously" because "it legalizes all wars of self-defense and it leaves to each nation the right to interpret self-defense. That," he concluded, "will cover practically any war, past or future." See Roger Baldwin to Mary B. Orr, 2 Feb. 1929, WPU Papers, SCPC, reel 88.2.

26. U.S. Section, WILPF, Minutes, National Board Mtg., 14–15 Oct. 1928, WILPF Papers, SCPC, 5, series A2, box 2.

27. Dorothy Detzer, "News of the United States Section," *Pax International* (Sept. 1928), WILPF Papers, SCPC, series E2, box 1.

28. Selig Adler, *The Uncertain Giant 1921–1941: American Foreign Policy Between the Wars* (New York: Macmillan, 1965), 91.

29. Dorothy Detzer, "News of the United States Section," *Pax International* (Sept. 1928), WILPF Papers, SCPC, series E2, box 1.

30. Dorothy Detzer, "Report of the Executive Secretary," Oct.–Nov. 1928, WILPF Papers, Univ. of Colo., 1, series III, box 32; Dorothy Detzer to Branches, 31 Oct. 1928, WILPF Papers, SCPC, 1, series E4, box 1.

31. Emily Greene Balch to Senate Foreign Relations Committee, n.d. [Dec. 1928], WILPF Papers, SCPC, 1–2, series C1, box 5.

32. Dorothy Detzer, "News of the United States Section," *Pax International* (Dec. 1928), WILPF Papers, SCPC, series E2, box 1.

33. Ellis, *Republican Foreign Policy*, 227.

34. Roger Baldwin to Mary B. Orr, 2 Feb. 1929, WPU Papers, SCPC, reel 88.2.

35. "How to Make the Kellogg Pact a Reality, Proposed Programme, W.I.L.P.F. Congress 1929," Aug. 1929, WILPF Papers, Univ. of Colo., series III, box 32.

7. Disarmament Hopes Dashed

1. Ellis, *Republican Foreign Policy*, 164. Shearer was hired by three U.S. companies, Bethlehem Steel, Newport News Shipbuilding, and the New York Shipbuilding Company. According to Shearer, he was to go to Geneva in 1927 "to see that the United States should 'get out their side of the story' at the conference, to obtain a treaty of parity, if possible, but failing that, no treaty at all. The consideration was $25,000 a year." See H. C. Englebrecht and F. C. Hanighen, *Merchants of Death: A Study of the International Armament Industry* (New York: Dodd, Mead, 1934), 207.

2. Dorothy Detzer to Branches, 3 Oct. 1929, WILPF Papers, SCPC, 1–2, series E4, box 1; George Seldes, *Iron, Blood, and Profits: An Exposure of the World-Wide Munitions Racket* (New York: Harper and Brothers, 1934), 158; Engelbrecht and Hanighen, *Merchants of Death*, 212–17.

3. Seldes, *Iron, Blood, and Profits*, 159.

4. Dorothy Detzer, *Appointment on the Hill* (New York: Henry Holt, 1948), 89.

5. Dorothy Detzer to Mary Sheepshanks and A. R. Burrows, 18 Feb. 1930, WILPF Papers, Univ. of Colo., series IV, box 2.

6. Mary Sheepshanks, "Women's Deputations to the Naval Conference," *Pax International* 5 (Feb. 1930), WILPF Papers, Univ. of Colo., series V, box 3.

7. Madeleine Z. Doty to Mary Sheepshanks, 13 Feb. 1930, WILPF Papers, Univ. of Colo., series IV, box 2.

8. Detzer, *Appointment on the Hill*, 89–90.

9. Ibid., 90–91.

10. Ibid., 91–97.

11. Ibid., 97–99. There was a perfectly good reason why Hoover could not respond any more positively to Detzer's suggestions than with a feeble "I can't." As Charles Chatfield has so succinctly put it, "Indeed he could not, for two days earlier, on April 22, the United States had signed the treaty." Detzer, of course, was not made privy to this fact. See Chatfield, *For Peace and Justice*, 160.

12. Laura Puffer Morgan, "Memorandum," 31 Oct. 1930, WILPF Papers, Univ. of Colo., 1–2, series IV, box 2. In this memorandum Morgan recounted a conversation with Dr. Edouard Benes, Foreign Minister of Czechoslovakia, in which he expressed satisfaction with the outcome of the conference as quoted.

13. WPU, "Mrs. Tone's Report of the Meeting of the Pacifist Action Committee on Friday April 25, 1930," WPU Papers, SCPC, 1, reel 88.1.

14. Dorothy Detzer, "Memorandum on the Findings of the War Policies Commission and the Statement of the Women's International League for Peace and Freedom to the Commission," May 1931, WILPF Papers, SCPC, 1, series A2, box 2.

15. Arthur A. Ekirch, Jr., "Introduction," in *Death and Profits: A Study of the War Policies Commission*, ed. Seymour Waldman (1932, New York: Warren reprint, New York: Garland, 1971), 3; Dorothy Detzer, "Resumé of History and Campaign of Women's International League in Munitions Investigation," n.d. [probably Mar. 1934], WILPF Papers, SCPC, 1, series A2, box 1.

16. Waldman, *Death and Profits*, 100.

17. Ekirch, "Introduction," 3.

18. Dorothy Detzer to Emily Greene Balch, 26 May 1931, WILPF Papers, SCPC, 1–2, series C1, box 6.

19. Waldman, *Death and Profits*, 103.

20. Dorothy Detzer to Emily Greene Balch, 26 May 1931, WILPF Papers, SCPC, 2, series C1, box 6. That the representatives from the peace groups were deliberately not "cross-questioned" was, in Detzer's words, "carefully stricken from the record" when the WPC published the hearings in fall 1931. See Dorothy Detzer, "Report of the Executive Secretary," June–Oct. 1931, WILPF Papers, SCPC, 1, series A2, box 2.

21. Dorothy Detzer, "Memorandum on the Findings of the War Policies Commission. . . ," May 1931, WILPF Papers, SCPC, 1–3, series A2, box 2.

22. Waldman, *Death and Profits*, 120.

23. Ibid., 21.

24. Dorothy Cook, "At the Wheel," *Pax International* (Sept. 1931), WILPF Papers, SCPC, series E2, box 1.

25. Ibid.

26. U.S. Section, WILPF, press release, 10 Oct. 1931, WILPF, SCPC, series A4, box 4.

27. Ibid.

28. D. Detzer, *Appointment on the Hill*, 104.

29. Dorothy Detzer to Emily Greene Balch, 18 Dec. 1931, WILPF Papers, SCPC, 1, series C1, box 6.

30. Carrie Chapman Catt to Hannah Clothier Hull, 25 Nov. 1931, Hannah Clothier Hull Papers, SCPC, 2, box 6.

31. Dorothy Detzer to Carrie Chapman Catt, 28 Nov. 1931, Hannah Clothier Hull Papers, SCPC, 1, box 6.

32. Detzer, *Appointment on the Hill*, 105.

33. The foregoing discussion of the meeting between Detzer and Rogers is taken from *Appointment on the Hill*, 106–8, and from Detzer's letter to Balch, 28 Dec. 1931, WILPF Papers, SCPC, series C1, box 9. Emphasis in original.

34. U.S. Section, WILPF, press release, 11 Jan. 1932, WILPF Papers, SCPC, series A4, box 4.

35. "Resolution Adopted at Mass Meeting Called by Women's International League, Belasco Theater, January 10, 1932," WILPF Papers, SCPC, series A4, box 4.

36. Henry R. Winkler, "Arthur Henderson," in *The Diplomats*, Vol. 2, *The Thirties*, ed. Gordon C. Craig and Felix Gilbert (New York: Atheneum, 1971), 341.

37. Detzer, *Appointment on the Hill*, 110.

38. Ibid. Amy Woods to Fellow Workers for World Disarmament, 30 Apr. 1932, WILPF Papers, SCPC, 2, series A4, box 4.

39. Detzer, *Appointment on the Hill*, 111.

40. Ibid., 112. Emphasis in original. Amy Woods, WILPF representative for the United States at the conference, made a telling observation about Claude Swanson of the U.S. delegation when she wrote home that the senator and soon-to-be secretary of the Navy in the Roosevelt administration "eulogized our American war ships as 'more precious than rubies'." Amy Woods, "On Coming World Disarmament," n.d. [early 1933], WILPF Papers, Univ. of Colo., 8, series IV, box 2.

41. Dorothy Detzer to Emily Greene Balch and Hannah Clothier Hull, 15 Nov. 1932, WILPF Papers, SCPC, 1, series C7, box 8.

42. Dorothy Detzer to Camille Drevet, 14 Nov. 1932 WILPF Papers, Univ. of Colo., series III, box 32; Lola Maverick Lloyd, "Another Way," Autumn 1932, WILPF Papers, Univ. of Colo., Boulder, series III, box 32.

43. Amy Woods to Hannah Clothier Hull, 30 Nov. 1932, Hannah Clothier Hull Papers, SCPC, 2, box 2. Amy Woods, "Copy of my Recommendation to the National Board Meeting Today in Washington," 10 Dec. 1932, WILPF Papers, Univ. of Colo., series III, box 32.

44. Jane Addams quoted in Amy Woods, "Letter From the United States," 11 July 1932, WILPF Papers, Univ. of Colo., 2, series III, box 32.

45. U.S. Section, WILPF, "Traffic in Arms," *The Pax Special* 1 (June 1925), WILPF Papers, SCPC, series E2, box 1,

46. Detzer, *Appointment on the Hill,* 152.

8. Tensions of Transition

1. Dorothy Detzer, "Report of Executive Secretary," May 1926, WILPF Papers, SCPC, 2, series A2, box 1.

2. Dorothy Detzer to Emily Greene Balch, 28 Mar. 1927, WILPF Papers, SCPC, 1, series C1, box 5.

3. Dwight F. Davis to Hannah Clothier Hull, 17 May 1926, Hannah Clothier Hull Papers, SCPC, box 6.

4. Frederick J. Libby to Dwight F. Davis, 29 May 1926, Hannah Clothier Hull Papers, SCPC, 1–2, box 6.

5. "League for 'Peace and Freedom' Opposed;" "National Defense Number;" "Resolutions," *Monahan Post News,* Apr. 1926, WILPF Papers, Univ. of Colo., series III, box 31.

6. Dorothy Detzer to Forest Bailey, 24 Nov. 1926, WILPF Papers, SCPC, 1, series C1, box 5.

7. Dorothy Detzer to Jane Addams, 22 Nov. 1926, WILPF Papers, SCPC, 2, series C1, box 4.

8. Dorothy Detzer to Madeleine Z. Doty, 24 Nov. 1926, WILPF Papers, Univ. of Colo., 2, series III, box 31.

9. Dorothy Detzer, "Report of Executive Secretary," May 1926, WILPF Papers, SCPC, 1, series A2, box 1.

10. Emily Greene Balch, "Women's International League for Peace and Freedom—Some Things That It Is and . . . Is Not," n.d. [summer 1926], Hannah Clothier Hull Papers, SCPC, 2–3, box 6.

11. Dorothy Detzer, "Report of Executive Secretary," Oct. 1926, WILPF Papers, SCPC, series A2, box 1.

12. Carrie Chapman Catt, "An Open Letter to the D.A.R.," reprinted by the WILPF from *The Woman Citizen,* July 1927, WILPF Papers, SCPC, 1, series C1, box 5.

13. The following discussion of the DAR's "red-baiting" activities is taken primarily from Catt's "Open Letter." Emphasis in original.

14. DAR, "Doubtful Speakers (Women)," n.d., WILPF Papers, SCPC, 1–2, series C1, box 5.

15. Eleanor S. Patterson to Hannah Clothier Hull and Lucy Biddle Lewis, 16 Mar. 1928, Hannah Clothier Hull Papers, SCPC, box 2.

16. Eleanor S. Patterson (Mrs. J.A. St. Omer Roy), "Remarks Made by Mrs. George Thatcher Guernsey . . . ," 17 Apr. 1928, WILPF Papers, SCPC, 1–2, series C1, box 5.

17. Emily Greene Balch to Valeria Parker, 9 May 1929, WILPF Papers, SCPC, series C1, box 6.

18. Otis J. Baughn to Mary B. Orr, 9 Feb. 1929, WPU Papers, SCPC, reel 88.2.

19. Madeleine Z. Doty, "The Attack on the W.I.L.," *Pax International* 4, no. 4 (Feb. 1929):2, WILPF Papers, Univ. of Colo., series V, box 3.

20. For the connection between the Allies Inn, the American Legion, and the U.S. Army, see p. 115. of this chapter.

21. Detzer, *Appointment on the Hill,* 67.

22. Dorothy Detzer to Henry L. Stimson, 3 July 1929, WILPF Papers, SCPC, series A2, box 2.

23. Lucy Biddle Lewis to Jane Addams, 30 Sept. 1922, WILPF Papers, SCPC, 1, series C1, box 1. Hannah Clothier Hull to Amy Woods, 22 Nov. 1924, Hannah Clothier Hull Papers, SCPC, box 1.

24. Emily Greene Balch to Branches, 29 Oct. 1924, WILPF Papers, SCPC, 1, series E4, box 1.

25. Dorothy Detzer, "Chapter II Corrections and/or Suggestions" [from letter to Rosemary Rainbolt, n.d., probably 1976], WILPF Papers, SCPC, 1, 3, series A2, box 3; John Woolfenden, "Service With Quakers in Russia Led to a Lifetime Devoted to Peace," *Sunday Peninsula Herald Weekend Magazine* [Carmel, CA], 16 Mar. 1977, WILPF Papers, SCPC, 3, series A2, box 3.

26. Madeleine Z. Doty to Hannah Clothier Hull, 5 Jan. 1925, Hannah Clothier Hull Papers, SCPC, box 1.

27. Hannah Clothier Hull to Jane Addams, et.al., 6 May 1925, Hannah Clothier Hull Papers, SCPC, box 1.

28. Frederick B. Tolles, "Partners For Peace. William I. Hull and Hannah Clothier Hull," untitled journal, n.d., Hannah Clothier Hull Papers, SCPC, box 8.

29. Karl Detzer, *Myself When Young* (New York: Funk and Wagnalls, 1968), 201.

30. "Statement of Mrs. Helen O. Weed . . . ," n.d. [1924?], WILPF Papers, SCPC, series C1, box 5.

31. U.S. Section, WILPF, Minutes, Board Mtg., 15 June 1928, WILPF Papers, Univ. of Colo., 3, series III, box 32. One indication of Thomas's attitude toward Detzer—and vice versa—can be found in a letter written by Detzer in which she says of Thomas, "It was she who told Eleanor Brannan that she did not think I should be allowed to work in Congress any more as I was too young. Her idea is to have as decrepit an old party as possible to interview Senators." Dorothy Detzer to Bessie Kind, 23 Mar. 1928, WILPF Papers, SCPC, series C7, box 8.

32. Mary Louise Marriott, "Report of the Secretary to Miss Detzer," 10 Sept.–10 Oct. 1928, WILPF Papers, Univ. of Colo., series III, box 32.

33. Eleanor S. Patterson, "Report of the Office Secretary," Oct.–Nov. 1928, WILPF Papers, Univ. of Colo., series III, box 32.

34. Dorothy Detzer, "Work to be Done by the National Office . . . ," 14–15 Oct. 1928, WILPF Papers, SCPC, 1–2, series A2, box 2. Emphasis added.

35. Dorothy Detzer to Emily Greene Balch and Hannah Clothier Hull, 28 Jan. 1930, WILPF Papers, SCPC, series C1, box 6.

36. Katherine Devereaux Blake, "Report of the Committee on Personal Disarmament," 23 May 1930, WILPF Papers, Univ. of Colo., series III, box 32.

37. Dorothy Detzer to Hannah Clothier Hull, 7 Jan. 1933, Hannah Clothier Hull Papers, SCPC, 2, box 2.

38. Dorothy Detzer Denny to Dr. Barbara Solomon, 27 Jan. 1979, Dorothy Detzer Papers, SCPC, 2–3, series ACC81A-24, box 1.

39. "Varsity Swarthmoreans," *Garnet Letter,* Feb. 1943, People's Mandate to Governments Committee Papers (hereafter cited as People's Mandate Papers, SCPC), box 1.

40. According to Susan D. Becker, *The Origins of the Equal Rights Amendment: Ameri-*

can Feminism Between the Wars (Westport, Conn.: Greenwood Press, 1981), 90, it was a "minor disagreement" in 1930 among NWP leaders that "led Mabel Vernon and the headquarters staff to resign." Apparently the dispute was at heart a question of who was going to direct the organization, Alice Paul or Mabel Vernon. This controversy ought to be kept in mind as the story of Vernon's role in the WILPF unfolds here.

41. Katherine Devereaux Blake to Hannah Clothier Hull, 23 Aug. 1930, WILPF Papers, SCPC, 2, series C1, box 6.

42. Dorothy Detzer to Mildred Scott Olmsted, [Sept.?] 1930, WILPF Papers, SCPC, 1–2, series C7, box 8. Vernon was only ten years older than Detzer, but there is substantial evidence that the latter, appearing much younger than she really was, did not correct others in their assumption that the appearance was the reality.

43. Mildred Scott Olmsted to Emily Greene Balch, 17 Feb. 1932, WILPF Papers, SCPC, 2, series C1, box 6.

44. Dorothy Detzer to Mildred Scott Olmsted, [Fall?] 1931, 3, and 6 Nov. 1931, WILPF Papers, SCPC, series C7, box 8.

45. Mildred Scott Olmsted to Emily Greene Balch, 17 Feb. 1932, WILPF Papers, SCPC, 2, 3, series C1, box 6.

46. Ibid., 3.

47. Mildred Scott Olmsted to Emily Greene Balch, 11 Apr. 1932, WILPF Papers, SCPC, series C1, box 6.

48. Emily Greene Balch to Madeleine Z. Doty, n.d. [1926], WILPF Papers, Univ. of Colo., series III, box 31.

49. Dorothy Detzer to Emily Greene Balch, 19 Dec. 1929, WILPF Papers, SCPC, series C1, box 6.

50. Ibid., 2.

51. Hannah Clothier Hull, "To Those who attended the Board Meeting . . . ," 22 Jan. 1934, Hannah Clothier Hull Papers, SCPC, 1, box 2.

52. Lola Maverick Lloyd to Hannah Clothier Hull, 5 Feb. 1934, Hannah Clothier Hull Papers, SCPC, 1, box 2.

53. Hannah Clothier Hull, "To Those who attended the Board Meeting . . . ," 22 Jan. 1934, Hannah Clothier Hull Papers, SCPC, 1, box 2.

54. Lola Maverick Lloyd to Hannah Clothier Hull, 5 Feb. 1934, Hannah Clothier Hull Papers, SCPC, 1–2, box 2,

55. Dorothy Detzer, "Annual Report," from Minutes, Annual Meeting, 21–24 May 1930, WILPF Papers, SCPC, 3, series A2, box 2.

56. Ibid.

57. Dorothy Detzer to Emily Greene Balch, 15 Oct. 1934, WILPF Papers, Univ. of Colo., 1, series III, box 32.

58. Hannah Clothier Hull and Lucy Biddle Lewis to Dorothy Detzer, Mildred Scott Olmsted and Mabel Vernon, 29 Jan. 1935, WILPF Papers, SCPC, series C4, box 2.

59. Mildred Scott Olmsted to Emily Greene Balch, 13 May 1935, WILPF Papers, Univ. of Colo., series III, box 33.

60. Mildred Scott Olmsted to Emily Greene Balch, 7 Mar. 1935, WILPF Papers, Univ. of Colo., 1, series III, box 33.

61. Hannah Clothier Hull to Emily Greene Balch, 9 May 1935, Hannah Clothier Hull Papers, SCPC, 1, box 3.

62. Dorothy Detzer to Emily Greene Balch, 6 June 1935, WILPF Papers, Univ. of Colo. 1, series III, box 33.

63. Hannah Clothier Hull to Emily Greene Balch, 9 May 1935, Hannah Clothier Hull Papers, SCPC, 1, box 3. Mildred Scott Olmsted to Emily Greene Balch, 13 May 1935, WILPF Papers, Univ. of Colo., series III, box 33.

64. Dorothy Detzer, Br. Ltr. No. 16, 20 May 1935, WILPF Papers, SCPC, 2, series E4, box 1.

65. Petition, "Peoples Mandate to Governments," n.d., WILPF Papers, Univ. of Colo., series IV, box 10.

66. Lola Maverick Lloyd to Emily Greene Balch, 29 May 1935, WILPF Papers, Univ. of Colo., 1, series III, box 33.

67. Hannah Clothier Hull to Co-Worker in Peace, 12 Aug. 1935, People's Mandate Papers, SCPC, series B, box 10.

68. Hannah Clothier Hull to Co-Worker, 23 Oct. 1935, WILPF Papers, SCPC, series C1, box 19.

69. Hannah Clothier Hull to Gertrude Baer, 4 Nov. 1935, Hannah Clothier Hull Papers, SCPC, box 3.

70. Hannah Clothier Hull to Dorothy Detzer, 5 Nov. 1935, Hannah Clothier Hull Papers, SCPC, 1, box 3.

71. Hannah Clothier Hull to Mabel Vernon, 11 Nov. 1935, Hannah Clothier Hull Papers, SCPC, 1–2, box 3.

72. Hannah Clothier Hull to Mabel Vernon, 13 Nov. 1935, People's Mandate Papers, SCPC, series B, box 10.

73. U.S. Section, WILPF, untitled job descriptions for the three National Secretaries, n.d. [May 1934], Hannah Clothier Hull Papers, SCPC, box 3.

74. Mildred Scott Olmsted to Hannah Clothier Hull, 3 July 1935, Hannah Clothier Hull Papers, SCPC, 1, box 3.

75. Mildred Scott Olmsted to Helen Beardsley, 19 July 1935, WILPF Papers SCPC, series C1, box 33.

76. Mildred Scott Olmsted to Eleanor Eaton, 8 July 1936, WILPF Papers, SCPC, series C4, box 2.

77. Ibid., 2.

78. Ibid.

79. Anne Martin to Hannah Clothier Hull, 30 June 1936; Anne Martin to Board Member, 30 July 1936, in Amelia R. Fry, *Mabel Vernon: Speaker for Suffrage and Petitioner for Peace*, Suffragists Oral History Project, the Bancroft Library Regional Oral History Office (Berkeley: Univ. of California, 1976), 258–60.

80. See, for example, John K. Nelson, *The Peace Prophets: American Pacifist Thought, 1919–1941* (Chapel Hill: Univ. of North Carolina Press, 1967), 30; Merle Curti, *Peace or War: The American Struggle 1636–1936* (New York: W. W. Norton, 1936), 241, 271; Robert Edwin Bowers, "The American Peace Movement 1933–1941" (unpublished Ph.D. diss., Univ. of Wisconsin, 1947), 20; Charles Chatfield, *For Peace and Justice*, 256–86; Robert A. Divine, *The Illusion of Neutrality: Franklin D. Roosevelt and the Struggle Over the Arms Embargo* (Chicago: Quadrangle Books, 1962), 27–29, 36–37, 63–66.

81. Hannah Clothier Hull to Mabel Vernon, 22 July 1936, Hannah Clothier Hull Papers, SCPC, 1–2, box 3; Dorothy Detzer to Hannah Clothier Hull, 20 July 1936, Hannah Clothier Hull Papers, SCPC, 4, 8, box 3.

82. Dorothy Detzer to Hannah Clothier Hull, 29 July 1936, Hannah Clothier Hull Papers, SCPC, 13–14, box 3.

83. Hannah Clothier Hull to Dorothy Detzer, 31 July 1936, Hannah Clothier Hull Papers, SCPC, box 3.

84. Dorothy Detzer to Hannah Clothier Hull, 5 Aug. 1936, Hannah Clothier Hull Papers, SCPC, box 3.

85. Hannah Clothier Hull to Mabel Vernon, 6 May 1937, Hannah Clothier Hull Papers, SCPC, 1, box 4.

86. Hannah Clothier Hull, "Report of the National President, . . ." Jan, 1937, WILPF Papers, Univ. of Colo., series IV, box 7.

87. As introduced in Congress in December 1923, the ERA stated: "Men and women shall have equal rights throughout the United States, and every place subject to its jurisdiction." See "Historical Sketch of the National Woman's Party," National Woman's Party Papers, microfilm, 1, Ohio State Univ., Columbus (hereafter cited as NWP Papers, Ohio State Univ.).

88. Ibid., 4.

89. Hannah Clothier Hull, "Annual Report," May 1935, WILPF Papers, SCPC, 3 series E4, box 1.

90. Hannah Clothier Hull to Mrs. Stephen Pell, 4 Nov. 1934, NWP Papers, Ohio State Univ., series I, reel 55.

91. Alice Paul to Lola Maverick Lloyd, 15 April 1935, NWP Papers, Ohio State Univ., series I, reel 56.

92. Alice Paul to Florence Bayard Hilles, 27 Feb. 1935, NWP Papers, Ohio State Univ., 2 series I, reel 55.

93. Anita Pollitzer to Alice Paul, 31 May 1935, NWP Papers, Ohio State Univ., 1, series I, reel 56.

94. Ibid. Jane Norman Smith to Florence Bayard Hilles, 7 May 1935, NWP Papers, Ohio State Univ., series I, reel 56.

95. Lola Maverick Lloyd to Betty Gram Swing, 31 May 1936, NWP Papers, Ohio State Univ., series I, reel 57.

96. Winifred LeSueur to All Affiliated Societies of the Open Door International, 18 Mar. 1937, NWP Papers, Ohio State Univ., 2, series I, reel 59. As the NWP put it with respect to the contradictions in the charter, it "espouses full political and civil rights, full opportunity for education, full opportunity of employment, equal pay for equal work and security of livelihood. At the same time it limits these freedoms and virtually defeats its purpose by refusing to declare for an equal status in the field of paid labor. It upholds special privileges for women, but not for men, special safeguards for the health of women but not for men, special wage and hour laws for women but not for their male competitors and emphasizes the physical differences between men and women. These two approaches to the problems and objectives of women are obviously incompatible and inconsistent." See NWP to Clarence E. Hancock, "The Women's Charter vs. The Equal Rights Amendment and Treaty, An Open Letter," Mar. 1937, NWP Papers, Ohio State Univ., 2, series I, reel 59.

97. Mary Wilhelmine Williams to Martha Souder, 26 Mar. 1937, NWP Papers, Ohio State Univ., series I, reel 59.

98. Martha Souder to Lola Maverick Lloyd, 15 Apr. 1937, NWP Papers, Ohio State Univ., series I, reel 59.

99. U.S. Section, WILPF, Minutes, Annual Mtg., 30 Apr.–3 May 1937, WILPF Papers, Univ. of Colo., 8, series III, box 33.

100. Ibid., 9.

101. Mary Wilhelmine Williams to Martha Souder, 7 Apr. 1938, NWP Papers, Ohio State Univ., series I, reel 61.

9. Repression at Home and Abroad

1. Jane Addams, *Democracy and Social Ethics*, ed. with Introduction by Anne Firor Scott (1907; reprint, Cambridge: Belknap Press), 6, 11 (page citations are to reprint edition).

2. Mary Church Terrell, *A Colored Woman in a White World* (Washington, D.C.: National Association of Colored Women's Clubs, 1940), 328–29. All subsequent quotations concerning Terrell and the Zurich Congress are taken from this autobiography, 328–35.

3. Emily Greene Balch to Mildred Scott Olmsted, 11 Jan. 1929, WILPF Papers, SCPC, series C1, box 6.

4. All quotations concerning the petition are from Terrell, *Colored Woman*, 360–64.

5. U.S. Section, WILPF, "Accomplishments During the Year 1925," with Dorothy Detzer to Branches, 13 May 1926, WILPF Papers, SCPC, series E4, box 1; James Weldon Johnson, "The Race Problem and Peace," May 1924, WILPF Papers, Univ. of Colo., series IV, box 4. It may be that Alice Dunbar-Nelson, elected to the Board in Sept. 1925, was black; this is suggested by the context in which her name appears in the minutes of the Sept. and May 1926 board meetings. It is difficult to know for certain because characteristics such as the race of WILPF members is never specifically noted. In fact, the WILPF considered it a point in its favor that there was no indication "on cards of members whether white or colored." See "W.I.L. Record on Race Recognition," 1 July 1930, WILPF Papers, SCPC, series C1, box 6.

6. Addie W. Hunton to Mildred Scott Olmsted, 20 Dec. 1928, WILPF Papers, SCPC, series C1, box 6.

7. Dorothy Detzer, Minutes, Board Mtg., 6 June 1929, WILPF Papers, Univ. of Colo., 3, series III, box 32.

8. Emily Greene Balch, Statement of Policies, Annual Mtg., 24–27 Apr. 1929, WILPF Papers, SCPC, 2–3, series A2, box 2.

9. Dorothy Detzer to Board Members, 18 Mar. 1930, WILPF Papers, SCPC, 1–2, series A2, box 2.

10. U.S. Section, WILPF, Minutes, Board Mtg., 23 May 1930, WILPF Papers, SCPC, series A2, box 2.

11. "W.I.L. Record on Race Recognition," 1 July 1930, WILPF Papers, SCPC, series C1, box 6.

12. "News of the United States Section," *Pax International* 5, no. 7 (May 1930):2, WILPF Papers, SCPC, series A2, box 2.

13. Dorothy Detzer to Branches, 19 Mar. 1934, 2, and 1 Feb. 1934, WILPF Papers, SCPC, 2, series E4, box 1.

14. Emily Greene Balch to Franklin D. Roosevelt, 9 Nov. 1934, WILPF Papers, Univ. of Colo., 1–2, series III, box 33.

15. Dorothy Detzer, Br. Ltr. No. 6, 31 Dec. 1934, WILPF Papers, Univ. of Colo., 2, series III, box 33.

16. Dorothy Detzer to Emily Greene Balch, 14 Dec. 1934, WILPF Papers, Univ. of Colo. 2, series III, box 33.

17. Dorothy Detzer, Br. Ltr. No. 7, 11 Jan. 1935, 1–2, and No. 9, 12 Feb. 1935, WILPF Papers, SCPC, 3, series E4, box 1.

18. Addie W. Hunton, "Report of the Inter-Racial Committee," May 1935, WILPF Papers, SCPC, 1–4, series E4, box 1.

19. "Report of Dorothy Detzer, May, 1935" WILPF Papers, Univ. of Colo., 2, series III, box 33; Dorothy Detzer to Huldah [Randall], 15 Mar. 1980, Dorothy Detzer Papers, SCPC, 2–3, series ACC81A-24, box 1.

20. U.S. Section, WILPF, "Program and Policies 1935–36," WILPF Papers, SCPC, 2, series A2, box 2.

21. Dorothy Detzer, Br. Ltr. No. 24, 4 Feb. 1936, WILPF Papers, SCPC, 1–3, series E4, box 1.

22. Dorothy Detzer, Br. Ltr. No. 27, 28 May 1936, WILPF Papers, SCPC, 4–5, series E4, box 1.

23. Lois Jameson, "Sharecroppers and the Terror Belt of Arkansas," from Dorothy Detzer, Br. Ltr. No. 27, 28 May 1936, WILPF Papers, SCPC, series E4, box 1.

24. Eleanor Fowler, "Report . . . on the American Federation of Labor Convention," from Dorothy Detzer, Br. Ltr. No. 34, 23 Dec. 1936, WILPF Papers, SCPC, 1–5, series E4, box 1.

25. Ibid., 2.

26. U.S. Section, WILPF, "Resolutions Adopted by the Annual Meeting . . . , Apr. 30–May 3, 1937," WILPF Papers, Univ. of Colo., 2, series III, box 33.

27. Dorothy Detzer, Br. Ltr. No. 43, 2 Apr. 1937, WILPF Papers, SCPC, 1–2, series E4, box 2.

28. Dan T. Carter, "Law and Order" (excerpted from his book, *Scottsboro: A Tragedy of the American South*), in *The Segregation Era 1863–1954: A Modern Reader,* ed. Allen Weinstein and Frank Otto Gatell (New York: Oxford Univ. Press, 1970), 189.

29. Hannah Clothier Hull and Dorothy Detzer to Attorney General, 25 Jan. 1939, Hannah Clothier Hull Papers, SCPC, box 5.

30. Dorothy Detzer, "Report of the Executive Secretary," June–Sept. 1930, WILPF Papers, SCPC, 2, series A2, box 2.

31. Dorothy Detzer to Mary Sheepshanks, 19 Aug. 1930, WILPF Papers, Univ. of Colo., 1, series II, box 9. Harris's assertion that Ras Tafari offered slave labor to the J. G. White Company was based on James E. Baum's *Savage Abyssinia* and was thus second-hand evidence. And according to Dunn, "the extract from Baum's book [to which Harris referred] was not a definite quotation from Tafari himself." See Detzer to Sheepshanks, 19 Aug. 1930.

32. "Brief Report of the United States Section's Activities," 1 Sept. 1929–1 Apr. 1932, WILPF Papers, Univ. of Colo., 1, 2, series III, box 32.

33. Statement issued by J. G. White Company, 15 Aug. 1930, with W. R. Castle to Dorothy Detzer, 7 Feb. 1933, WILPF Papers, SCPC, series C1, box 4.

34. Dorothy Detzer[?], "The Rape of Liberia," n.d. [late summer or early fall 1933], WILPF Papers, SCPC, 1, series A2, box 1. A League of Nations commission would subsequently put the value of this land at fifty cents an acre. See Detzer, *Appointment on the Hill,* 125.

35. I. K. Sundiata, *Black Scandal: America and the Liberian Labor Crisis 1929–1936* (Philadelphia: Institute for the Study of Human Issues, 1980), 38.

36. Ibid., 1.

37. Raymond Leslie Buell, *The Native Problem in Africa* (New York: Macmillan, 1928).

38. Sundiata, *Black Scandal,* 44, 45–46.

39. Ibid., 47, 49, 1, 54.

40. Emily Greene Balch to [Benjamin] Gerig and Balch to [Ernest] Gruening, 16 Mar. 1932, Emily Greene Balch Papers, microfilm, Swarthmore College Peace Collection, series II, reel 9 (hereafter cited as Emily Greene Balch Papers, SCPC). *The Crisis* is the NAACP journal.

41. Sundiata, *Black Scandal,* 61.

42. Detzer, *Appointment on the Hill,* 130–31.

43. Sundiata, *Black Scandal,* 65, 66-67.

44. Detzer, *Appointment on the Hill,* 132.

45. Sundiata, *Black Scandal,* 70.

46. Detzer, *Appointment on the Hill,* 132.

47. Dorothy Detzer, "Memorandum on Liberia," 6 June 1933, WILPF Papers, SCPC, 4-5, series E4, box 1.

48. Sundiata, *Black Scandal,* 93.

49. Dorothy Detzer to L. A. Grimes, 25 Sept. 1933, WILPF Papers, SCPC, 1, series A2, box 2.

50. Hannah Clothier Hull, Dorothy Detzer, and Mabel Vernon to "Selected List of People Interested in Negro," 26 Sept. 1933, WILPF Papers, SCPC, series A4, box 4.

51. C. A. Casell and M. M. Parker to Dorothy Detzer, 15 Sept. 1933, Emily Greene Balch Papers, SCPC, series II, reel 9.

52. Dorothy Detzer to L. A. Grimes, 9 Nov. 1933, WILPF Papers, SCPC, series A2, box 2. Detzer was deeply moved by the offer to be personally decorated by the African nation, but regretfully declined to accept the honor, noting that "it would be wiser for me as an individual not to accept any honor from a government. I think it is very important," she explained, "that I should never be put in the position in which there could be any possible criticism from my Government with regard to my actions. . . . I am sure that you and your Government will understand that I am doing so in order that I may better serve the interests of Liberia." She did suggest, however, that if an organization could be the recipient of such an honor, she saw no reason why the WILPF could not accept such a "token."

53. Sundiata, *Black Scandal,* 98, 57. In 1930, for example, the State Department was unwilling to ignore the Liberian issue because, in William Castle's words, "Negroes would be furious and would turn bitterly against the administration."

54. Ibid., 98.

55. Dorothy Detzer, to Prentiss Gilbert, 19 Aug. 1933, WILPF Papers, Univ. of Colo., 1, series III, box 31.

56. Detzer, *Appointment on the Hill,* 77.

57. Auguste Kirchoff, "Anti-Semitism, An Aftermath of the War," n.d.; WILPF, "Resolutions Passed at the Congress held in Washington, May 1-8, 1924"; WILPF, "Resolutions and Manifesto of the Washington Congress," 1-7 May 1924, WILPF Papers, Univ. of Colo., 5, series I, box 14.

58. [Mary H. Ingham], Chair, National Committee, International Congress to Calvin Coolidge, 30 Jan. 1924, WILPF Papers, SCPC, series C1, box 2.

59. German Section, "Work of the W.I.L. National Sections," *Pax International* 4, no. 7 (Aug. 1929), WILPF Papers, Univ. of Colo., series V, box 3.

60. Dorothy Detzer, "News of the United States Section," *Pax International* 9, no. 10 (Sept. 1930), WILPF Papers, SCPC, series E2, box 1.

61. Dorothy Detzer to WILPF members, 13 May 1930, WILPF Papers, Univ. of Colo., series III, box 32.

62. Dorothy Detzer to Emily Greene Balch, 20 Mar. 1931, Hannah Clothier Hull Papers, SCPC, 2, box 6.

63. Francis Ralston Welsh to Marcia Sternbergh, 6 May 1931; Francis Ralston Welsh, "The Women's International League for Peace and Freedom," 7 May 1931, WILPF Papers, SCPC, series C1, box 5.

64. E. H. Shaffer to Lowell Mellett, 26 May 1931, WILPF Papers, SCPC, 1, series C1, box 5.

65. Dorothy Detzer, "War Department v. State Department," "News of the United States Section," *Pax International* (Aug. 1931), WILPF Papers, SCPC, series E2, box 1.

66. James H. Bishop to Whom It May Concern, 10 May 1932; James H. Bishop, "The Board of Christian Education, Wilmington Conference . . . ," 10 May 1932, WILPF Papers, SCPC, series C1, box 5.

67. Hamilton Fish to Dorothy Detzer, 8 Mar. 1933, WILPF Papers, SCPC, series C1, box 5.

68. WILPF, press release, 14 July 1932, WILPF Papers, Univ. of Colo., series III, box 32; Dorothy Detzer to Chairmen, 16 Nov. 1932, WILPF Papers, SCPC, 1, series E4, box 1.

69. Dorothy Detzer to Emily Greene Balch and Hannah Clothier Hull, 15 Nov. 1932, WILPF Papers, SCPC, 1, series C7, box 8.

70. Emily Greene Balch to Franklin D. Roosevelt, 31 Jan. 1933, WILPF Papers, SCPC, series C7, box 23.

71. Emily Greene Balch, "Germany Revisited," Nov. 1931, WILPF Papers, Univ. of Colo., 1–4, series III, box 32.

72. Gertrude Baer, "The German Section and the Elections for the Reichstag," n.d. [early Aug. 1932], WILPF Papers, Univ. of Colo., 1–2, series III, box 10.

73. Dorothy Detzer to Hannah Clothier Hull and Emily Greene Balch, 31 Aug. [1932], WILPF Papers, SCPC, series C7, box 8.

74. Anne Zueblin Forsythe to Florence Taussig, 7 Mar. 1933; Anne Zueblin Forsythe to Ellen Starr Brinton, 7 Mar. 1933, WILPF Papers, Univ. of Colo., series III, box 32.

75. Emily Greene Balch to Secretary of State, 14 Mar. 1933 WILPF Papers, Univ. of Colo., series III, box 32.

76. Dorothy Detzer to Charge d'Affairs, 18 Mar. 1933 WILPF Papers, Univ. of Colo., series III, box 32.

77. George Sylvester Viereck to Provisional Committee, 27 Mar. 1933, Emily Greene Balch Papers, SCPC, series II, reel 9. The other members of the committee were Lincoln Steffans, Robert Morss Lovett, George W. Kirchwey, Alvin Johnson, and John Haynes Holmes.

78. Kate Dewing to Hans Luther, 25 Apr. 1933, WILPF Papers, Univ. of Colo., series III, box 32.

79. Emily Greene Balch, untitled letter or report, 1 June 1933, WILPF Papers, Univ. of Colo., 2, series III, box 32.

80. Anne Zueblin Forsythe to Emily Greene Balch, 7 Mar. 1933; Anne Zueblin Forsythe to [Kate] Dewing, 12 June 1933; Anne Zueblin Forsythe to Dorothy Detzer, 27 June 1933, WILPF Papers, Univ. of Colo., series III, box 32.

81. Anne Zueblin Forsythe to Florence Taussig, 23 June 1933, WILPF Papers, Univ. of Colo., series III, box 32.

82. International WILPF, Minutes, Exec. Comm. Mtg., 12 Apr. 1933 and 13 Apr. 1933, WILPF Papers, Univ. of Colo., 1–2, series I, box 7.

83. Ibid., 13 Apr. 1933, WILPF Papers, Univ. of Colo., series I, box 7; Amy Woods, "Political Situation of the United States," n.d. [Spring 1933], WILPF Papers, Univ. of Colo., 1–2, series III, box 32; Emily Greene Balch to Camille Drevet, 19 Oct. 1932; Amy Woods to Camille Drevet, 9 Dec. 1932 and 4 Nov. 1933; Amy Woods to Anne Zueblin Forsythe, 27 Nov. 1933, WILPF Papers, Univ. of Colo., series III, box 32.

84. WILPF International Secretary to Franklin D. Roosevelt, 14 Apr. 1933, WILPF Papers, Univ. of Colo., 1, series I, box 7.

85. Exec. Comm., WILPF, "Sanctions," and "Resolutions on Anti-Semitism," 11–15 Apr. 1933, WILPF Papers, Univ. of Colo., series I, box 7.

86. Dorothy Detzer to Branches, 19 Mar. 1932, WILPF Papers, SCPC, 4, series E4, box 1.

87. Dorothy Detzer to Branches, 1 June 1933, WILPF Papers, SCPC, 1, series E4, box 1.

88. Hannah Clothier Hull to Lillian Canter, 4 Dec. 1933, Hannah Clothier Hull Papers, SCPC, 2, box 2; Hannah Clothier Hull to Mrs. Mark Harris, 2 Nov. 1933, Hannah Clothier Hull Papers, SCPC, 1, box 2.

89. Amy Woods and Dorothy Detzer to Edgar L.G. Prochnik, 7 Mar. 1934, WILPF Papers, Univ. of Colo., series III, box 32.

90. Katherine Devereaux Blake to Hans Luther, 3 Oct. 1934, WILPF Papers, Univ. of Colo., series III, box 32.

91. Dorothy Detzer to Hans Luther, 19 Dec. 1934, Emily Greene Balch Papers, SCPC, series II, reel 9.

92. Dorothy Detzer to Gertrude Baer, 1 Feb. 1935, 1; Blanche Roulet to Dorothy Detzer, 19 Jan. 1935, WILPF Papers, Univ. of Colo., series III, box 32.

93. Dorothy Detzer to Kirby Page, 1 Nov. 1933, WILPF Papers, Univ. of Colo., series III, box 32.

10. Munitions and Manchuria

1. David Burner, *Herbert Hoover: A Public Life* (New York: Knopf, 1979), 293–94.

2. Mary Beard, "The Japanese-American Crisis," *The Pax Special* 1 (June 1925):4, WILPF Papers, SCPC, series E2, box 1.

3. Dorothy Detzer, "Report of the Executive Secretary," June–Oct. 1931, WILPF Papers, SCPC, series A2, box 2.

4. Detzer, *Appointment on the Hill*, 141.

5. Dorothy Detzer to Camille Drevet, 17 Oct. 1931, WILPF Papers, Univ. of Colo., series IV, box 7.

6. Dorothy Detzer to Secretary of State, 11 Nov. 1931, WILPF Papers, Univ. of Colo., series IV, box 7.

7. Ibid.

8. Dorothy Detzer, "The War in Manchuria," n.d., WILPF Papers, SCPC, series A2, box 1.

9. Dorothy Detzer to Branches, 19 Nov. 1931, WILPF Papers, SCPC, 1, series E4, box 1.

10. Cor Ramondt-Hirschmann to vice presidents, 9 Nov. 1931, WILPF Papers, Univ. of Colo., series II, box 9.

11. Dorothy Detzer to Branches, 19 Nov. 1931, WILPF Papers, SCPC, 2, series E4, box 1.

12. Ibid., 4.

13. "The League and the Manchurian Question," *Pax International* 7 (Jan. 1932), WILPF Papers, Univ. of Colo., series V, box 3.

14. Dorothy Detzer, "Report," 12–13 Dec. 1931, WILPF Papers, SCPC, 2, series A2, box 2. The Interorganizational Council on Disarmament included, besides the WILPF, the AAUW, American Community, American Ethical Union, AFSC, American Unitarian Association, Anglo-American Committee for International Discussion, Central Conference of American Rabbis, Commission on International Justice and Goodwill of the Federal Council of Churches of Christ in America, Commission on International Relations of the Congregational and Christian Churches, Committee on Educational Publicity, Com-

mittee on Militarism in Education, FOR, First Humanist Society, Foreign Policy Associa-
tion, Friends' Peace Committee of Philadelphia, League for Independent Political
Action, League of Nations Association, National Board of the YWCA, National Commit-
tee on Churches and World Peace, NCCCW, NCPW, National Federation of Business and
Professional Women's Clubs, National Federation of Temple Sisterhoods, Teachers'
Union of New York City, YMCA, Union of Orthodox Jewish Congregations, Women's
Branch of the WRL of America, WPS, World Alliance for International Friendship
through the Churches, World Peace Commission, World Peace Foundation, World Peace
Posters, Inc.

15. Dorothy Detzer to Emily Greene Balch, 28 Jan. 1932, WILPF Papers, SCPC,
series C1, box 6.

16. Dorothy Detzer, "Report," 15–16 Jan. 1932, WILPF Papers, Univ. of Colo., 2,
series III, box 32.

17. Ibid.

18. Emily Greene Balch to Edith M. Pye, 26 Jan. 1932, WILPF Papers, SCPC, series
C1, box 6.

19. Emily Greene Balch and Hannah Clothier Hull to Herbert Hoover, 18 Jan.
1932, WILPF Papers, SCPC, series E4, box 1.

20. Dorothy Detzer to Interorg. Council, 10 Feb. 1932, WILPF Papers, SCPC, 2,
series E4, box 1.

21. Ibid.

22. Divine, *Illusion of Neutrality*, 28.

23. Dorothy Detzer to Friends, 12 Feb. 1932, WILPF Papers, Univ. of Colo., 1,
series V, box 7.

24. Detzer, *Appointment on the Hill*, 149.

25. Dorothy Detzer to Clarence Pickett, 18 Feb. 1932, WILPF Papers, SCPC, 1,
series C1, box 5.

26. Dorothy Detzer to Emily Greene Balch, 5 Feb. 1932, WILPF Papers, SCPC,
series C1, box 6.

27. Dorothy Detzer, "Memorandum of Conversation with Assistant Secretary of
State James Grafton Rogers . . . ," 19 Mar. 1932, WILPF Papers, Univ. of Colo., 1–3,
series IV, box 2.

28. Divine, *Illusion of Neutrality*, 32.

29. Dorothy Detzer to Herbert Hoover, 20 Dec. 1932, WILPF Papers, SCPC, series
C7, box 8.

30. Dorothy Detzer to Mildred Scott Olmsted, 24 Dec. 1932, WILPF Papers, SCPC,
series C7, box 8.

31. Dorothy Detzer to Herbert Hoover, 20 Dec. 1932, WILPF Papers, SCPC, series
C7, box 8.

32. Divine, *Illusion of Neutrality*, 33.

33. Ibid.

34. Ibid., 35.

35. Ibid., 37.

36. Dorothy Detzer to Branches, 15 Feb. 1933, WILPF Papers, SCPC, 2, series E4,
box 1.

37. Dorothy Detzer to Branches, 7 Apr. 1933, WILPF Papers, SCPC, series E4, box
1.

38. According to Divine, "the significance of the failure of the arms embargo resolution is that even a small step in the direction of a more active American policy toward

the world proved unattainable in 1933. The strength of the Wilsonian tradition, embodied in the sincere efforts of men like Hull . . . , could not dissolve the grip of isolation on the people, the Congress and the President." Divine, *Illusion of Neutrality*, 56. For other works that discuss U.S. isolationism in the 1930s, see the Selected Bibliography.

39. The National Peace Conference was organized in Mar. 1933 in the attempt to form "a more permanent and substantial coordination of the peace forces," and was originally chaired by Dr. Walter VanKirk. At its founding on 30 Mar., it was composed of twenty organizations: AAUW, Church Peace Union, Council of Women for Home Missions, Federal Council of Churches, Foreign Policy Association, General Federation of Women's Clubs, Institute of International Education, Institute of Pacific Relations, League of Nations Association, National Board of YWCA, National Federation of Business and Professional Women's Clubs, NCCCW, National Council of Jewish Women, NCPW, National Council of YMCA, National League of Women Voters, WCTU, WILPF, World Alliance for International Friendship Through the Churches, and World Peace Foundation. Also invited were the CEIP, the Catholic Peace Association, the Central Conference of American Rabbis, the Jewish Welfare Board, the Federation of Women's Boards of Foreign Missions, and the National Catholic Welfare Council. See "Organizations Represented at Group Meeting March 30, 1933" and "Agenda for Meeting March 30, 1933," National Peace Conference Papers, Swarthmore College Peace Collection, box 2, Swarthmore, Penn. (hereafter cited as NPC Papers, SCPC).

40. Detzer, *Appointment on the Hill*, 153.

41. Katherine Devereaux Blake to Camille Drevet, 23 Nov. 1932, WILPF Papers, Univ. of Colo., series III, box 32.

42. Detzer, *Appointment on the Hill*, 154–56.

43. Ibid., 157.

44. Dorothy Detzer to Branches, 8 Mar. 1934, WILPF Papers, SCPC, series E4, box 1.

45. Detzer, *Appointment on the Hill*, 159.

46. Ibid.

47. Ibid., 163.

48. Divine, *Illusion of Neutrality*, 61.

49. Detzer, *Appointment on the Hill*, 165.

50. Ibid., 166.

51. Drew Pearson and Robert S. Allen, "Washington Merry-Go-Round," *Washington Post*[?], 4 Sept. 1934, WILPF Papers, SCPC, series A2, box 1.

52. John Wiltz, *In Search of Peace: The Senate Munitions Inquiry, 1934–1936* (Baton Rouge: Louisiana State Univ. Press, 1963), 24.

53. Chatfield, *For Peace and Justice*, 166.

54. Chatfield quoting Stone in ibid.

55. Ibid.

56. Russell J. Clinchy, "The Plight of the DuPonts," *The Christian Century*, 3 Oct. 1934, 1234, WILPF Papers, SCPC, series A2, box 1.

57. Detzer, *Appointment on the Hill*, 169.

58. Clinchy, "Plight of the DuPonts," 1235.

59. John K. Nelson, *The Peace Prophets: American Pacifist Thought, 1919–1941* (Chapel Hill: Univ. of North Carolina Press, 1967), particularly ch. 2, "Pacifism and the Nature and Causes of War," 40–72.

60. Clinchy, "Plight of the DuPonts," 1235.

61. Dorothy Detzer to Branches, 19 Oct. 1934, WILPF Papers, SCPC, series E4, box 1.

62. Dorothy Detzer to Branches, 13 Dec. 1934, WILPF Papers, SCPC, 1, series E4, box 1.

63. Dorothy Detzer to Branches, 6 Dec. 1934, WILPF Papers, SCPC, 1, series E4, box 1.

64. Dorothy Detzer to Branches, 13 Dec. 1934, WILPF Papers, SCPC, 2, series E4, box 1.

65. Ibid.

66. Ibid., 3.

67. Dorothy Detzer to Emily Greene Balch, 14 Dec. 1934, WILPF Papers, Univ. of Colo., 1, series III, box 32.

68. Dorothy Detzer to Branches, 18 Mar. 1935, WILPF Papers, SCPC, 3, series E4, box 1.

69. Divine, *Illusion of Neutrality*, 57.

11. The Search for Neutrality

1. Divine, *Illusion of Neutrality*, 93.

2. Dorothy Detzer, Br. Ltr. No. 15, 15 May 1935, WILPF Papers, SCPC, 1, series E4, box 1.

3. Dorothy Detzer to Wilbur Thomas, 28 May 1935, WILPF Papers, SCPC, 1–2; Wilbur K. Thomas to Dorothy Detzer, 21 May 1935, WILPF Papers, SCPC, 1, series C1, box 19.

4. Emily Greene Balch, untitled statement regarding accusations of communism against the WILPF, 10 May 1935, WILPF Papers, Univ. of Colo., series II, box 19.

5. Dorothy Detzer to Miss Seelman, 9 Oct. 1934, WILPF Papers, SCPC, 1–2, series C6, box 1.

6. Dorothy Detzer to Kirby Page, 1 Nov. 1933, WILPF Papers, Univ. of Colo., 2, series III, box 32.

7. WILPF, Minutes, International Exec. Comm. Mtg., 12 Sept. 1935, WILPF Papers, SCPC, 10, series I, box 8.

8. NPC, "Statement of Principles . . . ," May 1935, NPC Papers, SCPC, 3, box 1.

9. Dorothy Detzer, Br. Ltr. No. 18, 7 July 1935, WILPF Papers, SCPC, 1, series E4, box 1.

10. Divine, *Illusion of Neutrality*, 95.

11. Mildred Scott Olmsted, Br. Ltr. No. 19, 1 Aug. 1935, WILPF Papers, SCPC, 2, series E4, box 1.

12. Mildred Scott Olmsted, Br. Ltr. No. 20, 23 Sept. 1935, WILPF Papers, SCPC, 1, series E4, box 1.

13. U.S. Section, WILPF, Minutes, National Board Mtg., 19–20 Mar. 1933, WILPF Papers, Univ. of Colo., 12, series III, box 31.

14. U.S. Section, WILPF, Minutes, National Board Mtg., 12 Oct. 1935, WILPF Papers, Univ. of Colo., 5, series III, box 31.

15. Dorothy Detzer, "What Neutrality Means," *The Nation* 141 (4 Dec. 1935): 642, WILPF Papers, SCPC, series A2, box 3.

16. Divine, *Illusion of Neutrality*, 135–36.

17. Dorothy Detzer, "United States and Neutrality," *Pax International* 11 (Jan.–Feb. 1936), WILPF Papers, Univ. of Colo., series V, box 3.

18. Divine, *Illusion of Neutrality*, 160.

19. Of the original twenty members of the NPC in 1933, four apparently were no longer participating by Dec. 1935—the Federal Council of Churches, the General Feder-

ation of Women's Clubs, the Institute of Pacific Relations, and the National League of Women Voters. An additional seventeen groups had joined (two on a "consultative" basis): the AFSC, the American Unitarian Association, the CEIP, the Central Conference of American Rabbis, the Council for Social Action of the Congregational and Christian Churches, the Committee on Militarism in Education, the Committee on Women's Work of the Foreign Missions Conference, the Department of International Justice and Goodwill of the Federal Council of Churches, the FOR, the Intercollegiate Council on International Cooperation, the International Society of Christian Endeavor, the National Federation of Temple Sisterhoods, the National Student Federation, the Public Action Committee, the World Peace Commission of the Methodist Episcopal Church, and World Peaceways. The two consultative organizations were the Foreign Policy Association and the Catholic Association for International Peace. Included among the NPC's "Cooperating Organizations" were the Connecticut Council on International Relations, the New Jersey Committee on the Cause and Cure of War, the New Jersey Joint Council on International Relations, and the Rhode Island Council for Peace Action. See "Organizations Represented in the National Peace Conference . . . ," n.d. [early 1936], NPC Papers, SCPC, 5, box 1.

20. Among the groups that attended the Buck Hill Falls meeting were the No Frontier News Service, Bureau on Negro Affairs, Federal Council of Churches, Church of the Brethren, YMCA, WILPF, FOR, AFSC, League for Industrial Democracy, Central Conference of American Rabbis, NCPW, and the American Student Union. See "Emergency Peace Campaign Policy Forming Council," n.d., Emergency Peace Campaign Papers, Swarthmore College Peace Collection, microfilm, reel 72.1, Swarthmore, Penn. (hereafter cited as EPC Papers, SCPC).

21. "Concerning Functions of the NPC and EPC," n.d., EPC Papers, SCPC, reel 72.1.

22. "The Need for Vigorous Nation-Wide Pacifist Program to be Undertaken Immediately," Dec. 1935, EPC Papers, SCPC, reel 72.1.

23. Ray Newton, "Why the Campaign?" Apr. 1936, EPC Papers, SCPC, 2, reel 72.3.

24. NPC, Minutes, 16 Mar. 1936, NPC Papers, SCPC, 1, box 2.

25. Newton, "Why the Campaign?"

26. "Planks on Peace Approved by the National Peace Conference . . . ," 18 May 1936, WILPF Papers, SCPC, 1-2, from Dorothy Detzer, Br. Ltr. No. 28, 29 May 1936, series E4, box 1.

27. NPC, Minutes, 15 June 1936, NPC Papers, SCPC, 2, box 2; "Party Platform on Peace Issues—1936," NPC Papers, SCPC, box 12.

28. U.S. Section, WILPF, "Program and Policies," July 1936, Hannah Clothier Hull Papers, SCPC, 1, box 3; "Miss Detzer's Final Draft of the Programs and Policies, . . ." n.d. [summer 1936], WILPF Papers, SCPC, 1, series C1, box 22.

29. Hannah Clothier Hull to Chase Kimball, 25 Mar. 1936, Hannah Clothier Hull Papers, SCPC, 1, box 3.

30. Martha Helen Elliott to Emily Cooper Johnson, 28 Apr. 1936, WILPF Papers, SCPC, 1, series C7, box 23; Mildred Scott Olmsted to Mrs. Orlando Cole, 29 Apr. 1936, WILPF Papers, SCPC, 1, series C7, box 33; Hannah Clothier Hull to Mrs. Harry D. Reed, 27 June 1936, WILPF Papers, SCPC, 1-2, series C7, box 33.

31. Hannah Clothier Hull to Editor, Philadelphia *Inquirer*, 19 Aug. 1936, Hannah Clothier Hull Papers, SCPC, box 3.

32. Dorothy Detzer to Emily Cooper Johnson, 9 Oct. 1936, WILPF Papers, SCPC, series C7, box 8.

33. Dorothy Detzer and Hannah Clothier Hull to Franklin D. Roosevelt, 15 Aug. 1936, Hannah Clothier Hull Papers, SCPC, 1 box 3; Hannah Clothier Hull to Franklin D. Roosevelt, 14 Sept. 1936, box 3.

34. Dorothy Detzer to Friends, 14 Nov. 1936, WILPF Papers, Univ. of Colo., series III, box 33.

35. EPC, "The Neutrality Fight is On—1937," EPC Papers, SCPC, 1-2, reel 72.8.

36. Dorothy Detzer, "What Neutrality Means," *The Nation* 141 (4 Dec. 1935): 642, WILPF Papers, SCPC, series A2, box 3.

37. EPC, Minutes, Council Mtg., 9 Jan. 1937, EPC Papers, SCPC, 1, reels 72.1 and 72.2.

38. EPC, "No-Foreign-War Crusade," n.d. [spring 1937], EPC Papers, SCPC, reel 72.8.

39. DeBenedetti, *Peace Reform*, 131-32.

40. Dorothy Detzer, Br. Ltr. No. 46, 7 May 1937, WILPF Papers, SCPC, 2, series E4, box 2.

41. Ibid.

42. Divine, *Illusion of Neutrality*, 198.

43. Hannah Clothier Hull to Eleanor Fowler, 15 June 1937, Hannah Clothier Hull Papers, SCPC, box 6.

44. Eleanor Fowler to Emily Greene Balch, 30 July 1937, Emily Greene Balch Papers, SCPC, series II, reel 10,

45. Dorothy Detzer to Roger Baldwin, 10 Dec. 1936, WILPF Papers, SCPC, series C1, box 22.

46. Dorothy Detzer to Mrs. Newlin F. Paxson, 16 May 1938, WILPF Papers, SCPC, series C1, box 26.

47. Dorothy Detzer, "President Roosevelt's Chicago Speech," 1 Nov. 1937, WILPF Papers, SCPC, 2, series A2, box 1.

48. NCPW, World Peaceways, WILPF, FOR, EPC, Committee on Militarism in Education, press release, 7 Oct. 1937, WILPF Papers, SCPC, 2, series E4, box 2.

49. Dorothy Detzer, "President Roosevelt's Chicago Speech," 1 Nov. 1937, WILPF Papers, SCPC, 2, series A2, box 1.

50. Dorothy Detzer, "We Prepare For War," 12 Nov. 1937, WILPF Papers, SCPC, 2, series A2, box 1.

51. Jessie Ash Arndt, "Miss Detzer Tells Barnard Club of District [What] Liberal Pacifists Do," *Washington Post*, 21 Nov. 1937, WILPF Papers, SCPC, series A2, box 3.

52. U.S. Section, WILPF, to Members of International Executive, 28 Dec. 1937, WILPF Papers, Univ. of Colo., 3, series I, box 8.

53. Emily Greene Balch to International WILPF, 15 Mar. 1938, WILPF Papers, Univ. of Colo., series II, box 10.

54. Dorothy Detzer, "Dress Rehearsal For War," n.d. [Jan. 1938], WILPF Papers, SCPC, 1, 3; Dorothy Detzer[?], untitled article concerning *Panay* incident and war referendum, n.d. [Jan. 1938], WILPF Papers, SCPC, 10, series A2, box 1; Dorothy Detzer, Br. Ltr. No. 59, 27 Jan. 1938, WILPF Papers, SCPC, 1-2, series E4, box 2.

55. Dorothy Detzer, Br. Ltr. No. 63, 2 Apr. 1938, WILPF Papers, SCPC, 1-2, series E4, box 2; Dorothy Detzer, "Statement on Neutrality," *Pax International* 12 (15 Oct. 1937) WILPF Papers, Univ. of Colo., 5, series V, box 3.

56. WILPF, Minutes, International Exec. Comm. Mtg., 7-11 Sept. 1938, WILPF Papers, Univ. of Colo., 1, 3-4, series I, box 8.

57. Clara Ragaz, Gertrud[e] Baer, K.E. Innes, Circular Ltr. No. 23, 1 Oct. 1938, WILPF Papers, Univ. of Colo., 1-3, series I, box 8.

58. Dorothy Detzer, Br. Ltr. No. 65, 1 Oct. 1938, WILPF Papers, SCPC, 1–2, series E4, box 2.

59. Divine, *Illusion of Neutrality*, 230–31.

60. Dorothy Detzer[?], two untitled articles concerning increase in military spending, [Oct.] 1938, WILPF Papers, SCPC, series A2, box 1.

61. Dorothy Detzer to Gertrude Baer, 2 Dec. 1938, WILPF Papers, SCPC, 2, series C1, box 26.

62. Eleanor Fowler, "General Motors and Civil Liberties," 11 Feb. 1937, WILPF Papers, SCPC, 3, series A5, box 7a.

63. Dorothy Detzer, Annual Report, 30 Apr. 1937, Dorothy Detzer Papers, SCPC, 2, series ACC80A-54.

64. Eleanor Fowler, "General Motors and Civil Liberties," 11 Feb. 1937, WILPF Papers, SCPC, 2, 4, series A5, box 7a.

65. "W.I.L. Labor Front" was issued only twice, in Feb. and Mar. 1937. In Apr. 1937 the Executive Committee decided to incorporate all labor issues in the regularly issued branch Letters. See Eleanor Fowler, "Annual Report," 30 Apr. 1937, WILPF Papers, Univ. of Colo., 2, series III, box 33.

66. Ibid., 1. Dorothy Detzer, Annual Report, 30 Apr. 1937, Dorothy Detzer Papers, SCPC, 10, series ACC80A-54.

67. Eleanor Fowler, Annual Report, 30 Apr. 1937, WILPF Papers, Univ. of Colo., 2–3, series III, box 33.

68. Eleanor Fowler, Labor Ltr., 10 Mar. 1937, WILPF Papers, SCPC, 1, series E4, box 2.

69. Eleanor Fowler, Labor Ltr., 15 Mar. 1937, 1; Dorothy Detzer, Br. Ltr. No. 46, 7 May 1937, WILPF Papers, SCPC, 3, series E4, box 2.

70. Dorothy Detzer, Br. Ltr. No. 46, 7 May 1937, WILPF Papers, SCPC, 1, series E4, box 2.

71. Eleanor Fowler, Labor Ltr., 15 Mar. and 9 June 1937, WILPF Papers, SCPC, series E4, box 2.

72. Hannah Clothier Hull to Edward J. Kelly, 17 June 1937 and Dorothy Detzer, Br. Ltr. No. 51, 23 June 1937, WILPF Papers, Univ. of Colo., series III, box 33.

73. Dorothy Detzer, Br. Ltr. No. 51, 23 June 1937, WILPF Papers, Univ. of Colo., 2, series III, box 33; *W.I.L. Labor Front* (Vol. 1, No. 1), Feb. 1937, WILPF Papers, Univ. of Colo., series III, box 33.

74. Eleanor Fowler, Labor Ltr., 11 Aug. 1937, WILPF Papers, Univ. of Colo., 1, series III, box 33.

75. Robert Justin Goldstein, *Political Repression in Modern America. 1870 to the Present* (New York: Schenkman, 1978), 239.

76. Dorothy Detzer, "Memorandum on Interview with Homer Chaillaux," Jan. 1939, WILPF Papers, Univ. of Colo., 1, series III, box 34.

77. Dorothy Hammel to Gertrude Baer, 3 Mar. 1939, WILPF Papers, Univ. of Colo., series III, box 34. The WILPF resigned from the ALAWF in disagreement over the group's position on U.S. neutrality; in Nov. 1937 the ALAWF became the American League for Peace and Democracy. See U.S. Section, WILPF, Minutes, National Board Mtg., 23–24 Oct. 1937, 4, and Eleanor Fowler, Br. Ltr. No. 52, 12 July 1937, WILPF Papers, Univ. of Colo., 4, series III, box 33.

78. U.S. Section, WILPF, Minutes, National Board Mtg., 23–24 Oct. 1937, WILPF Papers, Univ. of Colo., 5, series III, box 33.

79. NCPW, World Peaceways, WILPF, Labor Anti-War Council, Youth Committee

Against War, KAOWC, FOR, press release, 2 Feb. 1939, WILPF Papers, Univ. of Colo., series III, box 33.

80. Dorothy Detzer[?], "Members of the W.I.L. accept certain basic principles," n.d. [Jan. 1939], WILPF Papers, SCPC, 4, series A2, box 1.

81. Dorothy Detzer, "Statement Before Foreign Relations Committee of the Senate," 4 May 1939, WILPF Papers, SCPC, 3-4, 7, 8, series A2, box 1.

82. "National Legislative Program, 1938-1939 as authorized by Annual Meeting, U.S. Section, May, 1938," WILPF Papers, SCPC, 1, series A, microfilm.

83. U.S. Section, WILPF, Minutes, Annual Mtg., 4-6 May 1939, WILPF Papers, Univ. of Colo., 9, series III, box 34.

84. Ibid., 9, 10-11, 13, 19.

85. Divine, *Illusion of Neutrality*, 265.

86. Dorothy Detzer, Br. Ltr. No. 75, 20 June 1939, WILPF Papers, SCPC, series E4, box 2.

87. Divine, *Illusion of Neutrality*, 270.

12. Keep America Out of War!

1. U.S. Section, WILPF, untitled statement of response to outbreak of World War II, n.d. [Sept. 1939], WILPF Papers, Univ. of Colo., 2, series III, box 34.

2. Dorothy Detzer, radio address, 21 Oct. 1939, WILPF Papers, SCPC, series A2, box 1.

3. Walter VanKirk, radio address, 20 Sept. 1939, NPC Papers, SCPC, 1-2, box 12.

4. Ibid., 3.

5. Dorothy Detzer, Br. Ltr. No. 77, 9 Sept. 1939, WILPF Papers, SCPC, 1, series E4, box 2.

6. Ibid., 2.

7. KAOWC, Minutes, Governing Comm. Mtg., 14 and 29 Sept. 1939, Keep America Out of War Congress Papers, SCPC, Swarthmore College, Swarthmore, Penn. (hereafter cited as KAOWC, SCPC). 1, 3, box 1.

8. Dorothy Detzer, Br. Ltr. No. 80, 11 Oct. 1939, WILPF Papers, SCPC, 2, series E4, box 2.

9. Mildred Scott Olmsted, "Memorandum for the National Peace Conference," 18 Sept. 1939, WILPF Papers, SCPC, 1-3, series E2, box 2; Mildred Scott Olmsted, Org. Ltr., 22 Sept. 1939, WILPF Papers, SCPC, series E2, box 2.

10. KAOWC, press releases, 23 Sept. 1939 and 23 Oct. 1939, KAOWC Papers, SCPC, 2, 1; KAOWC, "Peace Groups Ask Arms Embargo Against Russia," 29 Sept. 1939, KAOWC Papers, SCPC, 1.

11. Dorothy Detzer, Br. Ltr. No. 80, 11 Oct. 1939, WILPF Papers, SCPC, 1, series E4, box 2.

12. Divine, *Illusion of Neutrality*, 313 and 324.

13. Dorothy Detzer to Gertrude Baer, 31 Oct. 1939, series III, box 34, WILPF: Boulder.

14. Divine, *Illusion of Neutrality*, 327.

15. Ibid., 335.

16. Dorothy Detzer, Br. Ltr. No. 81, 25 Nov. 1939, WILPF Papers, SCPC, 1, series E4, box 2.

17. William L. Langer and S. Everett Gleason, *The Challenge to Isolation 1937-1940* (New York: Harper and Brothers, 1952), 48.

18. Dorothy Hommel to Gertrude Baer, 3 Mar. 1939, WILPF Papers, Univ. of Colo., series III, box 34.

19. Dorothy Detzer, Br. Ltr. No. 80, 11 Oct. 1939, WILPF Papers, SCPC, 2, series E4, box 2.

20. Cor Ramondt-Hirschman, "Newsletter No. 8," Nov. 1939, WILPF Papers, Univ. of Colo., 2, series V, box 3.

21. Dorothy Detzer, radio address, 21 Oct. 1939, WILPF Papers, SCPC, series A2, box 1.

22. Dorothy Hommel to Gertrude Baer, 26 Oct. 1939, WILPF Papers, Univ. of Colo., series III, box 34.

23. Dorothy Detzer, Br. Ltr. No. 81, 25 Novn 1939, WILPF Papers, SCPC, 1, series E4,'box 2; Dorothy Detzer, untitled statement re: military build-up, [Oct.] 1938, WILPF Papers, SCPC, 6, series A2, box 1.

24. Dorothy Detzer, Br. Ltr. No. 81, 25 Nov. 1939, WILPF Papers, SCPC, 1, series E4, box 2.

25. KAOWC, Minutes, General Staff Mtg., 8 Jan. 1940, KAOWC Papers, SCPC, 2, box 1.

26. KAOWC, press release, 31 Aug. 1940, KAOWC Papers, SCPC, box 2.

27. John T. Flynn to Affiliated and Cooperating Orgs., 12 Mar. 1940, KAOWC Papers, SCPC, 2, box 2.

28. Dorothy Hommel, to Br. Chairs, 5 June 1938, WILPF Papers, SCPC, 1, series C4, box 2.

29. The term "intervenationalist" comes from DeBenedetti, *Peace Reform*, 134.

30. Dorothy Detzer to Hannah Clothier Hull, 27 Jan. 1940, Dorothy Hommel and Gertrude Baer, Hannah Clothier Hull Papers, SCPC, 2, box 5.

31. Hannah Clothier Hull and Dorothy Detzer to Franklin D. Roosevelt, 18 Nov. 1938, WILPF Papers, Univ. of Colo., series III, box 33.

32. Mildred Scott Olmsted to Gertrude Baer, 17 Nov. 1938, WILPF Papers, SCPC, 2, series C1, box 26.

33. "The U.S.A. Section and Refugees," *Pax International* (Vol. 13, No. 11), Dec. 1938, WILPF Papers, Univ. of Colo., series V, box 3.

34. Dorothy Detzer, "Calling America For Peace," 15 May 1939, WILPF Papers, SCPC, 3, series A2, box 1.

35. Esther Alsop Harris, Minutes, National Refugee Comm. Mtg., 12 Sept. 1939, WILPF Papers, Univ. of Colo., 2, series III, box 34; Margaret E. Jones, "Important Memo From the Refugee Committee," 26 Sept. 1939, WILPF Papers, SCPC, series E2, box 2.

36. Clara Ragaz, Gertrude Baer, Kathleen E. Innes to Franklin D. Roosevelt, 30 Sept. 1939, WILPF Papers, Univ. of Colo., series I, box 8.

37. Gertrude Baer to U.S. Section, 11 Dec. 1939, WILPF Papers, Univ. of Colo., series III, box 34.

38. Eva Wiegelmesser to National Refugee Comm. and Chairs, Local Refugee Comms., 15 Dec. 1939 and 18 Jan. 1940, WILPF Papers, Univ. of Colo., 2, series III, box 34.

39. Alice L. Dodge, Minutes, General Staff Mtg., 8 Jan. 1940, KAOWC Papers, SCPC, 3, box 1; Eva Wiegelmesser to National Refugee Comm. and chairs, Local Refugee Comms., 18 Jan. 1940, WILPF Papers, Univ. of Colo., 2, series III, box 35.

40. Alice L. Dodge, Minutes, General Staff Mtg., 19 Feb. 1940, KAOWC Papers, SCPC, 3, box 1.

41. Dorothy Detzer, "Pittsburgh Speech," 29 Apr. 1940, WILPF Papers, SCPC, 2, series A2, box 1.

42. Ibid., 3.

43. Alice L. Dodge, Minutes, Governing Comm. Mtg., 12 June 1940, KAOWC Papers, SCPC, 4, box 1.

44. Dorothy Detzer, Br. Ltr. No. 91, 3 July 1940, WILPF Papers, SCPC, 1, series E4, box 2.

45. "Peace Planks Adopted Unanimously by 300 delegates from 19 States at Anti-War Mobilization June 7, 1940—Washington, D.C.," KAOWC Papers, SCPC, box 2.

46. "Statement by F.O.R. Council," 20 Apr. 1940, the Fellowship of Reconciliation Papers, Swarthmore College Peace Collection, 4, box 2, Swarthmore, Penn. (hereafter cited as FOR Papers, SCPC).

47. Dorothy Detzer, Br. Ltr. No. 91, 3 July 1940, WILPF Papers, SCPC, 1, series E4, box 2.

48. "Statement by Walker VanKirk before the Resolutions Committee of the Democratic National Convention," 12 July 1940, NPC Papers, SCPC, 1–2, box 12; Arthur D. Reeve, Jr., "Report of the Executive Secretary, Sept. 1939–Sept. 1940," NPC Papers, SCPC, 3, box 1.

49. Charles A. Beard, *President Roosevelt and the Coming of the War* (New Haven: Yale Univ. Press, 1948), 3. Emphasis in original; Robert Dallek, *Franklin D. Roosevelt and American Foreign Policy 1932–1945* (New York: Oxford Univ. Press, 1979), 250.

50. Dorothy Detzer, "Speech at AntiWar Mass Meeting," 7 June 1940, WILPF Papers, SCPC, 1, 3, series A2, box 1. Emphasis in original.

51. Dorothy Detzer, Br. Ltr. No. 91, 3 July 1940, WILPF Papers, SCPC, 2, series E4, box 2.

52. Langer and Gleason, *Challenge to Isolation*, 680.

53. Catherine FitzGibbon, "Statement Made Before the Military Affairs Committee of the Senate," 10 July 1940, WILPF Papers, SCPC, 2, Series E4, box 2, from Dorothy Detzer, Br. Ltr. No. 92, 31 July 1940, WILPF Papers, SCPC, 4–5, series E4, box 2.

54. Dorothy Detzer, "Statement Made Before the Military Affairs Committee of the House," 30 July 1940, WILPF Papers, SCPC, 1–2, series A2, box 1.

55. Mildred Scott Olmsted to Annette Roberts, 12 July 1940, WILPF Papers, SCPC, 2, series C7, box 33.

56. John T. Flynn, Frederick J. Libby, Dorothy Detzer, A. J. Muste, Abe Kaufman, Fay Bennett, "Statement on Conscription Issued July 25, 1940, by National Peace Leaders," KAOWC Papers, SCPC, box 1.

57. Emily Greene Balch to Mildred Scott Olmsted, n.d. [July 1940], WILPF Papers, SCPC, 1, series C4, box 2.

58. Committee on Militarism in Education, "A Declaration Against Conscription," n.d. [Aug. 1940], FOR Papers, SCPC. 1, box 13.

59. Dorothy Detzer, Br. Ltr. No. 95, 28 Sept. 1940, WILPF Papers, SCPC, 1–2, series E4, box 2.

60. KAOWC, press release, "1,000 Attend Anti-War Rally," 5 Oct. 1940, KAOWC Papers, SCPC, 1, box 2.

61. Alice L. Dodge, Minutes, Governing Comm. Mtg., 23 Sept. 1940, KAOWC Papers, SCPC, 1, box 1.

62. Pauli Murray, "Labor and National Defense," 27 Sept. 1940, KAOWC Papers, SCPC, 1, box 2.

63. Alice L. Dodge to Local Affiliated and Cooperating Orgs., 18 Sept. 1940, KAOWC Papers, SCPC, 2–3, box 2.

64. James MacGregor Burns, *Roosevelt: The Lion and the Fox* (New York: Harcourt, Brace and World, 1956), 438–39.

65. Dorothy Detzer, Br. Ltr. No. 95, 28 Sept. 1940, WILPF Papers, SCPC, 3, series E4, box 2. Frederick J. Libby, "The Next Step in Our Campaign For Peace," 9 Sept. 1940, KAOWC Papers, SCPC, box 2.

66. Libby, "The Next Step."

67. Burns, *Lion and Fox*, 451, 454, 455.

68. Alice L. Dodge, Minutes, Governing Comm. Mtg., 13 Nov. 1940, KAOWC Papers, SCPC, 2, box 1.

69. Dorothy Detzer, Br. Ltr. No. 96, 16 Nov. 1940, WILPF Papers, SCPC, 3, series E4, box 2.

70. KAOWC, "Memorandum to Local Organizations," 27 Nov. 1940, KAOWC Papers, SCPC, 1, box 2.

71. Alice L. Dodge, Minutes, Governing Comm. Mtg., 13 Nov. 1940, KAOWC Papers, SCPC, 2, box 1, Alice L. Dodge to Mildred Scott Olmsted, 25 Nov. 1940, WILPF Papers, SCPC, 2, series C4, box 3.

72. Alice L. Dodge, Minutes, Governing Comm. Mtg., 13 Nov. 1940, KAOWC Papers, SCPC, 1, box 1.

73. Dorothy Hommel to Mrs. Katherine M. Arnett, 5 June 1938, WILPF Papers, SCPC, 1, series C7, box 29.

74. U.S. Section, WILPF, Br. Ltr. No. 98, 27 Jan. 1941, WILPF Papers, SCPC, 1, series E4, box 2.

75. Beard, *President Roosevelt*, 13, 15–16.

76. U.S. Section, WILPF, Br. Ltr. No. 98, 27 Jan. 1941, WILPF Papers, SCPC, 1, series E4, box 2; KAOWC, press release, "Flynn Says President Proposes War," 7 Jan. 1941, KAOWC Papers, SCPC, 1, box 2.

77. Beard, *President Roosevelt*, 20, 71.

78. Dorothy Detzer, Br. Ltr. No. 99, 12 Feb. 1941, WILPF Papers, SCPC, 1, series E4, box 2.

79. Dorothy Detzer, speech, Forum of the Air, 16 Mar. 1941, WILPF Papers, SCPC, 2, series A2, box 1.

80. KAOWC, "An Appeal to the American People," 21 Feb. 1941, KAOWC Papers, SCPC, 2, box 1.

81. A. J. Muste, "Report of Co-Secretary," 12 Dec. 1940 to 25 Mar. 1941, 34, and 28 Mar. to 29 May 1941, FOR Papers, SCPC, 1, box 2.

82. Drew Pearson and Robert Allen, "Washington Merry-Go-Round," *Philadelphia Inquirer*, 25 Jan. 1941, WILPF Papers, SCPC, series C7, box 33.

83. Emily Greene Balch to Robert Allen, 27 Jan. 1941; Emily Greene Balch to Drew Pearson, n.d. [Jan. 1941], Emily Greene Balch Papers, SCPC, series II, reel 11.

84. A. J. Muste, "Report of Co-Secretary," 12 Dec. 1940 to 25 Mar. 1941, FOR Papers, SCPC, 34, box 2.

85. Alice L. Dodge, Minutes, Governing Comm. Mtg., 6 Jan. 1941, KAOWC Papers, SCPC, 1, box 1.

86. Alice L. Dodge, Minutes, Governing Comm. Mtg., 3 Mar. 1941, KAOWC Papers, SCPC, 2, box 1.

87. "Resolutions Passed by Delegates at the Second National Anti-War Congress, Plenary Session in Press Club Auditorium, June 1, 1941, Washington, D.C.," KAOWC Papers, 10–11, box 1.

88. Ibid., 11.

89. Frederick J. Libby to Mary Hillyer, 12 June 1941, KAOWC Papers, SCPC, 1–2, box 1.

90. Alice Thacher Post to Mrs. C. E. Woodruff, 3 June 1941, Emily Greene Balch Papers, SCPC, series II, reel 11.

91. "Resolution Passed by the Executive Committee of WRL," 28 July 1941, War Resisters League Papers, Swarthmore College Peace Collection, box 2, Swarthmore, Penn. (hereafter cited as WRL Papers, SCPC); Mildred Scott Olmsted, Org. Ltr., 18 June 1941, WILPF Papers, SCPC, 2, series E2, box 2; A. J. Muste, "Report of Co-Secretary," 28 March 1941 to May 1941, FOR Papers, SCPC, 2, box 2.

92. KAOWC, press release, 30 May 1941, KAOWC Papers, SCPC, 1, box 2; Mary Hillyer to "Friend," 19 May 1941, KAOWC Papers, SCPC, box 2.

93. Beard, *President Roosevelt*, 118–19.

94. Mildred Scott Olmsted, Org. Ltr., 27 Aug. 1941, WILPF Papers, SCPC, 1, series E2, box 2.

95. Emily Greene Balch, Gertrude Baer, and Dorothy Detzer, "Comments on the Roosevelt-Churchill Eight Points," from Dorothy Detzer, Br. Ltr. No. 109, 14 Oct. 1941, WILPF Papers, SCPC, 2–3, series E4, box 2.

96. Dallek, *Roosevelt and Foreign Policy*, 285; James MacGregor Burns, *Roosevelt: The Soldier of Freedom 1940–1945* (New York: Harcourt Brace Jovanovich, 1970), 132.

97. Beard, *President Roosevelt*, 138–39.

98. KAOWC, press release, 10 Sept. 1941, KAOWC Papers, SCPC, box 2.

99. Beard, *President Roosevelt*, 140.

100. U.S. Section, WILPF, "The President's Speech," Br. Ltr. No. 108, 16 Sept. 1941, WILPF Papers, SCPC, 1, series E4, box 2; KAOWC, press release, 10 Sept. 1941, KAOWC Papers, SCPC, box 2.

101. U.S. Section, WILPF, "Resolutions Passed by the National Board," 18–19 Oct. 1941, WILPF Papers, SCPC, 1, series E4, box 2.

102. Beard, *President Roosevelt*, 159.

103. Dorothy Detzer, Br. Ltr. No. 111, 7 Nov. 1941, WILPF Papers, SCPC, 3, series E4, box 2.

104. "Two of the most flagrant cases" of such incidents, notes Beard, "were those of the tanker *Salinas* on October 30, 1941, and the *Reuben James* on the night of October 30–31." Beard, *President Roosevelt*, 148.

105. Detzer, *Appointment on the Hill*, 238.

13. World War II

1. U.S. Section, WILPF, untitled statement regarding Pearl Harbor, 8 Dec. 1941, and "The Following Statement Was Adopted at an Emergency Meeting . . .," 10 Dec. 1941, WILPF Papers, SCPC, series A2, reel 100.11.

2. Dorothy Detzer, Br. Ltr. No. 112, 13 Dec. 1941, WILPF Papers, SCPC, 1, series E4, box 2.

3. John Toland, *Infamy: Pearl Harbor and Its Aftermath* (Garden City, N.Y.: Doubleday 1982), 13.

4. Beard, *President Roosevelt*, 141.

5. Ibid., 143–44, 147–48.

6. KAOWC, press release, "The President is Responsible," n.d. [late Apr. 1941], KAOWC Papers, SCPC, box 2.

7. The controversy over whether the attack at Pearl Harbor came as a surprise to top U.S. military and civilian leaders still rages, and the response of military historian Colonel Trevor N. Dupuy to allegations of "conspiracy" is typical of supposedly informed

Americans on the subject: "Although I am not an apologist for the late President Roosevelt," wrote Dupuy in 1962, "it is simply ridiculous to suggest that he, who loved the navy perhaps more than did any of our Presidents, would deliberately offer the Pacific Fleet as a sacrifice to entice Japan into war, and that this scheme was abetted by other responsible military men and statesmen."

Yet in his article entitled "Pearl Harbor: Who Blundered?" Dupuy provides a wealth of evidence, all of which he terms "blunders," that, read with a little less naïveté and wishful thinking, easily points to a conspiracy even for the most uninitiated of readers. See Colonel T. N. Dupuy, "Pearl Harbor: Who Blundered?" *American Heritage* 113, no. 2 (Feb. 1962): 64–107.

8. KAOWC, press release, 2 Dec. 1941, KAOWC Papers, SCPC, box 2.

9. FOR, "Public Statement by Executive Committee . . . ," 10 Dec. 1941, FOR Papers, SCPC, 1, box 2.

10. Jessie Wallace Hughan and Abe Kaufman, "Our U.S.A. Movement Since Pearl Harbor," May 1942, WRL Papers, SCPC, 1, box 2.

11. WRL, "A Communication From the Executive Committee . . ." 19 Dec. 1941, WRL Papers, SCPC, 1, box 2.

12. U.S. Section, WILPF, untitled statement regarding Pearl Harbor, 8 Dec. 1941, WILPF Papers, SCPC, series A2, reel 100.11.

13. U.S. Section, WILPF, "The Following Statement Was Adopted at an Emergency Meeting . . . ," 10 Dec. 1941, WILPF Papers, SCPC, series A2, reel 100.11.

14. NPC, "1942 Statement of Purpose of the NATIONAL PEACE CONFERENCE," n.d. [Jan. 1942], NPC Papers, SCPC, box 1; Mildred Scott Olmsted, Org. Ltr., 16 Jan. 1942, WILPF Papers, 2, series E2, box 2.

15. PWWC, Gov. Comm., 2 Mar. 1942, Post War World Council Papers, Swarthmore College Peace Collection, microfilm, reel 90.1, Swarthmore, Penn. (hereafter cited as PWWC, SCPC); Dorothy Detzer, "Our Future Policies," 28 Dec. 1941, WILPF Papers, SCPC, series A5, box 4.

16. Frederick J. Libby to Ray Newton, 1 July 1942, WILPF Papers, SCPC, series C4, box 4.

17. Dorothy Detzer to Roger Baldwin, 2 July 1942, WRL Papers, SCPC, box 25; John Nevin Sayre to James Vail, 27 July 1942, FOR Papers, SCPC, 1, box 19.

18. Mildred Scott Olmsted to Dorothy Detzer, 24 July 1942, WILPF Papers, SCPC, 1–2, series C4, box 4; Dorothy Detzer to Mildred Scott Olmsted, 28 July 1942, WILPF Papers, SCPC, 1, series C4, box 4.

19. Roger Baldwin to A. J. Muste, 19 Aug. 1942, and Arthur Garfield Hays and Roger Baldwin to L. M. C. Smith, 18 Aug. 1942, FOR Papers, SCPC, 1–2, box 19.

20. Burns, *Soldier of Freedom*, 213, 216, 266–68.

21. PWWC, Minutes, Exec. Comm. Mtg., 3 Mar. 1942, PWWC Papers, SCPC, 2; PWWC to Franklin D. Roosevelt 30 Apr. 1942, PWWC Papers, SCPC, 1–2, reel 90.1.

22. Mary W. Hillyer to Henry L. Stimson, 10 June 1942, PWWC Papers, SCPC, 2, reel 90.1.

23. For an excellent first-hand report of the evacuation process, see Hideo Hashimoto to FOR, 18 Apr. 1942, FOR Papers, SCPC, 1–3, box 3.

24. Statement Adopted by Conference on Japanese Evacuation . . . ," 18 June 1942, PWWC Papers, SCPC, reel 90.1.

25. Quoted in Mildred Scott Olmsted, Org. Ltr., 19 June 1942, WILPF Papers, SCPC, 2–3, series E2, box 2.

26. Mildred Scott Olmsted, Org. Ltr., 20 Feb. 1943, WILPF Papers, SCPC, 2, series

E2, box 2; Gladys D. Walser to WIL Leader, 31 Jan. 1944, Emily Greene Balch Papers, SCPC, 1, series IV, box 47.

27. Gladys D. Walser to WIL Leader, 28 May 1943, WILPF Papers, SCPC, 1, series A5, box 5; Gladys D. Walser to WIL Leader, 20 July 1943, Emily Greene Balch Papers, SCPC, series IV, box 47.

28. U.S. Section, WILPF, "Principles, Policies and Program . . . ," May 1942, WILPF Papers, Univ. of Colo., 1, series III, box 35.

29. Mercedes Randall to W.I.L. Friend, 27 Apr. 1943, WILPF Papers, SCPC, 1–2, series A5, box 5.

30. Dorothy Detzer to Chairs, International WILPF sections, 1 July 1943, WILPF Papers, Univ. of Colo., 3–4, series III, box 35.

31. Mildred Scott Olmsted, Org. Ltr., 1 July 1943, WILPF Papers, SCPC, 1–2, series E2, box 2.

32. Mercedes Randall to Friend, 19 Apr. 1943, WILPF Papers, SCPC, 1–2, series A5, box 5.

33. Ibid., 2. See Arthur D. Morse, *While Six Million Died: A Chronicle of American Apathy* (Woodstock, N.Y.: Overlook Press, 1983), 50–63, for details of the 1943 Anglo-American Conference on Refugees in Bermuda. As Morse notes, "The Bermuda Conference authorized only one definite action on refugees: twenty-one thousand refugees in Spain would be removed to North Africa. . . . In 1965 [Richard Kidston Law, who headed the British delegation] . . . was asked to recall the events at Bermuda. 'It was a conflict of self-justification,' he said, 'a facade for inaction. We said the results of the conference were confidential, but in fact there were no results that I can recall.' "

34. Edith Reeves, "Some Volunteer Civilian Services For Women . . .," with Mildred Scott Olmsted, Org. Ltr., 24 Apr. 1942, WILPF Papers, SCPC, 3, series E2, box 2.

35. Grace Rhoads, "Report of Committee on Conscientious Objection," with Mildred Scott Olmsted, Org. Ltr., 1 Sept. 1942, WILPF Papers, SCPC, 5, series E2, box 2.

36. Grace Rhoads to Abe Kaufman, 13 Jan. 1942, WRL Papers, SCPC, box 25.

37. Jessie Wallace Hughan and Abe Kaufman, "Our U.S.A. Movement Since Pearl Harbor," May 1942, WRL Papers, SCPC, 7, 8, box 2.

38. Ibid., 8.

39. Ibid., 9, 10.

40. A. J. Muste to Dorothy Detzer, 1 Dec. 1942, National Committee on Conscientious Objectors of the American Civil Liberties Union Papers, Swarthmore College Peace Collection, 1–3, box 9, Swarthmore, Penn. (hereafter cited as NCCO Papers, SCPC); LSCO, "Statement of Purpose," 14 Dec. 1942, NCCO Papers, SCPC, box 1.

41. Ibid.

42. Albert W. Hamilton to A. J. Muste, 10 Jan. 1943, NCCO Papers, SCPC, 1–2, box 9.

43. Albert W. Hamilton, Minutes, Washington Comm. of NCCO, 20 Jan. 1943, NCCO Papers, SCPC, 1–2, box 1; Willis Giese, Minutes, Washington Comm. of NCCO, 25 Jan. 1943, NCCO Papers, SCPC, 2, box 1.

44. Dorothy Detzer, "Report to the National Committee on Conscientious Objectors, . . ." 5 Mar. 1943, NCCO Papers, SCPC, box 1.

45. Dorothy Detzer to Fowler Harper, 22 Apr. 1943, NCCO Papers, SCPC, 1–3, box 9.

46. R. Boland Brooks, "Report and Conclusions with Respect to the Work of the Washington Office of the N.C.C.O.," 24 Aug. 1943, NCCO Papers, SCPC, box 1.

47. Dorothy Detzer, Br. Ltr. No. 114, 23 Feb. 1942, WILPF Papers, SCPC, series E4, box 2.

48. Dorothy Detzer, Br. Ltr. No. 115, 1 Apr. 1942, WILPF Papers, SCPC, series E4, box 2.

49. Dorothy Detzer, Br. Ltr. No. 114, 23 Feb. 1942, WILPF Papers, SCPC, series E4, box 2.

50. Dorothy Detzer, Br. Ltr. No. 115, 1 Apr. 1942, WILPF Papers, SCPC, series E4, box 2.

51. Ibid., 3.

52. Mildred Scott Olmsted, Org. Ltr., 27 Mar. 1942, WILPF Papers, SCPC, 1, series, E2, box 2.

53. Mildred Scott Olmsted, Org. Ltr., 1 Dec. 1942, WILPF Papers, SCPC, 2, series E2, box 2.

54. Dorothy Detzer, Br. Ltr. No. 124, 11 Feb. 1943, WILPF Papers, SCPC, 1, series E4, box 2.

55. Ibid., 2.

56. Dorothy Detzer to Mildred Scott Olmsted, 11 Feb. 1943, Women's Committee to Oppose Conscription Papers, Swarthmore College Peace Collection, series C, box 2, Swarthmore, Penn. (hereafter cited as WCOC, SCPC); Marjorie Littell Himes, "Memorandum to Workers in the Drive Against the Conscription of Women," 19 Feb. 1943, with Mildred Scott Olmsted, Org. Ltr., 20 Feb. 1943, WILPF Papers, SCPC, 4, series E2, box 2.

57. Mildred Scott Olmsted, Org. Ltr., 17 Mar. 1943, WILPF Papers, SCPC, 2, series E2, box 2 and 18 Jan. 1943, WILPF Papers, SCPC, 1, series E2, box 2.

58. Dorothy Detzer to A. J. Muste, 3 Mar. 1943, NCCO Papers, SCPC, box 9.

59. Mildred Scott Olmsted to Committee Member, 1 Apr. 1943 and 22 Mar. 1943, WCOC Papers, SCPC, series A, box 1.

60. Mildred Scott Olmsted to A. J. Muste, 16 Mar. 1943; Mildred Scott Olmsted to Committee Member, 11 May 1943 and 1 Apr. 1943, WCOC Papers, SCPC, series A, box 1.

61. Mildred Scott Olmsted, "Statement on House Resolution 1742, . . ." n.d. [May 1943], with Mildred Scott Olmsted to Committee Member, 11 May 1943, WCOC Papers, SCPC, series A, box 1.

62. Oswald Garrison Villard, "Shall We Conscript Women?" *The Christian Century*, 4 Aug. 1943, 886–87, WCOC Papers, SCPC, series A, box 1.

63. Mildred Scott Olmsted, Org. Ltr., 1 July 1943, WILPF Papers, SCPC, 2, series E2, box 2.

64. "Brief Summary Report, Seminar on Conscription, Coercion and Disarmament, Pendle Hill," Oct. 1943, FOR Papers, 1, box 6. The discussion of the conference that follows is taken from this report.

65. Elsie Elfenbein, "Report of Executive Director, . . ." 6 Jan. 1944, PWWC Papers, SCPC, 1, reel 90.1.

66. Ibid.; Abe Kaufman, Minutes, Exec. Comm. Mtg., 8 Dec. 1943, WRL Papers, SCPC, 2, box 2.

67. Norman Thomas, "Conscription, the Test of Peace," Jan. 1944, WCOC Papers, SCPC, 5–6, series A, box 1.

68. Mildred Scott Olmsted, "The Drafting of Women for the Armed Forces," 3 Feb. 1944, WCOC Papers, SCPC, 1–2, series A, box 1.

69. PWWC, "News Bulletin," Vol. 111, No. 9, Sept. 1944, WCOC Papers, SCPC, series A, box 3; Dorothy Detzer, Br. Ltr. No. 143, 10 Nov. 1944, WILPF Papers, SCPC, series E4, box 2.

70. Dorothy Detzer, Br. Ltr. No. 144, 12 Dec. 1944, WILPF Papers, SCPC, 2, series E4, box 2.

71. New Jersey WILPF, "The Fight Is On!" *New Jersey News*, Dec.–Jan. 1945, Vol. 3, no. 1, WCOC Papers, SCPC, series A, box 4.

72. Dorothy Detzer, Annual Report, April 1944, 2, from Br. Ltr. No. 138, 16 May 1944, WILPF Papers, SCPC, series E4, box 2.

73. Ibid., 3, 7, 8. Dorothy Detzer[?], Br. Ltr. No. 136, 25 Feb. 1944, WILPF Papers, SCPC, series E4, box 2.

74. Dorothy Detzer, Br. Ltr. No. 125, 19 Mar. 1943, 3; No. 128, 16 June 1943, WILPF Papers, SCPC, 1–2, series E4, box 2; Dorothy Detzer, "Memorandum on Work for the Hearings on Senate Resolution 100," n.d. [Nov. 1943], WILPF, SCPC, series A2, box 1; Dorothy Detzer, Annual Report, Apr. 1944, WILPF Papers SCPC 8, series E4, box 2, with Br. Ltr. No. 138, 16 May 1944, WILPF Papers, SCPC, series E4, box 2.

75. Dorothy Detzer, Br. Ltr. No. 139, 8 June 1944, WILPF Papers, SCPC, 2, series E4, box 2.

76. Dorothy Medders Robinson and Dorothy Detzer to Franklin D. Roosevelt, 12 Feb. 1944, WILPF Papers, SCPC, series A5, box 5; CPS, *Information* (1, no. 9) (2 Sept. 1943), WILPF Papers, SCPC, 2, series E2, box 2.

77. U.S. Section, WILPF, "Draft Proposal For Peace Terms . . . ," n.d. [Feb. 1944], WILPF Papers, SCPC, 1–2, series A5, box 5.

78. Dorothy Detzer, "Memorandum on conversation with Mr. Edward R. Stettinius, Jr.," 10 Mar. 1944, WILPF Papers, SCPC, series A2, box 1.

79. Dorothy Detzer, "Memorandum on Conversation with Mr. Edward R. Stettinius, Jr. Under-Secretary of State," 6 June 1944, WILPF Papers, SCPC, series A2, box 1.

80. NPC, "Planks For Foreign Policy Platforms. . . . ," n.d. [early summer 1944], NPC Papers, SCPC, box 12.

81. [John Paul Jones], "An Appeal to Organizations Which Have Voted Against the Support of the National Peace Conference Planks for Foreign Policy . . .," n.d. [ca. 15 May 1944], NPC Papers, SCPC, box 12.

82. Dorothy Detzer, Annual Report, Apr. 1944, 5, with Br. Ltr. No. 138, 16 May 1944, WILPF Papers, SCPC, series E4, box 2.

83. Ibid. Dorothy Detzer, Br. Ltr. No. 141, 31 Aug. 1944, WILPF Papers, SCPC, series E4, box 2.

84. WRL, "The Dumbarton Oaks Proposals," 27 Nov. 1944, WRL Papers, SCPC, box 2.

85. U.S. Section, WILPF, pamphlet, "Speak Now or Hold Your Peace Until the Third World War," n.d. [Oct. 1944], FOR Papers, SCPC, box 21.

86. Abe Kaufman, Minutes, Exec. Comm. Mtg., 27 Nov. 1944, WRL Papers, SCPC, box 2.

87. "Statement on the Dumbarton Oaks Proposal by the National Council of the Fellowship of Reconciliation," 9 Dec. 1944, FOR Papers, SCPC, box 19.

88. Edith Wynner, "Searchlight on Dumbarton Oaks," *Common Sense*, Dec. 1944, WILPF Papers, SCPC, 423–28, series E2, box 2.

89. Dorothy Detzer, Report of the National Secretary, 20–22 Oct. 1944, WILPF Papers, SCPC, series A2, box 1.

90. A. J. Muste, "Dumbarton Oaks Will Not Do," n.d. [Dec. 1944], FOR Papers, SCPC, box 19.

91. WRL, "The Dumbarton Oaks Proposals," 27 Nov. 1944, WRL Papers, SCPC, box 2.

92. A. J. Muste, "Personal Comment on the U.C.C.D. Statement on Dumbarton Oaks," n.d. [Nov. 1944], FOR Papers, SCPC, box 19; Edith Wynner, "Searchlight on Dumbarton Oaks," WILPF Papers, SCPC, series E2, box 2.

93. "Statement on the Dumbarton Oaks Proposal by the National Council of the Fellowship of Reconciliation," Dec. 1944, FOR Papers, SCPC, box 19.

94. Dorothy Detzer, Br. Ltr. No. 147, 2 Mar. 1945, WILPF Papers, SCPC, series E4, box 2; A. J. Muste, "What is the Alternative to Dumbarton—Yalta?" 15 Mar. 1945, FOR Papers, SCPC, 1, box 19.

95. Mildred Scott Olmsted, Org. Ltr., 5 Jan. 1945, WILPF Papers, SCPC, 1, series E2, box 2; PWWC, press release, 20 Feb. 1945, PWWC Papers, SCPC, 3, reel 90.7.

96. PWWC, press release, 20 Feb. 1945, 3–4, PWWC Papers, SCPC, reel 90.7.

97. Dorothy Detzer, Br. Ltr. No. 147, 2 Mar. 1945, WILPF Papers, SCPC, 1, series E4, box 2.

98. Ibid.

99. Dorothy Detzer, Annual Report, May 1945, 5–6, WILPF Papers, SCPC, series E4, box 2.

100. Ibid.

101. Ibid. Mildred Scott Olmsted, Org. Ltr., 30 Apr. 1945, WILPF Papers, SCPC, 2, series E2, box 2.

102. FOR, "V-E Day Statement," 8 May 1945, FOR Papers, SCPC, 1, box 3.

103. "Statement of Executive Committee Fellowship of Reconciliation on Proposals for International Organization," 9 May 1945, FOR Papers, SCPC, 2, box 3.

104. Dorothy Detzer to Mildred Scott Olmsted, et. al., 11 May 1945, WILPF Papers, SCPC, 4–5, series C1, box 36.

105. Dorothy Detzer, Annual Report, May 1945, WILPF Papers, SCPC, 2, series E4, box 2.

106. NPC, "Statement on the United Nations' Charter," 16 July 1945, NPC Papers SCPC, box 13.

107. U.S. Section, WILPF, "Proposed Program and Policies," [May] 1945, WILPF Papers, Univ. of Colo., 4, series III, box 35.

108. PWWC, press release, 24 May 1945, PWWC Papers, SCPC, 3, 4, reel 90.7.

109. Mildred Scott Olmsted, Org. Ltr., 6 June 1945, WILPF Papers, SCPC, 1, series E2, box 2.

110. Frank Olmstead to Fellow Worker to End War, 10 Aug. 1945, WRL Papers, SCPC, box 4.

111. Dorothy Detzer, Br. Ltr. No. 150, 13 Aug. 1945, WILPF Papers, SCPC, 1, series E4, box 2.

112. Mildred Scott Olmsted, Org. Ltr., 5 Jan. 1945, WILPF Papers, SCPC, 1, series E2, box 2.

113. PWWC, press release, 12 Aug. 1945, PWWC Papers, SCPC, reel 90.7; Hanson W. Baldwin, "Atomic Bomb Responsibilities," New York Times, 12 Sept. 1945, reprinted by the NCPW, FOR Papers, SCPC, box 21.

114. "The Use of the Atomic Bomb," 20 Aug. 1945, reprinted from unnamed journal, Sept. 1945, Emily Greene Balch Papers, SCPC, 161, series IV, box 31.

115. Dorothy Detzer, Br. Ltr. No. 150, 13 Aug. 1945, WILPF Papers, SCPC, 1, series E4, box 2; A. J. Muste to Harry Truman, 17 Aug. 1945, FOR Papers, SCPC, 1, box 12; WRL, "Excerpts of Comments Received, . . . ," n.d. [Aug. 1945], WRL Papers, SCPC, 1, box 2.

116. Dorothy Detzer, Br. Ltr. No. 150, 13 Aug. 1945, WILPF Papers, SCPC, 1, series E4, box 2; WRL, "Excerpts of Comments Received, . . ." n.d. [Aug. 1945], WRL Papers, SCPC, 4, box 2.

117. A. J. Muste to Harry Truman, 17 Aug. 1945, FOR Papers, SCPC, 2, box 2; A. J. Muste to John Bennett, 15 Aug. 1945, FOR Papers, SCPC, 1-2, box 12.

118. WRL, Minutes, Exec. Comm. Mtg., 24 Aug. 1945, WRL Papers, SCPC, 1, box 2.

119. Dorothy Detzer, "Tentative Statement on the Atomic Bomb," 1 Oct. 1945, Emily Greene Balch Papers, SCPC, 2, series IV, box 31; WRL, "Excerpts of Comments Received . . . ," n.d. [Aug. 1945], WRL Papers, SCPC, 1, box 2.

120. Reinhold Niebuhr to A. J. Muste, 21 Aug. 1945, FOR Papers, SCPC, box 12.

121. PWWC, press release, 21 Dec. 1945, PWWC Papers, SCPC, 1-2, reel 90.7; PWWC, Minutes, Board of Gov. Mtg., 19 Dec. 1945, PWWC Papers, SCPC, 4, reel 90.1.

122. Charles L. Mee, Jr., "The Cold War," in *Historical Viewpoints*, Vol. 2, *Since 1865*, ed. John A. Garraty (New York: Harper and Row, 1987), 287–88.

123. Noam Chomsky, address at The Midway, Univ. of Chicago, "The United States and the Third World: Illusion and Reality," 1981, taped copy in personal file of Carrie Foster, Hamilton, Ohio. Emphasis added.

124. Mildred Scott Olmsted, Org. Ltr., 24 Aug. 1945, WILPF Papers, SCPC, 1, series E2, box 2.

125. Addams shared the Nobel Peace Prize with Nicholas Murray Butler in 1931, and Balch shared it with John Raleigh Mott.

126. "Address by Emily Greene Balch, Philadelphia—Apr. 26, 1947," WILPF Papers, Univ. of Colo., 1-5, series II, box 12.

14. Conclusion

1. Jane Evans, "Notes from San Francisco," 10 June 1945, NPC Papers, SCPC, 2, box 13.

2. See Anne Firor Scott, "Jane Addams: Urban Crusader," in *Historical Viewpoints*, vol. 2, *Since 1865*, ed. John A. Garraty (New York: Harper & Row, 1983), 160–75; and Madeline Z. Doty, *Society's Misfits* (New York: Century, 1914).

3. Detzer, *Appointment on the Hill*, 5.

4. See George Seldes, *Lords of the Press* (New York: Julian Messner, 1938), 122–26.

5. Dorothy Detzer[?], "The United States and Neutrality," n.d. [probably 1936], WILPF Papers, Univ. of Colo., 1, series III, box 33.

6. George Seldes, *One Thousand Americans* (New York: Boni and Gaer, 1947), 75.

7. Dorothy Detzer, radio address, n.d. [Armistice Day 1935], WILPF Papers, SCPC, 1, series C1, box 19.

8. Madeleine Z. Doty, "Five Power Naval Conference," *Pax International* 5 (Feb. 1930), WILPF Papers, Univ. of Colo., series V, box 3.

9. Hannah Clothier Hull to Mrs. Norman Storer, 28 Jan. 1935, Hannah Clothier Hull Papers, SCPC, 1-2, box 6.

10. Ibid., 2.

11. Reinhold Niebuhr, *Moral Man and Immoral Society: A Study in Ethics and Politics* (New York: Charles Scribner's Sons, 1932), xiv–xvii.

12. Detzer, *Appointment on the Hill*, 131.

13. Ibid., 139–40.

14. Richard Gregg, "Moral Jiu-Jitsu," in *The Pacifist Conscience*, ed., Peter Mayer (Chicago: Henry Regnery, 1966), 230. Originally from Gregg, *The Power of Non-Violence* (1934; reprint, Nyack, N.Y.: Fellowship, 1959).

15. Michael Parenti, *Democracy for the Few* (New York: St. Martin's Press, 1988).

16. Quoted from George Fitzhugh in Kenneth Stampp, *The Peculiar Institution: Slavery in the Ante-Bellum South* (New York: Vintage Books, 1956), 420.

17. Dorothy Detzer, radio address, "America and the Next Peace," 27 Mar. 1940, WILPF Papers, SCPC, series A2, box 1. Emphasis added.

18. Gregg, "Moral Jiu-Jitsu," 231.

19. See Charles Beard, *An Economic Interpretation of the Constitution of the United States* (New York: Macmillan, 1913, 1935); Ferdinand Lundberg, *Cracks in the Constitution* (Seacaucus, N.J.: Lyle Stuart, 1980); Jerry Fresia, *Toward an American Revolution: Exposing the Constitution and Other Illusions* (Boston: South End Press, 1988); and Bertell Ollman and Jonathan Birnbaum, eds., *The United States Constitution: 200 Years of Anti-Federalist, Abolitionist, Feminist, Muckraking, Progressive, and Especially Socialist Criticism* (New York: New York Univ. Press, 1990).

Selected Bibliography

Manuscript Collections

Berkeley, Calif. University of California. Anne Martin Papers. Suffragists Oral History Project. The Bancroft Library Regional Oral History Office.
Boulder, Colo. University of Colorado. Women's International League for Peace and Freedom Papers.
Columbus, Ohio. Ohio State University. National Woman's Party Papers.
Swarthmore, Penn. Swarthmore College Peace Collection.
   Jane Addams Papers.
   Emily Greene Balch Papers.
   Dorothy Detzer Papers.
   Emergency Peace Campaign Papers.
   Fellowship of Reconciliation Papers.
   Hannah Clothier Hull Papers.
   Keep America Out of War Congress Papers.
   National Committee on Conscientious Objectors of the American Civil Liberties Union Papers.
   National Conference on the Cause and Cure of War Papers.
   National Peace Conference Papers.
   Mildred Scott Olmsted Papers.
   People's Mandate to Governments to End War Papers.
   Post War World Council Papers.
   Women's International League for Peace and Freedom Papers.
   Women's Committee to Oppose Conscription Papers.
   Women's Peace Society Papers.
   Women's Peace Union Papers.

Interviews and Correspondence

Denny, Dorothy Detzer. Telephone conversation. September 1980.
Olmsted, Mildred Scott. Interview. June 1980. Moylan, Penn.
———. Letter to author. 20 August and 2 September 1983. Personal file of
author.

Miscellaneous

Chomsky, Noam. Speech. University of Chicago, 1981. Taped copy in personal
file of author.

Books

Addams, Jane. *Democracy and Social Ethics.* New York: Macmillan, 1907. Reprint.
Edited by Anne Firor Scott. Cambridge, Mass.: Belknap Press, 1964.
———. *Newer Ideals of Peace.* New York: Macmillan, 1907.
———. *Peace and Bread in Time of War.* Boston: G. K. Hall, 1922. Reprint. 1960.
———. *Twenty Years at Hull House.* New York: Phillips Publishing and Mac-
millan, 1910. Reprint. New York: New American Library.
———. Emily G. Balch, and Alice Hamilton. *Women at The Hague: The Interna-
tional Congress of Women and Its Results.* Reprint. New York: Garland, 1972.
Adler, Selig. *The Isolationist Impulse: Its Twentieth-Century Reaction.* New York: Ab-
elard-Schuman, 1957.
———. *The Uncertain Giant 1921–1941: American Foreign Policy Between the Wars.*
New York: Macmillan, 1965.
Allen, Frederick Lewis. *The Lords of Creation.* Chicago: Quadrangle Books, 1935.
———. *Only Yesterday.* 1931. Reprint. New York: Bantam Books, 1959.
Agee, Philip. *CIA Diary: Inside the Company.* New York: Stonehill, 1975.
———. *On the Run.* Secaucus, N.J.: Lyle Stuart, 1987.
Alonso, Harriet Hyman. *The Women's Peace Union and the Outlawry of War, 1921–
1942.* Knoxville: Univ. of Tennessee Press, 1989.
Alperovitz, Gar. *Atomic Diplomacy.* New York: Viking Press, 1985.
Bartlett, Ruhl J. *The League to Enforce Peace.* Chapel Hill: Univ. of North Carolina
Press, 1944.
Beard, Charles. *An Economic Interpretation of the Constitution of the United States.*
1913. Reprint. New York: Macmillan, 1935.
———. *President Roosevelt and the Coming of the War, 1941.* New Haven: Yale
Univ. Press, 1948.
Becker, Susan. "International Feminism Between the Wars: The National
Woman's Party versus the League of Women Voters." In *Decades of Discon-
tent: The Women's Movement, 1920–1940,* edited by Lois Scharf and Joan M.
Jensen, 223–42. Westport, Conn.: Greenwood Press, 1983.
———. *The Origins of the Equal Rights Amendment: American Feminism Between the
Wars.* Westport, Conn.: Greenwood Press, 1981.

Bernstein, Barton J., ed. *Towards a New Past: Dissenting Essays in American History.* New York: Pantheon Books, 1968.

Blackstock, Nelson. *COINTELPRO. The FBI's Secret War on Political Freedom.* New York: Vintage Books, 1976.

Blake, Katherine Devereaux, and Margaret Louise Wallace. *Champion of Women: The Life of Lillie Devereaux Blake.* New York: Fleming H. Revell, 1943.

Blum, John Morton. *Woodrow Wilson and the Politics of Morality.* Boston: Little, Brown, 1956.

Blum, William, *The CIA: A Forgotten History.* London: Zed Books, 1986.

Bolt, Ernest C., Jr. *Ballots Before Bullets: The War Referendum Approach to Peace in America 1914–1941.* Charlottesville: Univ. Press of Virginia, 1977.

Borg, Dorothy. *The United States and the Far Eastern Crisis of 1933–1938.* Cambridge: Harvard Univ. Press, 1964.

Boyer, Richard O., and Herbert M. Morais. *Labor's Untold Story.* New York: United Electrical, Radio & Machine Workers of America, 1955.

Breckinridge, Sophonisba P. *Women in the Twentieth Century.* New York: McGraw-Hill Book Co., 1933. Reprint. New York: Arno Press, 1972.

Brock, Peter. *Pacifism in the United States: From the Colonial Era to the First World War.* Princeton, N.J.: Princeton Univ. Press, 1968.

——. *Twentieth Century Pacifism.* New York: Van Nostrand Reinold, 1970.

Brockway, Fenner. *The Bloody Traffic.* London: Victor Gollancz, 1933.

Buell, Raymond Leslie. *The Native Problem in Africa.* New York: Macmillan, 1928.

Burner, David. *Herbert Hoover, A Public Life.* New York: Knopf, 1979.

——. *Politics and Provincialism: The Democratic Party in Transition, 1918–1932.* New York: Knopf, 1970.

Burns, James MacGregor. *Roosevelt: The Lion and the Fox.* New York: Harcourt, Brace and World, 1956.

——. *Roosevelt: The Soldier of Freedom 1940–1945.* New York: Harcourt Brace Jovanovich, 1970.

Bussey, Gertrude, and Margaret Tims. *Pioneers For Peace: Women's International League for Peace and Freedom 1915–1965.* 1965. Reprint. London: WILPF British Section, 1980.

Carter, Dan T. "Law and Order." In *The Segregation Era 1863–1954: A Modern Reader,* edited by Allen Weinstein and Frank Otto Gatell, 185–96. New York: Oxford Univ. Press, 1970.

Carter, Paul. *The Twenties in America.* Arlington Heights, Ill.: AHM, 1968.

Catton, Bruce. *The War Lords of Washington.* New York: Harcourt, Brace, 1948.

Chafe, William Henry. *The American Woman: Her Changing Social, Economic, and Political Roles, 1920–1970.* New York: Oxford Univ. Press, 1972.

Chambers, Clarke A. *Paul U. Kellogg and The Survey: Voices for Social Welfare and Social Justice.* Minneapolis: Univ. of Minnesota Press, 1971.

——. *Seedtime of Reform: American Social Service and Social Action 1918–1933.* Minneapolis: Univ. of Minnesota Press, 1963.

Chatfield, Charles. *For Peace and Justice: Pacifism in America 1914–1941.* Knoxville: Univ. of Tennessee Press, 1971.

————, ed. *International War Resistance Through World War II*. New York: Garland, 1975.

————, ed. *Peace Movements in America*. New York: Schocken Books, 1973.

Churchill, Ward, and Jim VanderWall. *Agents of Repression: The FBI's Secret Wars Against the Black Panther Party and the American Indian Movement*. Boston: South End Press, 1988.

Cohen, Joshua, and Joel Rogers. *On Democracy: Toward a Transformation of American Society*. New York: Penguin Books, 1983.

Cole, Wayne S. *America First: The Battle Against Intervention 1940–1941*. Madison: Univ. of Wisconsin Press, 1953.

————. *Charles A. Lindbergh and the Battle Against Intervention in World War II*. New York: Harcourt Brace Jovanovich, 1974.

————. *Senator Gerald P. Nye and American Foreign Relations*. Minneapolis: Univ. of Minnesota Press, 1962.

Conlin, Joseph R. *American Anti-War Movements*. Beverly Hills: Glencoe Press, 1968.

Conway, Jill. "Jane Addams: An American Heroine." In *The Woman in America*, edited by Robert Jay Lifton, 247–66. Boston: Houghton Mifflin, 1964.

Cook, Blanche Wiesen. "Democracy in Wartime: Antimilitarism in England and the United States, 1914–1918." In *Peace Movements in America*, edited by Charles Chatfield, 39–56. New York: Schocken Books, 1973.

————. "Female Support Networks and Political Activism: Lillian Wald, Crystal Eastman, Emma Goldman." In *Women's America: Refocusing the Past*, edited by Linda K. Kerber and Jane DeHart Mathews. New York: Oxford Univ. Press, 1982.

Cook, Blanche Wiesen, ed. *Crystal Eastman on Women and Revolution*. New York: Oxford Univ. Press, 1978.

Cott, Nancy F. *The Grounding of American Feminism*. New Haven: Yale Univ. Press, 1987.

Craig, Gordon A. "The British Foreign Office from Grey to Austen Chamberlain." In *The Diplomats 1919–1939*, Vol. 1, *The Twenties*, edited by Gordon A. Craig and Felix Gilbert, 15–48. 1953. New York: Atheneum, 1971.

Craig, Gordon A., and Gilbert, Felix, eds. *The Diplomats 1919–1939*. 2 vols. 1953. Reprint. New York: Atheneum, 1971.

Current, Richard N. "The United States and 'Collective Security': Notes on the History of an Idea." In *Isolation and Security: Ideas and Interest in Twentieth-Century American Foreign Policy*, edited by Alexander DeConde, 32–53. Durham, N.C.: Duke Univ. Press, 1957.

Curti, Merle. *Peace or War: The American Struggle 1636–1936*. New York: W. W. Norton, 1936.

Dabringhaus, Erhard. *Klaus Barbie*. Washington, D.C.: Acropolis Books, 1984.

Dallek, Robert. *Franklin D. Roosevelt and American Foreign Policy, 1932–1945*. New York: Oxford Univ. Press, 1979.

Dallek, Robert, ed. *The Roosevelt Diplomacy and World War II*. New York: Holt, Rinehart and Winston, 1970.

Davis, Allen F. *American Heroine: The Life and Legend of Jane Addams.* New York: Oxford Univ. Press, 1973.

DeBenedetti, Charles. "Alternative Strategies in the American Peace Movement in the 1920s." In *Peace Movements in America,* edited by Charles Chatfield, 57–67. New York: Schocken Books, 1973.

———. *Origins of the Modern American Peace Movement, 1915–1929.* New York: KTO Press, 1980.

———. *The Peace Reform in American History.* Bloomington: Univ. of Indiana Press, 1980.

DeConde, Alexander, ed. *Isolation and Security: Ideas and Interest in Twentieth-Century American Foreign Policy.* Durham, N.C.: Duke Univ. Press, 1957.

Degen, Marie Louise. *The History of the Woman's Peace Party.* Baltimore: Johns Hopkins Univ. Press, 1939.

Dellinger, David. *Vietnam Revisited: Covert Action to Invasion to Reconstruction.* Boston: South End Press, 1986.

Denny, Ludwell. *We Fight For Oil.* Westport, Conn.: Hyperion Press, 1928.

Detzer, Dorothy. *Appointment on the Hill.* New York: Henry Holt, 1948.

Detzer, Karl. *Myself When Young.* New York: Funk and Wagnalls, 1968.

Divine, Robert. *The Illusion of Neutrality: Franklin D. Roosevelt and the Struggle Over the Arms Embargo.* Chicago: Quadrangle Books, 1962.

———. *The Reluctant Belligerent: American Entry into World War II.* New York: John Wiley and Sons, 1965.

———. *Roosevelt and World War II.* Baltimore: Penguin Books, 1969.

Doty, Madeleine Z. *Behind the Battle Line: Around the World in 1918.* New York: Macmillan, 1918.

———. *Short Rations: An American Woman in Germany, 1915 . . . 1916.* New York: Century, 1917.

———. *Society's Misfits.* New York: Century, 1914. Reprint. 1916.

Eagan, Eileen. *Class, Culture, and Classroom: The Student Peace Movement of the 1930's.* Philadelphia: Temple Univ. Press, 1981.

Ekirch, Arthur A., Jr. "Introduction." In *Death and Profits: A Study of the War Policies Commission,* edited by Seymour Waldman, 1–7. 1932. Reprint. New York: Garland.

Ellis, L. Ethan. *Republican Foreign Policy, 1921–1933.* New Brunswick, N.J.: Rutgers Univ. Press, 1968.

Engelbrecht, H. C., and F. C. Hanighen. *Merchants of Death: A Study of the International Armament Industry.* New York: Dodd, Mead, 1934.

Farrell, John C. *Beloved Lady: A History of Jane Addams' Ideas on Reform and Peace.* Baltimore: Johns Hopkins Univ. Press, 1967.

Fensterwald, Bernard, Jr., with Ewing, Michael. *Coincidence or Conspiracy?* New York: Zebra Books, 1977.

Ferrell, Robert H. *Peace in Their Time: The Origins of the Kellogg-Briand Pact.* New Haven: Yale Univ. Press, 1952.

Flacks, Richard. *Making History: The Radical Tradition in American Life.* New York: Columbia Univ. Press, 1988.

Flexner, Eleanor. *Century of Struggle: The Woman's Rights Movement in the United States*. Cambridge: Belknap Press, 1950.

Foster, Catherine. *Women for All Seasons: The Story of the Women's International League for Peace and Freedom*. Athens: The Univ. of Georgia Press, 1989.

Freedman, Estelle B. "The New Woman: Changing Views of Women in the 1920s." In *Decades of Discontent*, edited by Lois Scarf and Joan M. Jensen, 21–42. Westport, Conn.: Greenwood Press, 1983.

Fresia, Jerry. *Toward an American Revolution: Exposing the Constitution and Other Illusions*. Boston: South End Press, 1988.

Fry, Amelia R. *Mabel Vernon: Speaker for Suffrage and Petitioner for Peace*. Berkeley: Suffragists Oral History Project, Bancroft Regional Oral History Office, 1976.

Gardner, Lloyd C. "American Foreign Policy 1900–1921: A Second Look at the Realist Critique of American Diplomacy." In *Towards a New Past: Dissenting Essays in American History*, edited by Barton J. Bernstein, 202–31. New York: Pantheon Books, 1968.

———. *Economic Aspects of New Deal Diplomacy*. Madison: Univ. of Wisconsin Press, 1964.

———. *Safe For Democracy: The Anglo-American Response to Revolution, 1913–1923*. New York: Oxford Univ. Press, 1984.

Gluck, Sharon. "Socialist Feminism Between the Two World Wars: Insights From Oral History." In *Decades of Discontent*, edited by Lois Scharf and Joan M. Jensen, 279–97. Westport, Conn.: Greenwood Press, 1983.

Goldstein, Robert Justin. *Political Repression in Modern America, 1870 to the Present*. New York: Schenkman, 1978.

Goodman, Walter. *The Committee: The Extraordinary Career of the House Committee on Un-American Activities*. New York: Farrar, Straus and Giroux, 1968.

Graham, Otis L., Jr. *An Encore For Reform: The Old Progressives and the New Deal*. New York: Oxford Univ. Press, 1967.

———. *The Great Campaigns: Reform and War in America, 1900–1928*. Englewood Cliffs, N.J.: Prentice-Hall, 1971.

Grantham, Dewey W., Jr. "The Progressive Era and the Reform Tradition. In *Progressivism: The Critical Issues*, edited by David M. Kennedy, 109–21. Boston: Little, Brown, 1971.

Greene, Felix. *The Enemy: What Every American Should Know About Imperialism*. New York: Vintage Books, 1971.

Gregg, Richard. "Moral Jiu-Jitsu." In *The Pacifist Conscience*, edited by Peter Mayer, 225–34. Chicago: Henry Regnery, 1966.

Gregory, Ross. *The Origins of American Intervention in the First World War.* New York: W. W. Norton, 1971.

Gurtov, Melvin. *The United States Against the Third World*. New York: Praeger, 1974.

Halperin, Morton H., et al. *The Lawless State: The Crimes of the U.S. Intelligence Agencies*. Middlesex, England: Penguin Books, 1976.

Hentoff, Nat. *Peace Agitator: The Story of A. J. Muste*. New York: Macmillan, 1963.

Herman, Sondra K. *Eleven Against War: Studies in American Internationalist Thought, 1898–1921*. Palo Alto: Stanford Univ. Press, 1969.

Higham, Charles. *Trading With the Enemy*. New York: Delacorte Press, 1983.

Irwin, Inez Haynes. *Angels and Amazons: A Hundred Years of American Women*. New York: Doubleday, Doran, 1933.

———. *Up Hill With Banners Flying*. Reprint. Penobscot, Maine: Traversity Press, 1964.

Jensen, Joan M. "All Pink Sisters: The War Department and the Feminist Movement in the 1920s." In *Decades of Discontent: The Women's Movement, 1920–1940*, edited by Lois Scharf and Joan M. Jensen, 197–221. Westport, Conn.: Greenwood Press, 1983.

Jonas, Manfred. *Isolationism in America, 1935–1941*. Ithaca: Cornell Univ. Press, 1966.

Josephson, Hannah. *Jeanette Rankin: First Lady in Congress*. New York: Bobbs-Merrill, 1974.

Josephson, Matthew. *The Money Lords: The Great Finance Capitalists 1925–1950*. New York: Weybright and Talley, 1972.

Kennedy, David. *Over Here: The First World War and American Society*. New York: Oxford Univ. Press, 1980.

Kennedy, David, ed. *Progressivism: The Critical Issues*. Boston: Little, Brown, 1971.

Kerber, Linda K., and Jane DeHart Mathews, eds. *Women's America: Refocusing the Past*. New York: Oxford Univ. Press, 1982.

Kimball, Jeffrey P. *To Reason Why: The Debate about the Causes of U.S. Involvement in the Vietnam War*. New York: McGraw-Hill, 1990.

Kolko, Gabriel. *The Roots of American Foreign Policy*. Boston: Beacon Press, 1969.

Kraft, Barbara. *The Peace Ship: Henry Ford's Pacifist Adventure in the First World War*. New York: Macmillan, 1978.

Kuehl, Warren F. *Seeking World Order: The United States and International Organization to 1920*. Nashville: Vanderbilt Univ. Press, 1969.

Lafore, Laurence. *The End of Glory: An Interpretation of the Origins of World War II*. New York: J. B. Lipincott, 1970.

Lane, Mark. *Rush to Judgment*. New York: Holt, Rinehart and Winston, 1966.

Langer, William L., and S. Everett Gleason. *The Challenge to Isolation 1937–1940*. New York: Harper and Brothers, 1952.

Lasch, Christopher. *The New Radicalism in America 1889–1963: The Intellectual as a Social Type*. New York: Vintage Books, 1965.

Lasch, Christopher, ed. *The Social Thought of Jane Addams*. New York: Bobbs-Merrill, 1965.

Lasky, Victor. *It Didn't Start With Watergate*. New York: Dell, 1977.

Lemons, J. Stanley. *The Woman Citizen: Social Feminism in the 1920's*. Urbana: Univ. of Illinois Press, 1973.

Libby, Frederick J. *To End War: The Story of the National Council for Prevention of War*. Nyack, New York: Fellowship, 1969.

Lifton, Robert Jay, ed. *The Woman in America*. Boston: Houghton Mifflin, 1964.

Link, Arthur S. *Wilson: Campaigns for Progressivism and Peace 1916–1917.* Princeton, N.J.: Princeton Univ. Press, 1965.

Link, Arthur S. "Wilson and the Struggle for Neutrality." In *The Impact of World War I,* edited by Arthur S. Link, 8–28. New York: Harper and Row, 1969.

———. *Woodrow Wilson and the Progressive Era 1910–1917.* New York: Harper and Row, 1954.

Link, Arthur S., ed. *The Impact of World War I.* New York: Harper and Row, 1969.

Link, Arthur S., and Richard L. McCormick. *Progressivism.* Arlington Heights, Ill.: Harlan Davidson, 1983.

Linklater, Magnus, et al. *The Nazi Legacy: Klaus Barbie and the International Fascist Connection.* New York: Holt, Rinehart and Winston, 1984.

Litwack, Leon. *The American Labor Movement.* Englewood Cliffs, N.J.: Prentice-Hall, 1962.

Lucaites, John Louis, and Lawrence M. Bernabo. *Great Speakers and Speeches.* 2d ed. Dubuque: Kendall/Hunt, 1989, 1992.

Lundberg, Ferdinand. *America's Sixty Families.* 1937. Reprint. New York: Halcyon House, 1939.

———. *Cracks in the Constitution.* Secaucus, N.J.: Lyle Stuart, 1980.

McGehee, Ralph. *Deadly Deceits: My 25 Years in the CIA.* New York: Sheridan Square Publications, 1983.

Maddox, Robert James. *William E. Borah and American Foreign Policy.* Baton Rouge: Louisiana State Univ. Press, 1969.

Marchand, C. Roland. *The American Peace Movement and Social Reform 1898–1918.* New Jersey: Princeton Univ. Press, 1972.

Marchetti, Victor, and John D. Marks. *The CIA and the Cult of Intelligence.* New York: Dell, 1974.

Marks, John D. *The Search for the Manchurian Candidate: The CIA and Mind Control.* New York: McGraw-Hill, 1980.

Marrs, Jim. *Crossfire: The Plot That Killed Kennedy.* New York: Carroll and Graf, 1989.

Marshall, Jonathan, et al. *The Iran-Contra Connection: Secret Teams and Covert Operations in the Reagan Era.* Boston: South End Press, 1987.

May, Henry F. *The End of American Innocence.* Chicago: Quadrangle Books, 1959.

Mayer, Peter, ed. *The Pacifist Conscience.* Chicago: Henry Regnery, 1966.

Meagher, Sylvia. *Accessories After the Fact: The Warren Commission, the Authorities, and the Report.* New York: Bobbs-Merrill, 1967.

Mee, Charles L., Jr. "The Cold War." In *Historical Viewpoints,* Vol. 2, *Since 1865,* edited by John A. Garraty, 278–93. New York: Harper and Row, 1987.

Millis, Walter. *Road to War: America 1914–1917.* Boston: Houghton Mifflin, 1935.

Morison, Elting E. *Turmoil and Tradition: A Study in the Life and Times of Henry L. Stimson.* New York: Atheneum, 1966.

Morse, Arthur D. *While Six Million Died: A Chronicle of American Apathy.* Woodstock, N.Y.: Overlook Press, 1983.

Murray, Robert. *The Harding Era: Warren G. Harding and His Administration.* Minneapolis: Univ. of Minnesota Press, 1969.

————. *Red Scare: A Study of National Hysteria, 1919–1920.* New York: McGraw-Hill, 1955.

Nearing, Scott, and Joseph Freeman. *Dollar Diplomacy: A Study in American Imperialism.* New York: B. W. Huebsch and Viking Press, 1925.

Nelson, John K. *The Peace Prophets: American Pacifist Thought, 1919–1941.* Chapel Hill: Univ. of North Carolina Press, 1967.

Nichols, Beverley. *Cry Havoc!* Garden City, New York: Doubleday, Doran, 1933.

Niebuhr, Reinhold. *Moral Man and Immoral Society: A Study in Ethics and Politics.* New York: Charles Scribner's Sons, 1932.

O'Connor, Raymond G. *Diplomacy For Victory: FDR and Unconditional Surrender.* New York: W. W. Norton, 1971.

O'Neill, William L. *Everyone Was Brave: The Rise and Fall of Feminism in America.* Chicago: Quadrangle Books, 1969.

Parenti, Michael. *Democracy For the Few.* New York: St. Martin's Press, 1988.

————. *The Sword and the Dollar: Imperialism, Revolution, and the Arms Race.* New York: St. Martin's Press, 1989.

Patterson, David S. *Toward a Warless World: The Travail of the American Peace Movement 1887–1914.* Bloomington: Indiana Univ. Press, 1976.

Peterson, H. C., and Gilbert C. Fite. *Opponents of War, 1917–1918.* 1957. Reprint. Seattle: Univ. of Washington Press, 1971.

Polenberg, Richard. *War and Society: The United States, 1941–1945.* Philadelphia: J. B. Lippincott, 1972.

Randall, Mercedes M., ed. *Beyond Nationalism: Social Thought of Emily Greene Balch.* New York: Twayne, 1972.

————. *Improper Bostonian: Emily Greene Balch.* New York: Twayne, 1964.

Resek, Carl, ed. *The Progressives.* New York: Bobbs-Merrill, 1967.

Rieselbach, Leroy N. *The Roots of Isolationism: Congressional Voting and Presidential Leadership in Foreign Policy.* New York: Bobbs-Merrill, 1966.

Robertson, Esmonde M., ed. *The Origins of the Second World War.* London: Macmillan, 1971.

Rothman, Sheila. *Woman's Proper Place: A History of Changing Ideals and Practices, 1870 to the Present.* New York: Basic Books, 1978.

Rupp, Leila J., and Verta Taylor. *Survival in the Doldrums: The American Women's Rights Movement, 1945 to the 1960s.* New York: Oxford Univ. Press, 1987.

Russett, Bruce M. *No Clear and Present Danger: A Skeptical View of the U.S. Entry Into World War II.* New York: Harper Torchbooks, 1972.

Ryan, Mary P. *Womanhood in America.* New York: New Viewpoints, 1975.

Salzman, Jack, ed. *Years of Protest: A Collection of American Writings of the 1930's.* New York: Bobbs-Merrill, 1967.

Scharf, Lois, and Joan M. Jensen, eds. *Decades of Discontent: The Women's Movement, 1920–1940.* Westport, Conn.: Greenwood Press, 1983.

Scott, Anne Firor. "Jane Addams: Urban Crusader." In *Historical Viewpoints,* Vol. 2, *Since 1865,* edited by John A. Garraty, 160–75. New York: Century, 1914.

————. *Making the Invisible Woman Visible.* Urbana: Univ. of Illinois Press, 1984.

Scott, Peter Dale. *Crime and Cover-Up: the CIA, the Mafia, and the Dallas-Watergate Connection.* Berkeley: Westworks, 1977.

Seldes, George. *Facts and Fascism.* New York: In Fact, 1943.

————. *Iron, Blood and Profits: An Exposure of the World-Wide Munitions Racket.* New York: Harper and Brothers, 1934.

————. *Lords of the Press.* New York: Julian Messner, 1938.

————. *One Thousand Americans.* New York: Boni and Gaer, 1947.

————. *The People Don't Know: The American Press and the Cold War.* New York: Gaer Associates, 1949.

————. *You Can't Do That!* New York: Modern Age Books, 1938.

————. *You Can't Print That! The Truth Behind the News 1918–1928.* 1929. Reprint. Grosse Pointe Woods, Mich.: Scholarly Press, 1968.

Shannon, David, ed. *The Great Depression.* Englewood Cliffs, N.J.: Prentice-Hall, 1960.

Stavrianos, L. S. *Global Rift: The Third World Comes of Age.* New York: William Morrow, 1981.

Stone, I. F. *Business As Usual. The First Year of Defense.* New York: Modern Age Books, 1941.

————. *The Truman Era.* New York: Vintage Books, 1953, 1973.

————. *The War Years 1939–1945.* Boston: Little, Brown, 1988.

Sundiata, I. K. *Black Scandal: America and the Liberian Labor Crisis 1929–1936.* Philadelphia: Institute for the Study of Human Issues, 1980.

Tansill, Charles Callan. *Back Door to War: The Roosevelt Foreign Policy 1933–1941.* Chicago: Henry Regnery, 1952.

Tate, Merze. *The United States and Armaments.* 1948. Reprint. New York: Russell and Russell, 1969.

Terrell, Mary Church. *A Colored Woman in a White World.* Washington, D.C.: National Association of Colored Women's Clubs, 1940.

Thomas, Norman, and Bertram Wolfe. *Keep America Out of War: A Program.* New York: Frederick A. Stokes, 1939.

Toland, John. *Infamy: Pearl Harbor and Its Aftermath.* Garden City, N.Y.: Doubleday, 1982.

Valentine, Douglas. *The Phoenix Program.* New York: William Morrow, 1990.

Waldman, Seymour. *Death and Profits. A Study of the War Policies Commission.* 1932. Reprint. New York: Garland, 1971.

Weinstein, Allen, and Frank Otto Gatell. *The Segregation Era 1863–1954: A Modern Reader.* New York: Oxford Univ. Press, 1970.

Wells, Anna Mary. *Miss Marks and Miss Woolley.* Boston: Houghton Mifflin, 1978.

Wiebe, Robert. *The Search for Order 1877–1920.* New York: Hill and Wang, 1967.

Williams, William Appleman. *The Contours of American History.* Chicago: Quadrangle Books, 1966.

————. *The Roots of the Modern American Empire.* New York: Vintage Books, 1969.

————. *The Tragedy of American Diplomacy.* 1959. Reprint. New York: Dell, 1962.

Wilson, Joan Hoff. *Herbert Hoover, Forgotten Progressive.* Boston: Little, Brown, 1975.

Wiltz, John E. *From Isolation to War, 1931–1941.* Arlington Heights, Ill.: AHM, 1968.

———. *In Search of Peace: The Senate Munitions Inquiry, 1934–36.* Baton Rouge: Louisiana State Univ. Press, 1963.

Winkler, Allan M. *Home Front U.S.A.: America During World War II.* Arlington Heights, Ill.: Harlan Davidson, 1986.

Wise, David. *The American Police State: The Government Against the People.* New York: Vintage Books, 1976.

———. *The Politics of Lying: Government Deception, Secrecy, and Power.* New York: Vintage Books, 1973.

Wittner, Lawrence S. *Rebels Against War: The American Peace Movement, 1941–1960.* New York: Columbia Univ. Press, 1969.

Wohlstetter, Roberta. *Pearl Harbor: Warning and Decision.* Palo Alto: Stanford Univ. Press, 1962.

Wolfe, Bertram D. *A Life in Two Centuries: An Autobiography.* New York: Stein and Day, 1981.

Wreszin, Michael. *Oswald Garrison Villard: Pacifist at War.* Bloomington: Indiana Univ. Press, 1965.

Young, Rose, ed. *Why Wars Must Cease.* New York: Macmillan, 1935.

Periodicals

Ambrosius, Lloyd. "Wilson's League of Nations." *Maryland Historical Magazine* 65 (Winter 1970): 369–93.

Baker, Paula. "The Domestication of Politics: Women and American Political Society, 1780–1920." *American Historical Review* 89 (June 1984): 620–47.

Carlton, David. "Great Britain and the Coolidge Naval Disarmament Conference of 1927." *Political Science Quarterly* 83 (December 1968): 573–98.

Carroll, Berenice A. "The Outsiders: Comments on Fukuda Hideko, Catherine Marshall and Dorothy Detzer." *Peace and Change* 4 (Fall 1977): 23–26.

Chamberlain, Mary. "Women at The Hague." *The Survey* 34 (June 1915): 940–92.

Cook, Blanche Wiesen. "The Woman's Peace Party: Collaboration and Non-Cooperation." *Peace and Change* 1 (Fall 1972): 36–42.

Chatfield, Charles. "World War I and the Liberal Pacifist in the United States." *American Historical Review* 65 (December 1970): 1,920–37.

Cott, Nancy F. "Feminist Politics in the 1920s: The National Woman's Party." *The Journal of American History* 71 (June 1984): 43–67.

Davis, Allen F. "Welfare, Reform, and World War I." *American Quarterly* 19 (Fall 1967): 516–33.

DeBenedetti, Charles. "Borah and the Kellogg-Briand Pact." *Pacific Northwest Quarterly* 63 (January 1972): 22–29.

———. "The First Detente: America and Locarno." *The South Atlantic Quarterly* 75 (Autumn 1976): 407–23.

———. "The $100,000 American Peace Award of 1924." *Pennsylvania Magazine of History and Biography* 98 (April 1974): 224–49.

———. "The Origins of Neutrality Revision: The American Plan of 1924." *The Historian* 35 (November 1972): 75–89.

———. "Peace History in the American Manner." *The History Teacher* 18 (November 1984): 75–110.

Doenecke, Justus. "Non-Interventionism of the Left: The Keep America Out of War Congress, 1938–41." *Journal of Contemporary History* 12 (April 1977): 221–36.

Dubay, Robert William. "The Geneva Naval Conference of 1927: A Study of Battleship Diplomacy." *Southern Quarterly* 8 (January 1970): 177–99.

DuPuy, T.N. "Pearl Harbor: Who Blundered?" *American Heritage* 13, no. 2 (February 1962): 64–107.

Forcey, Linda Rennie. "Women as Peacemakers: Contested Terrain for Feminist Peace Studies." *Peace and Change* 16 (October 1991): 331–54.

Freedman, Estelle B. "Separatism as Strategy: Female Institution Building and American Feminism, 1870–1930." *Feminist Studies* 5 (Fall 1979): 512–29.

Hogan, Michael J. "Corporatism." From "A Roundtable: Explaining the History of American Foreign Relations." *The Journal of American History* 77 (June 1990): 153–60.

"Is the Women's Movement 'Silly and Base'?" *Literary Digest* 50 (May 1915): 1022–23.

Jennings, David H. "President Harding and International Organization." *Ohio History* 75 (Spring–Summer 1966): 149–65.

Johnson, Dorothy E. "Organized Women as Lobbyists in the 1920's." *Capitol Studies* I (Spring 1972): 41–58.

Koistenen, Paul A.C. "The 'Industrial-Military Complex' in Historical Perspective: The Interwar Years." *The Journal of American History* 56 (March 1970): 819–39.

Leffler, Melvyn P. "American Policy Making and European Stability, 1921–1933." *Pacific Historical Review* 46 (May 1977): 207–28.

Lemons, J. Stanley. "Social Feminism in the 1920s: Progressive Women and Industrial Legislation." *Labor History* 14 (Winter 1973): 83–91.

Lerner, Gerda. "Placing Women in History: Definitions and Challenges." *Feminist Studies* 3 (Fall 1975): 5–14.

McGett, Michael. "Political Style and Women's Power, 1830–1930." *The Journal of American History* 77 (December 1990): 864–85.

Maddox, Robert James. "Another Look at the Legend of Isolationism in the 1920s." *Mid-America* 53 (January 1971): 35–43.

———. "William E. Borah and the Crusade to Outlaw War." *The Historian* 29 (February 1967): 20–37.

Nasmyth, George W. "Constructive Mediation, An Interpretation of the Ten Foremost Proposals." *The Survey* 33 (March 1915): 616–20.

Patterson, David S. "Woodrow Wilson and the Mediation Movement, 1914–17." *The Historian* 33 (August 1971): 535–56.

———. "The United States and the Origins of the World Court." *Political Science Quarterly* 91 (Summer 1976): 279–95.

Rainbolt, Rosemary. "Women and War in the United States: The Case of Dorothy Detzer, National Secretary W.I.L.P.F." *Peace and Change* 4 (Fall 1977): 18–22.

Rosenberg, Emily S. "Gender." From "A Round Table: Explaining the History of American Foreign Relations." *The Journal of American History* 77 (June 1990): 116–24.

Scott, Anne Firor. "On Seeing and Not Seeing: A Case of Historical Invisibility." *The Journal of American History* 71 (June 1984): 7–21.

Trattner, Walter I. "Julia Grace Wales and the Wisconsin Plan For Peace." *Wisconsin Magazine of History* 44 (Spring 1961): 203–13.

Van Alstyne, Richard W. "Woodrow Wilson and the Idea of the Nation State." *International Affairs* 37 (July 1961): 293–308.

Van Meter, Robert H., Jr. "The Washington Conference of 1921–22: A New Look." *Pacific Historical Review* 46 (Nov. 1977): 603–24.

Werner, Emmy E. "Women in Congress: 1917–1964." *Western Political Quarterly* 19 (March 1966).

Williams, William Appleman. "The Legend of Isolationism in the 1920's." *Science and Society* 18 (Winter 1954): 1–20.

Wilson, Joan Hoff. "'Peace is a Woman's Job . . .' Jeannette Rankin and American Foreign Policy: The Origins of her Pacifism." *Montana: The Magazine of Western History* 30 (Winter 1980): 28–41.

"A Woman's Peace Party Full Pledged for Action." *The Survey* 33 (January 1915): 433–34.

Yavenditti, Michael J. "The American People and the Use of Atomic Bombs on Japan: The 1940s." *The Historian* 36 (February 1974): 224–47.

Young, Louise M. "Women's Place in American Politics: The Historical Perspective." *Journal of Politics* 38 (August 1976): 295–335.

Dissertations

Bowers, Robert Edwin. "The American Peace Movement, 1933–41." Ph.D. diss., Univ. of Wisconsin, 1947.

Pois, Anne-Marie. "The Process and Politics of Organizing For Peace: The U.S. Section of the Women's International League For Peace and Freedom, 1919–1939." Ph.D. diss., Univ. of Colorado, 1988.

Index